This study explores the subtle, many-faceted interplay of power in Tibullus' first book of elegies. A series of power relationships are created by the text (lover and beloveds, poet and patron), and the processes through which power of various sorts can be exercised are brought to the foreground. Such powerplay within the text of Tibullus I has ramifications well beyond the erotic sphere. Gender categories, rural life, religion, *militia*, patronage are among the areas subsumed within and determined by the operation of power dynamics in this consistently underrated Augustan text. As secure meaning becomes elusive, the reader also is drawn into this nexus of power-play. Taking a linear reading of Book One as its basis, this study uncovers the shifting, unstable ground of Tibullan elegy. The result is a picture of the poet and text of Book One far removed from the bland, safe and urbane 'Tibullus' of previous criticism.

PARSHIA LEE-STECUM is Lecturer in Classics at the University of Melbourne.

T0382439

CAMBRIDGE CLASSICAL STUDIES

General Editors
M. F. BURNYEAT, P. E. EASTERLING, M. K. HOPKINS,
M. D. REEVE, A. M. SNODGRASS

POWERPLAY IN TIBULLUS

POWERPLAY IN TIBULLUS
Reading *Elegies* Book One

PARSHIA LEE-STECUM

CAMBRIDGE UNIVERSITY PRESS
Cambridge, New York, Melbourne, Madrid, Cape Town, Singapore, São Paulo, Delhi

Cambridge University Press
The Edinburgh Building, Cambridge CB2 8RU, UK

Published in the United States of America by Cambridge University Press, New York

www.cambridge.org
Information on this title: www.cambridge.org/9780521103183

First published 1998
This digitally printed version 2009

A catalogue record for this publication is available from the British Library

ISBN 978-0-521-63083-2 hardback
ISBN 978-0-521-10318-3 paperback

Who but a weakling would analyse power?

Allen Wheelis, *The Path Not Taken*

CONTENTS

PREFACE

This book is a substantial revision and expansion of a 1995 Cambridge doctoral thesis. In my time at Cambridge I received particular direction and inspiration from Michael Reeve and John Henderson (my own personal Scylla and Charybdis). The insights which they tried to foster and the methodological rigour which they encouraged are, I hope, still visible in the best parts of the present work. I am also grateful to Maria Wyke, Peter Davis and Pat Easterling for reading and commenting upon drafts at different stages, and especially to Kathleen Coleman whose valiant efforts, against strong resistance, to channel my unintelligible gibbering into eloquent prose have, I fear, not entirely succeeded. Thanks also to Pauline Hire, Muriel Hall and other members of Cambridge University Press for the work they have put into turning my manuscript into the artefact you now see before you. Suffice it to say, any problems which remain are entirely due to my own obtuse and stubborn nature.

During my time in Dublin while preparing this text for publication I was warmed and welcomed by my colleagues in the School of Classics, Trinity College. My gratitude to them for providing a stimulating working environment is considerable: a finer, kinder bunch of people were never assembled within the same academic department. Thanks, as well, to my students, for keeping me interested and on my toes: a valuable gift and one I am very much aware of even if it doesn't always seem that way.

Finally, for her care and support (and for convincing me *not* to start this book with a quotation from Barthes' *Lover's Discourse*), my thanks and love to Siân, whom all this has been done to impress. I don't know, I guess it's just a power thing ...

ABBREVIATIONS

OLD *Oxford Latin Dictionary.* Oxford, 1968–82.
RE   *Real-Encyclopädie der classischen Altertumswissenschaft.* Stuttgart, 1893–1980
TLL *Thesaurus Linguae Latinae.* Leipzig, 1900–

Abbreviations of journal titles correspond to those used in *L'Année Philologique.*

INTRODUCTION

Collecting the set

Tibullus Book One presents the reader with ten poems, one after another.[1] In the same way, this study takes the form of a linear reading of those ten poems, one after another. To some this approach may seem simply common sense: it is a well tried and still popular technique of literary criticism, and particularly criticism of classical texts.[2] To others it may seem overly rigid, anachronistic, even naive. At any rate, such an approach should not be taken for granted; it needs some explanation and defence.

On a basic level, this linear approach finds support in the physical nature of the ancient 'book'. The mechanics of the book roll demanded that a reader move through that roll's contents in a linear motion. The reader could only '[un]roll' through. To get from point A to point C (or vice versa) there was no other way for it but to go through point B: 'The roll imposes linear movement through or back. No skipping around or dipping in.'[3] This physical imperative to read texts in a linear fashion is echoed in the theory of the so-called 'Reader Response' school of literary criticism, where the physical

---

[1] There is general agreement on the sequence of the poems in the manuscript tradition. The only serious attempt to challenge the physical sequence of poems offered by the manuscripts seems to have been that of Doncieux (1887), which has gained little, if any, critical support: see Ball (1983) 225. On the other hand, Scaliger's rearrangement of the poems into *internal* orders which conformed to a structure and meaning matching the editor's expectations (Scaliger (1577)) stood until the manuscript authority was restored by Volpi (1749); for an overview of the history of editing Tibullus, which I have followed here, see Ball (1983) 12ff.

[2] One of the classic examples of this is Putnam (1970). More recent, and more immediately relevant to the approach taken here, are Henderson (1991) and (1992), a two-part, consecutive, linear reading of two consecutive elegiac texts (Ovid *Amores* 2.7 and 2.8).

[3] Van Sickle (1980) 5.

I

'unfolding' of the book is tied to the process of reading and the reader's construction of meaning from the text. A statement of Michael Riffaterre makes clear this connection, and the exemplary nature of ancient 'books' in this regard:

One can never give enough stress to the importance of a reading that runs in the direction of the text, i.e. from beginning to end. If one ignores this 'one way' sign, one is missing a vital element of the literary phenomenon: namely that the book unfolds (just as in antiquity the scroll materially unrolled) and that the text is the object of a progressive discovery, a dynamic and constantly changing perception, whereby the reader not only advances from surprise to surprise, but at the same time sees as he advances how his comprehension of what he has read changes, because each new element lends a new dimension to preceding elements by repeating, contradicting or developing them.[4]

The physical layout of the book, and in particular the ancient book roll, conditions the reading process, and provides a necessary context for interpretative responses such as this present study.

But, as these words of Riffaterre suggest, the process of reading is not that simple, and neither the linear approach nor even the particular assumption that a poetic collection should be treated as a single entity is unproblematic. 'Reading is not a straightforward linear movement, a merely cumulative affair.'[5] It has now almost become a truism in certain branches of literary criticism that every reading, especially the reading of a collection, is a re-reading.[6] The 'dynamic and constantly changing perception' which Riffaterre finds in the reading process entails constant re-reading of what is already read, and even reading forward as expectations of what is yet to be read are formed and re-formed. 'One might simplify by saying that each intentional sentence correlative opens up a particular horizon, which is modified, if not completely changed, by succeeding sentences. While these expectations arouse interest in what is to come, the subsequent modification of them will

[4] Riffaterre, quoted in Iser (1978) 222.
[5] Eagleton (1983) 77.
[6] '[T]here is no *first* reading, even if the text is concerned to give us that illusion by several operations of suspense, artifices more spectacular than persuasive', Barthes (1974) 16.

also have a retrospective effect on what has already been read. This may now take on a different significance from that which it had at the moment of reading.'[7] Reading, as Iser describes it here, is a constant process of re-reading of previous readings (and re-readings of readings of readings and so on).[8]

While this study takes the form of a straight reading from poem one through to poem ten in order, it is necessarily as much a reading back as it is a reading forward. In the reading of a collection of poems the constant process of re-reading which Iser and others have examined often at the level of interaction between sentences within a unified (or at least 'monolithic') text[9] also takes place on another, larger and thus perhaps more obvious, level. This is the interaction within any reading of the various individual poems of the collection. The nature of such a reading has been well described by Paul Miller in his recent book on Lyric texts: 'The reader of the collection is led from one poem to another, constantly posing the questions: what is the relation of this poem to those which came before and those which will follow after; are these experiences related to one another; what is the nature of the subjectivity projected by these poems that integrates them into a meaningful whole?'[10] There are problems with the approaches of Iser and Miller which will be discussed below, but it is basically this reading process (or, rather, the attempt to read this way) which this study seeks to examine, question and enact through the method of a linear reading of each poem from start to finish. The questions which Miller sees the lyric collection as posing, and others like them, are the flesh of any reading and will be the fuel of this study. (Criticism, by these terms, is carnivorous, if not cannibalistic.)

---

[7] Iser (1980) 53–4.
[8] See also Barthes (1974) 11: 'To read is to find meanings, and to find meanings is to name them; but these named meanings are swept towards other names; names call to each other, reassemble, and their grouping calls for further meaning: I name, I unname, I rename: so the text passes: it is a nomination in the course of becoming, a tireless approximation, a metonymic labor.'
[9] Iser, for example, makes extensive use of Ingarden's notion of 'intentionale Satzkorrelate', Iser (1980) 52ff; see also Iser (1978) 111.
[10] Miller (1994) 55.

The multiplicity of complex inter-relations between poems and facets of poems, each opening up further possibilities in turn (and so on, and so on in an accelerating spiral), will be pursued, as vigorously as space allows, in the course of this reading. But, at the same time, I am aware of and hope to draw attention to the ironies and problems inherent in the circular nature of such a reading. As Miller puts it, 'these separate readings qualify one another in such a way that the speaker's projected experience is constantly recycled as a paradigm of that experience's own intelligibility. Each moment is always interpreted in light of the others known to the reader. Thus the action or sentiment described in one poem frequently only becomes fully intelligible in light of the actions or sentiments described in another poem and vice versa'.[11]

Of course, the 'actions or sentiments' of one poem may in fact be made less intelligible by their inter-relation with other poems or even passages within the *same* poem. The danger of viewing reading as a process, as Riffaterre, Iser and Miller (in the context of a poetic collection) do, is that it becomes equated with progress.[12] This would imply that all the shifting re-readings, the modifications of expectations, the dissemination of competing possibilities, however they might destabilise any reading as it moves through the text, will finally be resolved into certainty when the reader reaches the end. This is the quality, for instance, which Barthes equates with the classic or 'readerly' text: 'here [in the readerly text] dissemination is not the random scattering of meanings toward the infinity of language but a simple – temporary – suspension of affinitive, already magnetized elements, before they are summoned together to take their place, economically, in the same *package*'.[13] In the readerly text, according to Barthes, meaning becomes clear in the end, however obscure or ambiguous it may seem in the beginning and middle. The reading of a

---

[11] Miller (1994) 57.
[12] See Culler (1982) 79, for a discussion of this tendency of reader response criticism.
[13] Barthes (1974) 182.

collection as of any text, however, is not necessarily a march towards enlightenment. Possibilities can remain open, questions remain unanswered, the language of the text and the comparison of and interaction between poems and passages within poems can escape any final certainty, fail to resolve into the neat 'package' of which Barthes speaks.[14] It is one of the contentions of this study that the Tibullan text dramatically fails to resolve itself into Barthes' category of the 'readerly text'.

Despite these qualifications, Miller's central point, that the inter-relation of the poems of a collection effectively forms the context for the meaning of those poems (reading forming the context of itself), largely stands. This is what Duncan Kennedy calls, specifically in the 'context' of Tibullus' first book, 'the piquant circularity of extrapolating "reality" from the text and then using it to assess the viewpoint from which that "reality" has been presented'.[15] The ironies and discrepancies which this 'hermeneutic circle' can foster are necessary parts of any reading and, as I intend to argue, are particularly visible in the reading of Tibullus Book One. Kennedy's words will seem appropriate at many points in the course of this study.

Techniques which seek out formal patterning within ancient collections have also stressed the inter-actions between poems within the Tibullan first book. But this approach and the static, closed, often diagrammatic nature of many of the grouping strategies employed by various critics[16] will be largely rejected here as unproductive representations of the reading process. Ironically, it is only when the bewildering variety of conclusions which this approach to the collection has spawned is viewed collectively that the shifting and expanding number of

---

[14] 'This overpowerfulness as the life of the signifier is produced within the anxiety and the wandering of the language always richer than knowledge, the language always capable of the movement which takes it further than peaceful and sedentary certitude.' Derrida (1978) 73.

[15] Kennedy (1993) 15.

[16] Those who wish to pursue such an approach to the collection are referred to: Littlewood (1970); Powell (1974); Grondona (1975); Ball (1979); Dettmer (1980); also see Ball (1983) 225ff. and the survey of 'recent structural studies' in Ball (1989).

possibilities which the reading of a collection opens up start to suggest themselves. It is one of my prime contentions in this study that Tibullus Book One destabilises precisely this desire to fix meaning, to diagrammatise the relations between poems or sections of poems, which these grouping strategies display. This sort of confidence finds no safe home in the world of Tibullan elegy. As Iser has claimed, 'selection automatically involves exclusion.'[17] To fix finally upon any meaning, any one possibility, demands that all other possibilities which the text may suggest be excluded. This is particularly true, I will argue, of the Tibullan text. The only way to achieve final control over the meaning of Tibullus' first book is to ignore the 'overflow of possibilities'[18] which the text spawns. As Shoshana Felman noted in her reading of James's *Turn of the Screw*: 'To *master*, then, (to become the Master) is, here as elsewhere, to *refuse to read* the letters; here as elsewhere, to "see it all" is in effect to "shut one's eyes as tight as possible to the truth"; once more, "to see it all" is in reality to *exclude*.'[19] Such inter-relations within Tibullus Book One as the various grouping strategies propose are, I would argue, a necessary part of reading the collection, but where they are formed they exist, for as long as they do exist, in a constant state of flux, metamorphosis, insecurity and danger of collapse: 'The play between truth and fiction, reader and text, message and feint, has become impossible to unravel into an "unequivocal" meaning.'[20] This 'play' is part of what I want to trace through this linear study of the ten poems, one after another.

The whole and the sum of its parts

The examination of the first Tibullan collection (in particular) as an inter-related sequence has a distinguished critical pedigree. This approach to Tibullus was first established by Ludolf Dissen in 1835.[21] It was Dissen who made the first sustained

---

[17] Iser (1978) 126. [18] Iser (1978) 126. [19] Felman (1982a) 194.
[20] Johnson (1982) 501. [21] Dissen (1835).

attempt to construct meaning from the poems in the order in which they appear in the manuscripts. While at times this mission led to the smoothing out, or forced reconciliation, of disruptive or conflicting elements in the cause of creating a unified meaning for the poems[22] (just as Scaliger had sought to do by the physical re-positioning of various lines and passages, or in more recent years Walter Wimmel[23] by re-ordering and grouping the poems in their supposed chronological order), in its fundamental linear approach to the text, and to the construction of meaning from that text by means of such a sequential reading, Dissen's work is the prototype of this present study as it has been of much of the Tibullan criticism of the last one hundred and fifty years.

More recently, one of the strongest arguments for approaching the first Tibullan collection *in order*, as an entity of necessarily inter-related facets, has been made by Eleanor Leach.[24] Leach herself exploits and moves on from attempts to find symmetrical patterns in the arrangement of the poems (in particular the work of R. J. Littlewood)[25] to argue for the sequential development of the collection.[26] The first book of Elegies is seen as the developing statement of Tibullus' poetic credo. It follows that this 'thematic development'[27] necessitates a linear reading of the collection: 'the *ars poetica* of Tibullus' first book [is] a poetic statement in evolution inseparable from the order of the poems.'[28] Like the structural, symmetrical patterning strategies from which she draws the impetus for her own approach, Leach's concept of linear development draws a stable, complete meaning for the collection

---

[22] For example, see below, 68–9.
[23] For his first attempt at this approach to Tibullus see Wimmel (1968); a similar re-ordering is employed (explicitly or implicitly) in the approaches of other critics to various elements of the Tibullan text: see, for example, Schiebe's approach to the Tibullan poet's presentation of the 'ideal life', Schiebe (1981).
[24] See especially, Leach (1978) 79–105; (1980a) 79–86; and (1980b) 47–69.
[25] Littlewood (1970).
[26] Leach (1980a) 80.
[27] Leach (1980a) 81.
[28] Leach (1980a) 80.

from the inter-relation of its parts. The difference in Leach's case is that this stability of meaning comes only after the reader has made it to the last line of the final poem. Rather than simply a set pattern, the collection is thus seen as a thematic journey with shifts, moments of apparent self-contradiction and ambiguity, but a strong teleological sense. All is made clear in the end, at last. Here, for example, is Leach's summary of her linear reading of the collection:

> The *ars poetica* of Tibullus' book thus involves the hypothetical creation of an ideal poet, a self-assured figure who has assessed the weaknesses of his predecessor and confidently assumed control over his own fate. The order of the poems presents a structure of experiences by which this control is challenged, fails, is reconstituted and is at last brought into accord with reality.[29]

The 'final resolution'[30] which this reading produces is seen as characteristic of the early Augustan poetic collection, and particularly the collection of ten poems. Both the *Eclogues* of Virgil and Horace's first book of *Satires* are described by Leach in similar terms. Of Horace, for instance, Leach claims: 'the general progress of his plot may be described as the emergence of the satirist Horace *in propria persona* from beneath the impersonal mask of the diatribe satirist worn in the initial poems.'[31] In the same way, in the case of the *Eclogues* Leach writes of the 'sense of progressive change in the book'.[32]

While I do not want to deny that each of these collections involves the construction of poetic identity and the questioning of the nature of poetry itself, and I fully accept Leach's emphasis on the necessity of reading the poems in order, her picture of a final safe harbour of meaning to be reached at the end of such a reading, like Miller's ultimate 'intelligibility' created by reading each poem in the light of each of the others,

---

[29] Leach (1980a) 91.
[30] Leach (1978) 98. See also Ross (1975) 162: 'Conflicts and tensions are finally resolved'.
[31] Leach (1980a) 81.
[32] Leach (1980a) 81.

produces too stable and confident an analysis of the collection. As I hope I made clear above, this does not accurately reflect the process of reading Tibullus' first book as I see it. The sequential reading of the collection emphasises, rather, the difficulties of channelling the possibilities raised by the poems and the interaction between poems into a single, uni-directional master-meaning. The interplay and multiplication of meaning thus involves the reader, and especially the critic, of the Tibullan collection in a power struggle. Meaning can only be pinned down, finalised, fixed, at the cost of repressing the evasive, ambiguous, even self-contradictory aspects of the text: '[it is] an unfolding ... of meanings which irreversible, linear consecution, moving from present point to present, could only tend to repress, and (to a certain extent) could only fail to repress.'[33] While my own reading cannot perhaps avoid involvement in this repression, this struggle, it is also, for the same reason, uniquely placed to trace it. The reading which *this* sequential study produces is one in which such confidence in a complete and recoverable meaning is specifically destabilised, rather than confirmed, by the ironies and complexities of a linear procession through each poem, one after another.

Reading (Tibullan) Elegy: the last thirty years

In recent years, relatively few developed critical models of reading Tibullan elegy, or indeed Augustan elegy in general, have been successfully propagated. One model, of which Francis Cairns is the leading constructor,[34] represents the poems as varied sets of literary conventions, traditional subjects and motifs, subtly handled and grouped by the poet[35] but, in the final analysis, Hellenistic, Alexandrian or, at any

---

[33] Derrida (1978) 217.
[34] The central work which presents this model is Cairns (1979). See also Bulloch (1973); Luck (1969) ch. 1; and Wimmel (1960).
[35] For example, 'Certainly Tibullus is consistently original in his combinations and modifications of the standard topoi which he inherited from the Hellenistic world,' Cairns (1979) 23.

rate, traditional: and, hence, decodable in those supposedly understood terms. This is clear not only from the title of Cairns' major work on Tibullus, but in the first chapter of that work, where even the fact that 'not all the characteristics of Hellenistic poetry are alluded to in Tibullus 1.1'[36] provides legitimisation for this model: 'This makes the elegy all the more valuable as a literary manifesto in that it allows something of Tibullus' place within the great range of Hellenistic poetry to be understood.'[37]

There is of course a tension apparent in the aims of Cairns, and others who follow a similar model of reading, such as A.W. Bulloch. This consists primarily of the attempt to reconcile a reading practice which foregrounds the depiction of 'Hellenistic' elements in Latin elegy, and Tibullus in particular, with what seems to be for them another important critical task, the location of originality. This tension has been addressed by critics in various ways.[38] Bulloch's statement that 'the Roman elegists stood at the beginning of their own tradition, and it is understandable that they should have looked for so much guidance to Greek culture'[39] sums up the nature of the critical 'pull in both directions'. The depiction of Latin elegy as a development in some way from its Hellenistic models is the most common means of overcoming this perceived tension, often using Gallus, and his conveniently absent elegiac works, as a bridge. Cairns, for example, states: 'The very sophisticated and almost wholly subjective love-elegies of Tibullus Book One also imply that Tibullus is building on the work of a predecessor – Gallus – who had gone far beyond the Greek achievement.'[40] Expressions throughout *Tibullus: A Hellenistic Poet at Rome*, such as 'In the Roman elegists this principle is carried even further ...',[41] reinforce this model.

This need to assert the *Roman* elements of Roman Erotic Elegy, to pinpoint in some way the *originality* of the Roman

---

[36] Cairns (1979) 11.   [37] Cairns (1979) 11.
[38] For example see Day (1938); and Luck (1969).   [39] Bulloch (1973) 83.
[40] Cairns (1979) 227.   [41] Cairns (1979) 24.

contribution, is associated with a series of historical and aesthetic assumptions. Again, Cairns states this most clearly:

The work of any great artist must represent, symbolise or incorporate the
overall concerns of the age in which he lives. Tibullus' contribution in this
area can be seen in relation to the form and content of his poetry. He is a
Roman citizen writing elegiac love-poetry: his personality and life are
therefore those of a man torn between and sometimes contriving to reconcile the twin poles of private and public life, of leisure and active service of
the state, of town and country, of duty and love, of war and farming.[42]

Although this statement, which is based on 'Tibullus' status in
antiquity as the greatest of the Roman elegists',[43] depends
on an assumption about what a 'great' artist 'must' do, and
although it might seem to conflict with Cairns' own earlier
warning against the conflation of the poet's life and poetry,[44]
it also asserts the tension (which is also a tension of this particular critical model) between the Roman specificity of the
text and the elements of poetic form and content which Cairns
elsewhere calls 'Hellenistic'.

But it is the location of these Hellenistic elements which, for
this particular model, remains the basis of reading Tibullus,
and Elegy more generally. From the first chapter, Cairns'
primary concern is to list and explain clearly which Hellenistic
motifs and themes *are* present in Tibullus ('Another area of
subject-matter important in Hellenistic poetry is ...'),[45] and
which are not ('Of the features not found in Hellenistic poetry
but present in Tibullus ...').[46] Similarly Luck and Bulloch[47]
are concerned mostly with the location of such elements.[48]

---

[42] Cairns (1979) 229.
[43] Cairns (1979) 228. Cairns seeks to prove this in the opening pages of his
book, (1979) 1–6, basing his proof on the famous passage from Quintilian
(*Inst. Or.* 10.1.93), Velleius Paterculus (2.36.3) (where Tibullus is given equal status
with Ovid), the *Vita Tibulli* (which is medieval), Diomedes (whose use of Tibullus'
first couplet as an example of the elegiac metre is taken by Cairns as evidence
for 'Tibullus' pre-eminence in Roman elegy'), and Ovid (esp. *Am.*1.15.27; 3.9;
*Tr.*2.445ff.), all of which might be contested as reliable pointers to the judgement
of their respective ages.
[44] 'confusion between Tibullus the man and Tibullus the poet' Cairns (1979) 3.
[45] Cairns (1979) 17.
[46] Cairns (1979) 29.
[47] Bulloch (1973) in his examination of poem eight of Book One, for example,
focuses on the observation of 'mostly conventional material', 88.
[48] See Bulloch's (1973) list of examples, 74–8; see also Luck (1969), ch. 1.

In each case, the text is approached with the categories of Hellenistic 'convention' in mind, and the location of those conventions there thus becomes the aim and culmination of this critical model. It is not my intention here to deny or ignore the important influence of Hellenistic poetry on Roman Erotic Elegy, as on all other genres of Roman Augustan poetry. The details of this influence are not, however, the primary interest of this study, nor is the tracing of the literary ancestry of particular themes, motifs or perceived poetic forms seen as an end in itself. Where such intertextual elements become significant, the focus will be on their place in the reading process outlined above and on their relation to the issues central to my approach to the text which are to be introduced below.

Another approach which is exploited here only with qualifications foregrounds elegy's professed function as a tool designed to persuade a beloved to comply with the poet's wishes, i.e. as the poetry of 'courtship'. This approach is represented centrally by Stroh and summed up in the title of his book *Die römische Liebeselegie als werbende Dichtung*.[49] While the 'Nützlichkeitstopik'[50] will not be assumed to explain the significance of the text in itself, or even be privileged as its central concern, the role of persuasion in the delineation and operation of the power structures of the *amor*-relationships in Tibullus Book One forms an important issue in this study. This is not to accept that elegy should be considered a real practical tool of courtship addressed to a real woman masked by a pseudonym,[51] but neither does it deny such a rhetorical role to the text in the elegiac world of *amor*-relationships and the power structures which those relationships represent.

Paul Veyne's approach to Augustan elegy presents another possible model for reading Tibullus. Veyne's assertion that

---

[49] Stroh (1971).

[50] Stroh (1971). The term is first introduced on page 8. For a similar view, see Conte's characterisation of elegy: 'The poetry that is produced by the poet-lover's direct experience and resembles his life should at the same time perform a practical function and serve as a means of courtship', Conte (1994a), 323–4.

[51] See Stroh's speculations about this issue (1971), chs. 6 and 7.

'elegy was a witty genre, a literary game'[52] presents a model
of elegy, the 'game' model, which projects a set of rules, which
might be labelled 'generic rules', shared by poet and 'implied
reader': 'the codes that govern the role of the elegiac text's
reader and narrator in the construction of literary meaning'.[53]
The elegiac poet-persona is a playful and self-parodic figure
whom the reader laughs at without looking beyond elegy's
function as a 'pleasing falsehood'.[54] The acknowledgement of
the largely unproblematic relationship of poet and implied
reader, and of the operation of this set of rules, thus becomes
the critical mission. The meaning of an elegiac text becomes
located in its aim: to amuse.[55] This model ignores the complex tensions in any relationship between reader and poet,
or, more precisely, reader and text, the negotiations and re-
negotiations (the 'powerplay') of meaning in the elegiac text
which it is one of the central concerns of this study to examine. While I accept Veyne's separation of the text from the
poet's life, the assertion of the poet as 'Ego's editor',[56] and
elegy as 'A fiction, no less systematic than the erotic lyrics of
the troubadours or Petrarchian poetry',[57] his statement that
'Roman erotic elegy does not depict anything'[58] again ignores
possible tensions and interplay between the text and anything
external to it, anything to which it might be read as referring.[59] The assumption of the inevitability of such an interplay in any reading of the text is one of the underlying principles of my reading of Tibullus and distinguishes it from the
model constructed by Veyne.[60]

The examination of the various representational strategies
of elegy undertaken by Maria Wyke[61] and more recently, and

---

[52] Veyne (1988) 154.
[53] Wyke (1989a) 167 on Veyne.
[54] Veyne (1988) 86.
[55] Elegy is 'insincere, written to amuse, it is an amusing paradox' Veyne (1988) 188.
[56] Veyne (1988) 95–6.
[57] Veyne (1988) 85.
[58] Veyne (1988) 7.
[59] See Wyke (1989a) 169–70, for this criticism of Veyne.
[60] For a more extensive critique of Veyne's model see Kennedy (1993) 91–100.
[61] See especially Wyke (1989b) 25–47.

with particular reference to the Delia poems of Tibullus,[62] by Duncan Kennedy has had a fundamental influence on the approach my reading has taken to Tibullus Book One. There are two principal ways in which this influence is apparent. First in the treatment of elegiac texts not as mimetic reflections of Roman reality but as discourse. The word 'discourse' has come to assume a variety of meanings in contemporary literary studies, and in choosing to use it here I am aware that, while its utterance may cause a warm, comfortable feeling in some, there are others who, hearing the word 'discourse', reach for their gun. Here I understand discourse to mean, in simple terms, a way of talking or writing about a subject.[63] This may seem a very broad definition, possibly too broad to be useful, but it has several consequences for our understanding of the texts which are part of such a discourse, or perhaps several such discourses at once, which the treatment of them as mimetic representations of Roman reality does not. A discourse, such as elegy, does not mirror 'flesh-and-blood'[64] Roman society, but neither is it unconnected to the cultural context in which it arises. Discourse is fundamentally involved with the ideologies of that culture, forming, articulating and contesting them. Its relationship with those ideologies is always more dynamic than the mimetic model allows, because it is not simply a representation of reality, but a construction and reconstruction of it. The ideologies through which a society sees, experiences and writes about reality are 'generated out of a process of constant contestation'.[65] Discourses are how a culture forms reality. 'The production of meaning is a social phenomenon; the meanings of words are affirmed and challenged in every utterance, and this process of contestation is itself part of the meaning of language-in-use.'[66]

---

[62] Kennedy (1993) 13–22.
[63] For one classic discussion of what discourses are, see Foucault (1972).
[64] See Wyke's comments on the depiction of women in Ovidian elegy, Wyke (1989c) 128; and Kennedy's discussion of Wyke's work, Kennedy (1993) 5ff.
[65] Kennedy (1993) 37
[66] Kennedy (1993) 25.

A central issue in this articulation and contestation of meaning is power:

> From this perspective, power is never an absolute, but it is always generated out of what it depicts itself as needing to control, and figures of power must constantly negotiate their position within the discourses which constitute them as a focus of power.[67]

The issue of power is raised both by the narrative aspects of elegy, the description of the control exercised by the beloved or the patron over the poet-lover, and by the relation to this of the performative aspect, what the poet-lover's discourse represents itself as doing or attempting to do: 'the struggle of the lover through his discourse to control the beloved, to mould her into the fulfilment of his desires'.[68] To this might be added, as I intend to argue, the reception of the poet's performance by the reader. Issues of power are part even of reading and the processes of interpretation which it involves. This is especially true of the kind of interpretation which is attempted by this study. As Kennedy recognises, 'scholarly discourse seeks mastery.'[69]

It is an extension of this concern with power in the elegiac texts which provides the second major contribution of the work of Kennedy and Wyke to the present study. In Tibullus Book One various areas or elements, such as *amor*, the rural world, religion, patronage or military achievements, are placed in a relation of both similarity and difference to one another. This is most visible, as it is in other elegiac texts, in the language used of each, notably the motifs of *militia amoris* and *seruitium amoris*: 'Talking about love ... involves using terms that are also applicable to other things.'[70] While this study will pay close attention to the complexities of such linguistic linkage, it is also my contention here that such similarities of language between different areas such as love and war, or love and slavery, signal and are made possible by similarities in the power structures and processes involved in each case. Such structures and processes are part of elegiac dis-

[67] Kennedy (1993) 37.   [68] Kennedy (1993) 72.   [69] Kennedy (1993) 82.
[70] Kennedy (1993) 47.

course's articulation and contestation of cultural ideologies. As Maria Wyke has suggested in the case of the two examples used above: 'The metaphors of *militia* and *seruitium amoris* are *not* timeless and transcendent but firmly grounded in the cultural discourses of Augustan Rome.'[71] The interplay between the areas which share these power structures and processes in Tibullus Book One is part of what I am investigating in the present study and hope to explain more fully below. The Tibullan elegiac discourse, it is the aim of this study to suggest, is more broadly a 'discourse of power',[72] with all the ambiguities and difficulties for final categorisation and limitation which that term suggests. My aim is to present my own reconceptualisation of how this discourse works in one particular text: Tibullus Book One.

Genre

The concept of genre, expressed or unexpressed, is central to all of these recent approaches to elegy, just as it is to many current approaches to classical literature in general. In the case of Roman elegy, 'where texts cluster thickly within a brief historical moment',[73] the issue of genre is particularly focused and intense. Its importance to a reading of this type is clear. Expectations of generic form and content influence the reading process, and are in turn modified in that process. Genre according to this view is a dynamic, fluid element within

---

[71] Wyke (1989a) 173.

[72] The danger in this approach, as Kennedy has pointed out, is that the way we read this 'discourse of power' is affected by our own understanding of power, which is itself ideologically constructed: 'Important as the term is, it is equally important to be aware of the dangers of integrating, or collapsing, everything into a single master discourse, the discourse of "power". The definition of "power", it must not be forgotten, is itself ideologically determined', Kennedy (1992) 35. While an effort will be made in the following pages to outline what is understood in this study by power in the Roman context and to make explicit the role which more recent sociological studies of power have taken in the formation of this reading, the influence of my own modern conception of power on the reading given here confirms the continuing involvement of the text in precisely the sort of construction and contestation of ideology which, I claim, would have been present in its 'original' Roman context.

[73] Leach (1995) 200.

reading, not a set of fixed, abstract rules existing outside the text. Such a view, for instance, deprives Veyne's 'implied reader' of the apparently unchangeable generic parameters which allow him or her to understand the text.[74] The rules of the elegiac game are destabilised. As Gian Biagio Conte has recently formulated it, genre exists only in its individual realisation within a text. This approach avoids the danger of forcing individual works into strict abstract categories, a series of predetermined rules against which those works are judged. It points instead to the way genre is exploited, modified, and reformed in each text. It suggests that genre is not a set of inflexible rules, but a dynamic force at work within, and reconstituted by, the reading process.

Each text can affiliate itself to one or a number of genres, and it is through this particularly intense form of intertextuality that the generic expectations of a reader are raised. An individual text, then, by associating itself with the form or themes of other texts, calls such expectations into being at the same time as it may modify or possibly entirely overturn and undercut them.[75] These expectations and the processes by which they are exploited or played with in the text are thus important to any study which purports to examine how that text may be read. Similarly, two or more genres may intersect, overlap or appear side by side in any one text, and the interplay of various sets of generic expectations can equally influence how the reader constructs meaning from the text. Both these aspects of the role of genre in reading, the raising and modification of generic expectation and the interplay of multiple, sometimes competing, sets of such expectations, are certainly present in the Tibullan text. The intersection of different genres and the manipulation of generic expectation in the opening poem of Book One signal these as virtually programmatic elements of Tibullan elegy.

Equally important to this study is another aspect of genre

---

[74] Conte (1994b).
[75] This approach to genre has obvious similarities with the more general theories of reader response mentioned above, 1–4.

which various theorists have drawn attention to: the relation of a genre to the socio-cultural environment in which it is realised. The Bakhtinian view of genre stresses this relationship between cultural reality and the literary genre: 'the thematic unity of the work is inseparable from its primary orientation in its environment, inseparable, that is to say, from the circumstances of place and time.'[76] '[E]very genre has its methods and means of seeing and conceptualizing reality',[77] its own 'system of the imagination and grammar of things',[78] but these methods and means, this system, must necessarily draw on the cultural fabric and structures of the society in which it is generated. As Todorov has put it, 'genres bring to light the constitutive features of the society to which they belong.'[79] These may of course be modified by different realisations of any given genre over time, and even the generic elements of a single text may be differently received by readers from different historical periods or cultures.[80] But this further underlines, rather than disproves, the relation of generic form and content to socio-cultural context. The relation of a particular set of cultural structures and ideologies to the formation of genre is particularly significant for a genre like Roman elegy, a group of texts which is relatively specific in its historical and cultural context. Such a relation is also of particular interest to this study, which takes as its thematic focus the realisation, in a single elegiac text, of relationships and processes fundamental to the cultural structures of Roman society.

---

[76] M.M. Bakhtin/P.N. Medvedev, in Morris (1986) 178.
[77] M.M. Bakhtin/P.N. Medvedev, in Morris (1986) 178.
[78] Conte (1994b) 132.
[79] Todorov (1990) 19. Todorov, however, can be too inflexible in his view of the 'institutionalisation' of genres (18–19). See also Miller (1994) 50: 'genres function as "literature's organs of memory", and, in doing so, reveal the basic categories of thought and feeling present in the societies which produce, receive, and preserve them'.
[80] See Miller (1994) 44: 'Genres can now be seen as variable, linguistic responses to the changing conditions of communal life, which derive their evolutionary and recombinatory possibilities from the set of accepted patterns of usage available to a given socio-cultural grouping at a particular time.'

Power

Writing recently of the relationship between slave and master in the Roman world, K. R. Bradley defended his decision to examine slavery as an institution partly by pointing to the pervasiveness of such a power structure in Roman culture: 'The relationship was just one, as it happens, of a sequence of asymmetrical relationships in Roman society that tied individuals together.'[81] Roman elegy is a genre which in its most characteristic elements exploits the ideology of such power structures, not least of course the master-slave relationship itself. The relationships described by the first Tibullan collection (and this does not mean just the relationships of lover and beloved) at once settle into the asymmetrical power structure familiar from other Roman social relationships, and at the same time significantly transform, invert or destabilise such relationships. The most obvious case of this transformation of the conventional power structure is summed up by Catharine Edwards: 'The usual elegiac scenario presents the man (conventionally the dominant partner) as slave to the woman – a piquant inversion of relations of domination as traditionally conceived, which also serves to problematize the relationship between power and sexual desire.'[82] As I hope to demonstrate in the course of this study, this is only part of a network of power-relationships which are exploited and often transformed or destabilised in Tibullus' first book. It is one of the central aims of this work to trace and examine this process, and to argue that the ways in which conceptions of power are constructed, exploited and transformed in the text are of vital significance to an understanding of Tibullus Book One and how it interacts with the conventional power structures of Roman culture. The words which Bradley uses of the master-slave relationship seem even more appropriate. to elegiac power-relationships: 'if the master-slave relationship was only

[81] Bradley (1994) 4.   [82] Edwards (1993) 65 n.4.

a variation on a theme in the Roman mind, the degree of variation in this case was highly significant.'[83]

Similar conclusions have been reached by Richard Saller in his work on personal patronage, another power relationship with an important place in Roman culture. The relationship of patronage is an 'asymmetrical'[84] relationship, where one member is in a more powerful position. Apart from its obvious importance to Tibullus Book One, where the poet's own patron Marcus Valerius Messalla Corvinus plays a major role, the importance of patronal relationships to the operation of Roman society which Saller has identified demonstrates the widespread and deep penetration of the structure and operation of such power relationships into Roman cultural identity. 'Patronal language and ideology permeated Roman society.'[85] It is in the context of this vital and deep-rooted cultural structure, the asymmetrical power relationship, that Tibullus' first book stands. It is my contention that this structure permeates Book One just as it permeates Roman society more generally. But there is another aspect of this asymmetrical cultural structure suggested by Saller which is important to understanding power relationships in Tibullus' first book: the concept of *'reciprocal* exchange'.[86] The expectation of exchange or the characterisation of relationships in terms of exchange again links many ostensibly different social and religious relationships. The structure in each case is similar, and often, as Saller points out, this similarity extends to the language used of such relationships:

> [T]he language of reciprocity did not become exclusively 'un jargon de fonctionnaires et de mandarins' in the Principate. Romans continued to use words such as *beneficium* and *gratia* in their private lives to conceptualize social roles involved in man-god, familial and friendship relations.[87]

Dominated as Book One is by relationships of a similar asymmetrical structure, one specifically a patronal relationship

---

[83] Bradley (1994) 5.   [84] Saller (1982) 1.   [85] Saller (1982) 37.
[86] Saller (1982) 1.   [87] Saller (1982) 26.

and the others *amor*-relationships, the expectation of such a process of reciprocity or exchange and its importance to the structure and operation of power relationships is at the centre of the elegies' involvement with cultural norms of power. This study thus sets out to trace the treatment of such processes in Book One against the background of their importance to Roman culture more generally.

The examination of power relationships and the processes which establish and maintain them has of course been a concern of sociologists for many years, and much work has been done to provide a theoretical basis for the study of such relationships. One such conception of social power which is relevant to the structures and processes which appear in Tibullus Book One has been expressed by Peter Blau:

> Exchange processes, then, give rise to differentiation of power. A person who commands services others need, and who is independent of any at their command, attains power over others by making the satisfaction of their need contingent on their compliance. This principle is held to apply to the most intimate as well as the most distant social relationships.[88]

The conception of power which Blau describes here, and one aspect of which is examined in the Roman context by Saller, goes beyond the understanding of power as simply physical coercion to a view of power as being socially established and operating within a variety of social relationships. Physical coercion is still, of course, the ultimate means of asserting power even within some relationships of social exchange.[89] Physical power and power through social exchange overlap. Slavery, for instance, in its day to day operation, is a relationship of exchange in which service is given by the slave in exchange for the withholding of punishment, the expression of the master's physical power over the slave's body. It is thus

---

[88] Blau (1964) 22.
[89] See Blau's comparison of power through exchange and power through physical coercion: 'unilateral services that meet basic needs are the penultimate source of power. Its ultimate source, of course, is physical coercion. While the power that rests on physical coercion is more absolute, however, it is also more limited in scope than power that derives from met needs.' Blau (1964) 22.

INTRODUCTION

both a relationship of direct physical coercion and, in what
Bradley might call its operation as a social institution, a relationship of social exchange. The power defined and contested
through relationships of social exchange is central to a society's operation and identity. It perpetuates itself in the social
structures most fundamental to that culture. In the Roman
context such structures include, as Saller and others have
shown, patronage, and familial and religious relationships, as
well as more obvious economic processes by which money as
a standard element of exchange becomes equated with power.
In elegy, too, power is generated through relationships.

Feminist studies have done much to highlight the operation
of power within social relationships. A distinction made by
Marilyn French, between 'power-to' and 'power-over', helps
to clarify the different ways in which power can operate and
be understood. In a passage discussing feminist reconsidera-
tions of 'the meaning of power', French writes:

> To begin with, there are different sorts of power: there is power-to, which
> refers to ability, capacity, and connotes a kind of freedom, and there is
> power-over, which refers to domination. Both forms are highly esteemed in
> our society.[90]

It is French's own proviso that '[p]ower-to overlaps with
power-over'[91] which suggests how such a distinction might
help towards an understanding of the different forms which
power takes in Tibullus Book One and the interplay and interconnection between those different forms. Power-to suggests
the power of an individual or group to affect their outward
environment, the 'power to create' for instance. But it can also
suggest the power to affect other individuals or groups, to
manipulate, to persuade, or in extreme cases to force. In both
cases such power can easily become power-over. A farmer's
power to raise a crop can be seen as power over the natural
world, for instance. A general or army's power to defeat other
armies can be seen as power over an enemy. Power-to can also
be institutionalised into power-over. As the passage from Blau

suggested, an individual or group's power to achieve or provide something is an asset around which processes of exchange, and thus relationships of exchange, can form and solidify into fundamental social structures. Both the distinctions between these different conceptions of power, and their essential interrelation, are important to how power is constructed in Tibullus Book One. Power-to and power-over overlap; one makes possible the other.

The conception of power which emerges from Tibullus' first book is not simply one in which individuals possess power which they wield independently, i.e. not simply power-to. Instead, power is generated and expressed through relationships and the processes of exchange which structure them. 'Power is not something that is acquired, seized, or shared, something that one holds on to or allows to slip away; power is exercised from innumerable points, in the interplay of nonegalitarian and mobile relations.'[92] There are both similarities and differences between the various manifestations of such power relationships in Tibullus' first book, as there are in Roman culture more generally. They inter-connect with each other through a shared structure, but operate in different social spheres and, in Roman elegy, can radically reverse the conventional roles played by particular figures within such relationships.

Power in Tibullus Book One, then, is manifested in a series of relationships which can be conceived as relationships of exchange. But this is not the only way in which power in the elegies can be understood, nor does it fully take account of the complex ties between such relationships and the generation of power through struggle or conflict. In an often-quoted passage of the Introduction to *The History of Sexuality* Michel Foucault writes:

It seems to me that power must be understood in the first instance as the multiplicity of force relations immanent in the sphere in which they operate and which constitute their own organisation (*la multiplicité des rapports de force qui sont immanents au domaine où ils s'exercent, et sont constitutifs de*

[92] Foucault (1979) 94–5.

leur organisation); as the process which, through ceaseless struggles and confrontations, transforms, strengthens, or reverses them; as the support which these force relations find in one another, thus forming a chain or a system, or, on the contrary, the disjunctions and contradictions which isolate them from one another ...[93]

Inevitably, the formulation of power which is employed in this study owes a great deal to Foucault, as it does to recent studies of power in other areas of Roman culture, some of which I have mentioned, studies that have themselves been influenced either directly or indirectly by Foucault's work. His model of power as being constantly negotiated and redefined through struggle, and the process of the interplay of power-relations which he highlights, contributes another insight into how power operates which can be usefully applied to Tibullus Book One. The central relationships in the elegies can be seen not just as processes of exchange, but as power struggles. One player in such a relationship seeks to gain the compliance of the other. This may involve submitting to other relationships of exchange, and so various power relationships inter-connect, support each other or conflict. In this way the two conceptions of power, as process of social exchange or as power struggle, may co-exist and even merge within the same relationship or set of relationships in the same way that power-to and power-over inter-relate. Or, to put it in specifically elegiac terms, *seruitium amoris* exists alongside and intersects with *militia amoris*.

Powerplay in Tibullus: A reading of *Elegies* Book One

So the issues which this study focuses on involve the construction and negotiation of various power relationships. These might stem from the 'narrative' elements of the poems, the description of the relationship of poet/lover and beloved, for example, and in some respects that of poet and patron. Or they might stem from the role of the poet/author as constructor of the text, what might be termed the 'performative'

---

[93] Foucault (1976) 92–3.

aspect, including the relationship of reader and poet/text (the ongoing contestation of meaning which merges with the other relationships through its inevitable consequences for them) and the relationship of the poet to the expectations which surround the elegiac genre and, again, to the patron. The separation of these two categories, the narrative and the performative, and of all the discrete power relationships which arise in each case, is of course a consequence of the particular reading strategies brought to the text, and an effort will be made in the course of this study to suggest the interplay of such constructs and the elision of separation within the 'discourse of power'.

Issues of authority, in all these respects, merge and conflict with each other in the elegiac discourse, creating tensions and resonances (differences and similarities), which in turn allow the construction of networks for the articulation and contestation of power. Fundamental to the contestation of power within the frames suggested by these relationships are the processes by which power is constructed and maintained, the processes which describe it. These are what Foucault has described as 'the rules of power':[94]

[I]n a society such as ours, but basically in any society, there are manifold relations of power which permeate, characterise and constitute the social body, and these relations of power cannot themselves be established, consolidated nor implemented without the production, accumulation, circulation and functioning of a discourse.[95]

Tibullus Book One exploits and plays with this discourse. The similarities between the ostensibly *different* processes and between the ostensibly *different* areas of power struggle cause them, again, to merge in a tense, problematic interplay of structures and models which are set for the realisation and operation of power.[96] The interweaving of Messalla's world of traditional, official Roman power (of generals, patrons and magistrates) with the power structures of the world of elegiac *amor*-relationships encourages in Tibullus' first book, more

---

[94] Foucault (1980) 94.
[95] Foucault (1980) 93.
[96] '[T]he interplay of the rules that make possible the appearance of objects during a given period of time', Foucault (1972) 32–3.

than in the early works of any of the other extant elegists, the examination and direct comparison of the regimes of power which operate in each of these areas.

These processes are the focus of this linear study of the ten poems of the first book of Tibullus. In the course of the study of each poem, issues relating to this reading of the discourse of power will come to the fore at various points: knowledge, gender, genre, the patron, the relation of the elegies to other literature etc. For reasons of space and to avoid unnecessary repetition, each of these various aspects will be emphasised at particular times, and passed over more briefly at others. The thesis proceeds in the knowledge that this is only one possible reading of the Tibullan collection and that many other models for reading must be suppressed in the cause of propagating this particular model. But it is also an aim of this study to suggest the centrality and complexity of questions of power, of how power is to be constructed and understood, in any reading of elegy. While these questions have also been recognised in broader contemporary studies of Roman culture[97] which have influenced the terms and direction of this study and provide wider resonances for any conclusions it draws or suggestions it makes, the focus here is primarily on a single text, Tibullus Book One. The central concerns and practice of the reading of the poems through the collection will be more fully introduced and discussed in the specific reading of poem one which follows.

---

[97] In addition to the studies already mentioned, Saller (1982) and Bradley (1994), see, for example, Edwards (1993) esp. 24–32, on the centrality of questions of power relations within the various forms of Roman moral discourse; Beard & North (1990); and White (1993), who also employs exchange theory in his discussion of the relationship between poet and patron, although he particularly argues that the relationships of 'friendship' which existed between Roman poet and Roman 'patron' were less 'power-oriented' than the patron-client relationship as it is understood in modern sociology, 14ff and 270–1.

POEM ONE

Power and process

Diuitias alius fuluo sibi congerat auro
et teneat culti iugera magna soli,
quem labor assiduus uicino terreat hoste,
Martia cui somnos classica pulsa fugent:
me mea paupertas uitae traducat inerti
dum meus assiduo luceat igne focus.   (1-6)[1]

The first lines of Tibullus' first elegy (1.1.1-4) describe a conventional process by which a Roman male citizen might achieve power, a process which is in explicit opposition to the lifestyle desired by the poet. The power comes in the form of wealth – *diuitiae*, the very first word – which consists of gold and lands. My choice of the label 'power' at this initial stage is based not only on the obvious potential opened up by the possession of such wealth ('purchasing power'), but on the inscription of wealth within the discussion of power at Rome (as in many societies and eras, including our own). Wealth is commonly grouped in Roman texts with the instruments, signs and goals of social and political power. This can be seen particularly in the literature of Tibullus' generation and the generation which preceded it. Perhaps the most important example is Lucretius' fifth book, which formulates the emergence of wealth (there also consisting of property and gold) as a moment when the terms of power relations fundamentally changed:

> Posterius res inuentast aurumque repertum,
> quod facile et ualidis et pulchris dempsit honorem;
> diuitioris enim sectam plerumque sequuntur

---

[1] Unless otherwise stated, the text used throughout is that of Lee (1990).

quamlibet et fortes et pulchro corpore creti.
quod siquis uera uitam ratione gubernet,
diuitiae grandes homini sunt uiuere parce
aequo animo; neque enim est umquam penuria parui.
at claros homines uoluerunt se atque potentis,
ut fundamento stabili fortuna manere
et placidam possent opulenti degere uitam.   (5.1113–22)

The same set of associations can be seen in the *De Officiis* of
Cicero, a work which attempts to formulate and control
action (including the exertion of power over others and over
the environment) through a discourse of moral responsibility.[2]
Cicero places *diuitiae* with other terms commonly related to
power: *regna, imperia, nobilitas, honores, diuitiae, opes* ...
(2.115). Similarly, at *Georgics* 2.500–12 Virgil groups wealth
(and the wealthy) with laws, the forum (and *populi tabularia*),
sea-trade and war, as well as the plots of courtiers and the
political (or other) support expressed through ovations. This
passage contains a line which is perhaps recalled by the first
line of Tibullus' elegy (*condit opes alius defossoque incubat
auro, G.* 2.502); see also *G.* 2.495–9,[3] and Horace's fourth
Epode, where wealth, which includes both cash (*Ep.* 4.5) and
vast lands (*Ep.* 4.13), is instrument and sign of the ex-slave's
rise to power (to tribuneship).

The *alius* with whom the Tibullan poet contrasts himself
would, as the poet pictures it, heap up his wealth (*congerat*)
and take possession of the land (*teneat*). He is not only an
active figure, as indicated by the verbs, but is also fully in
control. The poet's choice of the term *iugera* to describe these
lands is also interesting in this context, as it derives, according
to some ancient etymologies,[4] from the *iuga* of the oxen which
plough it, the instrument by which those oxen are controlled.
So too, the earth is *cultus*, it is tamed and under the control
of the *alius*. Read in this way the 'other man's' control over

[2] On *De Officiis* see Douglas (1964) 148–9, and Wood (1988) 68.
[3] Here too it is in the context of an opposition between the trappings and concerns of (urban) power-play and the concerns of the *agricola* which are specified at G.2.513ff.
[4] See Putnam (1973) 50; and also Pliny, *N.H.* 18.9. For this and alternative etymologies see Maltby (1991) 316.

the land expresses and extends the power constituted by his wealth;[5] or, read in more general terms, it reflects the culmination of the human domestication of nature.[6] Hence, the control of the land expressed in these lines reinforces and is reinforced by the common association of *diuitiae* with power.

The hypothetical 'other man', then, judging from the nature of his possessions and the vocabulary chosen to describe both them and him, possesses security and power. But, as the next couplet shows, this has been achieved at the cost of a period of temporary vulnerability and lack of control. The hardship (*labor assiduus*) and the imminent danger (*uicino hoste*) of military life are emphasised. The lack of comfort and the violence of sudden awakening are captured both in the image of broken sleep itself (line 6) and in the vocabulary chosen to express it, as with the unusual use of *pulsa* to describe the trumpet.[7] In this phase of his career, the *alius* is forced into a passive role. He is the one being terrified (*labor ... terreat*), *his* sleep is put to rout (*classica pulsa fugent*). The process by which the power of the other man may be achieved is now fully delineated. It is a straight trade-off: a relatively temporary period (or periods) of discomfort, danger, the threat of sudden and violent death exchanged for the wealth (precious metal and real estate) which in Roman terms is a major constituent of, and basis for, power. Lack of control of life and environment during military service wins corresponding power, security and control over life and environment purchased by the booty from that military service.

The poet has already, in the very first lines, stated that this life is not for him, although he has said nothing to condemn it or discount it for everyone (he says *alius* not *nemo*), and in the following couplet (lines 5–6) he puts forward an alter-

---

[5] For a comparable expression of agricultural power see the farmer of the *Georgics*, whose exertion of power over the land is often described in distinctly military terms (see especially *G.* 2.273–87).

[6] This reading might be encouraged by Lucretius Bk 5. See also Beagon on Pliny the Elder: 'At times, the whole of *Natura*, not just *Terra*, seems to be little more than a servant to man's initiative' Beagon (1992) 201.

[7] On the oddness of *pulsa* in this context see *TLL* X.1019.42ff.; on its connotations of violence particularly in poetic usage see *TLL* X.1017.62ff., and also Murgatroyd (1980) 53.

native process of his own. Lack of wealth (*paupertas*) leads to inaction (*uita iners*). Such a life is without war, without glory, without power, and thus, according to one strand of conventional Roman morality, morally worthless.[8] The poet is entirely passive: *me ... traducat.*[9] The result of this process is comfort. The *assiduus ignis* is in direct opposition to the discomfort of *assiduus labor*. Its importance in the 'alternative' lifestyle corresponds to the importance of *assiduus labor* in the first. The similarity and opposition of these two sets of terms thus signal that lines 5–6 are presenting a direct alternative to the lifestyle of the *alius*. The images of hearth, fire and light (*luceat*) bring the reader back from the larger landscape of the *iugera multa* and faraway battlefields to the highly personalised sphere of the poet's *focus*. The personal nature of the poet's desires is emphasised by the frequency of personal pronouns, *me mea* (the first two words of the couplet) and *meus* in the space of two lines. The poet's goal, then, is the minimum (*dum ...*) for *personal* security and comfort,[10] not control over other things or people.

This preferred lifestyle (or perhaps 'process of life' would be a more appropriate term) is an inversion, both in content and structure, of that attributed to the *alius*. The consequence of the *alius*' lifestyle (wealth) is the opposite of the initial element of the poet's preferred way of life (*paupertas*) while the initial element of the *alius*' lifestyle (action, discomfort and danger) is the opposite of the consequence of the poet's ideal process of life (inaction and comfort). The inversion is emphasised by the description in lines 1–4 of the effect first, then the cause, while in lines 5–6 the cause is mentioned before the effect. In these opening six lines the process underlying a conventional Roman career path is first revealed then comprehensively transformed.

As I suggested earlier, this should not be seen as a complete

---

[8] See Lyne (1980) 155.
[9] See Murgatroyd (1980) 53 for the (ironic?) military connotations of *traducat*.
[10] A goal which, in contradiction of the poet's distinction here between a life of struggle (of the *alius*) and a life of ease (his own), Cicero cites as the first goal of power struggle for mortals (*De Officiis* 1.11).

condemnation of normal Roman *militia* and the power founded upon it (or the processes of acquisition underlying it). But, precisely by presenting an alternative to it, the poet gives it normative force.[11] He tries to place himself outside the conventional position, but to do this must define his own position in terms of the orthodox processes. Further complications can be read into the poet's position since, as Leach notes,[12] the initial formulation of the poet's rural life attracts to it connotations of the pious Catonian *rusticus* explicitly linked in Roman ethical discourse with precisely the military life the poet had figured himself as turning away from.[13] This could be read as an inversion, a usurpation of a conventional Roman moral type, presenting a poet who dynamically transforms these conventions to suit his own desires.[14] An alternative reading, however, might locate an ambivalence on the poet's part to setting himself outside or even in opposition to established moral or social categories. If the first reading is to be upheld, the distinct formulation of the two processes in lines 1–6 (inverted and opposite) must be seen to assert aggressively[15] the difference between the two lifestyles, setting up a discourse of opposition.

Such a reading might be complicated if, for example, these opening lines were read against Horace's recent *Satires* I.I. That poem also formulates the process of enduring hardship for money (*Sat.* I.I.28–32), of which *both* farming *and* soldiering are examples. In both cases security in later life is the aim[16] and Horace gives the process ethical validity partly through analogy with the ant at lines 32–8. There is (in this

[11] 'Where there is power there is resistance, and yet, or rather consequently, this resistance is never in a position of exteriority to power', Foucault (1976) 95.
[12] Leach (1980a) 86.
[13] I.e. rural life is good training for being a soldier; cf. Cato, *De Agricultura* I.I.
[14] See Lyne (1980) 153, who suggests that Tibullus usurps the term *rusticus*, normally associated in the Roman mind with hard work and simple, upright morality (cf.Cato, *De Agricultura* I.I), using it to describe a life of *otium*, and thus further inverting conventional Roman socio-moral types. This (the 'reinterpretation' of traditional values) is also the conclusion of Leach (1980a) 86.
[15] The poet could thus be seen as replacing the aggressive process of *militia* with his own aggressive counter-attack.
[16] Just as security (the avoidance of injury and the satisfaction of basic needs) was the foremost aim of all humans according to Cicero at *De Off.* I.II.

reading of *Satires* 1.1) *no* opposition between the two life-styles. Only when the process is invalidated by the excessive pursuit of money for its own sake does Horace criticise the hardship-for-money trade-off. In cases of such excess, greed (whether of the miser or the spendthrift) converts wealth *in itself* to a source of vulnerability and insecurity rather than, as in the conventional process, the final guarantee of *security* (power) bought by initial hardship, vulnerability or insecurity (*Sat.* 1.1.38–60). Horace concerns himself with delimiting the conventional process, not with fundamentally transforming the process itself. It is the conflict and power struggle between individuals which the *excessive* pursuit of wealth creates (and consists of) that Horace criticises (*Sat.* 1.1.108–16). The commonality asserted in *Satires* 1.1 for the processes (or lifestyles) of farming and soldiering presents a different system from the oppositional one which is asserted in Tib. 1.1.1–6. In *Satires* 1.1 *both* lifestyles are schematically an exchange of hardship or vulnerability for security. The Tibullan reading of opposition between two separate processes could be compared to a similar scheme in the *Georgics*, where the pursuit of military or political power is at some points set explicitly in opposition to the farmer's life (for example at *G.* 2.513ff.; see the note above). But within the *Georgics* itself a tension might be read between this assertion of separation or difference on the one hand, and the force exerted by the farmer to gain control of the land on the other, since this force itself can in fact be seen as *parallel* to military struggle and the pursuit of political power (see, for example, *G.* 2.273–87).

These differences and correspondences also suggest one reading strategy which these lines might encourage and which I in the preceding interpretation have to some extent been following. The juxtaposition of different lifestyles in lines 1–6 of Tibullus 1.1 and the implication that the poet *is* satisfied with his lot has affinities in at least this respect with the opening lines of *Satires* 1.1 (especially lines 1–12), where those who complain about their lot are criticised. This perhaps suggests that the opening lines of Tibullus' poem may also be introducing a moral programme of the type explicit in

Horace's *Satires* Book One. The resonances with Lucretius Book Five and the *Georgics* would thus cement these lines' place in an ethical discourse.[17] This, then, might be one way in which to read this elegy (or collection): as part of a discussion about how to live. The opening of Tibullus' first elegy could then be seen as inscribing itself within an ethical discussion which not only provides a context for the poem as a whole but opens tensions and contradictions which allow the choices and formulations of the poet in lines 1–6 to be read in a variety of ways.

In this way the opening lines draw out the contradictions within the various Roman ethical discourses. The link between *rusticus* and *miles* seen in *Satires* 1.1 is present at least as early as the Catonian discussion of lifestyles which opens *De Agricultura*. There the two, and the values invested in the two, are the same: *At ex agricolis et uiri fortissimi et milites strenuissimi gignuntur* (*De Agricultura*, 1). The distinct separation of rural life from *militia* in Tib. 1.1.1–6, the placement of rural life *outside* the sphere of power struggle inhabited by the soldier, finds tension in its own expression. The power of the *alius* actually consists of *rural* estates (*iugera*) gained through *militia*. This tension is reinforced if compared to similar attempts to separate the rural and the military/political spheres in other recent poetic works. The separation of the two spheres in the *Georgics*, for example, is problematic, and in the *Eclogues* the rural or pastoral world (see especially *Eclogues* 1 and 9) becomes precisely the *site* and *prize* of power contest rather than an escape from it.[18] This stands in contrast to what might be expected from the pastoral world, just as it stands in contrast to the poet's formula at Tib. 1.1.1–6.[19] The opening of Tibullus' first elegy works within the gaps and contradictions of these various ethical expressions of

---

[17] This reading strategy – on my part – is implicit also in the references to Cicero above.

[18] For similarities between the military and agricultural spheres in the *Georgics* see Betensky (1979); for the rural world as focus of power contest and a victim of its effects see Boyle (1975b).

[19] Alternatively, such a separation could be seen as one of the failed ideals of the *Eclogue* collection.

sameness and/or difference. As the poet takes a position towards them, the text invites readers (through the process of
reading) to find their own position. In exactly what does the
sameness or difference consist? Are the apparent contradictions of the poet's position within such a moral discussion
to be drawn out and exploited, or is the assertion of opposition and separation to be upheld? It is within the dynamic of
such a discussion that these opening lines move and may be
read.

Pius rusticus

Ipse seram teneras maturo tempore uites
  rusticus et facili grandia poma manu,
nec Spes destituat, sed frugum semper aceruos
  praebeat et pleno pinguia musta lacu:
nam ueneror seu stipes habet desertus in agris
  seu uetus in triuio florida serta lapis,
et quodcumque mihi pomum nouus educat annus
  libatum agricolam ponitur ante deum.
flaua Ceres, tibi sit nostro de rure corona
  spicea quae templi pendeat ante fores,
pomosisque ruber custos ponatur in hortis
  terreat ut saeua falce Priapus aues.
uos quoque, felicis quondam, nunc pauperis agri
  custodes, fertis munera uestra, Lares;
tunc uitula innumeros lustrabat caesa iuuencos,
  nunc agna exigui est hostia parua soli:
agna cadet uobis, quam circum rustica pubes
  clamet 'io, messes et bona uina date'.   (7–24)

  From line 7 the poet starts to fill in some of the details of
his proposed lifestyle. The work which the poet would do as a
rusticus would be relatively easy: the vines are *tenerae* and he
sets trees *facili manu*. Nor is the work continual, as the *labor
assiduus* of warfare is; instead it will occur only at the proper,
seasonal time(s) (*maturo tempore*). Yet the abundance which

the poet would never cease to hope for does not fit comfortably under the name of *paupertas*. The *acerui frugum* perhaps recall the heaped up gold of the first line and certainly suggest more than simple self-sufficiency, as does *pinguia*,[20] an opulent word to describe the new wine in the full (*plenus*) vat.[21] What's more, such abundance is not hoped for merely sometimes but *semper*. Here can be read a working definition of *paupertas* and the poet's desired level of comfort which is rather more than the reader might have expected back in line 5. Already the reader finds that the value or meaning which she/he is encouraged to give to words may shift in the process of reading as the text reveals more.

Is such minimal effort as described in 7–8 enough to ensure the level of comfort and security the poet seems to desire? Apparently not. The power of a third party is required. The poet is unwilling or unable to achieve such abundance by himself. He openly declares the reason he holds out hope for such plentiful produce: *nam ueneror* ... The first present indicative verb of the poem illustrates the poet's attempt to ensure prosperity, to control the future vicariously, by venerating the gods in whom ultimate power lies. Just as it was *Spes*, not the poet, who would supply (*praebeat*) the fruits at 10, it is the rural gods who are the true power-wielders in the poet's countryside. Hence, the offering of the first fruits to win the power of the gods over to his side takes the place of the *labor assiduus* of the *alius* to win the power base of wealth and land. The separation and assertion of difference which underlay the formulation of these processes (rural life and *militia*) in the opening lines may now be eroding. Rural piety is substituted for military service, but the goal (except perhaps in degree) is essentially the same: to ensure a beneficial future outcome. The riches of produce (lines 8–10) and the riches of

[20] Assuming the 'normal' expectations surrounding *paupertas* given by Cairns (1979) 20 as 'simple sufficiency without surplus', *pinguia* is a strikingly inappropriate word, carrying as it does connotations of overabundance and obesity.
[21] The succession of 'p's (*praebeat et plena pinguia*...), forming a full sound in the mouth, perhaps also gives the impression, verbally, of fullness, even opulence, although such verbal effects are always difficult to interpret.

lines 1–2 need not be seen as so very different in nature. But the results of the poet's attempts to achieve, or at least win to his side, some power without disturbing his own comfort or following the normal career path of a high class Roman are uncertain. For, while he speaks of the attempt itself (his veneration) in very thorough[22] and definite terms, his hopes for rural life remain in the subjunctive. The action of *Spes* (uncertain by its very nature) is doubly indefinite coupled with these subjunctives (*nec destituat* and *praebeat*). The poet does not have the power to make his alternative lifestyle a success, and must rely on other factors, such as the gods, who, while he may appeal to them and expect his appeals to be successful, are not under his direct control.

Yet the power of the rural gods, which the poet appeals to in his address to Ceres, is clearly of a different kind to the gold and estates garnered by warfare. Ceres is *flaua*, perhaps recalling the colour of gold in line 1 (*fuluum*), but the crown she is offered is not of gold, but of corn (*spicea*). Similarly, the cameo of Priapus (lines 17–18) is a parody of warfare as it is described in lines 3–4. The phallic god is to be stationed as a sentry (*custos ponatur*), but it is not on the battlefield nor even in hostile territory but *in hortis*, a phrase implying not so much even an open field but an ordered, controlled and secure environment. The image is *ruber*, but not with blood; he is armed with a *falx* (the traditional Priapan 'falx-symbol'), but its description as *saeua* is so clearly inappropriate as to push the couplet even further into the realms of the mock-heroic. The word *terreat* directly recalls line 3. The birds, like the soldiers, are frightened. But, of course, they are only birds and in this alternative, burlesque version, unlike real war, no real harm is done, no blood is shed. The very use of humour itself creates a gentler atmosphere than the description of war earlier in the poem. But perhaps more importantly, Priapus here is in control and acting on behalf of the poet to negate a possible

---

[22] He is careful to pray at every deserted stump and to garland any old crossroad stone he may come across.

threat (the *aues*), and the result of this action, while again being an alternative to gold and lands, is just as real:[23] *pomosi horti*, words which again speak of abundance. But the use of subjunctives still leaves the successful realisation of such a picture in doubt. It is all still at the hypothetical stage.[24]

The address to the Lares (at lines 19–20) directly contrasts past and present (*quondam ... nunc ... tunc ... nunc*). Questions are immediately raised: why has there been a change from prosperity to *paupertas*? Does this mean that the offerings to the gods have failed to ensure their support in the past? Do the gods not really possess such power in the first place? Or is this the result of something outside the rural sphere? The comparison of present and past has immediate consequences for our understanding of the future. The Lares are enlisted, perhaps even obliged, to lend their power for the prosperity and security of the estate (and thus, as we have seen, the comfort of the poet).[25] They are *custodes*, just as Priapus is *custos*, and the other rural gods might be called the same. The poet pays them for the service: *fertis munera uestra*, *fertis* being a solid indicative after another run of subjunctives. But the results of this are seeming less and less solid and certain as the poem progresses. Lines 21–2 undercut the poet's hopes for the future even further: if *innumeri iuuenci* offered to the gods were not sufficient to ensure continued prosperity in the past (since that prosperity has diminished to present *paupertas*), the meagre offering of the present (*exigui ... hostia parua soli*) is even less likely to do so. The poet is for the first time placed within the context of a social group (*rustica pubes*) as the ultimate aim of his piety, to control a future outcome (in this case the harvest), is pronounced in direct speech through the com-

---

[23] Parody in itself only functions (of course) if *similarity* is recognised as well as difference: 'parodic representations expose the model's conventions and lay bare its devices through the coexistence of the two codes in the same message' Ben-Porat (1979) 247 (quoted in Hutcheon (1984) 49). See also Rose (1993) 29–36 for the parodic interplay of imitation and incongruity.

[24] And in the comic treatment of Priapus the poet might be seen laughing at his own hopes.

[25] For the *Lares familiares* as guardians of the *familia* and country estate see *RE* 'Lares' 814.1–818.57.

mon voice of the rural community: *io, messes et bona uina date*. It may be uncertain whether the entire rustic community thinks as he does, but the comfort and security which the poet seems to desire from a rural life, while being presented as an alternative to power itself in the conventional Roman sense, does require a certain amount of power to achieve. Given the limited amount of work the poet himself is willing to put into mastering the land, he must rely upon a third party, the gods, to exercise this power. The process of amassing personal power then is replaced with one of surrogate power, the support of the gods. While the process of exchange is similar, power in each case is expressed differently: directly in the case of the *alius*; indirectly (through the gods) in the case of the poet, who would gain the control over the future which he desires by controlling, through piety and specifically offerings, the actions of the gods.[26] The uncertainties which surround the *poet's* process of pious exchange might suggest that it is actually the apparent solidity or certainty of the exchange of *militia* for wealth which presents the *major difference* between the two schemes, while in other significant respects they are similar. This makes possible an ironic re-reading of the assertion of difference or separation between them in lines 1–6.

Past and present

Iam modo, iam possim contentus uiuere paruo
    nec semper longae deditus esse uiae,
sed Canis aestiuos ortus uitare sub umbra
    arboris ad riuos praetereuntis aquae.
nec tamen interdum pudeat tenuisse bidentem
    aut stimulo tardos increpuisse boues;
non agnamue sinu pigeat fetumue capellae
    desertum oblita matre referre domum.   (25–32)

---

[26] More complexity can be read into these similarities and differences. While in some ways the produce the poet desires corresponds to the wealth of the *alius* (the ends of the exchange), in another respect the support of the gods corresponds to that wealth since both make possible their possessors' control, whether of the land, the future, or in broader terms.

Iam modo immediately throws a new element into the picture: the contrast between the poet's hopes and his past behaviour. The insistence of *iam modo, iam*[27] with the subjunctive *possim* suggests both that, in the past, he was not *contentus uiuere paruo* and that, in fact, he finds it difficult to do this. Again this might recall the Lucretian passage quoted earlier which asserts a re-definition of *diuitiae* that is invalidated by the continued human pursuit of the wealth which bestows power:

> diuitiae grandes homini sunt uiuere parce
> aequo animo; neque enim est umquam penuria parui. (Lucr. 5.1118–19)

The poet's attempt to re-define and transform his own past behaviour in this direction may now be read into the formulations and reformulations of the elegy's opening lines. But at the same time this attempt at self-improvement is brought into doubt and destabilised by the poet's implicit tendency (in the past?) *not* to be *contentus uiuere paruo*. These tensions might be further drawn out by the re-reading now of the relationship between this elegy (up to this point) and Horace's first satire. The Tibullan poet has *not*, after all, been content with his lot, but is in the process of changing careers. The poet could now be seen as parallel to the figure at *Sat.* 1.1.14–19 who claims a desire to change his lifestyle, but ultimately does not carry that desire through. This parallel further destabilises the poet's reformulation of his lifestyle (and thus his reformulation of the conventional process of the opening lines). He portrays himself as a powerless, passive victim (*deditus*),[28] while the phrase *longa uia* suggests travel undertaken for military or commercial purposes with the objective of personal gain.[29] The poet is not the simple lover of country comfort as the reader may have been led to believe. His desire for a rural

---

[27] See Murgatroyd (1980) 299, for a defence of this reading, although his placement of this line between lines 6 and 7 seems unnecessary.

[28] If the poet has so little control over what he may or may not be 'content' with that, as this phrase suggests, he can only hope (*iam modo iam ...*) to control how he will now live, then the possibility is opened up that it is elements of his own character which make him inherently powerless.

[29] Compare similar meanings of *uia* at Propertius 3.21.2 and *longa uia* at Ovid *Am.* 1.9.9.

life is relatively new. Another Horatian resonance, that of *Epode* 2 and of Alfius the moneylender and would-be farmer whose transformation into a *rusticus* lasts about two weeks (*Epode* 2.67–70), might also raise questions about the Tibullan poet's ability to maintain the changes and reformations he has claimed to desire. Or to put it slightly differently, it might bring into doubt the poet's ability to enforce *in his own case*, and on the most basic level, the separation between the two lifestyles, or processes, set out in the opening lines. The earlier assertion of difference between the poet's chosen lifestyle and the process of power struggle in which the *alius* is involved can be seen to be eroding on several fronts. Not only can distinct similarities in the structures of the two supposedly opposed lifestyles be discerned, but at the same time the reader is also invited to doubt the poet's ability to exclude from his life involvement in precisely that process of power struggle (*militia* and the pursuit of wealth) which he had apparently rejected in the opening lines.

Even more questions may arise in a reader's mind at this point. If the poet has been away all the time (*semper*) on military or commercial ventures, is this perhaps the reason for the decline of his estate? Is it simply the victim of neglect? But the very fact that the couplet is rich in suggestion hinders certainty, and such possibilities where they might be seen remain open but unverified.

The poet returns to his desire for stillness and comfort, to escape the heat in the shade by running water. Lines 27–8 present a pastoral scene in contrast to the continual motion and hardship of the *longa uia*. This is interrupted by a very reluctant statement of 'georgic' intent (*nec tamen interdum pudeat*). The tension in these lines (25–32) between the pastoral and the georgic, between the enjoyment of the natural *locus amoenus* and the necessity of agricultural labour, suggests the poet's grudging and half-hearted recognition of the need for struggle and control even within such an apparently idyllic environment. This irrepressibility of the struggle for control, even of the half-serious kind advocated by the poet here, does in fact recall the two corresponding Virgilian poems, the one pastoral, the other georgic. The problematic division in the *Georgics* between agricultural force and power of other sorts (are they different? the same?), and the invasion of the pastoral sphere (ideally exterior to power contest) by the values and forces of power struggle in the *Eclogues*,[30] similarly suggest the difficulties of excluding force, control or power from any practical, ethical or poetic scheme. The Tibullan poet in lines 29–32 will exert his power and control (*tenuisse, stimulo increpuisse* being words which speak of control and, even military, discipline), but he doesn't seem to want to. He will do it only sometimes. It might be argued that a Roman farmer, unless truly a peasant, would not have the need to do these things. In this case the poet's statement that now and again he might come out and hurry up a few lazy cows with a goad presents a rather comic[31] demonstration of power over livestock in the same way that Priapus and his *saeua falx* present a comic depiction of armed combat. But part of the poet's wish is to be *himself* the *rusticus (ipse ... rusticus* 7–8), and a *rusticus* might be expected to work more often than *interdum*.[32] Again it is unclear how the pastoral security and comfort the poet desires might be gained without the necessary work or, as it is more particularly described, mastery and control of land and beast to produce the *frugum acerui* which seem to form, in the poet's mind, the minimum basis for that comfort.[33] The poet at lines 31–2 adds a demonstration of pastoral care in its fullest sense, although *non ... pigeat* suggests that this might not be looked upon as entirely reputable. The poet juxtaposes (or confuses) one system of values, that of the high-class Roman who might be ashamed to do such menial tasks, with another, that of the *rusticus* associated in traditional Roman morality with upright hard work (see Cato again). The poet does this by means of a notional change of role, from Roman estate-owner, accustomed to

[30] See also the echo at Tib.1.1.31–2 of *Ecl.*1.14–15.
[31] And, thus, not taken entirely seriously.
[32] See Lyne (1980) 155 and 157.
[33] The tension here between what might be called the pastoral and the georgic modes is reinforced by the recollections of Virgil in these lines; on which see Ball (1983) 34.

journeys (military or otherwise) on the *longa uia*, to humble peasant farmer devoted to his land and livestock. This confusion of roles may again draw readers into the contradictions and conflicts between the values and ethical positions attached to each role. The reader is thus involved within the enunciation and negotiation of the similarities or differences between those roles. In exploiting these contradictions, while again suggesting an ambivalence on the poet's part to the division of these lifestyles, the text demonstrates the difficulty of maintaining such a separation of lifestyles or ethical roles, and the tendency of one to contaminate the other. The poet at lines 31–2, still speaking in the subjunctive, represents himself protecting what is perhaps one of the archetypal images of vulnerability, the lamb or kid abandoned by its mother, and bringing it to the security of his home. He is thus representing in his own *sinus* and *domus* the role of security and comfort which he wants to discover for himself.

The power of appeal

At uos exiguo pecori, furesque lupique,
    parcite: de magno est praeda petenda grege.
hic ego pastoremque meum lustrare quotannis
    et placidam soleo spargere lacte Palem.
adsitis, diui, neu uos e paupere mensa
    dona nec e puris spernite fictilibus:
fictilia antiquus primum sibi fecit agrestis,
    pocula de facili composuitque luto.
non ego diuitias patrum fructusque requiro
    quos tulit antiquo condita messis auo:
parua seges satis est, satis est requiescere lecto
    si licet et solito membra leuare toro.   (33–44)

At, a qualification, breaks into the picture of serenity. There are threats to it. This lifestyle is vulnerable. The poet, having no power to prevent them himself, must appeal to these threats (*furesque lupique*) to spare him (*parcite*) just as he must appeal to various gods to support him. In connection with this, the poet reveals another reason for his dislike of wealth. Quite apart from the vulnerability and discomfort involved in achieving it, wealth itself, and hence its possessor, are vulnerable simply because that wealth is desirable:[34] *de magno est praeda petenda grege* (34). Such wealth would thus make his desire for security even more difficult to achieve. *Paupertas*, the *exiguum pecus*, may, he hopes, afford some protection (although the reader might wonder if wolves or thieves would be so obliging as to make the distinction). The conflicting and the common associations of both wealth and poverty (power, security, vulnerability) are brought to the surface in this appeal. Any reading must negotiate these contradictions and similarities. Is there in fact a relationship of *paupertas* to security just as there is of wealth to power? Is the poet's *paupertas* converted to security, which might itself be thought of as a form of power, through this assertion that it is beyond threat? Or does the impression of vulnerability remain?

Again piety, or, more exactly, recourse to the power of the gods, is offered as a safeguard. This time the poet's appeals are more vivid: *hic ego* ... The need for such an appeal is present and constant. He performs the rites regularly and is used to it (*quotannis ... soleo*), presumably when he is not off on the *longa uia*. The verb used of the poet's ritual purification of his shepherd (as at line 21) is *lustrare*, a word with strong connotations of light and brightness.[35] This may suggest safety, certainty or security, just as the *pastor* who is purified is himself a figure of security as protector of the flock (lines 31-2). But the presence of the gods is still only requested (*adsitis diui*). There is no evidence that divine aid is a present reality; the poet is still speaking in the subjunctive. The decline of the estate referred to at lines 19-22 might even encourage the deduction that divine assistance has been absent in the past. The future presence of the gods would thus seem unlikely, casting an ironic light upon the ritual endeavours of the pious Tibullan *rusticus* in this poem. In mentioning the pay-

---

[34] Again this intersects (and complicates itself) with the reading of *Satires* I.I.
[35] *Lustrare* can often mean simply 'to irradiate', see *TLL* VII.1877.12ff.

ment he gives the gods for their power, the *dona*, it seems clear
the poet himself sees some threat that his *paupertas* (such as it
may be) will not be enough to purchase him this power, hence
the shift into the imperative, *nec spernite*, as with *parcite* at
line 34. There may even be a hint that he is ashamed of the
moderate means which he had actively advocated in the
opening lines of the poem. The poet defends his offerings *e
puris fictilibus* by linking them with the morality of an earlier
time (*antiquus primum ... agrestis*). This suggests the poet's
alignment with a purer, 'Golden Age', morality. Apart from
arguing for the superior morality of his offerings, and thus for
their acceptance by the gods, the picture of the ancient coun-
tryman is one of self-sufficiency (*sibi fecit*) involving some
power for personal needs (*composuit*) but little work (*de facili
luto*). This would seem to match at least the *desires* of the poet
for his own life. The link with ancient times also establishes
the poet within a tradition which, along with the customs and
repeated forms of religion (*soleo ...*) often mentioned in the
poem, may provide another form of certainty or security.

The subject of ancient times brings the poet back to the
contrast between past prosperity and present *paupertas*. This
time the plenteous produce of the past is linked verbally with
the wealth (*diuitiae*) which the *alius* (line 1) would possess:
diuitias ... fructusque (41).[36] Thus, the suspicion that agriculture and *militia* are similar in structure and goal may be
strengthened in the continued interplay and intertwining of
similarity and difference, as separation even of vocabulary is
transgressed. Both rural prosperity and wealth acquired
through military service require a certain amount of power to
achieve (the control of a future outcome) and both give a
certain amount of power to the possessor, whether simply the
power of self-sufficiency or personal security, or more. Again
the reader may wonder why the change from past wealth to
contemporary *paupertas* has come about, possibly (if we read
auus as 'grandfather') in the space of a generation or so. The

---

[36] Also *condita* used of the harvest echoes the gold which the *alius* may heap up
(*congerat*).

link between the poet's ancestor and the Golden Age-like, pure world of the ancient cup-maker (*antiquus agrestis, antiquus auus*) also suggests that apart from a superior morality, the work was easier. The harvest seems to produce fruits for the *auus* of its own accord, *quos tulit antiquo condita messis auo* (42). This is something which the poet himself, as has been seen, seems to desire: plentiful, heaped produce and easy work to get it. Yet the poet claims that he does not pursue such prosperity (is this perhaps *why* the estate is no longer prosperous?) and again states the minimum level of comfort he desires (lines 43–4). He is insistent (*satis est, satis est ...*).[37] It is enough to have the minimum wealth needed to be comfortable and at rest (*requiescere ...|... membra leuare*). The word *securus* sums up his desires for security and comfort. Again his wish is to enjoy such comfort not sometimes, but often and possibly always (*solito lecto*; again there is some certainty to be gained by customary action). *Si licet*, however, may suggest there is some real threat that this might not be possible. Even such a minimum may be beyond the power of the poet to achieve. But why is the poet now willing to put up gladly with such a minimum when line 25 suggested that he has found it hard to remain content with relatively little in the past?[38]

Domina – puella – Delia

Quam iuuat immites uentos audire cubantem
 et dominam tenero continuisse sinu!
aut gelidas hibernus aquas cum fuderit Auster,
 securum somnos igne iuuante sequi!
hoc mihi contingat: sit diues iure furorem
 qui maris et tristes ferre potest pluuias.
o quantum est auri pereat potuisque smaragdi
 quam fleat ob nostras ulla puella uias!
te bellare decet terra, Messalla, marique
 ut domus hostiles praeferat exuuias:

---

[37] Who is the poet trying to convince?
[38] Although, as lines 9–10 implied, the 'little' he requires and desires for comfort is, even now, not so different from prosperity and plenty.

> me retinent uinctum formosae uincla puellae,
> et sedeo duras ianitor ante fores.
> non ego laudari curo, mea Delia; tecum
> dum modo sim, quaeso segnis inersque uocer.   (45-58)

Quam iuuat gives emotional emphasis to the couplet which introduces a new element into the reader's understanding of the poem so far: a part of the poet's 'minimum' for comfort unmentioned up to now. Again you have rest (*cubantem*), pleasure (*iuuat*), and ease (*tenero sinu*), detached from the harsh elements, which are only heard in the background. But now the wish is *dominam tenero continuisse sinu* (46). As yet this is only part of the poet's hopes. Yet a contradiction, or at least a tension, may immediately be read here. Firstly, the *domina*, a term which might lead the reader to picture a woman in control, the one doing the holding or restraining,[39] is herself being restrained (*continuisse*). Secondly, the picture is detached from the poet himself. He speaks generally of 'one lying' (*cubantem*), not himself. This perhaps suggests that this wish, for him, may be unrealisable.[40] This wish to lie with the *domina*, however, rates mention before the poet's wish to escape extreme weather (line 47; already mentioned at lines 27-8), and to sleep safely in the firelight, which recalls the opposite *lack* of sleep occasioned by military service[41] and the similar comfort gained from the fire at lines 4-6. In the passage in which it is introduced, therefore, sleeping with a *domina* takes precedence over all the reasons for the poet's choice of his 'alternative' lifestyle which the reader is already familiar with. This might prompt the reader to some re-evaluation, as the finality of *hoc mihi contingat* and the recollection of the poem's opening in the concession of wealth to those who can (*potest*) endure the process of discomfort (the *furorem* ...

---

[39] See Maltby (1991) 195 for the obvious etymological connections of *domina/ dominari/domo*. Particularly significant in this context is the use of *domina* in Propertius Book I (which was most likely published just previously to this poem); see, for example, 1.7.6ff. (See also Murgatroyd (1980) 62.)

[40] See also Lyne (1980) 158.

[41] *Sequi*, which has military overtones, also recalls the martial context of the previous occasion that sleep was mentioned in the poem.

maris et tristes ... pluuias) to gain it[42] (at lines 49–50) seem to enact a closure of sorts. Because of his own character and the very nature of his desires, it may seem uncertain, and even unlikely, that the poet will have the power, even through the gods, fully to realise those desires.

But any such attempt at reflection and re-evaluation is pre-empted. The apparent ending was false and the poet now bursts forth *o quantum* ... An initial reading of *o* ... as an emotional intensifier might suggest that what is to follow is what the poet feels most passionately (or at least deeply). And what is it? The poet does, for once, vehemently attack wealth itself (*pereat*), but it is an attack on wealth relative to women: *potius ... quam*. This is his essential objection to the search for wealth (*nostras uias* recalling *longa uia*): the woman in question (as yet only an indefinite *ulla puella*) would have to be left behind and would object to this (*fleat*). The *uia*, it seems, brings hardship for the girl as well as the departing man who would make the woman cry by leaving. But the picture is general, even though it is *nostrae uiae*, and the reader, her/his attention caught by the strength of the sudden 'outburst', might expect more specific details concerning the poet's own situation. Such details are not immediately given. The poet instead turns to his patron, Messalla: *te bellare decet* (lines 53). Again, there is nothing intrinsically wrong, in the poet's mind, with war and the wealth which comes from it (*hostiles exuuias*).[43] It is morally right (*decet*) for Messalla to pursue the conventional path, but an 'alternative' morality operates in the poet's case. Again, to support this reading, the assertion of separation (between lifestyles or ethical codes) must be upheld. As his sudden (and rather brusque)[44] address to Messalla suggests, the poet has more pressing demands on him than a great man's power to expect extended recognition

---

[42] Again this does not involve an attack on wealth *per se*; those who can undergo the necessary hardship and vulnerability are looked upon as winning it by right (*iure*).

[43] On the poet's rejection of war in these lines not being a general 'prescription for all Romans' see Cloud (1993) 117.

[44] It almost seems as if the poet hurries to add this quick qualification, suddenly realising that his rejection of the conventional socio-moral type which his patron represents may have offended Messalla.

or praise from his poet/client. Line 55 alone contains three words emphasising the poet's powerlessness: *me retinent uinctum ... uincla* (55). He is passive and entirely controlled by the girl. This is an extreme *seruitium amoris*.[45] The poet is a slave, a *ianitor*. It is a present fact (*sedeo*). We are now out of the realm of optative and potential subjunctives and (so the suggestion – of poet to patron, and of text to reader – goes) dealing with reality. Correspondingly, the *formosa puella*, still unnamed, is elevated to a level of power, at least of power over the poet, comparable with Messalla and even the gods. The poet himself is offered 'before the doors' (line 56) of the girl, while 'before the doors' (line 16)[46] of Ceres the poet hangs a crown of corn. Similarly, the girl is in the same position as Messalla in the immediately previous line (or is it that *Messalla* in the previous line is now seen to be in the same position as the girl?): just as he has the spoils of warfare outside his home, the *formosa puella* has the spoils of her conquest outside hers.[47] In this way, the reader is forced to recall and re-evaluate what the poet has already said in the light of this piece of new information. As the *puella* is implicitly compared to Messalla, so the poet can be contrasted to him. While Messalla takes care of his own *domus*, decking it with spoils, the poet *is* spoils outside another person's house. Again the reader might consider whether this neglect of his *own* home is the reason for its decline in prosperity (the neglect theory must by now be gaining strength). Similarly, the comparison of the *puella* and the goddess Ceres through the offering *ante fores* suggests that, just as the poet was forced to appeal to Ceres for enough produce to sustain his comfort, so he must appeal to the girl for security and comfort, at least as he sees it. The far greater offering in the second case (the poet's very self) suggests that it is the pleasure and comfort which the *puella* has the power to bestow which is by far the more desired by him. Furthermore, devotion to such a girl is hard work. He is

---

[45] See Bright (1978) 132.
[46] Both occurrences of the phrase come as the last two words of their respective couplets.
[47] See Putnam (1973) 58.

a slave in shackles, and the doors are *durae*, presumably because they will not open to him. Such a negation of comfort contradicts what the poet has said or suggested about himself before. It resembles nothing so closely as the temporary hardships of war endured with the prospect of gain, a process which the poet has already dismissed in favour of an alternative developed at great length. Again the difference, the separation, is elided. The reader might assume that the poet considers the prospective gain from his service as *ianitor* far more desirable than the *diuitiae* accumulated by military service or even the past *diuitiae* (41) of his estate.

Non ego laudari curo (57) directly recalls *non ego diuitias requiro* (41). Now praise is added to wealth, but the poet's lack of interest in the two is clearly related. What is the reason for this lack of interest? *Mea Delia.* The poet has seemed to be holding back details about his mistress, teasing the reader. At line 46 the reader first hears of a perhaps hypothetical *domina*; at line 52 an equally indefinite *nostrae puellae*; at line 55 a specific *puella* who has the poet in her power is mentioned; and finally now we have her name (line 57). The trickle of information up to this point about the poet's relationship to his mistress may have been due to his realisation that 'the facts' undercut the desires he has expressed and wishes to sustain. This trickle might be seen as an attempt to hold back these 'facts' to prevent them from interfering with those desires and principles. But the information finally breaks forth (the truth outs) and totally re-arranges any reading of what has gone before. This demonstrates the disruptive power of that relationship (and Delia herself), not simply through its disruption of the poet's rural scheme but through a more general disruption of the reading process.

Opening the elegiac collection

The expectations attached to 'Elegy' as a genre, assuming that it can usefully be called a 'genre' at the point when Tibullus Book One was produced, also contribute to any reading (or re-reading) at this point. Any attempt to construct a picture of pre-Tibullan 'Roman Elegy' is handicapped by the loss of all but a few lines of Gallan elegy,[48] but the contemporary Propertian first book of elegies might provide some tentative point of reference.[49] Propertius begins his book with the straightforward admission of the poet's domination by Cynthia: *suis ... me cepit ocellis* (Prop.I.I.I). There is a focus upon the relationship between the poet and a woman from the start, and a direct statement of the poet's domination by her. This contrasts with the situation in Tibullus where there is only a trickle of details which the reader, constantly re-evaluating what has preceded, must piece together. However, the description of the power-relationship in Propertius' first couplet is similar to the relationship, as it is now becoming apparent, in Tibullus I.I: compare *suis ... me cepit ocellis* with *me retinent uinctum formosae uincla puellae.*[50]

The addressee of the Tibullan poem has changed several times up to this point as the poet's focus shifts. At first he had seemed to be holding forth generally, then he addressed Ceres and the Lares directly, then another general passage was followed by an address to the perceived threats, thieves and wolves, and then to the gods as a whole. Another unaddressed statement of the poet's wishes leads into the address to Messalla, and now, after this protean series of shifts, the poet fixes emphatically on *Delia ... Delia ... Delia* (lines 57, 61, and 68) and will address her exclusively almost to the end of the poem. The poet's true focus now seems clear.[51] The reason for the poet's apparent moral choices (most immediately not caring to be praised and his choice of an inactive life of *paupertas*) *now* seems to be Delia *alone*: *tecum | dum modo sim* (57–8).

---

[48] For a discussion of the evidence concerning Gallus' elegies (published before the discovery of the Qasr Ibrim fragment) see Ross (1975) 39–50, and more recently Nicastri (1984).

[49] The question of which of Tibullus' and Propertius' first books was 'published' first seems largely unanswerable. See Murgatroyd (1980) 13–15 for an overview of the arguments on this question.

[50] In the Tibullan line, however, subservience seems both more tangible and more complete.

[51] That this is the personal focus of the poet is also clear from the sudden flurry of first person verbs, which have not been common in the poem to date: *curo ... sim ... uocer ... quaeso ... spectem ... teneam* (57–60).

Delia is the central figure dominating the poet's thoughts, desires and actions: *tecum* (57), *te* (59), *te* (60), *tu* (67) (all in emphatic positions as first or last word of a line), and *tibi* (64). It is because of her (his enforced vigil outside her door, his desire *only* to be with her) that he has a positive desire (*quaeso*) for inactivity (*segnis inersque*).[52] *Segnis inersque* here may be similar to *tardus* in Propertius 1.1.17 describing *Amor* in its influence *on the poet*. Both point to the powerlessness of the respective poets. *Segnis* and *iners*, which recall *uita iners* and the associated rejection of the typical career path at lines 5–6, are here equated with slavery to Delia (lines 55–8). The preceding verses can now be seen in a new light. All the moral and social choices made and elaborated by the poet (his rejection of the active career-process in favour of inertia and comfort; the attitude of powerlessness which necessitates his frequent appeals to the power of gods to support and predators to spare him; his acceptance of present *paupertas* instead of past wealth) seem determined by Delia and the poet's relationship to her. He is emotionally, morally and physically under her control.

The question of the generic inevitability of *amor* as the dominant (and dominating) subject of the elegiac poet bears directly on how the poem up to now might be read. If an apparently non-amorous subject is looked upon as exceptional, as in Propertius' first book, where only the last two short poems show no apparent link to (or, more significantly, determination by) *amor*, then surprise or even suspicion might be part of a reading of the Tibullan poet's apparent attempt initially to place his poem within an ethical frame not explicitly concerned with *amor*. Now (with the naming of Delia) such a reading might re-evaluate this as a failed attempt by the elegiac poet to separate elegy from *amor*, or himself to escape *amor*'s power.[53] Just as the content of Propertius 1.21 and

---

[52] Or at the very least he would have the reputation (*uocer*) for being lazy and inactive.

[53] As the money-lender of *Epode* 2, after an apparent discussion of rural life in ethical terms, goes back to money-lending, so the elegiac poet-lover goes back to *amor*.

(to some extent) 1.22 and their apparent separation from the subject of the earlier poems might lead the reader to re-examine such separation and assertion of difference (between, for example, *amor* and civil war),[54] so in Tibullus 1.1 the separation of such spheres is again elided.

The power of *amor* which prevents the poet's effective separation of these spheres could be seen as an effect of *amor's* determination and control of the ethical terms by which the poet lives (as well as its physical and emotional control of him). This interpretation might again be informed by reading the poem against contemporary Elegy. At Propertius 1.1.5–6, for example,[55] *Amor* teaches the poet (*docuit*). He is taught *castas odisse puellas*. However this is understood,[56] to 'hate' chaste girls is not a normally expected Roman moral position, and this suggests that *Amor* is the poet's intellectual and moral master, at least to some extent. However, as Prop.1.1.3–4 (*improbus Amor*) and his description of his own position at line 25 as *lapsus* suggest, the poet's own moral values are not entirely under the control of his love. Paradoxically, however, this could also be seen to underline *Amor's* control of him, since the poet does what love forces him to do and feel even against his better judgement. While the description of his behaviour as *hic furor* (7), and the statement *cogor* (8), further emphasise that he is driven and controlled (an essentially passive figure like the poet in Tibullus 1.1), they also show that he realises and disapproves of this state of affairs. The poet still preserves at least some moral autonomy (implying an element of struggle), even if he is powerless to act upon it.

In contrasting his own powerlessness with the situation of others (lines 31ff.), however, the Propertian poet suggests an alternative form of love. For these others there is no hardship involved in love (*in tuto amore*), no powerlessness because the power of a god, presumably *Amor*, has been granted on their

---

[54] See Prop. 1.6.5–6 and the separation of *militia* and *militia amoris*, and compare the interplay of similarity and difference at Tib. 1.1.51ff.

[55] See also the rejection of *militia* at line 6.

[56] See, for example, the different interpretations discussed by Sullivan (1976) 102–4.

side: *quibus facili deus annuit aure.* This power gives them safety (*in tuto amore*), constancy (*semper*) and thus certainty, and, most importantly, a balance of power (*pares*) in the love-struggle which the poet seems to think is close to an ideal situation (if, that is, the greater love on the part of the woman which he desired at line 22 is not forthcoming). Such a situation would free the man from being controlled, thus allowing him to maintain the social advantage which his gender gives him over his female counterpart. In other words nothing too unconventional (the *assuetus amor* of line 36). But, because he lacks equal, or even partial, influence over the object of his love, Venus (who, as a goddess, is a power figure perfectly suited to represent the power-struggle of love) creates hardship for the poet and thus bitterness: *in me nostra Venus noctes exercet amaras* (33). Without any control whatsoever in the relationship, the poet finds love unfulfilling, worthless and a waste. It is *uacuus Amor.* It produces a constancy not of safety or certainty, but of vulnerability: *nullo tempore defit* (34).

In the concluding lines of Propertius 1.1, the poet presents a view of *amor* which could be seen as moralistic. From a position of superior knowledge he perhaps has the power at least to help other men (*moneo*), although it seems too late now for them to help him. Flight from the possibility of a situation such as his is the only safe course (*hoc uitate malum*) since, as this implies and as the reader has already seen, there is no chance for the man to gain the upper hand in a face-to-face power-struggle of the sort the poet describes between himself and Cynthia. Paradoxically, the nature of this flight is non-movement: *sua quemque moretur | cura, neque assueto mutet amore locum* (35–6). *Sua cura* here implies the 'right' type of concerns, non-dangerous ones which, judging from lines 31–2, involve at the least an equality of love, and thus influence over each other, within the conventional male-controlled social context. Change and movement outside the customary forms of love are dangerous: *neque assueto mutet amore locum.* The poet distinguishes between unconventional love like his own,

53

where the woman[57] can withhold her love and thus have power over the love-possessed man, and the other, conventional,[58] constant love shared between man and woman and, in particular, safe for the man. It is the fault of the man, lines 37–8 imply, if he fails to avoid the snares of women and domination by *Amor*, and this failure is irreversible. The final four lines might be read as a confidence shared between males in the hope of protecting others from the menaces of unconventional love: that is, domination by *Amor* and an uncompliant woman. It thus presents a relatively conventional moral view in a male-centred society, a view which asserts that no man should surrender his freedom of thought and action, most especially to a woman. This finds no apparent parallel in Tibullus 1.1, which seems to present an entirely *Amor*-determined moral and social view without suggesting (as the Propertian poet emphatically does) that this is in any way wrong, or desiring (or advising) escape from it.

A reading of 'elegiac' *amor* as power struggle[59] (and ultimate domination or control) might suggest the terms in which a re-examination of the poet's formulation (and attempted separation) of the various spheres of *militia*, rural life, and now *amor* itself might proceed.[60] Just as *amor* might now be seen as the determinant of the poet's ethical or moral stance

---

[57] As regards social class or category, she may also not be the sort of woman a high-class Roman might be expected to form any sort of long-term relationship with. For discussion of this possibility see Lyne (1980), 1–18.

[58] And as such easily absorbed into the normal working social/moral order.

[59] Of Propertius Tracy (1976) 579 writes: 'The competitive character of their [the poet's and Cynthia's] relationship, as one tries to gain ascendancy over the other, produces a state of almost constant tension between them', although in the statement that 'the relationship is between equals (*inter pares*) and is characterised by *amor* rather than *voluptas*', 576, he seems overly impressed by the poet's claims in poems such as 1.4 rather than his manifested powerlessness (and disillusionment) in other poems. 'Power-struggle' does not necessarily imply an equality of success or preclude the ascendancy of one of the combatants (however the other might struggle or claim otherwise).

[60] Similarly, a reading back into Gallus' elegiac books from Virgil's presentation of him in *Eclogue* 10 might suggest that the interweaving of the spheres of *amor* and *militia* and the interplay of their similarities, as well as differences, was part of the 'elegiac' scheme, or at least that of Gallus (as the Qaṣr Ibrîm fragment also perhaps suggests).

(having taken it over in a sense),[61] power – the process of its establishment and operation – invades (or inhabits in the first place) all spheres: *militia*, the wealth of the *alius* or Messalla, rural life and piety ... These areas can be seen to operate in the same way as the power struggles inherent in *amor*-relationships **or** the power struggles which constitute *militia*, the amassing and exercise of wealth, and rural life can be seen to operate also in *amor*-relationships.

Playing dead

> Te spectem suprema mihi cum uenerit hora;
>   te teneam moriens deficiente manu.
> flebis et arsuro positum me, Delia, lecto,
>   tristibus et lacrimis oscula mixta dabis.
> flebis: non tua sunt duro praecordia ferro
>   uincta, nec in tenero stat tibi corde silex.
> illo non iuuenis poterit de funere quisquam
>   lumina non uirgo sicca referre domum.
> tu manes ne laede meos, sed parce solutis
>   crinibus et teneris, Delia, parce genis.
> interea, dum Fata sinunt, iungamus amores:
>   iam ueniet tenebris Mors adoperta caput. (59–70)

In the light of his subservience to Delia, an irony[62] of the picture of the poet's death at Tibullus 1.1.59ff. becomes apparent. It is in the throes of the ultimate hardship of death (*moriens*), enduring the ultimate discomfort (*arsuro positum ... lecto*, recalling and contrasting with the comfort of *requiescere lecto*), when he is at his most physically powerless (*deficiente manu*) and passive (being lifelessly placed, *positum*, on the pyre), that the poet believes he will have some power, at least emotionally, over Delia. He will no longer be held shackled outside her door, but will hold *her* (*te teneam* recall-

---

[61] The 'moral purpose' which a reading of the poem against Horace's *Satires* (and especially *Sat.*1.1) might have suggested now ironically turns out to be an '*amor*al purpose', controlled by and serving *amor*.

[62] An irony which is perhaps unapparent to the poet himself.

ing *teneat* (2); *tenuisse* (29); *continuisse* (46); *retinent* (55), all,
as has been suggested, implying power or control over an
object or person). Again, as at line 52 only now more definitely,[63] he will have the power to make her weep: *flebis* . . .
flebis repeated in emphatic positions, first words of consecutive couplets. She will give offerings of tears and kisses, as he
has given offerings to the gods and offers himself at Delia's
door. Now, or rather *then*, she is the one who will be doing the
giving. The poet even goes so far as to extend his power to
make people weep to the *iuuenes* and *uirgines* who he believes
will be present at his funeral,[64] and whom he believes his
death will render emotionally powerless: *non poterit* . . .[65] The
poet believes he will get such a response from Delia because
there is no hardness in her heart:

> non tua sunt duro praecordia ferro
> uincta, nec in tenero stat tibi corde silex   (63–4)

He believes it will be easy: the adjective *tener* is again prominent. But the words *duro* and *uincta* may return the reader's
attention to a recent couplet in which both words occur in a
very contradictory sense: Delia has *bound* the poet before her
hard doors. Judging from such behaviour, the reader may well
doubt the tenderness of Delia, at least towards the poet. The
initial subjunctives (*teneam* and *spectem*) also suggest he himself is not completely sure of its chances of realisation. Indeed,
the poet's own concern for Delia renders him unable to exercise fully such emotional power over her. Ironically, because
of this concern, the logical extent of such power would actually *harm* the poet (lines 67–8), who must therefore appeal
to *Delia's* power[66] to spare him: *manes ne laede meos, sed*

---

[63] Initially the poet pictures the scene in hopeful subjunctives (*spectem, teneam*), but
as he grows in power, at least in his imagination, he moves into more forceful in-
dicatives: *flebis . . . flebis, dabis.*

[64] This perhaps implies that he was not entirely serious when he claimed indifference
to praise, or that this is a different, non-conventional type of praise, not included
in line 57.

[65] Significantly, *referre domum* (at the end of a line) mirrors *referre domum* at the end
of line 32, where the poet was speaking of his power or security in the pastoral
context, protecting abandoned lambs and kids. Here at 65–6 it is youth again
upon which the poet exercises his influence.

[66] See Bright (1978) 132.

parce ... parce. This recalls his plea to the thieves and wolves (*parcite*) at lines 33–4, another instance where he is powerless to resist a threat and can only make an appeal. Most obviously, however, the poet must undergo the extreme suffering of death – a fact kept before the reader's mind (*moriens deficiente manu*; *arsuro positum me lecto*; *de funere*) – in order to reach this point of power. This might be compared to the career process of the *alius* (lines 1–4) who undergoes hardship for the prospect of wealth and power (again challenging the separateness of the two positions). But death might seem an extreme course, to say the least, and any sway over Delia's affections this might achieve would be short lived.

With the word *interea*, the poet returns to the poetic present. Here the poet presents a direct argument, an attempt to persuade Delia to accept the poet as a lover, and death is an imminent (*iam*), dark and unappealing threat. With *mors* love ends (lines 69–70).[67] Again, this provides room for re-evaluation of the preceding lines. Either, it seems, the poet is abandoning, or at least undercutting, his vision of himself and Delia on his death bed as being empty and unfulfilling in favour of the much more immediate and much more enjoyable prospect of love in the present, which is what he wants, or the immediately preceding section addressed to Delia has been designed as a subtle argument to win over Delia's compliance in the affair. Thus, it would represent an example of the poet's devotion to her (especially the perhaps slightly exaggerated lines 67–8) to excite her pity, while line 69 presents the point of the argument.

A re-reading of the poem so far in these terms – as itself a power strategy, an attempt to achieve the poet's desires, an attempt to persuade[68] – might be disorienting. Where would

[67] As Bright points out, (1978) 133 n., the picture of death here contradicts the deathbed scene which is recalled by the use of the same verb. With *tenebris* and *adoperta* darkness negates the poet's hopes that he might look upon Delia, *te spectem*. It also provides an opposite to the minor run of light = comfort imagery in the poem, from firelight, to the rituals of purification (*lustro*) designed to protect or enrich his estate through the gods' power.

[68] 'The lover's discourse attempts to fix a particular application of a term, particular "metaphors", as "reality", and the common self-portrait of the lover as "slave" and his beloved as his *domina*, his mistress, can be considered, from the point of

57

the persuasion start? Could what might have been read as the failure of the poet's attempt to claim independence from *amor* (to assert the separateness of his own from various other life-styles) now be seen as a *demonstration* (on the part of the poet) of the subservience of his ethical choices to *amor* and its epi-centre, Delia?[69] Such a reading might see the entire poem[70] as an assertion of devotion to Delia in the hope of her com-pliance with the poet's wishes, or even as part of a process of exchange of such devotion *for* her compliance. Even if this reading, or a less broad citing of the power strategy of per-suasion ('rhetoric'), is upheld, the question of its success or failure remains. The poet must appeal (again in the subjunc-tive) to Delia's power to give some certainty (a bond) to their relationship: *iungamus amores*.[71] But, just as such a move is entirely in Delia's control, so too both she and the poet, and indeed all humans, are under the power of forces determining their future: *dum Fata sinunt* (69). *Mors* is a power which cannot be resisted. Perhaps such universal forces render all strategies to construct and exercise power finally precarious.

The power of Elegy

The attempt to gain power over his situation, especially through appeal to others, has concerned the poet throughout Tibullus 1.1 and might be read as yet another tell-tale generic marker, pointing out (and entrapping) the 'elegiac poet'. At line 19 of Propertius' opening elegy, for example, the poet, desperate to win the struggle to gain Cynthia's compliance but powerless to do so by himself, must appeal to other powers,

view of its rhetoric, as supporting the lover's position in his manipulation of the balance of erotic power ... Referring to the beloved as *domina* ostensibly attributes all "power" to her whilst at the same time seeking to bind her into a relationship in which the exercise of that "power" is a function of the fulfilment of the lover's desire.' Kennedy (1993) 73.
[69] 'The lover's discourse emerges as an incessant attempt to control, to mould, to construct for the beloved an identity (an "object") that she will accept or reject in the same way, by "giving" herself to the lover.' Kennedy (1993) 74.
[70] If, for instance, lines 51–6, including its explicit address to Messalla, are read as directed at the notice of the *puella* herself.
[71] This perhaps suggests an image of military discipline; see Murgatroyd (1980) 68.

just as, in a rural context, the Tibullan poet must appeal to gods and predators alike to allow him the comfort he desires, and later appeals directly to Delia herself for her compliance. The alternative power-source which the Propertian poet turns to is magic. Those who exercise this magic have power over a natural element, *deductae lunae*,[72] and they toil (*quibus est labor*) to achieve their power through magic (*magicis focis*), just as Milanion toiled (*nullos fugiendo labores*) to achieve power over Atalanta by gaining her love.[73] What the poet wants is that Cynthia be *more* in love with him than he is with her: *facite illa meo palleat ore magis* (22). Again, love is seen as a power-struggle, and Cynthia is currently in control (*dominae nostrae*). His scepticism concerning the witches' power – only then (*tunc*), when he sees it himself, will he believe they have such power – might imply that he views Cynthia as a more powerful force to be dealt with than not only the moon, but *sidera et amnis*, which the poet will assume the witches are able to control (*posse ducere*) if they are able to manipulate Cynthia. The mere manipulation of stars, moon, and rivers seems far easier.

A shift of addressee (linked verbally to the address to the witches, *at uos ... et uos*) continues the poet's search for possible sources of power, this time not supernatural but entirely human: *amici*. But now, as if he despairs of ever having the power to make Cynthia love him, the *auxilia* he seeks (unlike any of the poet's desires in Tibullus 1.1) is escape from Cynthia's power altogether. Again, the poet does not hold out much hope. It may be too late: *qui sero lapsum reuocatis* (25). The poet is ready to suffer resolutely any hardship (*fortiter ... patiemur*) to escape the power of *Amor*, and thus Cynthia,

[72] The traditional control of the moon through magic in this context might suggest that the witches represent a power opposed to the chaste moon-goddess (possibly identified with Diana and also known by the name of Cynthia) and thus to Cynthia's refusal to succumb to the poet's wishes.

[73] But the powers of these witches are described as *fallacia*, suggesting their claims to power are empty and the poet is sceptical of their chances of success, even though he still hopes, just as the Tibullan poet's chances of successfully enlisting the power of other forces might seem unlikely despite his own hopes or even expectations.

over him. This implies that the effects of his passion and the power of Cynthia over him are much worse than *ferrum saeuos ... et ignis*. He resorts to the conventional trade-off of reward in return for toil (or suffering), a pattern which might express itself in terms of *militia* or merchant journey on the *longa uia* as in Tibullus, or be represented paradigmatically by the toils of Milanion as in Propertius. But, unlike Milanion, the Propertian poet no longer expects the reward of the beloved's love. That seems unattainable; he cannot master her (in contrast to Milanion at line 15). What the poet desires is strikingly different: *sit modo libertas quae uelit ira loqui* (28). This line, by hinting at the political connotations of the word *libertas*, suggests that Cynthia has deprived the poet of his freedom of speech like some tyrant, implying that the poet, as he enables the reader to do (by his use of emotive language like *libertas*), sees this as emphatically wrong in moral and social terms. Hence his *ira* at the situation. He is insistent in his desire to escape and his assertion that he cannot do this under his own power (note the repetition: *ferte ... ferte*). He wants to be as far away as possible (*per extremas gentis et ... undas*). More than any of the dangers of such extreme measures is his fear of remaining under the control of *Amor* and Cynthia. So great and obsessively complete is this fear that he wishes to go *qua non ulla meum femina norit iter* (30). This could be seen as a development, or at least extension, of the poet's attitude in the poem so far. It reveals a paranoid fear of *all* women, which views them as positively hostile, since it implies that if they *knew*[74] of his location they would pursue him to get him into their clutches. As their weapon they have the agency of *Amor*, giving them power over men, which is itself the inversion of the normal moral and social order. This not only takes the initiative away from men but causes those men themselves to desire such a state of affairs. (How close might this be to a definition of 'Roman Elegy'?) Thus, the poet desires to take a route to escape them, unlike the poet in

---

[74] Knowledge, rather than itself being power, gives the *opportunity* to exercise power.

Tibullus 1.1, who desires[75] the opposite course: to remain
with his *puella* rather than take the *uia* away from her as the
Propertian poet himself claims he is forced to do in 1.6 to his
cost (see Prop. 1.6.35–6). Reading the texts against one another in this way, the comparison might be stated in these
terms: the poet in Tibullus 1.1's enslavement to Delia shows in
action the mental, moral and emotional powerlessness which
the poet in Propertius 1.1 describes to Tullus and now views
from a more conscious, conventional moral perspective (while
still apparently gripped by it), although in poems such as 1.8b
or 1.4 he may occlude the element of power-struggle[76] which
erupts (through his delusions) explicitly in other poems.[77]

A generic element, which might be called the operations
of power (its strategies and effects: domination, exchange,
struggle ...), might play a part in any reading of Tibullus
poem one. It is possible to see such poetic imperatives themselves as part of the poet's entrapment or subservience. Can
an elegiac poet ever escape from the power (the demands) of
elegy any more than from the demands (the power) of the
mistress? Are the two any different?

Play time

Iam subrepet iners aetas, neque amare decebit,
    dicere nec cano blanditias capite.
nunc leuis est tractanda Venus, dum frangere postes
    non pudet et rixas inseruisse iuuat.
hic ego dux milesque bonus. uos, signa tubaeque,
    ite procul; cupidis uulnera ferte uiris.   (71–6)

In the lines which follow the statement of the power of
Mors and *Fata* at Tibullus 1.1.69, the poet is not only narrat-
ing backwards in time (lines 69–70 about *mors*, then lines 71–

---

[75] The chains of lines 55–6 externalise the desire which *amor* imposes: a will which is
against the will? Is this another element of the elegiac interplay of similarity and
difference?
[76] This is perhaps what prompts Tracy (1976) to label the relationship *inter pares*.
[77] See especially Prop. 1.5; 1.6; 1.11; 1.12; 1.13; 1.14; 1.15; and 1.18.

2 about *aetas*, then lines 73–4ff. about a relatively youthful
nunc), but is recalling different elements of the poem so far in
reverse order to match the reverse chronology. The description of *Mors*, as we have seen, can affect the reader's understanding of the deathbed scene pictured immediately before it.
Iners aetas, which is an even more immediate threat than
Mors (again *iam*), together with the element of slowness suggested by *subrepet*, recalls the poet's wish to be *iners* at line 58
and elsewhere. But now inertia is undesirable: it implies sexual
impotence. The significance the poet places on words (or that
can be read into the emphasis he places upon them) is flexible.
They may take on whatever meaning suits his argument or
disposition at the time. But, in a way, the poet's earlier inertia
could be seen as the same as that of age, since in both cases,
whether through physical decrepitude or from slavery to an
uncompliant mistress, he is, or will be, unable to get his hands
on Delia, let alone do anything once he has her. *Neque amare
decebit* recalls the moral distinction of line 53, where it was
right for Messalla to wage war, while the claims of the *puella*,
for the poet at least, took precedence. With the ageing process,
as with the progress of the poem, morality shifts, although the
reader might wonder exactly what difference there is, in fact,
between the poet's present position (*iners* with Delia out of his
reach) and the prospective position of *iners aetas*. In both
cases, under the cover of moral choice (*decet ... ne decebit*)
the poet has attempted to hide (or reveal, if the more extreme
reading of the poem as persuasion is upheld) that which he is
powerless to resist, whether the inertia of slavery to Delia or
the inertia of old age.[78]

From *iam ... iam* (70–5) and the prospect of a future which
cannot be resisted, the poet, still moving backwards in chronology, focuses again on the here and now: *nunc ... hic* (73–

---

[78] The suspicion that the poet may simply be shifting his moral position to suit his
argument may be strengthened by the expression *dicere blanditias*, one of the
pastimes of love excluded by age. The question might be raised: is this poem, or
this part of it, simply *blanditiae* to win Delia over, more or less independent of the
truth, and, if so, how much faith should we place in the poet's claims here?

5).[79] *Leuis est tractanda Venus* (73): love, in the person of Venus (a goddess and, thus, a figure of power) must be controlled, mastered (*tractanda*). Love, as the poet seems to see it, is a power struggle. The poet believes this is light work (*leuis*), recalling the light work he was prepared to do on his estate. But another meaning of *leuis*, 'fickle', hints that, as the reader may already have gathered from what has gone before (in this elegy and in 'Elegy'), the whole thing is just not that easy. An ironic reading of this line might suggest that the poet is deluding either himself or Delia. Similarly, the physical power suggested in the phrase *dum frangere postes | non pudet* (73–4) recalls and is contradicted by the last time doors were mentioned (lines 55–6), where the poet was bound, subdued and entirely under the control of the girl physically and emotionally (and, as I've suggested, morally). Ironically, he is the last person from whom such a show of physical power and decisive action might be expected to come. He is either bluffing (in which case it might be considered a pretty weak bluff) or engaging in a bit of wishful thinking. At the same time, the simple phrases *non pudet* and *iuuat* (and even the clause following *dum*) recall similar phrases at lines 29 and 45 (and possibly line 6) respectively, where, while the desired occupations of the poet do see him exerting an element of control, the context is that of a relatively peaceful, rural setting. Now, *frangere postes ... et rixas inseruisse*, placed in a decidedly

---

[79] The poet has been predominantly concerned with the relationship between past and future and the potential for actions and elements in the present to affect or control the future (or otherwise). Even in the case of the contrast of past and present earlier in the poem, the central focus, following the reading I have been advocating, is the bearing of the precedents of the past on the likelihood that present hopes and actions will produce the desired future outcome. This is contrary to the view of most critics, such as Cairns (1979), Lyne (1980), Bright (1978) and Ball (1983), who emphasise the division and contrast between the comparison of past and present in the first half of the poem, and comparison of present and future in the second. The comparison of past and present (*ante ... tum*, 2–3) is also familiar to the reader of Propertius 1.1, although there it is exclusively in relation to amatory concerns that the poet views past and present. Love has broken the constancy, and thus the certainty, of the poet's past assurance: *constantis fastus* (3). For a different view of time in Tibullus, that of the *blurring* of the distinction between past, present and future, see Musurillo (1967) 253–68.

63

urban environment, may remind the reader that, even while (as usual) the poet concentrates on the pleasure (*iuuat*) while ignoring the hardship, 'love' can be a dangerous, violent business.

The mention of quarrels (*rixae*) and the breaking of doors leads into the culmination of the military motif in the poem. First, the statement *hic ego dux milesque bonus* (75). This might seem to be a contradiction of the poet's earlier rejection of warfare as too dangerous and hardship-ridden for him, just as *hic ego* might seem to contradict the location and intent of *hic ego* at line 35. But in the following lines he dismisses the symbols of 'real' warfare (the *signa tubaeque*, which recall the *classica* which interrupt sleep and signal danger in line 4) and rejects again the 'wounds-for-wealth-or-power' trade-off[80] (*vulnera/opes*) described in lines 1–4. This suggests that in the *militia* of love (like the parody of war by Priapus at lines 17–18), no real harm is done, only the odd breaking of doors (line 73) and *rixae* which are a pleasure (*iuuat*) and in which (supposedly) no one is hurt. But, as the poet has found (lines 55–6), the *militia* of love can be quite damaging, and the process or trade-off which the poet is making (hard devotion to Delia chained outside her door in the hope of her eventual sexual compliance and fidelity) is essentially the same as the *vulnera*-for-*opes* trade mentioned here and at lines 1–4, although at the moment the real soldier might seem more likely to achieve success in his quest for wealth and power than the poet in his quest for possession of Delia.

The imperatives, *ite* and *ferte* (76), also suggest that these symbols (*signa tubaeque*) and consequences (*uulnera*) of the *real* dangers of *real* war are a present threat which, like other present threats or powers in the poem, must be appealed to directly and warded off. Furthermore, *cupidi uiri*, the first real pejorative used in connection with the desire for wealth, could perhaps more fittingly describe the poet himself *desiring* Delia[81] than soldiers desiring wealth. In such a reading *cupi-*

---

[80] The poet still suggests, however, that, if men are willing to endure such wounds, they have a right to have the wealth, and that there is nothing intrinsically wrong with this equation.

[81] A perhaps more likely ambiguity than the 'greedy husbands' of Lee (1990) 116.

dis uulnera ferte uiris may contain an irony not apparent to
the speaker, and all in all not bode well for his *militia amoris*
(though *ferte et opes*, if the *opes* are understood to be Delia,
might be, in the poet's mind, a fair swap).

Closing it up, opening it out

Ferte et opes: ego composito securus aceruo
    dites despiciam despiciamque famem.   (77–8)

In the last couplet, the poet returns to the concerns of the
first lines of the elegy and a rural context, which might strike
the reader oddly after the pre-occupation with the relationship
of poet and mistress in an apparently urban setting over the
last twenty-five lines or so.[82] Another re-reading of the ethical
terms of the rural context and the poet's relationship to and
involvement within it is invited. Here again is the desire for
comfort and security (*securus*), and the desire for heaped produce (recalling line 9) which may affect the reader's understanding of the poet's definition of *paupertas*. But now the
reader might seriously question the poet's power (and perhaps
even his inclination) to achieve such desires. The carefully
phrased, symmetrical final line of the elegy presents the most
forceful language yet in regard to the poet's view of wealth, or
more particularly wealthy men. Such *dites* are linked syntac-
tically with hunger (*fames*), both of which the poet wants to
disdain (*despiciam despiciamque*). Again, however, similarity
and difference co-exist and intertwine and strict separation is
prevented. On one level, the two are opposites and the poet is
hoping to avoid both extremes, to achieve the power of self-
sufficiency. On another level, the two are similar, as both involve hardship either in their very nature (*fames*) or in the
efforts required to achieve their position (*dites*). Similarly,

---

[82] In contrast, Propertius 1.1 focuses throughout on love, which, it is suggested,
dominates the poet's life in general. The Tibullan poet on the other hand first develops more general, or at least apparently non-amatory, themes (his desire for a
comfortable rural life, his rejection of the conventional career paths) before it is
gradually revealed that his outlook in these areas is determined, intellectually,
morally and socially, by his passion for Delia.

POEM ONE

given what the reader may have learnt of the poet, his desire
to disdain both could be thought to stem from a similar root:
he would look down on hunger because, assuming his *com-
positus aceruus*, it would not be an issue; and he would look
down on the wealthy because, his ethical choices[83] having
been forced upon him by his subservience to Delia, the question of pursuing riches and becoming one of the *dites* is simply
not an issue. In the poet's moral world, the ethos of *amor* is
superior to the more conventional ethos of military or other
capitalism, although the reason for this, the moral powerlessness of the poet, may not be ethically so idealistic. Given
his powerlessness, it is hardly deliberate choice on his part. So,
too, even this hope which ends the elegy is just that, a hope,
and, as at many points in the reading and re-reading of the
poem up to now, ambiguity concerning the poet's ability to
achieve it persists.

Constant re-evaluation, re-interpretation and the different,
sometimes sudden, directions the elegy can take allow various
opportunities for constructing a picture of the poet: powerless
to achieve his central aspirations, his social, moral, perhaps
even political[84] choices determined by his emotional, physical
and moral subservience to a figure about whom the reader yet
knows very little except her power over the poet.[85] The ethical
separation of lifestyles which began the elegy is challenged by
the similarity of the processes – of *militia*, and rural life and
piety – by which they operate, the processes of control by
which a desired outcome is achieved (what, in its broadest
sense, I am calling 'power' in each context). The assertion of
ethical choice itself evaporates under the influence of *amor*,
which can be seen as almost a paradigm of power struggle.
'Power' in these senses intrudes into each of the ethical categories and processes which the elegy formulates.

A reading which accepts that the presentation of *amor* as

[83] And *despiciam* is strikingly moral language; see *TLL* V.744.58ff.
[84] I.e. his reluctance to fight for Augustan Rome. But this is a dubious point. For a
brief but balanced assessment on the theme of 'anti-militarism' in Augustan elegy
see Cloud (1993) 113–26.
[85] 'The power of the *domina* is stressed rather than her individual bodily characteristics', Palmer (1977) 8.

power struggle, domination and control (or lack of it) is in the nature of 'Elegy' itself might locate a further expression of 'power' in the revelation of *amor*'s effective control of the poet's ethical choices. *Amor* asserts itself as the dominating subject for the 'elegiac' poet.[86] But (and this could be seen as another triumph of generic inevitability) *amor*, like rural life, is a power-struggle at which the poet does not seem to be very good. He constantly appeals to others with the power to aid or injure his desires: the gods, predators, and, most emphatically, Delia. But the possibility that the future may be determined by deliberate action, or even appeal, in the present might seem a flimsy one, judging from the terms in which those actions are presented, and the less than successful precedents which are suggested to readers.[87] The reader is involved in the shifting fabric of the elegy, where not everything allows itself to remain unchallenged, where statements and even individual words may change value and the meanings they suggest alter.[88] Is it in this way, then, that the first poem in the book is programmatic,[89] by introducing both the ambiguous terms in which the poet and his actions and relationships might be understood, and the terms in which the elegy itself might be approached and read?

Reading similarity and difference in Poem One

Critical attention has often focused on the various lifestyles or ethical positions treated in the first elegy, their relationships with one another, and the question of how programmatic the poem actually is. From Dissen[90] onwards commentators and critics have tended to accept a more or less strict reading of

---

[86] A later (and perhaps *the*) example of such a reading of 'Elegy' would be Ovid's first elegy, *Amores* I.I.

[87] The present, after all, is only the future from the perspective of the past.

[88] '... involving us in the piquant circularity of extrapolating "reality" from the text and then using it to assess the viewpoint from which that "reality" has been presented', Kennedy (1993) 15.

[89] Not necessarily in the sense that it introduces a series of themes which will recur in later poems.

[90] Dissen (1835).

opposition between *amor* and *militia*,[91] while on the whole a more complementary relationship between the poet's conceptions or ideals of rural life and *amor* has been accepted.[92] Little note has been taken of slippage, or the erosion of separation, between these various categories and their methods of operation. However, the grounds upon which such an examination might proceed has long been a central issue (if not *the* central issue) in the study of Tibullus, and Elegy in general: the operations of *amor*. Smith, who, like most commentators, follows love as the main theme, labels it the 'tyranny of love'.[93] But although Smith formulates in this way the terms by which the central element of the collection of elegies[94] operates (the terms of that which I have been labelling 'power'), he does not extend those terms to the interpretation of the other elements of the opening elegy. Smith accepts the separation of these spheres and, suppressing the disruptive power of *amor* over the poet's ethical choices, sees the poet's 'idyllic simplicity' as unproblematic.[95]

The work done in the 60s and 70s by Wimmel focused more directly on these contrasts, these 'life choices', although again the comparison was not in terms of their operation but was concerned rather with the reconciliation or integration (and 'poetical value')[96] of these conflicts within the development of the poet-persona.[97] As such their separation was maintained and a dynamic of ethical choice on the poet's part asserted. This position continued to be held in the cluster of important work done on Tibullus in the late 70s and early 80s, without any challenge to the separateness or any examination of the interplay of similarity and difference in the operation of these

---

[91] Dissen (1835) XLIV and 5.

[92] Dissen (1835), for instance, claiming thematic interdependence: *Nam rure natus Amor*, XLII.

[93] Smith (1913) 200. See also Dissen (1835) XLVI.

[94] The first elegy, as Smith sees it, displays 'the conventional programme of true love', 45, although he does not go on to analyse the nature of any generic element at work. See similarly, although 60 years later, Putnam (1973) 58 and 'more hardened elegiac "realities"'.

[95] Smith (1913) 184.

[96] 'Der poetische Gewinn', Wimmel (1968) 262.

[97] See Wimmel (1968), 262–3.

various ethical options. Cairns, for example, upholds the
'moral choice' of the poet[98] without exploiting the possibility
of *amor*'s power as an (or the) ethical determinant, or the
collapse (or at least slippage) of the poet's formulation of
these separate options. The soldier and the lover are seen
as antithetical[99] and, as with the most recent commentators
(Putnam and Murgatroyd), similarities in the processes by
which both spheres operate are integrated into this scheme
of opposites by emphasising the contrast, the difference.[100]
Putnam does not assume the successful fulfilment of the poet's
'dreams'[101] (like Bright, who also focuses on 'the gap between
fantasy and reality' in the first elegy),[102] but neither does he
analyse further the operation of the force (the dominating
power of *amor*) which threatens them, or any relationships or
similarities between that force and the actual operations of the
components of those 'dreams'.

The 'ideals' of the poet remain a focus of Tibullan criticism.
These ideals are used by Murgatroyd, for instance, to link the
two 'symmetrical' parts of the poem: the 'farming' ideal and
the 'love' ideal.[103] But while he sees the operation of rural
piety as an exchange to secure success, and the ethical affili-
ations of such a lifestyle to traditional Roman morality,[104]
he does not relate this to the process of *militia* outlined in lines
1–4, or the similar position of the *miles* in Roman ethical
discourse. Leach outlines these contradictions within the poet's
'active' choice of lifestyle in poem one,[105] and the ethical
force attached to both *militia* and the poet's picture of rural
life.[106] But this is seen as a re-moulding of 'Roman values'

---

[98] Cairns (1979) 145.
[99] Cairns (1979) 145.
[100] See Putnam (1973) 58 on the contrast of the spoils before Messalla's house and
the poet as 'spoils of another sort' chained before the house of Delia.
[101] Putnam (1973) 50 and 58.
[102] See Bright (1978) 125, who writes that *amor* is not the only theme, but is not
concerned to trace any underlying basis of the operation of these other themes or
of the poet's world. See also Mutschler (1985) 45, who sees *amor* set in a 'wider
frame', but does not look for interconnections within such a frame.
[103] Murgatroyd (1980) 48.
[104] Murgatroyd (1980) 56.
[105] Leach (1978) 83.
[106] Leach (1980) 86.

into what in effect becomes, through its assertion of personal freedom, a 'snub' to such 'orthodox' values.[107] The similarities which can be found between the processes operating beneath this interplay of ethical positions, and the force which determines the choices of the poet,[108] are not excavated by Leach.

Conclusion

It is these similarities and points of interconnection, and the relationship of these spheres to *amor* and its power, which this study, based on the terms in which this reading of poem one has proceeded, intends to pursue through the collection. Throughout this reading of the first elegy I have labelled with the term 'power' the operation of the processes by which the goals of the various separate fields (*militia*, the rural world, *amor*) are achieved. These processes provide a common basis for an examination of the dynamics of such themes in the elegies. The process of exchange which asserts itself most strongly in the behaviour of the elegiac poet/lover can be similarly used to analyse *militia* endured in return for wealth (and, as particularly in Messalla's case, for social or political power), or analyse rural piety. The terms of 'power', of struggle, control and domination (the terms of *amor*),[109] then, are to be used to examine the processes and relationships formed within and by the elegies. Eleanor Leach formulates Book One as a developing *ars poetica* in which the poet first assumes ('poetic') control of 'his fate', fails in that control,

---

[107] Leach (1980) 85.

[108] The second half of poem one, Leach writes, defies traditional expectations in its revelation of *amor* as the determinant of the poet's ethical choices, Leach (1980) 83–4. The force (or 'power') of generic expectation, like that of *amor* in this process, is not explored. On the contrary, the work is set against a Gallan generic model and is seen as a reaction to it, 82.

[109] Kennedy (1993) 44–5 suggests the possibilities in this direction: 'Just as Ovid's Amor is able to wander all over the world, we might rephrase our questions to read: "What *cannot amor*/'love' mean?" and "What discursive areas *cannot amor*/ 'love' be a signifier of?" We might even ask, as Ovid indignantly enquires of Cupid in *Amores* 1.1.15, *an, quod ubique, tuum est?* ("is it true that everything everywhere is yours?"), so long as we are prepared for the reply that anything whatsoever can be articulated in and through the language of *amor*/"love".'

CONCLUSION

then reconstitutes it, bringing it into accord with 'reality'. This formulation expresses,[110] at least in terms of poetics (the poet's approach to writing elegiac poetry), another element of struggle which I wish to examine in this study. The dynamics of such poetics might themselves be read in terms of struggle and power in respect of their involvement within the development of the poet-persona and determination (of the themes) of the elegiac 'game'.[111] The interconnections of these elements with the concerns of the poet and with the terms in which those concerns are formulated again suggest at least one direction which a reading of the elegies might take. The causal forces, the powers which might be seen to determine the poet-persona's life and the poetics of the elegiac genre (and the intertwining of all these elements) are the focuses of this study. The processes by which such powers operate will be traced through a linear reading of the collection, based on an assumption of interconnection between the ten poems. It is in this way that I will be giving programmatic force to my reading of the opening poem. Ultimately, however, the terms in which this reading of the first poem has proceeded suggest that any conclusions and assumptions gathered from the poem may be suddenly modified, shown from a new perspective, or even entirely undercut by what is about to be read in poem two. This might raise a further possibility, that the process of reading itself might be seen as a power-struggle: the struggle for the construction and control of meaning.

[110] Leach (1980) 93. No system succeeds in ordering experience or reality completely: that is the struggle according to Leach.
[111] See Veyne's examination of generic imperatives and the poet's involvement within this 'game': (1988), 85–6, 99, and 154.

71

POEM TWO

Setting the scene

Critical approaches to the second elegy have been dominated by two interrelated concerns. The function of the paraclausithyron form in the poem has been examined in detail, in particular by Copley[1] and Vretska,[2] neither of whom were able to draw firm conclusions about the meaning of the text from appeal to that genre. For Copley 'the incident is a literary formality, a convenient frame on which to hang a poem',[3] while Vretska points to the more general difficulty of establishing the context of the poem with any certainty: 'Gewiß, Tibull zeichnet die realen Situationen nirgends klar und genau aus, sondern begnügt sich oft mit wenigen Andeutungen.'[4] Vretska's comments lead into the second, more general concern: the nature of the poem's 'dramatic setting'. Copley, for example, sees the dramatic setting as certain and fixed: 'a dramatic scene that seems to transport the reader to the doorway and place him at the side of the *exclusus*'.[5] But the poem resists such attempts to pin it down conclusively, as Vretska and Bright[6] have pointed out. Kennedy, who cites the comments of Lee[7] (who in turn is influenced by Vretska), sees 'the subject-matter and rapid changes of scene ... [as] remi-

---

[1] Copley (1956) 91–107.
[2] Vretska (1955) 20–46, who also has a good summary of the views of earlier critics on the second elegy as a paraclausithyron and, more generally, on the dramatic setting of the poem; see also Yardley (1978) 19–34.
[3] Copley (1956) 91; see, however, Wimmel (1983), who believes that the paraclausithyron form is determined by the appearance of the *coniunx* and is a demonstration of the poet/lover's reaction to his consequent powerlessness, 107.
[4] Vretska (1955) 23.
[5] Copley (1956) 92.
[6] Bright (1978) 134.
[7] Lee (1990) 116.

niscent of mime',[8] but suggests of the possibilities of 'performance' (a 'notion ... [which is] entailed by and encoded in a phrase like "dramatic setting")[9] that 'neither its establishment nor its refutation would "fix" or guarantee the meaning of the text'.[10] The attempts of critics to 'fix' the meaning of the poem by establishing a certain dramatic setting for it are destabilised by the variety of possibilities which the text raises. As Kennedy puts it: '1.2 has placed considerable difficulties in the path of ... [such an] analysis'.[11]

The paraclausithyron 'frame' and the uncertain or shifting nature of the setting both suggest the power-struggles at work in the text. The basis of the paraclausithyron form is the initial powerlessness of the poet/lover,[12] locked outside the beloved's door, and his attempts to gain his desires (access to the beloved) through the power of his words. Thus, both an initial position in a power structure, and the enactment of power struggle, are inherent in the paraclausithyron. Similarly, the text's suggestion of dramatic setting only to create uncertainty as to its exact nature involves the reader, as it has the critics who have approached the poem, in a struggle to fix meaning. The uncertainty of the setting of the poem could, thus, be seen to indicate the reader's place in a power dynamic with the text, a struggle for meaning where the reader's position is destabilised and remains insecure. In this way, the central concerns or problems which critics of the poem have isolated foreground the power relationships set up by the text, relationships which involve both poet/lover and reader.

Knocking on the door

Adde merum uinoque nouos compesce dolores,
occupet ut fessi lumina uicta sopor;

---

[8] Kennedy (1993) 21.
[9] Kennedy (1993) 21.
[10] Kennedy (1993) 21.
[11] Kennedy (1993) 18.
[12] See Wimmel, who stresses this aspect of the paraclausithyron form in the second elegy (Wimmel (1983) 107).

neu quisquam multo percussum tempora Baccho
excitet, infelix dum requiescit amor:
nam posita est nostrae custodia saeua puellae,
clauditur et dura ianua firma sera.
ianua difficilis domini, te uerberet imber,
te Iouis imperio fulmina missa petant.
ianua, iam pateas uni mihi, uicta querelis,
neu furtim uerso cardine aperta sones;
et mala siqua tibi dixit dementia nostra,
ignoscas: capiti sint precor illa meo.
te meminisse decet quae plurima uoce peregi
supplice, cum posti florida serta darem.   (1–14)

The first word of the second elegy is a command (*adde*).
The initial command might suggest that the poet, in contrast
to the first elegy, is taking a dominant position from the start.
As Bright has pointed out, the language of lines 1–6 is vigorous, exploiting military vocabulary (*compesce*; *occupet*; *percussum*; *uicta*).[13] Again the separation of *militia* and *amor* is
elided by a shared vocabulary.[14] But while Bright sees such
expressions as likening the poet's vigil outside Delia's door
to a siege laid upon a city, the military language is in fact
directed against the poet's own state:

uinoque nouos compesce dolores,
occupet ut fessi lumina uicta sopor   (1–2).

The poet is attempting to use the power of wine to restrain
(*compesce*) his grief, enabling sleep (*sopor*) to take control (*ut
occupet*) of his eyes, conquered and enslaved by exhaustion
(*fessi uicta*). He wishes to be controlled by these relatively
beneficial forces rather than by *dolor*, which he wants to suppress. This maintains the impression given by the first elegy of
the poet as passive, needing the power of other forces, in this

---

[13] Bright (1978) 135–6.
[14] 'The surprise so often expressed that love should be described in terms also used
for war, a surprise that manifests itself by calling that use metaphorical, is indicative of a definition of love which wishes to exclude or disown notions of violence,
aggression, the desire to impose domination, or to have domination imposed ...',
Kennedy (1993) 55.

case wine and sleep, to achieve his desires, in this case to create some comfort by suppressing his grief. It is ironic, then, that he begins with an order, effectively commanding that he be controlled. In his description of this desired state he sees himself as acted upon violently by the power of wine (summed up by the metonymic name of the god Bacchus, a figure of power): *multo percussum tempora Baccho* (3). Again, rest is a desired state (*neu quisquam*[15] ... *[me] excitet*, and, as at 1.1.43, *requiescit*), although the poet has become so dominated by his love that he actually speaks of his own rest, his own *sopor*, as the rest of *infelix amor: infelix dum requiescit amor* (1.2.4). It is the effect that his sleep will have on *amor* which determines the poet's desire for *sopor*. *Amor* seems to have become so entirely a part of him that his rest *is amor*'s rest.

Lines 5–6 give the reason for the poet's *dolor: nam* ... The expression *noui dolores* might have led the reader to expect something other than the simple restraint before the mistress' door of poem one, and in a sense the situation[16] *is* different[17] – and worse. Not only is he excluded from entry, but there is another force ranged against him: *custodia saeua*. Unlike the situation in poem one, where the terms *custodes* and *custos* referred to the gods of the estate (the Lares), who, the poet at least hoped, would act on his behalf, the *custodia* of poem two is a power operating against the poet. It is not a potential or doubtful force, like the powers which the poet desires to come to his aid in the opening elegy, but real and harsh (*saeua*, just as the door again is *dura*). The door is strong and impervious to the poet: *clauditur et dura ianua firma sera* (6). The poet is powerless to overcome it, hence his *dolores*, and hence his need for the power of wine to suppress his grief and bring rest and comfort. It is clear that the sentinel has been deliberately placed (*posita est*) and the door closed. This picture of the

---

[15] This perhaps suggests there is a threat that such rest might be disturbed.

[16] At least the situation as it is now revealed; since it is possible that these elements, although not revealed by the poet in the first elegy, were present earlier.

[17] For a different view, see Henderson (1987) 21, who argues that the suggestion of 'newness' here is problematic and proposes the emendation *nouo* qualifying *uinoque*.

physical manoeuvres of love (like the more than physical enslavement of the poet by his love explicated in poem one) describes a struggle. Someone is acting against the poet and, at the moment at least, seems in control. The question which most immediately faces the reader is: who is this 'someone'? In poem one the poet was chained *outside* the door and the implication of his appeal to Delia to comply with his wishes (*iungamus amores*) was that it was *she* who was opposed to him in this. But the exact situation remained relatively ambiguous (not necessarily precluding Delia's willingness) and open to different readings. Similarly, the description of the sentinel as *nostra puella* could conceivably mean that he was placed either by her, or by another for her 'protection'. This is suggested by *domini*,[18] which denotes the possessor of the *ianua* and refers to some powerful male figure (at this stage possibly anything from a father to a husband or lover) who locks her in. This provides a contrastingly powerful male to the poet's passive one, and, by suggesting that it is this *dominus* who is responsible for the guard, it leaves open the possibility that Delia is willing. *Difficilis* suggests the power struggle between the poet/lover and the stronger forces of the door and its *dominus*.

The poet now changes addressee, blaming the door itself for his lock-out, still seeming hesitant to specify the human source of his suffering. First he curses. He wishes upon the door hardship, just as its being locked has caused him hardship (7–8). Once more, as in the first poem, the poet must rely upon the power of a third party, in this case the ultimate power of Jupiter: *Iouis imperio*. The violence of his wishes – whipping (*uerberet*) by rain and attack by lightning (*fulmina petant*) – demonstrates the fierce, warlike nature of the *amor*-struggle in these elegies (recalling the destruction of the door at 1.1.73). The poet/lover attempts to take on the power latent in the curse by voicing it. But, of course, the verbs are in the subjunctive and the reader may doubt the likelihood that Jove will enforce the poet's words, especially given the lines which

---

[18] Which I take with *difficilis*, as Lee (1990) 116.

follow. The poet appeals directly to the door: *ianua iam pateas*, with the words *uni mihi* suggesting the threat of rivals. This opens new possibilities for reading the poem to this point. Is it a rival who caused the poet's exclusion? The implication that the door itself has the power to grant the poet's wish is artificial, since the poem makes it clear there is human agency behind his exclusion. Still, the idea that the poet is at the mercy of an inanimate object emphasises his powerlessness.[19] The hope that the door be *uicta querelis* demonstrates that the complaints of the poet, his threats (curses) and appeals, are themselves an attempt to gain power over the door (*uicta ianua*) by coercion and persuasion. The poem itself is part of the power struggle. Victory in this particular skirmish, the tipping of the power balance in favour of the poet, would result in the opening of the door (*aperta*). But line 10 introduces another element, the necessity for secrecy: *neu furtim ... sones.* This suggests that even such a victory leaves the victor vulnerable. The knowledge of it must be concealed since, it is implied, that knowledge would enable those with the power to do so to act against him. This might suggest to the reader that knowledge is itself power of a sort, and correspondingly so is the ability to deceive. To gain such power (of self-protection) the poet must appeal to an inanimate object (10): a door. His position may not look strong,[20] especially since he has just cursed the same inanimate object he is depending upon, a fact he draws attention to in the next couplet (11–12). He seems ignorant himself of his curses, unsure whether he pronounced them or not: *mala siqua ... dixit.* It is *dementia nostra*, not the poet, that is the subject of *dixit.*[21] He describes himself as mentally, and therefore verbally, out of his own control.[22] He can now only appeal to the door to forgive him for having cursed it: *ignoscas.*[23] It could be seen as a mark of the general

---

[19] For a similar effect of the lover's address to the door in another Roman paraclausithyron see Propertius 1.16.17ff.

[20] Not to mention how comic it might appear.

[21] He has not been the subject of any finite verb in the poem so far.

[22] *Dementia* recalls the controlling power of *amor* over the lovers at *Eclogue* 2.69 and 6.47.

[23] The joke is, of course, that doors are not sentient in the first place.

weakness of his argument and in particular the weakness of his confidence in his own power to carry the curses through and gain access without the goodwill of other powers (i.e. the door itself) that the poet takes back his curses, after the space of only three or four lines, in an extremely self-abasing, apologetic way: *capiti sint precor illa meo* (12).

While the poet, in writing the elegy, takes on (or at least tries to take on) the controlling role, shaping the course of the verse, at the same time the text suggests that the poet/lover is powerless to control the course of the poem. Instead its course seems determined by the possible reactions of a door: caustic when the poet thinks it is adverse to him, grovelling when he thinks these curses may anger the door into excluding him in the future. Even when he is apparently aggressive (as with his initial curses against the door) the poet soon returns to passivity, potentially suffering from his own wishes.[24] The powerlessness of the poet is extended even to his ability to control the final target of his words. This suggests further complications to the power structures in which the poet and reader are involved. While the poet/lover is presented as powerless, as an object of humour for the reader, at the same time the poet (the author) is in control of this presentation. The reader is thus at once in a superior position in relation to the powerless poet/lover and is *being placed* in that position (and thus to some extent manipulated) by the poet/author.[25]

The recantation of the poet/lover's curses also suggests that the poem could be read as an argument in which the poet uses various techniques (such as cursing or appeal) to get his way. As one technique seems unsuccessful or likely to create more difficulties for him (by his supposedly offending the door, for example), it is rejected and disavowed in favour of another. The possibility of such a (perhaps) more guarded reading is certainly open. So too it is possible to understand this impas-

---

[24] In fact, if he remains outside Delia's door (and as yet there is no sign of his being admitted or going away) he has as much chance of being beaten by rain or even possibly hit by lightning as the door.

[25] For further discussion of these issues see my reading of poem five below, esp. 156–8, 164–5, 168–9, and 178–9.

sioned address to an inanimate object as comic.[26] The humour
may be deliberate on the poet/lover's part, in which case he
might seem less serious in his grief, or it may be unintentional,
in which case the poet/lover's position seems all the more
ridiculous and pathetic in its powerlessness.

Te meminisse decet suggests that the ability to determine
what is remembered, what is known, is connected directly to
the ability to control eventual action. The word *decet* (recalling 1.1.53 and 71) again brings before the reader the poet's
definition of morality (what is 'right') in terms of his desire for
Delia. The reason, the reader may think, that it is right for the
door to remember one thing and not the other is simply that
the one may lead to the poet's admittance (and supposedly his
possession of Delia) while the other will not. The emphasis is
again on the poet's resort to appeals to the power of others
(even objects, as in this case) in order to achieve what he
desires: *quae plurima uoce peregi | supplice*. The picture of him
as a suppliant, worshipping before Delia's door, is underlined
by reference to the floral garlands he has given, which recall
the garlands he dedicated before the door of Ceres in poem
one (1.1.15–16). This similarity suggests the goddess-like
power which Delia has over the poet's life, and points to the
shared process which underlies this similarity between the religious procedure (prayer/supplication) and operations within
the sphere of *amor*: the attempt to secure power.

Setting out the rules

> Tu quoque, ne timide custodes, Delia, falle;
>   audendum est: fortes adiuuat ipsa Venus
> illa fauet seu quis iuuenis noua limina temptat
>   seu reserat fixo dente puella fores.
> illa docet furtim molli decedere lecto,
>   illa pedem nullo ponere posse sono,
> illa uiro coram nutus conferre loquaces
>   blandaque compositis abdere uerba notis;

---

[26] Or as a set piece of the *exclusus amator*: an immediately recognisable representation of the situation (and grief) of the unrequited lover.

nec docet hoc omnes sed quos nec inertia tardat
nec uetat obscura surgere nocte timor.
en ego cum tenebris tota uagor anxius urbe

. . . . .

nec sinit occurrat quisquam qui corpora ferro
uulneret aut rapta praemia ueste petat.
quisquis amore tenetur eat tutusque sacerque
qualibet; insidias non timuisse decet.
non mihi pigra nocent hibernae frigora noctis,
non mihi cum multa decidit imber aqua;
non labor hic laedit, reseret modo Delia postes
et uocet ad digiti me taciturna sonum.   (15–34)

The addressee changes once more, with the words *tu quo-que*, as if the direct approach to Delia is a second thought,[27] as if perhaps the poet is reluctant to speak to her, or, having failed in his approach to the door, he must now try another approach. He appeals to another power to admit him: to Delia herself. Such an address, with its advice to the furtive lover, seems to imply that Delia is receptive to the poet's desires. *Ne timide custodes*, Delia implies that the poet believes she *does* at present fear them, that she does not wish them to be there. The poet thus expects Delia to achieve his desires for him: *custodes, Delia, falle. Audendum est* raises a question: why, then, has *the poet* not dared, but must rely upon Delia? Or has he dared and failed? As usual, the poet seems powerless, useless. He must rely on Delia's initiative and power, and assures Delia that, should she attempt this, she in turn will be supported by the power of a third party, the goddess Venus: *fortes adiuuat ipsa Venus* (16). But the examples of the goddess' favour (*illa fauet*) which the poet proceeds to give question this. The young man *quis ... noua limina temptat* is in a similar position to the poet,[28] yet the poet has been, so far, unsuccessful. Is it, perhaps, that he is not *fortis*; is the goddess'

---

[27] It may, perhaps, also mirror the wandering mind of someone who is drunk (1–6), but this is not clear.
[28] *Noua* recalls *nouos* of the first line, suggesting that the poet too has not been by the door long.

power insufficient, or is perhaps the statement (line 16) invalid? Whatever the case, as a result of such doubt the second example of Venus' favour, which corresponds to what the poet hopes will be Delia's position (line 18), seems far less certain or straightforward than the poet suggests.[29] The repeated *illa ... illa ... illa ... illa* (17, 19, 20, 21) suggests that Venus is in control, determining the rules of the game. It certainly appears that, in the poet's mind, his love (the power of Venus) is the central controlling force.

The poet (maintaining the relation of knowledge to power) goes on to suggest that part of Venus' power is bestowed upon mortals through teaching (*illa docet*). Secrecy is foremost: *furtim molli decedere lecto | ... pedem nullo ponere posse sono* (19–20, recalling line 10).[30] This suggests that the ability to conceal information is a positive power (in the amatory context at least), enabling lovers to achieve their desires without the threat of possibly stronger forces intervening. Lines 21–2 emphasise the importance of knowledge in this regard: knowledge shared by the lovers (*nutus conferre loquaces ... compositis uerba notis*) but not by such threatening figures as the *puella*'s *uir*[31] (*uiro coram ... abdere*). This is an ideal of lovers, not involved in a power struggle between themselves, but united and empowered by the knowledge which they control, the knowledge granted by Venus. The next couplet, however (even more than the detached, lecture-like tone of these lines),[32] brings into doubt the relevance of this ideal to the poet's own immediate situation. Venus does not empower everybody (*nec docet hoc omnes*), and those she does are defined by what they don't do:

> quos nec inertia tardat
> nec uetat obscura surgere nocte timor.   (23–4)

---

[29] As Bright (1978) 139–40 suggests, the whole passage seems detached from the reality of the situation.

[30] *Ponere posse* instead of simply *ponere* emphasises that Venus invests others with power through the knowledge she bestows rather than simply exercising power directly herself.

[31] This does not necessarily suggest as yet that Delia herself is in the power of such a *uir*, but such a suggestion could be read here.

[32] On which see Bright (1978) 139.

This seems to be an encouragement to Delia *not* to do these things (to be *fortis*) and assumes that she wants the power which Venus would bestow, that she wants to comply with the poet's desires. But the word *inertia* recalls the poet's professed desire to be *iners*, and his actual position 'chained' motionless outside Delia's door in poem one. By the first test of 'don'ts' the poet himself fails. Again there is a process, a trade: the absence of *inertia* and fear (*timor*) gains the favour and teachings of Venus (i.e. the power which the poet desires). The poet, however, simply fails to deliver the goods. Conclusion: by the first of his own criteria, he will not receive the knowledge to enable him to carry on an affair in secrecy. In this respect too he is powerless.

Given that he fails the first criterion, it is perhaps not surprising that he concentrates on the second: *nec obscura ... nocte timor*. Based upon this (absence of fear about getting about at night), he claims his own share of the power (the invulnerability) of lovers: *En ego cum tenebris* ... The example of 'protected' lovers comes from his own life (*en ego*) rather than, as might have occurred, myth. The power of his passion is immediate to him, he is exclusively concerned with its effects on him. *Vagor anxius* shows that he is not in full physical or mental control over himself. His love is the reason he submits to dangers (*tenebris*) in a threatening, entirely urban environment (*tota urbe*). But again there is a trade-off: in return for love's control of him, it also protects him[33] even from the threat of physical danger (*nec sinit occurrat ...*). He meets no one who would offer a direct violent physical threat to his body or possessions:

> qui corpora ferro
> uulneret aut rapta praemia ueste petat. (27–8)

The trade-off is set out fully in the next line. Whoever is passively under the control of love is safe and sacred and may go where they like: *quisquis amore tenetur eat tutusque sacerque | qualibet*. Since they are, however, controlled by *Amor*,

---

[33] Presumably the lost line stated something of this sort. I am assuming here, based on the close connection of sense from lines 25 to 27, that there is only one lost line.

eat qualibet might seem equivalent to 'wherever *Amor* makes
them go'. *Sacer* (rather an extension of the sense of the immediately preceding lines) suggests *Amor* as a god and, more
particularly, that its power is godlike and *all* those controlled
by that power are favoured by the god. The morality – the
code of feeling, of response, and of behaviour – which is
determined by love is described again in line 30, and again the
word *decet* is used:[34] *insidias non timuisse decet.*[35] The poet
has claimed invulnerability from direct violent physical attack,
deceitful attack and, in the next couplet (made insistent by the
repetition of *non mihi* at the beginning of each line), any natural discomfort or danger which the night (*hibernae noctis*)
might bring.[36] Apparently, then, he has no reason whatsoever
to fear the night (as line 24). There is, it seems, some power
attached to the poet's state. The reader may, by this point,
wonder why, then, *he* doesn't brave the guard, if that is the
only obstacle to his love. Is it only because of his powerless
inertia?

The apparently simple trade-off of no night-terrors or discomfort in return for being controlled by love does in fact
have another, overriding condition which is now revealed:

> non labor hic laedit, reseret modo Delia postes
> et uocet ad digiti me taciturna sonum.   (33–4)

The poet will not suffer from such hardships *only* (*modo*) if
Delia complies, if *she* is the active party and enables him to
enter the house. It is entirely reliant upon her. Effectively, it is
not the power of the god which bestows this, perhaps purely
psychological, invulnerability to such hardships, but the power
of Delia; and her compliance is not certain (again the verb is in
the subjunctive). Similarly, on another level, it could be argued
that the poet makes this statement to encourage Delia to take
pity on him and save him from such hardship by complying,
in which case the entire conceit of the love-possessed being

---

[34] For the moral connotations of *decet* see *TLL* V.131.42ff.
[35] It is ironic that it was the lover at lines 19–22 who was employing *insidiae* of his/
her own.
[36] This recalls the rain (*imber*) he wishes upon the door and then upon himself.

invulnerable has been related for her benefit. In such a reading, the course of the poem, indeed the whole reason the poet is writing, is determined by Delia. The power to control the poet and also the power of silence and secrecy[37] are in her fingers: *uocet ad digiti me taciturna sonum* (34). The text, however, has already suggested several strategies (and several objects of address: the door, Jupiter etc.) by which the poet/lover might attempt to gain some control in the power struggle which *amor* represents, and, rather than collapsing them into a single master-strategy, the appeal to Delia simply presents one possibility for the poet in that struggle.

> Parcite luminibus, seu uir seu femina fiat
> obuia; celari uult sua furta Venus.
> ne strepitu terrete pedum neu quaerite nomen
> neu prope fulgenti lumina ferte face.
> siquis et imprudens aspexerit, occulat ille
> perque deos omnes se meminisse neget;
> nam fuerit quicumque loquax, is sanguine natam,
> is Venerem e rabido sentiet esse mari.   (35–42)

It is the need for secrecy (rather than his dependence upon Delia)[38] which the poet now expands upon. Again he must appeal to others[39] for this: *parcite luminibus, seu uir seu femina fiat | obuia* (35–6). As before in such appeals, *parcite* is used. In one sense those addressed are being asked to spare the poet, by maintaining secrecy, while in another more literal sense they would be sparing *themselves*, their own eyes (*luminibus*). The reference to Venus' desire for secrecy suggests the mythologically renowned anger of a goddess when mortals see (or know) what they should not.[40] The poet is thus claiming the power of Venus (the threat of it) to support his appeal for secrecy. *Ne strepitu terrete pedum* suggests that, while (at least

---

[37] If, as the action suggests, the sound of fingers is meant to summon the poet without alerting the *custodia*; on this point see Murgatroyd (1980) 82.

[38] This might suggest he does not want too much attention drawn to this dependence.

[39] Here the poet changes addressee once more.

[40] Most notably Diana's towards Actaeon or Juno's toward Tiresias.

if Delia complies) the poet has no fear of physical attack, he can be terrified by the sound of a foot. He seems a vulnerable, perhaps even somewhat pathetic, figure. Again knowledge (the sight of the poet, and especially the poet's name) gives power: the power to reveal the poet's presence to the man who has 'control' over Delia (whether father, husband, or dominant lover). This would effectively end the poet's access to her. The poet is the prey of chance, of anyone who might happen to see or find out (*siquis et imprudens aspexerit*). Apparently, and perhaps surprisingly,[41] he is powerless to prevent such 'accidents', and again must appeal to those who would have that knowledge and thus be in a superior position: *occulat ille | perque deos omnes se meminisse neget* (39–40). This recalls line 13 and the importance of what is known (and thus remembered) as a source of power and/or a threat throughout the poem. The poet's willingness to accept falsehood if it suits his purposes is another example of the morality determined by the poet's 'love'. This might alert the reader to the possibility that the poet's words should not always be taken at face value. He again backs up his appeals with the threat of Venus' power. He claims that the 'knowledge' such a *loquax* will gain (*sentiet*) will, ironically, be to his own loss:

> is sanguine natam,
> is Venerem e rabido sentiet esse mari. (41–2)

Venus is as violent and deadly as war, just as in the first poem, despite the poet's claims that the two are different, the processes by which war and love operate were seen to have more similarities than simply vocabulary and imagery (including real sentries, violence, captives and suffering). This description of Venus (central power figure/goddess of love) has implications for the poet/lover himself who has suffered and is suffering[42] from his love.

Indeed, the poet/lover could himself be called *loquax*, since his desire for secrecy is made a nonsense of by the published

---

[41] It is surprising because the reader might expect them to meet in more private places.
[42] As *dolores* in the very first line of this poem suggests.

poem itself.[43] This may suggest that the poet is unable to control his own tongue, yet another manifestation of general powerlessness. On another level, of course, the revelatory nature of the poem may be accepted by the reader as simply part of the elegiac 'game'.

Magic and the powerful woman

Nec tamen huic credet coniunx tuus, ut mihi uerax
  pollicita est magico saga ministerio.
hanc ego de caelo ducentem sidera uidi;
  fluminis haec rapidi carmine uertit iter;
haec cantu finditque solum manesque sepulcris
  elicit et tepido deuocat ossa rogo.
iam tenet infernas magico stridore cateruas;
  iam iubet aspersas lacte referre pedem.
cum libet, haec tristi depellit nubila caelo;
  cum libet, aestiuo conuocat orbe niues.
sola tenere malas Medeae dicitur herbas,
  sola feros Hecatae perdomuisse canes.   (43-54)

Nec tamen huic credet coniunx tuus: finally the poet states directly something which has been suggested and implied ambiguously throughout the poem so far. Another male figure (probably husband or established lover)[44] holds the dominant position in Delia's life, controlling her movements, or at least is powerful enough to be a threat to any affair between Delia and the poet.[45] The question of belief is also raised more directly by this statement. The potential power of any information is dependent on belief, and what is believed may be unreliable. This is seen on several levels. The poet believes the *coniunx* will *not* believe the truth, because the poet trusts a *saga* whom he believes to be *uerax*: *ut ... pollicita est*. If the beliefs of the *coniunx* are unreliable, why not the poet's? This undercuts the poet's claims, or at least encourages doubt on

---

[43] The use of pseudonyms, however (if Delia *is* a pseudonym), may lessen this.
[44] See Murgatroyd (1980) 7-8 on the ambiguity here.
[45] Hence the emphatic desire for secrecy.

the part of the reader, who may think *uerax saga* is a contradiction in terms.[46] The reader is thus him/herself involved in the belief process.[47]

The description of the 'powers' of the witch (45–54) continues the concern both with power and with the basis for knowledge/belief. The witch has power over stars: *de caelo*[48] *ducentem sidera* (45). The poet's belief in this power is apparently based on direct sensory perception: *hanc ego ... uidi*. It is, however, only the power to lead down stars which the poet claims to have seen at first hand. He does not state how he 'knows' of the powers named in 46–52. The witch is said to have power over natural forces: her power is physical (*fluminis haec rapidi carmine uertit iter*) and violent (*haec cantu finditque solum*). *Carmine* and *cantu* indicate that it is through song (incantation) that this power is exercised. This stands in contrast to the poet's songs, which, at least as yet, have had no power to bring Delia to him. Yet the only persons the witch has power over are dead: *manesque sepulcris | elicit et tepido deuocat*[49] *ossa rogo* (47–8). The words *tepido ossa rogo* emphasise the lifelessness. But what is the exact relation between the sphere of *amor* and such unnatural powers over the realm of death? Either there is no relation and again the poet appears unlikely to gain any power by this route, or, if a witch skilled in the area of death[50] is suitable for amatory matters, this may suggest love and death are similar in nature.[51] This would be another area where separateness is elided by the similar workings of power in each context. The witch's power is emphasised by the initial position in succeeding lines of *iam*

---

[46] Compare the deceitful nature of the more high-profile witches of myth, Medea and Circe.
[47] The reader might also doubt whether the poet himself really does believe what he claims to. He may, for instance, simply be falling back on another argument (*tamen ...*) in case the talk of possible discovery put Delia off.
[48] This might suggest power even over the gods.
[49] *Vocare* and its compounds as indicators of the subject's power recur (34, 48, 52).
[50] In Roman terms this might well include every witch, the whole notion of witchcraft being surrounded by connotations of death, corpses and the macabre; see, for example, Horace *Epode* 5.
[51] For example, the *manes'* slavery to the *saga* (*deuocat*) is like the poet's slavery to Delia (*uocet*).

tenet ... iam iubet. Again her power is over the dead (*infernas cateruas*). Through the instrument of her sound/song (*magico stridore*) she makes them come and go (*referre pedem*) at will.[52] The four lines concerning her power over the dead are framed by couplets relating her power over natural elements or forces (lines 45–6 and 51–2). At lines 51–2 again her power is emphasised by repetition of the first words of the lines, *cum libet ... cum libet*, highlighting her power to achieve her will. As with the description of her manipulation of the dead, her power is both to disperse (*depellit*)[53] and summon (*conuocat*). The repetition *sola ... sola* (53–4) shows that she has sole, absolute power in these areas. Again, the verb illustrating her power is *tenere*, and *perdomuisse* denotes control, literal mastery over wild forces (*feros canes*). But here the poet is no longer claiming first-hand experience of her power, or even leaving the question of how he 'knows' these things open. Instead he states *dicitur*. The fact that he says this may indicate his own doubt. The basis of belief, which is necessary if knowledge is to be possessed, is seen to be on a less stable foundation than at line 45. It may also hint that the powers of lines 46–52 were also heard of at second hand by the poet.

The *malae herbae* of Medea and the *feri canes* of Hecate are also rather ill-omened presages of the witch's skills as far as love is concerned. This is especially true of the herbs of Medea, the archetypal combination of love and power, with wild destruction the result. This is suggestive both of love's destructive force and its operation as a power struggle. It is also significant that almost all the power figures in the poem, with the exception of the *custodia*[54] and Jove's brief appearance (line 8), have been female: Delia, Venus, *saga, Medea, Hecate.*[55] This might suggest that the poet, so dominated himself by a woman and his feelings towards her, can con-

---

[52] The ceremony of the dead *aspersae lacte* recalls the poet's ritual *spargere lacte Palem* at 1.1.36. Here, too, it is to gain power (implying that this is one central function of ritual), although in poem one it was the power of peace (*placidam Palem*) and, supposedly, prosperity.
[53] Again *caelo*; cf. n.48.
[54] The *coniunx*, as presented by the poet at any rate, is not entirely in control (43).
[55] This is true in the opening poem as well: Ceres, Pales, Delia.

ceive of power, in relation to *amor* at any rate, virtually only in female terms.

Studies of the female in elegy, especially where they look specifically at Tibullan elegy, tend to concentrate on the mistress, often with the goal of 'identifying' the social class which the mistress is supposed to occupy or her relation, more generally, to 'real' women in contemporary Roman society.[56] From a different perspective, however, Judith Hallett has observed the 'inversion' of the conventional power relations between genders in the depiction of the relationship between poet/lover and mistress by Tibullus and Propertius: 'by having women control them, they are sharply reversing social reality'.[57] She suggests that the elegists are making a social statement, projecting a 'counter-culture', by 'both their non-compliance with widely-accepted behavioral norms and their bent towards social innovation by consciously and deliberately (if sometimes ironically) inverting conventional sex roles in their poetry'.[58] Maria Wyke, however, has more recently argued that the depiction of the female in elegy is a function of the power structures being presented by the text: 'it is not the concern of elegiac poetry to upgrade the political position of women, only to portray the male narrator as alienated from positions of power and to differentiate him from other, socially responsible male types'.[59] While this view puts the emphasis on the powerlessness of the male, rather than on female power,[60] the network of female power figures which can be seen in the Tibullan text work not only to place the poet/lover on the periphery of society and power through his domination by and association with the peripheral figure of the powerful mistress, *lena* or *saga*, but by linking these peripheral figures (who disrupt and invert the social norms) with more central, conventional figures of female power, such

[56] See, for example, Lilja (1965), esp. 37–41.
[57] Hallett (1973) 113.
[58] Hallett (1973) 109.
[59] Wyke (1989b) 42.
[60] '[T]he elegiac texts take little interest in elaborating their metaphors in terms of female power, but explore, rather, the concept of male dependency' Wyke (1989b) 42.

as the goddess Venus, similarities between these anomalous power structures and those of conventional society are drawn which complicate the simple inversion of gender relations. The powerful female figures, and the poet/lover's adoption of the passive, powerless role normally associated with the female in Roman sexual discourses,[61] are both anomalous to the power structures supported by traditional Roman society and understandable (and described) in terms of those same structures. In this way, the depiction of power structures in the elegies, despite the apparently peripheral role of *amor* and the power-relations it creates, relates itself directly to the operation of power more generally in Roman culture.

> Haec mihi composuit cantus quis fallere posses;
>   ter cane, ter dictis despue carminibus:
> ille nihil poterit de nobis credere cuiquam,
>   non sibi, si in molli uiderit ipse toro.
> tu tamen abstineas aliis, nam cetera cernet
>   omnia, de me uno sentiet ille nihil.
> quid credam? nempe haec eadem se dixit amores
>   cantibus aut herbis soluere posse meos,
> et me lustrauit taedis, et nocte serena
>   concidit ad magicos hostia pulla deos.
> non ego totus abesset amor sed mutuus esset
>   orabam, nec te posse carere uelim.   (55–66)

The poet claims that the power of the witch *has* been given to him (*mihi*). That power consists of the manipulation of belief and thus the manipulation of the actions of other figures (i.e. the *coniunx*), and again the channel for that power is song (*composuit cantus ... carminibus*). But it is *not* actually power for *him*, rather it is in Delia's hands. He can only give her instructions (knowledge: see line 19) involving a somewhat ridiculous combination of singing and spitting (*ter cane, ter ... despue*) which the reader might well expect Delia to laugh at rather than comply with.[62] The object of the poet is to

---

[61] Wyke (1989b) 36.
[62] Petronius, for example, uses 'magic' spitting for comic effect at *Sat*.131.

remove from the *coniunx* (the *ille* of line 57) the power to believe[63] reports from others about any affair between Delia and the poet: *ille nihil poterit de nobis credere cuiquam.* But then the poet claims the *coniunx* will not even have the power to believe his own direct perception: *non sibi, si in molli uiderit ipse toro.* The verbal parallel between *uiderit ipse* and *ego . . . uidi* (45) raises a question: if the *coniunx'* interpretation of visual perception may not be correct (for one reason or another), then why should the poet's be trusted?[64] Furthermore, lines 59–60 could be read as the poet's attempt to fill up any possible loopholes in his argument (*tamen . . .*) and (slyly?)[65] to use the threat of the *coniunx'*s power[66] to protect his own interests. This opens the possibility that the whole tale of the witch has been made up by the poet as part of his argument to convince Delia not to fear the power of the *coniunx.* Contrary to the poet's implication throughout that Delia would come to him if it wasn't for the guard, these lines also suggest that she might wish to go to others rather than to the poet.[67] Has the poet been deluding himself, the reader, or both?

Quid credam? might well sum up the situation at this point for the poet and the reader.[68] Belief, by its nature, is not necessarily infallible and can be manipulated by other forces. Knowledge, and thus a solid base from which to act, is not easy to possess. The poet is somewhat dubious about the witch's claim that she has the power (through her instruments *cantibus aut herbis*) to dissolve his passion altogether.[69] His

---

[63] This would in turn prevent his exercise of other powers (e.g. the power to somehow separate Delia and the poet, or worse).

[64] Could he too have selective/distorted perception, perhaps due to the force of his passion, which controls every other element of his operation, emotional, mental, physical, moral?

[65] It might also be thought that the poet here is blundering. Suddenly realising that Delia might take notice of his encouragement for the sake of some other rival, the poet tries here to patch up his mistake. This reading might make the poet appear, as he often does, rather pathetic.

[66] Knowledge would empower the *coniunx* to act (*cernet . . . de me uno sentiet ille nihil*) to prevent the success of the poet's rivals.

[67] For this idea see Bright (1978) 142–3.

[68] And, of course, for the *coniunx.*

[69] *Amores . . . soluere . . . meos:* the idea that his love must be loosed from him implies that at the moment he is bound by it and not free.

doubt[70] that a fight between the witch and his love would come out in the witch's favour may be based on his experience of the invulnerable power of *amor*; or, on another level, it may be part of the argument to impress Delia with the implied strength of his passion for her.

At any rate, the poet has, it seems, gone through with the ceremony (lines 63–4). Again ritual is used as a means of gaining power. The process – purification and sacrifice (*lustrauit . . . concidit . . . hostia*) – is the same as the poet's ceremony to gain the power of the Lares at 1.1.21–2, only here the source of the power is different: the gods the ritual is aimed at are *magici* and the ritual itself takes place at night (*nocte serena*). Even the power of the witch, it seems, comes from a third party.

As if realising he has undercut his suggestion that his love is unflinching by admitting he has undergone a rite to release him from that love, the poet qualifies his words:

> non ego totus abesset amor sed mutuus esset
> orabam. (65–6)

The poet, these lines suggest, is so controlled by *amor* he cannot even wish his love to be gone (unlike Propertius 1.1.26ff.), but at the most he desires a balance of power, a balance of love (*mutuus*). He does not even *want* (*nec . . . uelim*) to have the *power* (*posse*) to go without her (*carere*, something the poem suggests he may be forced to do), so controlled is he mentally and emotionally by his love. His wish that love be made mutual between them immediately reveals that, at present, it is not mutual, that Delia does not love him in return. The suggestions that only the guards and *coniunx* stand in the way are entirely undercut. The appeals to Delia to take the active part, trick the guard and let the poet in are shown to be fairly hopeless. Whatever the reason for such suggestions in the first place (possibly the poet's self-delusion),[71] this destabilises the reader's certainty in any 'meaning' he/she might gain from the poet's words.

---

[70] On which see Putnam (1973) 69.
[71] It may be another case of wishful thinking. His belief too, it seems, is not on a solid foundation.

Ferreus ille

Ferreus ille fuit qui, te cum posset habere,
  maluerit praedas stultus et arma sequi.
ille licet Cilicum uictas agat ante cateruas,
  ponat et in capto Matria castra solo,
totus et argento contectus, totus et auro,
  insideat celeri conspiciendus equo:
ipse boues – mea si tecum modo Delia – possim
  iungere et in solito pascere monte pecus;
et te dum liceat teneris retinere lacertis,
  mollis et inculta sit mihi somnus humo.
quid Tyrio recubere toro sine amore secundo
  prodest, cum fletu nox uigilanda uenit?
nam neque tunc plumae nec stragula picta soporem
  nec sonitus placidae ducere possit aquae.   (67–80)

By contrast, the poet (67ff.) describes a man who was in
a position of power over Delia (*te cum posset habere*) and,
furthermore, *did* have the ability to go without her. He is
described as *ferreus*. This may mean that he was unfeeling to
leave Delia (a meaning which the poet himself, calling the
man *stultus*, probably intends), but it may also mean that the
man has enough strength (like iron) to resist being controlled
by love. The poet here, as in the first poem, is not entirely
rejecting warfare or military service. The rejection of *militia* is
only relative to love, where a direct choice is made between
them (*maluerit*). *Ille licet* ... suggests that the rewards of
militia are the man's right.[72] It is only *the choice* which
prompts the poet, from a love-determined moral perspective,
to brand the man *ferreus* and *stultus*. Like the process of
I.I.I–6, *militia* brings power. This power is first described in
terms of war and then, as in poem one, wealth. Unlike the
poet who is himself (see I.I.55), or wishes to be (see I.2.2),
uictus, the *ferreus* drives hordes of captives before him. *He* is
in complete control: *Cilicum uictas agat ante cateruas. Ponat*

---

[72] This recalls the position of Messalla at I.I.53–4.

castra also points to this command and control, and the fact that his camp is *in capto solo* underlines it. The poet emphasises (even exaggerates) the wealth (*praedas*) gained:[73] *totus et argento contectus, totus et auro.* The man is *conspiciendus.* No secrecy exists here. Knowledge seems uncomplicated. Everything seems right up front.

There is, however, uncertainty as to the exact identity of the *ferreus. Ille* is not necessarily, or even probably, the *coniunx*, but may be another lover (or simply a beloved of Delia, as Delia is of the poet). The uncertainty involved in the identification of this figure, which has been highlighted by critics such as Zelzer and Brouwers,[74] echoes the uncertainty of the poem's dramatic setting, and like it leaves that identification to the assumptions of the reader. But the several possibilities left open by the text will always render such assumptions finally unstable.

The word *ipse* at the beginning of line 73 underlines the contrast between the *ferreus* and the poet. The description of rural life continues the recollection of the opening poem, but here the determination and domination of such a lifestyle by Delia is declared from the very start (*mea si tecum modo Delia*) and is more intense. The poet's preference for the rural life here depends entirely on Delia. The *inculta humus* (78) suggests that it is something to be *suffered* in return for Delia.[75] The sole criterion for such a life is a degree of control over Delia: *et te dum liceat teneris retinere lacertis.*[76] Comfort for

---

[73] Perhaps there is a suggestion here that the poet himself might have pursued such a lifestyle and consequently accumulated such wealth had he not surrendered these great career prospects in order to devote himself to Delia. Again such devotion might form part of an argument encouraging her to return his love.

[74] Zelzer (1988); and Brouwers (1978), who provides a good discussion of the variety of critical views on this point, 398–400; see also Bright (1978), 144.

[75] It might, thus, be an attempt by the poet to win the mistress over by impressing her with the amount of suffering he is willing to endure for her love. To a certain extent Roman elegy in general could be read this way, and has been (see Stroh (1971)).

[76] Control of the oxen (*boues iungere*) may reflect the power the poet would have in controlling Delia. Thus he grows in control generally. On the other hand, it may simply contrast the more elaborate power of *ferreus ille.* The accustomed hill (*in solito monte*) also implies stability and certainty.

the poet lies entirely in this (note the adjective *tener*, as in the first poem, and *mollis somnus*, recalling the comfort of sleep at 1.2.2 and 1.1.48). All this is, of course, a wish: *possim*. He does not have the power to achieve it.

Quid Tyrio recubare toro sine amore secundo | prodest? (77) may be suggestive of the *ferreus* who has gone without love and might be able to afford Tyrian dye. It may also simply suggest that luxury without happy love is, in the poet's eyes, far worse than physical hardship *with* love. But it is also clearly indicative of the poet's immediate position *sine amore secundo*. This is supported by the picture of the lover *cum fletu nox uigilanda uenit* (78). This hypothetical lover suffers and is deprived of sleep just as the poet, suffering (*dolores*) and desiring the *sopor* of wine (at line 2), seems to be. The similarity suggests that this is the reality of the poet's own position, in contrast to the wish he has no power to realise (73–6). The poet's passive situation achieves nothing and leaves him powerless (*quid prodest?*). In a world determined by love and oriented towards the object of that love, elements normally gentle to the senses (*plumae*; *stragula picta*; *sonitus placidae aquae*), lose their power to bring comfort and relief, qualities which are here again embodied by sleep: *soporem | nec ... ducere possit*.

Looking for excuses

> Num Veneris magnae uiolaui numina uerbo
>   et mea nunc poenas impia lingua luit?
> num feror incestus sedes adiisse deorum
>   sertaque de sanctis deripuisse focis?
> non ego, si merui, dubitem procumbere templis
>   et dare sacratis oscula liminibus;
> non ego tellurem genibus perrepere supplex
>   et miserum sancto tundere poste caput.   (81–8)

The lines which follow perhaps suggest that the poet is himself aware that this is the reality of his own position. For now the poet searches for a reason for his suffering; since, as the reader now knows (or at least believes), Delia is non-compliant. The poet wonders if he has offended Venus and she is exacting punishment:

> Num Veneris magnae uiolaui numina uerbo
> et mea nunc poenas impia lingua luit? (81–2)

Here is another process, like many others which have been seen in this and the first elegy. But in this case, instead of service/reward, it is transgression/punishment. Unable to achieve the first, the poet embraces the transgression/punishment process, freely offering to pay penance in the hope of improving his (powerless) situation. The simple fact that the poet believes this is possible, and sees Venus as a hostile power, undercuts his invocation of Venus' power on his behalf earlier in the poem. In fact, instead of Venus punishing those who reveal his affairs (41–2), he sees *himself* as being possibly punished by her (*poenas luit*). Indeed, the possibility is raised that those earlier words about Venus (16ff. and 35ff.) were themselves the *uerba* (81) which infringed her authority. Or, the poet thinks, he may have been reported as having acted against her temple, either by entering it *incestus*, or by stealing its garlands. At the same time as it emphasises the unreliability of belief and report, this may remind the reader that the poet himself cannot always be taken at face value. (The more sceptical reader, at the mention of *serta*, might recall those at line 14 hung by the poet on Delia's door, and start to get suspicious.) Unable to resist the power of *amor*/Venus, the poet declares that if he had done these things (*si merui*) he would gladly abase himself and demonstrate physically his total subservience to Venus' power (85–8). The description of himself as *supplex* and the emphasis on the doorway (*liminibus ... poste*) recalls Delia's door and the poet's attitude before it (a suppliant, treating it as a shrine: lines 13–14). In a way, then, according to his own terminology the poet is already prostrate and subservient before the door of a temple. He suffers there (perhaps through his own fault) just as he would suffer in his submission to Venus' power: *et miserum sancto tundere poste caput.* In one respect his suffering before Delia's door *is* submission to Venus' power: the power of *amor.*

> At tu qui lentus rides mala nostra caueto.
> Mox tibi, non uni saeuiet usque deus.
> uidi ego qui iuuenum miseros lusisset amores
> post Veneris uinclis subdere colla senem,
> et sibi blanditias tremula componere uoce,
> et manibus canas fingere uelle comas;
> stare nec ante fores puduit caraeue puellae
> ancillam medio detinuisse foro.
> hunc puer, hunc iuuenis turba circumterit arta,
> despuit in molles et sibi quisque sinus.   (89–98)

But now the poet once more changes addressee (*At tu*, 89), and speaks to those who might mock him. He uses the legalistic imperative *caueto*, as if he is in a position of power. He suggests that he is under the malevolent attack (*saeuiet*) of the god (*deus*), presumably *Amor*, and states without qualification that the mocker will suffer the same (*mox tibi*). How does he know this? *Vidi ego*: from direct perception, which, it has already been suggested, is unreliable. This might immediately encourage the reader to be wary of the poet's claims. The picture of the mocker and his fate at lines 91–2 parallels that which the poet imagined for himself at lines 81–8. The infringement of Love's authority (*miseros lusisset amores*) leads to total submission to the power of Venus (*post Veneris uinclis subdere colla*). The physical weakness of old age accentuates the loss of power. *Blanditias tremula componere uoce,* | *et manibus canas fingere uelle comas*, implies that while the old man may want to act in this particular way, it may be as far beyond his physical power to do so as it is beyond what is deemed appropriate for the elderly. The mocker's behaviour will be determined entirely by love, regardless of how pathetic or ridiculous this behaviour may be (as in lines 93–4). The same will be true of his personal morality: *stare nec ante fores puduit* (95).[77] The elements of public debasement (as in line 96: *medio foro*) and inappropriateness are emphasised as a crowd of youths gathers close around (lines 97–8). Similarities can be drawn here with the poet/lover's present condition. Yet, in the case of the mocker, it is a clear, logical (and, in divine moral terms, fair) process of punishment for an offence against *amor*. The poet, however, has supposedly committed no such offence; his puzzled questions at 81–4 and *si merui* (85) imply as much. Indeed, if the poet has seen the fate of such mockers himself (91), presumably he joined the band of youths who turn to superstition (recalling the magic at 56) to prevent such a future for themselves: *despuit in molles et sibi quisque sinus* (98). From the evidence of these poems, no such apotropaic power was forthcoming, for the poet at least. It all does him no good; he is still enslaved by love. Is Venus illogical in her exertion of power, enslaving those innocent as well as guilty in her eyes? Was the poet himself a mocker earlier in his life?[78] Or is his statement of Venus' power here (used to threaten those who would mock him, and thus to prevent them from mocking) just as untrustworthy as those earlier, undercut by the revelation of Venus' (unexplained) enmity towards him?

> At mihi parce, Venus. semper tibi dedita seruit
> mens mea. quid messes uris acerba tuas?   (99–100)

These questions are left open, but the final couplet emphasises once more (in the first and only direct address to Venus) that the poet is at the goddess' mercy. He is mentally enslaved to her[79] (*semper tibi dedita seruit | mens mea*), and can only appeal to her to operate her power the way he desires: *At mihi parce, Venus* (99). While the central relationships involving

---

[77] *Ancillam detinuisse* may hint, in physical terms, at the power-struggle of *amor* (as well as the secrecy). It might also suggest that the man is socially debased by love, being forced to deal with slaves.

[78] This raises the question of how old the poet is supposed to be.

[79] The poet is enslaved to Venus by being enslaved to Delia through the agency of *amor*. This opens the possibility of identification of the two central power figures in the poet's cosmos: Delia and Venus. Is an address by the poet to Venus equivalent to an address to Delia and vice versa?

amor are *power*-relations, the normal operation of the normal processes by which power in other spheres is gained (the trade-offs) seems to have broken down, or perhaps simply cannot exist in the sphere of *amor*. In return for 'loyal' service the poet receives hostility and bitterness (*acerba*). The illogical, self-destructive nature of *amor*, as the poet knows it, is demonstrated in the final words of the poem: *quid messes uris acerba tuas?* (100). The force which creates these desires, and this enslavement of the poet, itself brings them to nothing. The result is suffering which, at the beginning of the poem, the poet wished to suppress by wine. As yet he has been powerless to do so. Here in the final line that suffering is still present, captured in the image of burning.

Conclusion

The examination of power through the second elegy develops into wider areas and opens wider questions. The separation of various fields in the first elegy (*militia*, rural life, *amor*) was (as with magic and *amor* in the second elegy) elided by the common operation of power relationships and the existence in all these fields, or at least the assumption of the existence, of the processes by which power is gained, exerted and maintained. But in the second elegy those processes of exchange seem to fail actually to secure power in the field of *amor*, in the poet's case at least.[80] This could be read as re-asserting the difference (the anomalous and unconventional nature of *amor*) and undercutting the commonality. But the continued depiction of *amor* as power struggle might suggest another reading. Could the illogical, absolute and arbitrary nature of *amor*'s power suggest something more general about the nature of power when it tends to such extremes?[81] Any understanding of *amor* and the operations of power in the second elegy must in-

---

[80] Their failure was suggested in the first poem, but in the second this failure is brought out into the open.
[81] This reading might be particularly forceful if, as was tentatively suggested in my reading of poem one (see above 66), *amor* is seen as actually *paradigmatic* of power-struggle.

corporate the similarity as well as the difference between *amor* and these other fields.

Questions of knowledge and belief and their relation to power (as vital instruments to strengthen, weaken, or make possible the exertion of power) also become immediate to the reader in the course of the second poem. Previous interpretations of the text are questioned, revised or overhauled, as they were in the first elegy. In the process of reading, control óver meaning remains precarious. This is emphasised in poem two by uncertainty over the dramatic setting and the identification of *ferreus ille* at line 67, which uncertainty destabilises any reading through the variety of possibilities which the text leaves open. Reading always involves gaps and blind-spots, but in the second elegy the uncertainties are central to the reader's negotiation of the text. The dynamic of the poem grows out of and draws attention to such uncertainties. The poet himself is uncertain (see lines 61, 81ff., 99–100). In fact, the reader's lack of complete control over the meaning of the text mirrors the powerlessness of the poet in general as Delia's true attitude to him undercuts his suggestions earlier in the poem and prevents him from achieving his desires. The resonances which the text creates, both within the poem itself and between it and poem one, multiply the shifting set of possible meanings. This is evident in the last line, which explicitly uses harvest (*messes*) as a metaphor for love. It might suggest an entirely new metaphorical reading of the rural motif in poem one, at the last moment destabilising the reader's previous assumptions and beliefs.

POEM THREE

The problem of unity

As Campbell observed over twenty years ago,[1] critics of the third elegy of Tibullus' first book have always tended to focus on one central problem, the 'episodic character' of the poem. This episodic nature has been seen as a problem because the relationships between the various episodes often appear tenuous. One thought can move abruptly to another. Connections can seem obscure, and development of thought hard to follow or non-existent. This threatens the elegy's unity, fragmenting the poem. To counter this, various critical strategies have been employed to suggest unity: Eisenberger's construction of the poet/lover's 'Gefühlsgründe',[2] 'der Gesamtaufbau der Elegie' suggested by Hanslik,[3] or Campbell's own assertion of the 'inner coherence'[4] of the poem in both its linear progression and its structural 'schematization' of present, past and future.[5] These concerns illustrate both the desire to construct and the difficulty of constructing a single, complete meaning for the elegy.

But discontinuity within the poem also parallels a larger problem. The poet/lover's departure on *militia* and the power structure of the *amor*-relationship which he presents in elegy three appear inconsistent with the situation and positions suggested in the earlier poems. This is immediately disruptive to a linear reading of the collection. The expectations which have been established through a reading of the first two elegies are undercut and the viability of a coherent reading of the collection is brought into question. At the same time, however, the alternative strategy of resisting such a reading, of isolating

---

[1] Campbell (1973) 147–9. [2] Eisenberger (1960) 197. [3] Hanslik (1970) 145.
[4] Campbell (1973) 149. [5] Ibid. 156.

individual poems or episodes and suppressing the interpenetration of the separate components, is also obstructed by the
third poem. Comparisons with the previous two elegies are
encouraged and links underlined. This is disorienting for the
reader's attempts to construct meaning from the text. The disorienting effect on the reader is reflected in the poet/lover's
insubstantial ideals and visions which dominate the poem. In
turn this ambivalence encourages the reader to re-evaluate the
power structures operating in the elegies, which seem here to
intersect and re-align. The disorientation is further emphasised
and represented by the third elegy's dramatic setting. After the
indistinct setting of the second elegy, the reader of poem three
is presented with a setting which is simultaneously a geographically distinct location and a literary world peopled by
insubstantial ideals and dreams of past, present and future.

Allotting the roles

> Ibitis Aegeas sine me, Messalla, per undas,
> o utinam memores, ipse cohorsque, mei!
> me tenet ignotis aegrum Phaeacia terris,
> abstineas auidas Mors modo nigra manus.
> abstineas, Mors atra precor: non his mihi mater,
> quae legat in maestos ossa perusta sinus;
> non soror, Assyrios cineri quae dedat odores;
> et fleat effusis ante sepulcra comis.   (1–8)

In the opening line of the poem, the poet is fixed geographically, in contrast to the motion of Messalla and his
followers evident in the first word: *ibitis*. The importance to
the poet of his patron and general is emphasised by his desire
that Messalla and company remember him (line 2). But as well
as the opposition between departing patron and immobile
poet there is a further contrast between the power in motion
of the *cohors* and its leader, and the power of Phaeacia, or
more particularly the unspecified sickness (*me aegrum*), which
holds the poet motionless: *me tenet*. The first couplet viewed

in isolation might suggest to a reader familiar with the poet's professions in the earlier poems (especially 1.1.51–6) that the poet is excusing himself from military campaigning so that he may stay with Delia. But these logical asssumptions are undercut by the implication of the poet's words at lines 3–4. He *has*, in fact, left Delia, and *has* followed Messalla on campaign (*militia*), despite his earlier words, such as his dismissal of the '*militia* for gain' process at 1.1.1–6. This inconsistency is emphasised by the allusion to the *Odyssey* in the reference to Phaeacia[6] and its implicit comparison of the poet with Odysseus. The poet has abandoned *his* beloved, as Odysseus left Penelope. Despite this superficial similarity, however, the previous two elegies would seem to suggest that neither does the poet approach in any way the heroic code or martial exploits of Odysseus, nor does Delia approach, at least in relation to the poet, the proverbial faithfulness of Penelope.[7] The gulf between the Homeric version of the myth and the Tibullan realisation of it reflects the gulf between the poet's professions and his actions.[8] In each case the reader's assumptions are displaced.

Even the allusion to Homer, which Bright and Eisenberger[9] see as fixing the poet's position in terms of the Odyssean story ('He [the poet] tells of *himself as Odysseus*'),[10] multiplies meanings and resists a single definitive reading. For, while the association of the poet with Odysseus on Phaeacia may be one function of the allusion, the comparison of the poet's position with the events of the *Odyssey* might suggest at least one other

---

[6] On allusions to the *Odyssey* in the third elegy see Bright (1971) 197–214; this is presented in revised form in Bright (1978) 17–37; see also Eisenberger (1960) 191 and 194.

[7] And, of course, Odysseus comes to Phaeacia on his way *towards* Penelope, while the poet is moving *away from* Delia when he comes to Phaeacia.

[8] Although for a slightly different view of the significance of Phaeacia to the poem see Mills (1974) 226–32, who argues that the 'ideal' of Phaeacia is ' "undercut" and ultimately rejected' in favour of the more 'suitable' ideals of Elysium and the golden age which occur later in the poem.

[9] Bright (1971) 198ff.; Eisenberger (1960) 191. Mills (1974) also sees it as 'contribut[ing] a consistency and unified perspective to the poem's total meaning' 232.

[10] Bright (1971) 211.

parallel. The poet might resemble the member of Odysseus'
crew, Elpenor (*Od*.10.552ff.), whose body is left behind on
the island of Circe and who re-appears in the underworld
(*Od*.11.51ff.). Like Elpenor, the poet is being left behind by his
leader. As in the case of Elpenor, who fell to his death immediately after Odysseus' departure, it seems that the poet's
death will quickly follow Messalla's departure. Later in elegy
three the poet claims that he will be transported to the afterlife, another parallel with Elpenor who meets Odysseus once
more in the Underworld in a scene which focuses (as lines 5–9
of poem three do) on the dead man's lack of proper burial.
The description of Elpenor as οὔτε τι λίην | ἄλκιμο ἐν πολέμῳ
οὔτε φρεσὶν ᾗσιν ἀγήνωρ (*Od*.10.552–3) might also seem to
parallel the character of the elegiac poet/lover.[11] The relationship is not a perfect analogy, but neither, as was suggested
above, is the association of the poet with Odysseus. The similarities with Elpenor would place Messalla in the role of
Odysseus and equate the poet/lover with a figure who is powerless and ill-suited to war, an isolated individual who dies igno-
miniously, as the poet implies he too is soon to do. This might
undercut the parallel which the poet/lover implicitly suggests,
especially later in the poem, between himself and Odysseus. But
more obviously it demonstrates the multiplication of meanings
which the allusion to Homer triggers, rather than the production of a single fixed and unproblematic parallel. This frag-
mentation of meaning is part of a general destabilisation of
the reader's control over meaning in the third elegy.

The poet's position in the opening lines is passive: he is held
(*me tenet*). It is a position of danger and uncertainty, two
notions linked by his possibly life-threatening illness *in ignotis
terris*. He is threatened by *Mors*, a dark, negative force (*nigra
... Mors atra*), which appears actively to seek his life (its
hands are *auidae*). The poet is powerless and can only appeal,
a signal of powerlessness familiar from similar and frequent
positions of powerlessness in the two earlier elegies: *abstineas*

---

[11] Elpenor's drunkenness, which occasions his death and abandonment (*Od*.10.553–
5), also recalls the poet/lover's desire to get drunk at the beginning of poem two.

... *abstineas*[12] | *precor* (5). He is dependent on *Mors'* mercy (*modo [abstineas]*), which might seem a distant prospect, given the characterisation of *Mors'* hands as *auidae*.

The picture of the poet's possible death at lines 5–9 is presented in terms of who and what will *not* be present,[13] and Delia is not the first mourner he thinks of, in contrast to the death scene at 1.1.59ff., where she is the only specified mourner and without question the focus of the scene. The mourners whom he misses (*mater*, *soror*, Delia) are all female. This perhaps suggests the traditional role of women, especially in the heroic world of literary epic (where the poet has notionally placed himself by reference to Phaeacia),[14] fitting them into a male-viewed social scheme where they perform functions centred upon the man, in this case the poet. Delia, in fact, is virtually defined and fixed within the social unit of the family. She is mentioned along with sister and mother. The emphasis on the destructive force and barrenness of death (*ossa perusta*) may suggest that the achievement in death of such a socially and emotionally well-defined relationship between himself and Delia may be empty.[15] The poet, at line 8, misses his sister's weeping: *non ... fleat effusis comis*, recalling the description of his death in the first poem, where he gains the power to make Delia cry, but appeals to her to spare her hair. This might indicate that the poet values Delia's beauty so much that he qualifies his emotional power over her. Alternatively, it may suggest that the poet must still ask Delia for concessions even when he is describing a situation where he has ideal emotional control over her. At any rate, it is noticeable that the state of the hair here (and elsewhere in the poem) indicates the role being played, in this case social, emotional, and ritual.[16]

---

[12] This also recalls one of the poet's previous appeals: to Delia at 1.2.59.

[13] This suggests the emotional deprivation of the poet's position.

[14] This 'heroic' role is reinforced by his involvement in a military campaign.

[15] See similar suggestions about the emptiness of the power over Delia to be achieved by the poet's death in the first poem, above 57.

[16] On this point see Bright (1978), who only partially appreciates the role of hair in Book 1, simply stating that it is a signal of character: 'In general, Tibullus speaks of hair more often than any other poet, using it as an indication of character as well as a descriptive detail' Bright (1978) 74.

Push and pull

Delia non usquam, quae me quam mitteret urbe
dicitur ante omnes consuluisse deos.
illa sacras pueri sortes ter sustulit: illi
rettulit e triviis omina certa puer.
cuncta dabant reditus, tamen est deterrita nusquam
quin fleret nostras respiceretque uias.
ipse ego, solator, cum iam mandata dedissem,
quaerebam tardas anxius usque moras:
aut ego sum causatus aues aut omina dira
Saturniue sacram me tenuisse diem.
o quotiens ingressus iter mihi tristia dixi
offensum in porta signa dedisse pedem!
audeat inuito ne quis discedere amore
aut sciet egressum se prohibente deo.　　　　　　(9–22)

Despite her being third mentioned, the poet obviously considers Delia an important necessity which would be missing from his funeral: *Delia non usquam* comes at the initial position of the couplet. The reader is familiar with the dominance of Delia in the poet's emotional life, and in his life in general, but the couplet goes on to suggest that she was concerned for the poet's safety, the reason implied for her consulting the gods. This clearly conflicts with her attitude in the earlier elegies. After ten lines of the poem several contrasts have been formed, both between this and other elegies and within the third elegy itself. *Me ... mitteret urbe*, taken on a literal level, raises the question of how much irony at the expense of the poet-persona is to be allowed into any reading. It might, for example, suggest to the reader an explanation for the poet's inconsistent behaviour in departing on military service which can be reconciled with Delia's apparent attitude in elegies one and two. Taking advantage of her control over him she has sent him away from the city to be rid of him. But this is clearly not what the poet himself is implying, as the lines which follow reveal. Supposedly she consults the gods (*omnes consuluisse deos*) because she is concerned for the poet's safety, although her exact motives are not specified. Indeed, it is not entirely certain that she really does want a favourable result as regards the poet's return. The qualification *dicitur* at line 10 recalls the unreliability of report highlighted in the second elegy. This makes it clear that the poet himself is not sure of Delia's actions. Whatever the case, the consultation of the gods is an attempt to know and, possibly, to affect (even control) the future. Similarly, carrying on the theme of knowledge from poem two, the *sacrae sortes* are an attempt, through religious ritual, to learn, and thus affect, the future. The emphasis on the ritual three (*ter ... triuiis*) recalls another attempt to ensure a desired outcome, that of the witch at 1.2.55–6. Here, however, the attempt is related to established religion (the *sortes* are *sacrae*). The desire for knowledge, for *omina certa*, is clear, but the certainty or all-inclusiveness of such signs is undercut by the poet's present unforeseen sickness in an explicitly unknown and uncertain environment.

The omens *cuncta dabant reditus*. The search for certainty through religious prophecy seems to be conclusive. Indeed, although it may seem doubtful at the moment of the poet's sickness, it is still quite possible he may return. But such certainty is limited and brings no emotional comfort to the poet or, as it seems, to Delia: *tamen est deterrita nusquam.* ... Yet, Delia's apparent attitude to the poet in the previous two elegies might suggest the possibility that the promise of the poet's return is actually the *reason* for her distress,[17] a possibility which conflicts with the poet's ideal presentation of her in this poem. But the second elegy has already suggested the unreliability of report, and especially of the words and implications of the poet. This approach would generate a strongly ironic reading of this passage. But there is another possible explanation for Delia's reaction which may occur to the reader. *Fleret nostras respiceretque uias* (14) directly recalls 1.1.52, where the poet stated his preference for staying with his beloved(s) rather than seeking gain on *militia*. Perhaps Delia weeps now

---

[17] This possibility becomes stronger if the reader is aware of the possible implications of the phrase *me ... mitteret urbe* discussed above 106.

because the poet, contrary to his protestations, is abandoning her. If this reading, or the poet's version of the caring, concerned Delia, is maintained, then she is not like the Delia of the previous poems. In which case one question which immediately arises is: why?

The poet now turns the emphasis upon himself: *ipse ego*. He is *solator*, taking upon himself the role of consoling the weeping woman. Both his implied control over Delia's emotions and his general orders (*iam mandata dedissem*) suggest that he is now in a position of some power.[18] Yet he is still *anxius*, and seeks *tardae morae*. This anxiety and hesitation hint that his nature, as in the earlier poems, is not entirely active or heroic. The tension between the *amor*-determined lifestyle of the poet in previous poems and the martial (possibly heroic) code is obvious. The poet wants to be passive. He hopes that the omens and superstitions he pretends to see (*sum causatus*) will hold him back (*me tenuisse*). This is a cynical, pragmatic use of these means of prediction. Clearly such methods of divination, which perhaps include the *sacrae sortes* mentioned earlier in the poem, are not entirely objective or reliable.

The exclamation *o quotiens* at line 19 suggests the emotional forces which were controlling at least his attempts to delay. Again, *dixi* may point to a gap between truth and report. The poet's report is the only basis for belief in the *offensus pes in porta* and his interpretation of it. The pretence involving the so-called *omina dira* at line 17 undermines the reliability of the poet's report on such issues. The reader might assume that the *offensus pes* is similarly a lie inspired by his personal desire to stay, a desire which is once more determined by his *amor*. Uncharacteristically, however, the poet *does* (or rather *did*) leave on military campaign in the end. The comparison with earlier elegies is further encouraged by *in porta*. This recalls the position which the poet was most accustomed to in elegies one and two and would like here to return to: before the doors (*ante fores*) of Delia's house. There

---

[18] It seems that the poet has become like the *ille* whom he considered *stultus* at 1.2.67ff.

is also the suggestion, in the poet's resistance to departure, that it is the power of Messalla's command, not his own will, which forces him into the martial sphere. It may be a reflection or even consequence of this inconsistency between the poet/lover's role in earlier elegies and the role he takes on or has forced upon him in this poem, that the poet's attempt to be active, martial, even heroic as the allusions to the *Odyssey* might suggest, ends pathetically. The poet is rendered sick and immobile before the fighting has even begun.

The picture of the poet's departure ends with an explicit statement of *Amor's* power. Those who do not let the god control them by allowing his will to become their will (*audeat inuito ... quis discedere amore*) sooner or later will feel that power levelled against them: *sciet egressum se prohibente deo*. *Amor*, the poet states, is a hostile, authoritarian and vengeful god from whom there is no escape, no *egressum*. The possibility of knowing the future is also raised again here. Knowledge of the god's power (*sciet*) comes unforeseen to the one who has tried to leave against *Amor's* will. The poet's present sickness is supposedly just such an unforeseen act of divine revenge. So now the poet's experience gives him the knowledge to generalise about the future, warning others and possibly allowing them to avoid a similarly disastrous outcome. Such wisdom after the event, of course, allows only a very limited and vicarious control of the future, especially by comparison with the control exerted by *Amor*.

A tension between various powers and their demands upon the poet can be seen here, reinforcing in retrospect the suggestion the reader might have seen in the first couplet, that it is *Amor* which causes the poet to make his excuses to Messalla (*ibitis sine me*). Messalla and the martial, social and political world in which he operates, and whose demands he represents, are ranged against the power of *Amor*. The struggle between the power of Messalla to lead the poet away on campaign, and the power of *Amor*, which according to the poet becomes finally evident in the avenging sickness of line 3, has ended in a victory for *Amor*. Meanwhile the poet is left like a pawn in the middle, immobile in Phaeacia.

Isis

Quid tua nunc Isis mihi, Delia, quid mihi prosunt
   illa tua totiens aera repulsa manu,
quidue, pie dum sacra colis, pureque lauari
   te (memini) et puro secubuisse toro?
nunc, dea, nunc succurre mihi – nam posse mederi
   picta docet templis multa tabella tuis –
ut mea uotiuas persoluens Delia uoces
   ante sacras lino tecta fores sedeat
bisque die resoluta comas tibi dicere laudes
   insignis turba debeat in Pharia.
at mihi contingat patrios celebrare Penates
   reddereque antiquo menstrua tura Lari.   (23–34)

The poet now focuses his address directly on Delia. The
goddess with whom she is now linked, *tua Isis*, is no help to
him (*quid mihi prosunt*). It follows that she either lacks the
power or is unwilling to help him. The focus upon Isis here
may call to mind the similarities between her mythic rescue
and resurrection of her brother/husband Osiris and the position which the poet pictures for Delia and himself. Like Osiris,
the poet is lost (in death/sickness) and, just as Osiris was saved
by the efforts of Isis, the poet hopes to be recovered through
Delia's[19] ministrations. Like the allusions to the *Odyssey*,
which notionally set the poet in a mythic-heroic world, the
mention of Isis links him with a divine-mythic world, which is
all the more distant (and mythical) because it is a foreign
cult.[20] The poet is concerned with present results: *nunc* ... It
is revealed that Delia has been engaging in rituals. This
is possibly an attempt on her part to ensure a prosperous
future,[21] although this is not certain. The poet, absorbed by

---

[19] On this point see Murgatroyd (1980), 108.
[20] See Veremans (1983), 547, who (significantly for my reading here) also observes
the importance of Isis' power for the poet: 'Zumindest bestätigt diese literarische
Vorstellung, da ungeachtet der Distanz, die Tibull der ägyptischen Gottheit gegen-
über bezeigt, Isis doch auf ihn eine bestimmte faszinierende Kraft ausstrahlt ...'
548.
[21] This is the same reason the poet appeals to the gods in poem one.

his own position, thinks only of its practical effect on the future which has now become present. Such effect, as he sees, is negligible. Delia seems to have been concerned with religious correctness: *pie dum sacra colis, pureque lauari*. The poet bases his report of her past behaviour on personal experience (*memini*). The last detail of Delia's ritual behaviour (*puro secubuisse toro*) may suggest why the poet remembers so well. This ritual purity was (one) cause of his exclusion from Delia's bed. Furthermore, the poet's own false use of religion and superstition for his own benefit (17–20), and Delia's previous non-compliance with the poet's wishes, might suggest that the ritual was an excuse for Delia to keep the poet from her. If this was the case, the seemingly reliable, experience-based report of the poet, or at least his interpretation of that experience, is misleading.[22]

Nunc ... nunc (27): the poet is still concerned with immediate results. Now he appeals for Isis' aid[23] (*succurre*). This plea for help comes almost immediately after his claim that Isis is of no assistance: the poet has undercut his position in advance. As many times before, he must appeal to another figure or force (again a god) for the power he needs. The evidence of the *tabellae* on her temple walls suggests that Isis *does* have the power to save him (*posse mederi*). This may imply that she *chooses* not to help; that is, if the evidence of others' past experience reported (*docet*) by the tablets is to be trusted and is relevant to the present. It is also possible that the poet's call to Isis is a sceptical 'test' of the power of the foreign goddess, that he does not really believe she is capable of the healing feats claimed on her temple walls. Either reading is possible.

This leads the poet in lines 29–30 to describe and offer a deal. It is a process of the sort which has already been delineated in different ways in the earlier elegies. He hopes that the healing power of the goddess will be granted in return for

---

[22] This is not necessarily due to deliberate intent on the poet's part, but possibly because he himself was deceived.

[23] There is perhaps a sign of desperation here, emphasised by the repetition of *nunc*.

service to be given to her by Delia. The language emphasises that this is a deal: *uotiuas persoluens ... uoces* (29); *debeat* (32). It seems that such processes are the way the world works, on both the human level and the divine. Again a ritual is to be used in an attempt to gain power: *bisque die*. The description of Delia as *insignis turba in Pharia* perhaps refers to her beauty, perhaps to the fact that she, in contrast to the crowd, is Roman, or perhaps it carries the implication that she transcends them in piety. This could be read as dismissive of the foreign worshippers and possibly their cult. Many possibilities are left open by the poet's reference to the cult of Isis in lines 23–32, and the reader is unable conclusively to reconstruct the poet's exact attitude to Isis and her cult.

In the poet's vision of her it is now Delia who is the one *ante fores*, the one without wealth, simply dressed (*lino tecta*).[24] In this vision the power relationship between the two seems to have shifted. The poet expects Delia to do all this for him, to pay off *his* debts, undergoing this discomfort.[25] As might now seem characteristic of him, and again reinforcing links with earlier elegies, he can achieve nothing for himself. He, in contrast (*at mihi*), desires to stay with the secure and familiar Roman gods of poem one (*patrios ... Penates ... antiquo ... Lari*). Yet, not only is there no indication that the Penates and Lares[26] have the power to save him in his present sickness, but it is not even in the poet's own power to continue his usual worship. This privilege, which would coincide with his return home, must be granted to him (*mihi contingat*), presumably by *Isis*. Accordingly it might appear unlikely that he will be saved without Delia's intercession and Isis' help. Such help he may or may not expect (and may or may not be dismissive of), but still needs. It may also be that the desire to worship the Lares and Penates, deities linked in the first elegy with the rural lifestyle and rejection of war, signals the poet's

---

[24] Again the state of her hair (*resoluta comas*) defines her religious function.

[25] It is perhaps significant that, again, the power most important to the poet is invested in a female figure (see above, 88–90); or rather two female figures: Isis to act, and Delia to repay her.

[26] In this case it is significant that the deities placed in opposition to the female world of Isis are male.

desire to return to the pursuit of that lifestyle and the security of accustomed, repeated ritual (*reddere menstrua tura*) after his failed venture into the martial arena.

The age of Saturn and the dominion of Jove

Quam bene Saturno uiuebant rege, priusquam
    tellus in longas est patefacta uias!
nondum caeruleas pinus contempserat undas,
    effusum uentis praebueratque sinum;
nec uagus ignotis repetens compendia terris
    presserat externa nauita merce ratem.
illo non ualidus subiit iuga tempore taurus,
    non domito frenos ore momordit equus;
non domus ulla fores habuit, non fixus in agris
    qui regeret certis finibus arua lapis;
ipsae mella dabant quercus, ultroque ferebant
    obuia securis ubera lactis oues;
non acies, non ira fuit, non bella, nec ensem
    immiti saeuus duxerat arte faber.   (35–48)

Quam bene Saturno uiuebant rege brings a shift in focus to an ideal time, a mythic, pre-heroic world. The description of life during the reign of Saturn is, however, linked to the preceding lines not only by the contrast of ideal past with immediate present, but by the previous allusions to the equally (literary- or divine-) mythic worlds of Odysseus and Isis, which were also evoked as contrasts to the poet's present state. So Saturn is *rex*, pre-imperial, pre-republic, outside the familiar Roman social, political and military spheres. The poet concentrates here on presenting the ideal. The reference to Saturn links this ideal with the poet's hopes of staying with Delia; he has already claimed Saturn's day as a reason for delaying his departure from her. This may lead the reader to question[27] the extent to which the poet's stated and implied picture of a devoted and caring Delia was also such an

---

[27] If the contrast with the situation of the previous poems, and the poet's previous unreliability, has not already raised the question.

ideal.[28] The term *longae uiae*, described as something definitely bad and outside the ideal, recurs at line 36. This recalls the poet/lover's inconsistency. Despite his hopes at 1.1.25–6, he *has* followed Messalla on the *longae uiae*. The Age of Saturn, however, was a time before the *possibility* of such journeys was available (*prius tellus est patefacta*). Thus the material rewards for which such journeys are undertaken were beyond reach. This may imply that it is only the unavailability of such journeys which prevents men from pursuing them, that men (like the poet) cannot resist them once the possibility is offered.

The emotional emphasis of the exclamation *quam bene uiuebant* suggests that the description of the Age of Saturn which follows provides a picture of how the poet himself wants to live. The word *nondum* suggests the moral force of primacy,[29] which was also apparent in the opening poem. That which was first is also that which is morally superior. This is confirmed by *contempserat*, suggesting an immoral transgression. The Age of Saturn was a less corrupt period before such transgressions. The travel alluded to by the word *undas* recalls the travel which the poet has undertaken with Messalla but cannot now complete (line 1). It is precisely this experience which has confirmed the poet's original opinions of travel expressed in elegy one. It has made Delia weep and brought the pseudo-moral vengeance of *amor* upon him in the form of his sickness. Accordingly travel is seen as morally wrong. This could, therefore, be seen as another example of the poet's *amor*-determined morality. Again the text exploits the similarities and differences between this and traditional ethical stances: travel is morally wrong, not because it is undertaken in pursuit of filthy lucre, but because it disrupts the poet's single-minded obedience to his passion and the pursuit of its object.

The impression given by this description is that the con-

---

[28] One solution, suggested by Jacoby (1905) 78, is that this is the ideal of a wandering, sick, perhaps slightly feverish mind.
[29] This is a common idea which underlies the Roman fascination with the Golden Age myth.

temporary world, in contrast with Saturn's reign, is based upon power struggles of various types. The power of contemporary humans exerted over the natural world (the waves and the wind) is obvious in lines 37–8. Similarly, the power of the *ualidus taurus* is subjugated by contemporary Man (*subiit iuga*), just as control is exerted over the horse: *domito frenos ore momordit equus.* Nor, in the Age of Saturn, was control and regulation exerted upon the land (*non fixus lapis ... qui regeret*) and artificial certainty and order (*certis finibus*) imposed by Man. A reason for this exertion of power is suggested by the picture of the *nauita.* He is *uagus* (uncertain,[30] vulnerable) in an unknown and thus threatening environment (*ignotis terris*), yet he still risks these dangers for personal benefit (*repetens compendia*). He is driven by greed to pack his ship with goods: *presserat externa*[31] *merce ratem.* The reference to the *ignotae terrae* mirrors the poet's position in line 3 and might hint at a parallel between the motives for their respective *longae uiae* as well. At any rate, it is perhaps not surprising that the poet should remove such struggles for power from his ideal life. As has been seen, it is such a struggle between the demands of Messalla and the (vengeful) force of *Amor* which has carried him away from the object of his passion and brought his present sickness, leaving him alone in an uncertain environment. As well as this, the comment that in the Age of Saturn *non domus ulla fores habuit* reminds the reader (humorously) of the poet's position in poems one and two. In such a Saturnine world he would not be kept, by closed doors, from access to Delia. Thus another power struggle would be removed to his benefit.

At line 45 the description changes from negative terms to positive. Oak trees would give honey of their own accord (*ipsae* 45) as if sentient. Sheep would offer milk to whomever

---

[30] *Vagus* can suggest a sense of uncertainty as well as physical wandering, *OLD* 8.
[31] Foreign lands are more dangerous to get to and return from. An interesting comparison can be made between the sailor who risks his safety in foreign territory for wealth, and the poet who offers the service of Delia to a foreign goddess earlier in return for his safety. The basis of each process is the same.

they met (lines 45–6). This is a response of the natural world to Man which is far from the enmity of 37–44.[32] The security of the people in such a world (*securis*) implies a degree of comfort, safety and pleasure such as the poet desired in poem one, and obviously still does here. This again suggests links between the poems of the collection. The signalled presence of comfort and security in the Age of Saturn, however, implies – according to the rhetoric of opposition at work in this passage – that it is *not* present or possible in the contemporary age. Yet, while the virtual sentience of oak trees might seem unreal enough, the picture of the sheep looking to give their milk away to whomever they bump into might be thought ridiculous, and certainly highlights the unreality of the ideal.[33] Line 47 returns to negatives, heaping up the destructive forces of the contemporary world which were not present in Saturn's time: *non acies, non ira fuit, non bella, nec ensem* ... These might be considered to be some of the causes of the poet being carried away from the demands of *Amor* on military service, and the consequent suffering he is enduring. It may, therefore, be more than the conventions of the myth which prompts him to banish such forces from his ideal world. The poet's ideals seem to be directly determined by the central realities of his life. Human power, because in this case synonymous with human cruelty (the *faber* is *saeuus*), is channelled through technology into destruction: *ensem | immiti duxerat arte*. *Ars* here is a power for discord and devastation.

Nunc Ioue sub domino caedes et uulnera semper,
    nunc mare, nunc leti mille repente uiae.

---

[32] Bearing in mind the absence of physical obstacle to the poet's passion (line 43), the willingness of trees and sheep to give their produce to humans may hint at a general willingness to give which, in this the poet's ideal world, might be extended to Delia's compliance with his desires, something which seemed impossible to achieve in poems one and two. It is also possible that the more compliant and caring impression that the poet tries to give of Delia in *this* poem is also part of such an 'ideal'.

[33] Compare this to the sheep who spontaneously change colour to save humans the trouble of dyeing them in *Eclogue* 4 (lines 42–5) and the possibility of this absurdity undermining the realisability of the ideal in that poem.

parce, Pater: timidum non me periuria terrent,
non dicta in sanctos impia uerba deos.
quod si fatales iam nunc expleuimus annos,
fac lapis inscriptis stet super ossa notis;
HAC IACET IMMITI CONSVMPTVS MORTE TIBVLLVS
MESSALLAM TERRA DVM SEQVITVRQVE MARI.

(49–56)

The contrast between the ideal, mythic past and the present
is underlined by the poet's insistent focus on the present conveyed in the repetition: *nunc ... nunc ... nunc ... Iove sub
domino*: it is no longer under the auspices of a *rex* that life is
conducted, but rather under those of a *dominus*.[34] The danger
and devastation is constant (*semper*). The destructive nature
of human *uiae* is underlined (*uiae leti*). The future is unforeseen, unpredictable (*repente*). The inability to obtain knowledge of the future, the extreme exertion of power, the process
of risk-for-gain embodied by the *uiae* are all present, and the
result is destruction: *caedes et uulnera semper*.

As with the appeal to Isis, the poet now turns to Jupiter for
aid, after apparently discrediting that god's reign. The word
used is *parce*, as it has been many times before. The poet
describes himself as *timidum me*. In this case it refers in particular to his fear of dying, but possibly, judging from his
passivity earlier in the book, it is a more widely and ironically
appropriate description of him. The poet assumes[35] his fate
must be a punishment, but claims there is no reason for it: *non
me periuria terrent | non dicta in sanctos impia uerba deos*. This
recalls 1.2.81, where the poet, unable to explain his situation,
was similarly powerless to resist it. But the poet seems to
forget, while the reader may not, that he himself stated that
the *deus* forbade his departure (1.3.21–2). This implies that his
illness is the revenge of *Amor*. Even the literal offence of *periuria* is not evaded, since the poet's actions have apparently
contradicted his protestations that he would leave warring to

---

[34] This parallels the control of the *domina* or *dominus Amor* over the poet.
[35] Does the poet here betray a guilty conscience?

Messalla and stay confined by his passion (1.1.53ff.). His position is thus undercut. His present state might seem to be his own fault, at least partly. If the poet himself recognises this, then there is a possibility that his prayer here may even be an attempt to mislead Jupiter in the hope of gaining release from sickness.[36] This might provide another suggestion that the words of the poet/lover, for whatever reason, can not always be trusted.

The *fatales anni* of line 53 suggest that the poet's time of death is pre-determined and thus out of his control. It comes on fast (*iam nunc*), unexpectedly and unpredictably. The poet is uncertain whether it really has come now or will come later: *si* ... In his instructions for his tomb and epitaph he attempts to ensure some certainty and fixity at least in death (*lapis stet* ... '*Hic iacet* ...').[37] The inscription presumably expresses what he wishes to be remembered for.[38] It perhaps comes as a surprise to the reader, then, that in 55–6 the poet chooses to be remembered for his unrealised military exploits with Messalla (*Messallam terra dum sequiturque mari*) rather than his (in all respects dominating) passion for Delia.[39] Several possibilities are offered. The poet may be giving in to Roman convention, viewing the military as the more noteworthy exploit. He may not be so devoted to Delia after all, which might seem unlikely given what has already been seen of their relationship. Or the epitaph may carry the implication that Messalla is to blame for bringing about the poet's death (*dum sequitur Messallam*). Acceptance of the operations of established power structures co-exists in these words with criticism

[36] For this (of course) he needs the power of another: yet again a god.

[37] Even this, however, is dependent on the power of Jove, to whom the poet is (presumably still) praying for this indulgence.

[38] 'The tendency of the epitaphs, as we have seen, is to present the dead in a favourable light, and this will account for the frequency in both languages of what might almost be described as boasts; for along with the attribution of virtues to the deceased in the name of the inscriber, we find numerous cases where the dead man declares, or is made to declare, his excellences ... As might be expected, there are a great many Latin inscriptions of this general type', Lattimore (1942) 285 and 288.

[39] This contrasts with the chosen epitaphs of other elegists: cf. Prop. 2.13b.35–6, Ov. *Tristia* 3.3.73ff.

of those same operations, allowing either or both to be read here. In any case, the poet himself is once more seen as a passive figure (*consumptus*), powerless against a hostile force which threatens all mortals (*immiti morte*).

Between heaven and hell

> Sed me, quod facilis tenero sum semper amori,
>   ipsa Venus campos ducet in Elysios.
> hic choreae cantusque uigent, passimque uagantes
>   dulce sonant tenui gutture carmen aues;
> fert casiam non culta seges totosque per agros
>   floret odoratis terra benigna rosis:
> ac iuuenum series teneris immixta puellis
>   ludit, et assidue proelia miscet Amor.
> illic est cuicumque rapax Mors uenit amanti,
>   et gerit insigni myrtea serta coma.   (57–66)

Sed introduces another contrast, a contrast between the harshness of death (*ossa*) and the physical reality of the tomb on the one hand, and another ideal of a better fate[40] (*in Elysios campos*) on the other. As with the earlier allusions to the *Odyssey*,[41] the picture of Elysium, which in literature is normally the home of dead heroes, continues the poet's re-shaping of the heroic (martial) ethos around his own position. He does not fit the old heroic mould, but instead of changing himself to accommodate it, he changes the ideal to suit himself. The description of himself as *facilis semper tenero amori* casts him again as passive and vulnerable (*facilis*) to the power of *Amor*, and *Amor*, especially in its effects upon the poet, has not always been *tener*. The suggestion that *ipsa Venus* will gain him access to Elysium may seem odd since in the second poem Venus appeared to be opposed to him. Why the change now? Would it be a reward for his endurance of her

---

[40] This time the ideal is set in the future (i.e. after death) rather than the mythic past. But in the sense that they *are* ideals both are equally remote.
[41] Compare the picture of the underworld in *Odyssey* Bk. 11 and the questioning of the ideal by Achilles at lines 487–91.

tortures? Or is the poet deluding himself? It is significant, in any case, that Venus is controlling the poet in death (*ducet*) as he was controlled by the forces she embodies in his life. The 'heroic' environment of Elysium has been usurped by the ethos of the lover. Violent, active, martial heroes have been replaced by passive, suffering lover heroes.

Elysium itself is described in terms of sensual pleasure. First, in lines 59–60 the emphasis is on sweet sound. In particular, and perhaps not surprisingly since this is the ideal of a poet/lover, this sound consists of *carmen*, which is given a high priority in Elysium: *hic choreae cantusque uigent* | ... *sonant ... carmen*. Then, in lines 61–2, the emphasis is on sweet scent (*casia* and *odoratae rosae*). The land produces without any control being exerted over it (*non culta*) and the bounty is complete (*totos*). The favourable response of the natural (or pseudo-natural) world (*terra benigna*) has obvious parallels with the picture of the Age of Saturn. The produce of the land in Elysium, however, is for sensual pleasure not sustenance, since shades need no sustenance. Elysium is, the poet suggests, the only environment in which such an ideal is now achievable, and not only must those who enter it be dead, which might suggest that it is a somewhat empty realisation of the ideal,[42] but it is exclusively for lovers. The ideal of Elysium is, then, determined by the poet's picture of himself. But, given the doubts about Venus' willingness to comply,[43] he does not necessarily fit even his own picture.

The continuing description of Elysium re-emphasises the motif of love as battle. This motif is given more resonance now, since the place of the martial hero in Elysium has been taken over by the lover. The inhabitants form in *series* as in battle, and *Amor* is still in full control of them: *proelia miscet Amor*. It is only a game (*ludit*) for pleasure. (Note the adjective *tener* again, a term which has often seemed inappropriate to the contexts it has appeared in so far in the elegies.) As the

[42] Compare 1.1.59ff. discussed above 55ff. (and see, again, Achilles' words at *Od*.11.487–91).
[43] The poet, of course, is powerless to realise this ideal by himself.

poet sees it, no one is hurt in this ideal place after death; though the reader has seen the suffering caused by real-life struggles of *amor* in the two preceding poems. *Miscet* points to the confusion and uncertainty created by *Amor*'s power. This power forces the inhabitants of Elysium to fight eternally (*assidue*). In this way the battles of the Elysian lovers resemble the many repetitive torments undergone by the inhabitants of Tartarus (some of whom will appear later in the poem).

The *myrtea*[44] *serta*, which recall the *serta* the poet has previously given to Delia, are placed upon the lovers' heads as if they were victors. In social terms the importance has been taken from the martial hero and placed upon the lover, just as in literary terms it has been taken from the heroic world of epic and assumed and re-shaped in elegy. The central focus for this is, of course, the figure of the poet himself, whose views on social role, religion, the afterlife, and poetry seem to be determined by *amor* and what that makes him. *Militia* and war are presented as a barren reality of stone and bone, while in contrast the ideal world of the lover/hero blooms (*floret*). The terms in which the poet thinks are clear. The 'code' of *amor* which the poet claims to follow (57–8) takes over the heroic code. The poet *claims* to follow this code and, as has been emphasised, in nearly all ways he is dominated by it. But even in this he is imperfect. Because of his inability to resist, demonstrated by his weak and unsuccessful attempts to delay at 15ff., he *did* go, or at least *tried* to go, on *militia*, on the *longa uia*.

> At scelerata iacet sedes in nocte profunda
>   abdita, quam circum flumina nigra sonant:
> Tisiphoneque impexa feros pro crinibus angues
>   saeuit et huc illuc impia turba fugit;
> tunc niger in porta serpentum Cerberus ore
>   stridet et aeratas excubat ante fores.
> illic Iunonem temptare Ixionis ausi
>   uersantur celeri noxia membra rota,

---

[44] The myrtle was sacred to Venus (for this and earlier associations of myrtle with Elysium see Murgatroyd (1980) 120).

porrectusque nouem Tityos per iugera terrae
   assiduas atro uiscere pascit aues.
Tantalus est illic, et circum stagna, sed acrem
   iam iam poturi deserit unda sitim;
et Danai proles, Veneris quod numina laesit,
   in caua Lethaeas dolia portat aquas.   (67–80)

Again a contrast is drawn at line 67. Now crime and immorality in general (*scelerata sedes*) are defined in terms of
amor. The image of darkness (*in nocte profunda*) is strongly
linked to such crime and the suffering of resulting punishment.
Similarly, the *sedes* is hidden (*abdita*), its location unknown
and thus, as has been seen of other uncertainties, threatening.
Tisiphone presents the reader with a violent (*saeuit*), unnatural
female figure of power. Again her hair is a definition of her
nature and function: *impexa feros pro crinibus angues*.[45] In
one way she may remind the reader of *Amor* in Elysium as she
creates confusion, but in her case it is grim and aimless: *huc
illuc impia turba fugit*. If this is not assumed to be *simply*
a restatement of a conventional moral picture, the question
might be raised of exactly what, as far as the poet is concerned,
makes the inhabitants of this Hell *impia*. The appearance of
Cerberus *in porta ... ante fores* is strangely reminiscent of the
poet's own accustomed position before Delia's door (in poems
one and two).[46] Cerberus here, in guarding the doorway, is
symbolic of exclusion, a lover's nightmare especially familiar
to the poet (as in poem two).

As in Elysium, there is sound in Hell (*sonant* line 68; *stridet*
line 72), but here it is harsh, threatening, violent and related in
each case to darkness (*nigra* line 68; *niger* line 71). At lines
75–8 the sensual emphasis is on taste, or the lack of it, but it
is agonising and foul. The birds, in contrast to the *aues* in
Elysium (60), feed on Tityos' entrails (*pascit*), and Tantalus is
deprived of the satisfaction of tasting water (*poturi deserit*)
resulting in dryness and barrenness (*acrem sitim*).

Ixion, the first suffering inhabitant of Hell mentioned in

---

[45] See Bright (1978) 30.
[46] Or perhaps, rather, it is reminiscent of the position of the *custos*, *excluding* the
poet from Delia's door.

detail, is described as *Ixion ausus*. This boldness was directed against a superior power, *Iunonem*. It is because of this fact that it *is* boldness. The nature of his *noxia* (74), therefore, is violence of a sexual nature against a god. The attempted rape and resulting punishment functions as a paradigm for a struggle motivated by sexual passion (by *amor*) where one party is totally overpowered by the other. Similarly, Tityos was overpowered[47] by a god in an erotic struggle, and now suffers foul pain (*atro uiscere*) and constant (*assiduas*) discomfort as a result. The crime of Tantalus, too, was certainly against the gods and possibly, given the tradition that he attempted to abduct Ganymede,[48] in the erotic sphere. In his case, then, the crime would not be directly against a god, but against a mortal supported (and in this case beloved) by the gods.[49] In the same way, although the act of the Danaids (79–80) was against mortals, it is emphasised by the poet that the real offence lay in the attack upon the power of Venus: *Veneris quod numina laesit*. It is clear that the poet's view of hell and morality is also charted in terms of *amor* and associated power relations.[50] It might be observed that the poet himself could be said to have offended the power of Venus (1.2.81) or at least to be suffering at her hands, and he certainly, within the scope of this poem, has attracted the wrath of *Amor*, or at least *a* god associated with love (1.3.21–2). Ironically, it is possible that the poet himself would be a more appropriate inhabitant of his Hell than of his Elysium.

The Lucretian interpretation

The exact nature of the influence of Lucretius on the poet/lover's depiction of the underworld, Elysium and the Golden

---

[47] He is stretched *per iugera*, perhaps as in poem one recalling the *iuga*, an instrument of control, or perhaps suggesting that the *aues* plough through Tityos' entrails just as oxen plough through a field.

[48] See Murgatroyd (1980) 120 and 123.

[49] In effect, then, Tantalus falls to the power of a superior, divine rival.

[50] This is denied, however, by Cilliers (1974) 74–9, who simply assumes that the 'common associations' (78) of the 'arch-sinners' would restrict contemporary readers to seeing them only as an example of 'utmost misery' in contrast to 'the happiness in Elysium' 79.

Age here has been the cause of a great deal of critical debate. Henderson has argued that the poet/lover's Tartarus is a refutation of Lucretian/Epicurean doctrine, 'that Tibullus is here concerned to make a stand against Lucretius' teaching on death and romantic love'.[51] Tibullus does this, Henderson argues, not only by the depiction of each inhabitant of Hell as 'a type of enemy of the lover', but by the assertion of an Elysium specifically for lovers.[52] Cilliers, on the other hand, attempts to deny the resonance with Lucretius on the unconvincing grounds that there is no direct reference to the earlier poet.[53] While the picture of Elysium and Tartarus might be set in opposition to the Lucretian view, the reference in the third elegy to the Golden Age is directly associated with the earlier poet's use of the motif by Bénéjam: 'Il s'inscrit dans la lignée de Lucrèce, comme ceux qui ont reconnu en l'âge d'or une image archétypale de l'ataraxie philosophique.'[54] The poet/lover's association of himself in the space of a few lines with aspirations towards ataraxia and the assertion of an anti-Lucretian erotic lifestyle might seem to undercut both these ideals. The recollection of Lucretius draws attention to the opposition of these two ideals. In the Lucretian/Epicurean world-view they are, after all, mutually exclusive. This implies that the loss of the Golden Age and its associated ataraxia could be blamed as much on the assurgency of the type of power structures and struggle associated with *amor*, as it is on the discovery of warfare and travel by sea.

But, despite the arguments of Henderson, the poet/lover's depiction of Tartarus *and* Elysium can be assimilated to the view presented by the Lucretian passage which it recalls (Lucr. 3.978–1023). Lucretius' explanation of the myth of

---

[51] Henderson (1969) 649.
[52] Henderson (1969) 651.
[53] Cilliers (1974), whose arguments for disregarding the resonances of the passage with the earlier treatment of Tartarus by Lucretius are confused: see especially Cilliers (1974) 78.
[54] Bénéjam (1980) 102.

Tartarus is made clear in the opening two lines of that passage:

> Atque ea nimirum quaecunque Acherunte profundo
> prodita sunt esse, in uita sunt omnia nobis.   (Lucr. 3.978–9).

As I have argued, the poet/lover's heaven and hell are described in terms of *amor* and its associated power relations as he has experienced them,[55] and as he would ideally reconstruct them. In this respect, they can easily be assimilated to the critique of these myths that Lucretius puts forward. Just as Lucretius claims, the poet constructs his Hell (and his Elysium) in the image of what he has experienced during life. The Lucretian passage, rather than being set in opposition to the poet/lover's construction of Tartarus and Elysium, can thus be seen to expose the dependence of that construction on the power of *amor* and the structures and struggles by which it operates.

> Illic sit quicumque meos uiolauit amores,
> optauit lentas et mihi militias.   (81–2)

The poet (at lines 81–2) wishes that any who violate his love be confined to that Hell. It *is*, of course, only a wish (*sit*) and as such may not necessarily be fulfilled. The poet effectively wishes that he be (or maybe even suggests that he *is*) supported by the power of a god, the power which has conveyed its present inhabitants to the poet's *scelerata sedes*. Thus, he must appeal for that power: *sit*. The phrase *quicumque meos uiolauit amores* admits that such a violation has occurred. This opens up the further possibility that the entire picture of Hell, which culminates in this threat to potential violators, might have been deliberately designed to scare off rivals.[56] *Militia* is now explicitly revealed to be a threat to the

---

[55] This is reflected even in details such as Cerberus excluding people from the gates of Tartarus (as well as keeping them in), which recalls the poet/lover's own exclusion *ante fores* in earlier poems.
[56] Perhaps even the poet himself does not believe his picture but is using it as he used the pretence of the *omina dira* earlier.

poet's 'love', through the possibility not just of his death, but of Delia's unfaithfulness. Indeed, the implication that the poet's *lentae militiae* would be a good thing for any potential rival suggests that the dream of Delia's faithfulness which follows is far from the truth.

Livy and the dream of return

At tu casta, precor, maneas sanctique pudoris
    assideat custos sedula semper anus.
haec tibi fabellas referat positaque lucerna
    deducat plena stamina longa colu,
ac circa, grauibus pensis affixa, puella
    paulatim somno fessa remittat opus.
tunc ueniam subito nec quisquam nuntiet ante
    sed uidear caelo missus adesse tibi.
tunc mihi, qualis eris, longos turbata capillos,
    obuia nudato, Delia, curre pede.   (83–92)

At (83ff.) brings the final contrast. Firstly, there is a direct contrast with the suggestion of infidelity in the previous two lines. But, as well as this, the hope for return expressed in this final passage provides a contrast to the picture of separation and departure at the beginning of the elegy. The poet, in a powerless position, must appeal (*precor*) for Delia's fidelity to him. This suggests that the picture of the faithful, loving Delia may not be entirely correct. The poet stresses constancy (*assideat ... semper*), and the description of the preservation of her chastity for him as *sanctus pudor*, immediately following the picture of Hell, may hint that he feels it necessary to threaten her also with such punishment if that 'sanctity' is infringed. Similarly, the presence of a third party, a *custos*, is needed, as it was in a different context in the first elegy. The *custos* is *continually* (*semper*) necessary. This implies that Delia cannot be trusted to remain *casta* on her own. Yet, the protective power of a *sedula anus* might seem a rather pathetic hope on the poet's part; or perhaps he is just secure enough in Delia's faithfulness that he can trust her to so weak a guard.

The entire statement, of course, pre-supposes that the poet is in a position where Delia *can* be guarded for him. It was not so in the previous poems. On the contrary, in poem two she was guarded *from* him. There is no indication they are married. This and the fact that she needs guarding suggests that Delia is no Penelope. Despite the weaving going on around her she does not, it seems, take part in it herself. It is possible, then, that the picture of Delia given here and in the elegy in general is like the fictions which the poet suggests the *anus* tell Delia (*fabellas referat*). This picture creates a cosy, dream-like (*somno fessa*) domestic environment with Delia *posita* at a distance from rivals, where the poet wants her, surrounded by the traditional pursuits of morally upright Roman women (*grauibus pensis affixa*), fixed in a conventional Roman female sphere.[57] Thus, these lines work in the same way as the death-bed scene at lines 6-9. But, like the poet's attempt at *militia*, this particular Roman stereotype seems unlikely to be realised in this particular case.

The Roman paradigm which combines the display of traditional female virtue within the domestic sphere and the sudden return of men from foreign campaign (as also in this passage, lines 89ff.) is the myth of Lucretia. Livy (1.57-9) provides a detailed description of this episode of Roman myth/history which was written and published at roughly the same time as Tibullus Book One:[58] *sed nocte sera deditam lanae [uiderant] inter lucubrantes ancillas in medio aedium sedentem inueniunt* (Livy, 1.57.9). Read against Livy's realisation of the Lucretia story, the contradictions within the poet's ideal become even more apparent. Lucretia's husband, Collatinus, is, like the poet, away on campaign and not fighting but idle during the siege of Ardea, although Collatinus' idleness is due to a lull in the fighting not sickness. But there is

---

[57] See Leach (1980a) 87, on the blending of the Roman and the literary (Homeric) strands here. Leach suggests that the piece is 'a psychological step backwards from reality' and that the poet's 'very ingenuity betrays the artificial and insubstantial nature of this solution to the divorce between reality and the hypothetically ideal life'.

[58] It is possible that Livy's first pentad was produced contemporaneously with Tibullus' first book; see Ogilvie (1970) 2.

a confusion of roles in the poet's position and aspirations. Like Collatinus, the poet hopes to return suddenly: *necopinato* (Livy, 1.57.7). In this respect he adopts the role of Collatinus and places Delia in the role of the virtuous Lucretia, implying that his return is a test of the woman's fidelity. But the sequel to Collatinus' sudden return hangs over the poet's allocation of roles. Tarquin also returns suddenly, and the depiction of Tarquin at Livy 1.58 in itself resembles the Hellenistic komastic lover. He enters the house secretly at night, uses physical violence (compare Tib.1.1.73–4) and at one point is described in terms directly applicable to the elegiac (and especially Tibullan) poet/lover: *tum Tarquinius fateri amorem, orare, miscere precibus minas, uersare in omnes partes muliebrem animum* (Livy, 1.58.3). Indeed, Delia's dishevelled appearance on the poet's return (*longos turbata capillos | obuia nudato ... pede* Tib.1.3.91–2) might suggest violation. The poet aspires to a role similar to that of Collatinus, but at the same time, if the details of this passage are compared more closely to those of the Lucretia story, he is type-cast in the role of Tarquin. To this confusion and conflict of roles, which mirrors the multiple meanings of the Homeric allusions, is added the ambiguity of Delia's position. The poet's ideal demands that she be cast as Lucretia. But, when read against the Livian realisation of the story, it is the other wives, whom the returning soldiers discover at dinner-parties with friends, who most resemble what might be the expected behaviour of an elegiac mistress. The interplay of elegiac roles with the poet's ideal here (again the interplay of similarity and difference) produces a confusion between asserted and conventional categories which interferes with the prospects of the poet's desires and any reading or interpretation of them.

In the final lines (89ff.), the poet suddenly breaks in (*tunc ... tunc*). It is unclear whether the poet foresees this ideal being realised during his life or imagines returning as a vision after his death. The second possibility might again suggest the insubstantiality of his ideal. In it he is definite, active, vaguely heroic, unlike his character as suggested elsewhere. For Delia in this imagined scene the future has been unpredictable. She has had no prior knowledge of the poet's arrival: *subito ... nec quisquam nuntiet ante*. This sudden appearance may also be a veiled threat to Delia not to be unfaithful, as he might burst in at any time. The poet would appear *missus caelo*, as if the gods, for once, *were* granting him power in the vein of returning god-supported heroes like Odysseus.[59] (As before, however, the poet and Delia both in their natures and their relationship seem ridiculously out of place in the roles of Odysseus and Penelope.) The description of Delia as she will be when he arrives (*longos turbata capillos,* | *... nudato ... pede*), especially the state of the hair (compare line 37), is reminiscent of a worshipper. She reacts to the now god-like poet with what the poet himself assumes will be an overwhelming desire to see him: *curre*.

Conclusion

It is clear that either the attitudes and power relationship of the poet and Delia have dramatically shifted or the dream of Delia's faithfulness and other implications of reports by the poet of her behaviour in the poem simply represent the hopes of the poet/lover, which lines 89ff. certainly are. They present an ideal picture which bears an ambiguous relation to the situation suggested in earlier poems. These tensions can be suppressed if it is assumed that the 'Delias' of individual elegies do not necessarily bear any relation to one another but are constituted entirely by the varying projections of the poet's aspirations and anxieties. But, like the chronological re-arrangement of the Delia sequence argued for by Wimmel, such a reading strategy attempts to suppress the very inconsistencies which give rise to it. The interpenetration of the elegies of the collection, as I have suggested above, is unavoidable even, or especially, in a reading which attempts to suppress such interaction. As in the second poem, inconsistencies in the poet/lover's presentation of the figure 'Delia'

---

[59] There is perhaps also in this allusion a threat to any would-be suitors. As noted, however, the poet is unlikely to be in the position in relation to Delia to issue, let alone carry out, such threats.

can be figured as the conflict between the poet/lover's delu-
sions/ideals and the disruptive 'reality' of the elegiac mistress'
attitude. The irony here is that this reality is itself projected by
the poet/author. The reader must thus first reconstruct the
reality projected by the poet to establish the delusion of the
poet-persona.[60] The effect on the reader may be disorienting
and forces a re-evaluation of the relations in the elegy and
their points of contact, such as the conflict between the power
of the conventional Roman world of martial demands and
exploits represented by Messalla and the power of *amor* and
the elegiac world represented by Delia. The third elegy foregrounds this conflict and thus encourages the direct comparison of the two sets of power structures. It is the interaction
of these power structures that determines the situation of the
elegy and the positions of the leading figures within the various relationships which the elegy presents.

> Hoc precor; hunc illum nobis Aurora nitentem
> Luciferum roseis candida portet equis.   (93–4)

The poet can only hope for his ideal to be realised (*hoc
precor*, line 93) and it is not exactly certain how much of the
preceding elegy he is including in that ideal. The future, as has
been shown throughout this elegy, remains unpredictable. The
picture of Aurora and Lucifer which concludes the elegy
emphasises images of brightness (*nitentem ... candida*) and
colour which recall the flowers of Elysium (*roseis*). These epic
formula-like lines complete the poem's reshaping of the heroic
in terms of *amor*. The poet's desire that Aurora bring (*portet*)
the day that his ideal is realised does not, judging by the many
suggestions within this elegy and the two earlier poems, seem
likely of fulfilment.

The problem of how to untangle one created reality, that of
the author Tibullus, from another, that of the poet-persona, is
central to the third elegy. The disorientation and uncertainty
which this creates mirrors the shifting world of possibilities
and the insubstantial attempts to re-construct reality which the

---

[60] See Kennedy (1993) 15.

poet/lover projects. This forces a continuous re-evaluation of the power relations which the poet/lover's words suggest. Within this unstable reading process any strategy which allows a reader (or critic) to satisfy the impulse to impose a single, coherent meaning upon the speaker's words, whether it is Eisenberger's Gefühlsgründe,[61] Hanslik's structural unity,[62] or Campbell's 'organized' alternation of past, present and future,[63] would be in tune with the strangely inconsistent sense of apparent hope with which the poet himself concludes, and would be open to the same tensions and uncertainties which undermine such a complete, controlled construction or re-construction of meaning.

---

[61] Eisenberger (1960) 197.   [62] Hanslik (1970) 145.   [63] Campbell (1973) 156.

POEM FOUR

Looking for answers

Commentators have emphasised the differences between the fourth elegy and the earlier elegies of the collection. Littlewood separates the fourth poem (with the seventh) in his structural arrangement of the collection, categorising it as a 'genre poem'.[1] Critics such as Dawson, Luck, Wimmel and others[2] have shown the influence of Hellenistic and earlier Roman models to be particularly extensive in poem four's case. There are indeed pronounced differences between the fourth elegy and those earlier in the collection. The poem is didactic in nature, it is concerned with pederastic *amor*, and it is dominated by a speaker other than the poet/lover. But while the form of the poem and its didactic approach differ from the previous three elegies, at the same time the problems being addressed, and the structure of the power relationships involved in the sphere of *amor*, suggest similarities.

> 'Sic umbrosa tibi contingant tecta, Priape,
>   ne capiti soles ne noceantque niues:
> quae tua formosos cepit sollertia? certe
>   non tibi barba nitet, non tibi culta coma est;
> nudus et hibernae producis frigora brumae,
>   nudus et aestiui tempora sicca Canis.'   (1-6)

---

[1] Littlewood (1970) 662ff. For the poem's foundation in the erotodidaxis 'genre' see Wheeler (1910) 440–50, and (1911) 56–77; and Cairns (1972) 72, 173–4, and (1979) 36–7; also Murgatroyd (1980) 129–31.

[2] Dawson (1946) 1–15; Luck (1969) 92–8; Wimmel (1968), especially 14, 22, 26, 30–2 and 34–5 n.56; see also Wilhelm (1896) 48–58; Jacoby (1910) 56–77; Leonotti (1980) 259–70; Pieri (1986) 69–88; and Cairns (1979) 36–7.

The opening lines of the fourth elegy reveal an approach familiar from the earlier poems.[3] It is an appeal to a god (in this case Priapus) for power. Unsurprisingly it is power in the erotic sphere which is sought, and this power is to be activated by knowledge. The opening lines also describe a prospective deal, a process which my reading of the earlier elegies has located at the basis of social, religious and, in a more ambiguous way, amatory relations. Here the poet suggests that protection in the form of security from the discomforts of nature (line 2) will be given to the god in return for knowledge: *sic ... contingant*. Or rather, as is apparent from the nature of the prospective benefit,[4] that protection will be granted to the *statue* of the god which the poet is addressing. The poet, however, does not specifically state that he *personally* will confer this benefit. The deal is offered in vague terms (*sic ... contingant*). This leaves some uncertainty as to whether such benefits are in the poet's power to bestow. His side of the bargain may consist simply of the *wish* that Priapus' statue be protected. This would be consistent with the picture, suggested by earlier elegies, of a poet unable to achieve almost anything under his own power.

The figure of Priapus here recalls the mock-heroic, ridiculous *custos* of the orchards presented at 1.1.17–18. The choice of a phallic god-statue as an interlocutor in itself creates a comic tone. This suggests that the 'god' and, by association, the person addressing him as if he is some great and powerful oracle are not to be taken too seriously.[5] The return of

---

[3] It is also similar in being a direct address from the poet to another figure, as were the openings of poems two and three.

[4] For this point see Murgatroyd (1980) 128.

[5] This is reinforced by the tone of poetry concerning Priapus elsewhere: in Hellenistic and Augustan writers as well as the *Carmina Priapea*, on which see Parker (1988), 41–4. (On the connections between the *CP* and poem four see Murgatroyd (1980) 129.) The comic tone of the passage may also be enlivened simply by the fact that Priapus here is only a statue after all and not a 'real' god. Compare Theocritus *Epigram* 4 where the weather-beaten statue of Priapus is presented with offerings and asked to help the lover (although it is not advice which is sought), but does not answer back. A statue of Priapus does speak, however, in *AP* 10.2, 16.236, 16.237, and 16.261, but not about love. Compare also the use of a talking statue of Priapus for comic effect in Horace *Satires* 1.8.

Priapus also raises the question of the poet's location. Is he now in the rural environment which he desired in the opening poem, or in urban *horti*, of a type which even the passage in poem one (1.1.17–18) seemed to suggest was the true domain of Priapus? Unlike the immediately previous poem, the setting of the fourth poem is uncertain. The text, as in the second poem, seems to raise several initial possibilities without allowing the reader to construct a stable context for the poet/lover. This renders any assumptions which the reader might make fragile and open to being challenged or undercut by alternative possibilities at any point.

The knowledge which the poet seeks is how to capture beautiful boys: *quae tua formosos cepit sollertia?* (3). While the question is consistent with the erotic nature of Priapus,[6] the poet's concern with this subject matter might conflict with the impression given of him by the earlier poems. Like the revelation (at the start of poem three) that he had gone on military campaign with Messalla despite protestations to the contrary, the question to Priapus seems to undercut the poet's apparently exclusive obsession with and domination by Delia.[7] Now, instead, he is interested in a form of relationship where he, according to accepted social roles, would be the dominant partner.[8] This, of course, assumes that the poet wants the knowledge for his own use, for its translation into control (*cepit*). This is suggested by the fact that *he* is doing the questioning, and there is no implication that he is acting for someone else at this stage. Such control (although not, of course, over

---

[6] The question also finds parallels in earlier, especially Hellenistic, literature (on which see Murgatroyd (1980) 129).

[7] Compare the situation of the lover Callignotus in Callimachus' epigram *AP*5.6 (= 25 Pf.). Although contrast the claims of Quinn on the possibility of one lover maintaining both a heterosexual and a pederastic *amor*-relationship simultaneously, Quinn (1972a) 249 (a view based exclusively on this poem, and quoted with approval by Lilja (1983)).

[8] As the older man the poet would be the dominant partner in a pederastic relationship. But the same might have been expected (wrongly as it turned out, and with degrading consequences for the poet) of the male-female *amor*-relationship of earlier elegies. On conventions of dominance and submission within Roman erotic relationships see Veyne (1985) 26; on the balance of power within ancient pederastic relationships more generally see Dover (1978) 100–109.

boys) has already been advanced as a favoured, if not quite successfully applied, use of knowledge in the earlier elegies.

Many new possibilities are opened by the shift in subject matter. Is the reader to assume that the persona of 'the poet' is not consistent from one poem to the next? The use of the name of the actual author of the entire collection to designate the 'I' of the elegy at 1.3.55, and the use of the name Delia to designate the single beloved in poems 1–3, might tend to suggest some unity. Or are the elegies to be read as separate, with no connection *except* a common central persona, let alone any chronological sequence? Is elegy four a set piece, 'entertainment', or genre poem,[9] as some critics suggest, and does it signal a change from the technique of the first three, Delia-dominated, poems to something new? Do the expectations of the elegiac genre smooth over the conflict and allow deviation from the 'obsession' as an unproblematic trope?[10] Or is the poet the same as in earlier poems, and is he here simply having a joke with, or at the expense of, Priapus? Is he sweet-talking the god into a mock-rhetorical enunciation of the code by which he (Priapus rather than the poet) lives? Whatever the relative likelihood of each of these or other possibilities in any reader's mind, this, like other pivotal moments in earlier elegies,[11] forces a re-evaluation of the assumptions which have built up around the poet, and the effect is disorienting. The reader is not in control of any final meaning. He/she cannot be sure what is going on behind the poet/lover's words. The dependence of any reading upon the reader's expectations, both of the genre and of the Tibullan poet/lover, is exposed.

The normal powers of physical attraction are not available to Priapus, or at least they are not present in his statue. He has no shining beard, and he exerts no control over his wayward hair (*non tibi culta coma est*). The poet assumes firstly,

[9] See above 132
[10] Compare the non-Cynthian, non-*amor*-centred ending of Propertius Bk 1 (poems 21 and 22); and the deviation from the obsession with a single mistress which Ovid plays with in *Amores* 2.7 and 2.8 and elsewhere; see also the Gallan 'inconsistency' between *militia* and devotion to a beloved highlighted in *Eclogue* 10.
[11] For example, the beginning of the third elegy, discussed above.

POEM FOUR

based perhaps on reputation, that Priapus *has* the power to capture beautiful boys, and so assumes, secondly, that this power must come from Priapus' knowledge (*sollertia*).[12] The repetition of *nudus* emphasises the physical vulnerability of the god-statue (battered by the forces of the natural environment),[13] which *is* after all a statue (if not *only* a statue) and perhaps slightly ridiculous in its naked, battered state. At the same time, the god's nakedness suggests his erotic proclivities and vulgar nature. If some degree of *grauitas* is expected from a divine source of knowledge, then this might further encourage the reader not to take Priapus, or the poet's approach to Priapus, all that seriously.

The voice of experience

Sic ego. tum Bacchi respondit rustica proles,
  armatus curua, sic mihi, falce deus:
'o fuge te tenerae puerorum credere turbae,
  nam causam iusti semper amoris habent.
hic placet angustis quod equum compescit habenis;
  hic placidam niueo pectore pellit aquam.
hic quia fortis adest audacia cepit; at illi
  uirgineus teneras stat pudor ante genas.   (7–14)

Sic ego signals that this will be a dialogue. This accentuates the humour of the situation: the statue will answer back! The reference to the *falx* recalls the mock-heroic terms in which Priapus was presented at 1.1.17–18. This and the mock-epic style of the description of the god-statue[14] (*tum Bacchi respondit rustica proles | armatus curua sic mihi falce deus*), especially the mock-heroic epithet *armatus*, might provide another

---

[12] See Murgatroyd (1980) 133.
[13] This recalls 1.1.27, where protection from extremes of weather was part of the comforts of the poet's essentially love-determined, but essentially unrealised, ideal. This also recalls the poet's idealised representation of the physical security of the love-controlled at 1.2.31–2. In poem two, however, this ideal is eventually undermined by the lover's overall powerlessness. The reminiscence here, then, may suggest that the role which the poet ascribes to (or assumes of) Priapus is like this ideal, determined by *amor* and ultimately unrealisable.
[14] On which see Murgatroyd (1980) 134–5.

136

opportunity to question the advice of such a ridiculous figure. There is the further possibility of comic inappropriateness in Priapus' link with the power of the Olympian gods through his descent, as *Bacchi proles*. In addition Priapus is characterised here as *rusticus*, and has been explicitly called upon to advise the poet on erotics. This combination of the rustic and the amatory within the figure of Priapus may in itself recall the attempted integration of a benign *amor* into the rural ideal in the first poem. There the attempt was shown, by the *reality* which *amor* determines, to be ultimately unrealisable. The reminiscence here might imply that what follows is of the same nature.

The first words of Priapus are a direct warning against letting yourself be controlled by the *turba puerorum tenera*: *o fuge te ... credere*. This perhaps comes as a surprise for the poet/lover, who implies a belief in the god's success over boys (*cepit*), and even for the reader,[15] who might find the stance inconsistent with the expectations built up by both the beginning of this poem and the general picture given of Priapus in earlier literature.[16] Priapus' words suggest that not only should trust not be placed in belief, as has been seen in other contexts earlier in the collection, but also that there is a danger of entrusting the self to the control of such boys. More specifically there is a danger of the poet (*te*) entrusting himself. The adjective *tener*, like the more specific *hic placet* at 11, suggests the attraction: the possibility of pleasure. This is vocabulary familiar from earlier descriptions of Delia and the possibility of pleasure which she represents to the poet/lover. But the god's warning here implies that the poet should not believe such pleasure will be gained. The boys of whom Priapus speaks have the power (*causam semper habent*) to affect older men, such as the poet and the god, with *iustus amor*. The previous three elegies already stand as an expression of how dominating *amor*'s power (at least in one type of heterosexual

---

[15] It has also come as a surprise for critics, who have argued, unnecessarily, for the emendation of this line; for their arguments see Murgatroyd (1980) 306-7.

[16] Expectations built up especially from the *Priapea* and the Hellenistic writers (see note 5 above).

relationship) can be. The description of it as *iustus* may suggest, as in earlier poems, that, in the lover's mind at least, *amor* determines what is 'morally' right. It may also suggest that the power of *amor* is at least equivalent to the power of law.[17]

The repetition *hic... hic... hic*, while maintaining the mock-rhetorical[18] tone of Priapus' words begun with the exclamation *o fuge...*, emphasises the present threat of the attracting, captivating power of boys. Appropriately, the boys described by Priapus are all shown exercising power of some sort. The first is applying direct control over the natural force of the horse: *compescit habenis*. The second violently disturbs the peace of water (*pellit placidam aquam*). *Placida aqua* has elsewhere been set up as representative of ideal peace and comfort (1.2.79–80). As in the second poem, where the realisation of the ideal represented by the peaceful water was prevented by *amor*'s disruptive force, here the attractive boy, a catalyst and object of *amor*, breaks the surface of the water itself. The instrument which the boy uses to strike the calm water is his physical beauty, albeit effeminate in Roman terms[19] (*niueo pectore*). This suggests a metaphorical link between the boy's effect upon the water and the effects of the *amor* which his physical beauty inspires in onlookers. Unlike the poet as he has appeared in earlier elegies, the boys described in these lines are active figures, engaged in 'manly' pursuits, even though they are young, possibly effeminate, and thus supposedly easy to control. The third boy captures through daring: *quia fortis adest audacia cepit*. He has the aggressive qualities of a soldier, and the power to capture and control (*cepit*). This

---

[17] Perhaps supporting this conclusion, there is a possible reference to, and contradiction of, the *Lex Scantinia* here; see Williams (1968) 551. The implication is that the morality/law of *amor* is more pressing and possibly more powerful than that of Rome. Compare the victory of *amor* in the struggle against the demands of Messalla, the poet's patron-general, in poem three. On the *Lex Sc.* see Edwards (1993) 72 and n. Particularly significant for my reading of the power dynamic of the *amor*-relationship is Veyne's comment on the *Lex Sc.*: 'Sex had nothing to do with the question. What mattered was being free and not being a passive agent', Veyne (1985) 29.

[18] *Mock*-rhetorical because such rhetorical devices seem inappropriate for a naked, rustic god-statue.

[19] Murgatroyd (1980) 136.

recalls the initial question asked by the poet (line 3). The lover (the older man) may wish, and try, to gain control over the beloved (the boy) but the boy is the one in control of the older, supposedly dominating, man. This control is itself the cause of the lover's desire, or rather the instrument of control *is* the older man's desire. As with heterosexual *amor* in earlier poems, *amor* here generates a power struggle, and the poet seems once more to be on the losing side. What could be seen as a traditional moral force (*uirgineus pudor*) is also levelled against him. *Pudor*, too, is like a soldier, a sentinel: *teneras stat pudor ante genas*. The idea that *pudor* stands guard *ante genas*, presumably to keep the lover away from the beloved boy, may recall earlier examples of the lover being denied access to the beloved by being kept chained *ante fores*. This further links the pederastic *amor* described here with the heterosexual *amor* of the first three elegies.

Taking your time

Sed ne te capiant, primo si forte negabit,
    taedia: paulatim sub iuga colla dabit.
longa dies homini docuit parere leones;
    longa dies molli saxa peredit aqua.
annus in apricis maturat collibus uuas;
    annus agit certa lucida signa uice.   (15–20)

But Priapus himself seems to be overcome by the power of the boys' attractions, for he cannot stand by his first advice, to avoid trusting oneself to such objects of love: *sed ne te capiant ... taedia*. The Delia-like resistance of the boy suggested at 13–14 and here (*primo si forte negabit*) should not cause the lover to give up in disgust. The use again of *capere* (*ne capiant taedia*) suggests the struggle of the lover's possible *taedia* against the power of *amor* and the boy's attractions which were mentioned earlier (*cepit*, line 13). Like the struggle to gain Delia's compliance, the struggle to gain the sexual compliance of boys is described in terms of power and dominance: *sub iuga colla dabit*.

Time, the *longa dies* emphasised by repetition at 17–18,[20] is similarly described as a powerful force in terms which compare it directly to the power of attraction possessed by the boys. In fact the repetition of *longa dies* at the initial position of both lines 17 and 18 recalls the recurrence of *hic*, and of the similar sounds *hic placet* ... *hic placidam*, as the first words of the lines describing the boys' powers of attraction at 11–13. The correspondences between the description of the boys' attractions and the effects of the *longa dies* continue in the examples of time's power given at lines 17–18. But in this case the power relationships at work are subtly different. In the first example (line 17), the *longa dies* has power over animals. This is not simply power over a horse as the boy has at 11, but over lions: *longa dies homini docuit*[21] *parere leones*. The second example, like the picture of the boy at 12, involves water. But instead of force being exerted upon the water, the power-relationship in the image is reversed and the water itself (empowered by time) is the active force: *longa dies molli saxa peredit aqua*. This suggests a reversal in the power-relationship between the boy and the older lover, brought about by time. Time is more powerful than the boy's resistance, just as the taming of lions demonstrates more power than the controlling of a horse. Time, now *annus* ... *annus*, determines the cyclical, seasonal alternation and thus its produce. Its power is described as certain (*agit certa lucida signa uice*) and fruitful (line 19).

Making promises

Nec iurare time: Veneris periuria uenti
irrita per terras et freta summa ferunt.
gratia magna Ioui: uetuit pater ipse ualere
iurasset cupide quicquid ineptus amor;

[20] As critics have suggested, the excessive use of repetition (again at 28–30) also enhances the mock-rhetorical tone of Priapus' words. For these observations see Murgatroyd (1980) 131–2.
[21] The use of *docere* may again hint at the role of knowledge as an empowering force. Here, however, knowledge is specifically a force which controls (*parere*) the one learning it.

perque suas impune sinit Dictynna sagittas
affirmes, crines perque Minerua suos.   (21–6)

The advice of Priapus in the following two lines recalls the behaviour and statements of the poet/lover in previous elegies. The use of oaths for the lover's own purposes (*nec iurare time*) is encouraged. The duplicity of such a strategy recalls the poet's similar pretence at 1.3.17ff. involving another supposedly god-sanctioned matter, omens. In a somewhat different manner, the claim that perjuries against Venus have no effect (*Veneris periuria uenti | irrita per terras et freta summa ferunt*) not only recalls but contradicts the poet's description of Venus' power[22] at 1.2.81ff. and throughout the second poem.[23] The interpenetration of the various elegies is set in play once more. Lines 21–2 cause the reader to re-evaluate the earlier presentation of the strictness of Venus' power when her authority is infringed, to mistrust Priapus' words, or to remain undecided. Again final meaning remains unfixed. Here the reading of one elegy cannot help but affect the reading of others. These readings become entangled in each other, and as a result meaning can become elusive.

At lines 23–4 Priapus claims that the useful invalidity of oaths is due to the ultimate power figure, Jupiter himself (*gratia magna Ioui: uetuit pater ipse ualere | iurasset cupide quicquid ineptus amor*). Jupiter's veto might be explained by his own, mythologically prominent, domination by *amor*, and thus the wish to use oaths for *his* own purposes.[24] Those purposes, of course, are determined by *ineptus*[25] *amor*. The terms of the invalid oaths, by which the power of invulnerability or impunity is gained (*impune sinit ... affirmes*), might seem to

---

[22] See above, 96–7.
[23] Indeed the expression *per terras et freta* may also recall the poet's plight in the third poem (1.3.55–6), where he is prey to the avenging power of *Amor* (see especially 1.3.22–3). In poem three the poet also claims that he fears no perjuries (1.3.51–2). But, as has been seen, the validity of this claim is doubtful.
[24] For this suggestion see Murgatroyd (1980) 139–40.
[25] *Amor* is *ineptus* here in the effect it produces in the lover. Or possibly *amor* is *ineptus* (absurd) in its actual nature, again suggesting (like *o fuge* at line 9) that it is not entirely desirable.

be ridiculous[26] legislative loopholes (*perque suas Dictynna sagittas ... crines perque Minerua suos*). This might encourage the reader to take Priapus' claim less seriously. The two female, virgin, goddesses employed in the terms of such oaths appear to be unrelated and even antipathetic to the world of *amor*. As such they might appear reluctant to support deceitful lovers. Alternatively, it may be that their non-involvement in amatory affairs is precisely what makes such oaths safe for lovers, since those goddesses may well be disinclined to enforce them.

Keeping up

At si tardus eris errabis. transiet aetas
    quam cito! non segnis stat remeatue dies.
quam cito purpureos deperdit terra colores!
    quam cito formosas populus alta comas!
quam iacet, infirmae uenere ubi fata senectae,
    qui prior Eleo est carcere missus equus!
uidi iam iuuenem premeret cum serior aetas
    maerentem stultos praeteriisse dies.
crudeles diui. serpens nouus exuit annos;
    formae non ullam Fata dedere moram.
solis aeterna est Baccho Phoeboque iuuentas,
    nam decet intonsus crinis utrumque deum. (27–38)

At line 27, as frequently in the third poem, a contrast is introduced. In fact it is an apparent contradiction: *si tardus eris errabis*. Although *aetas* at 27 may not be of the same extent as the *longa dies* or *annus* of lines 17–20, the injunction not to be slow might seem at first inconsistent with the statement that amatory domination of boys takes time. That same power of time is ally *and* enemy to the older lover. There is no fixity, no constancy. The day now, rather than being *longa*, does not last: *non segnis stat remeatue dies*. This also suggests that the poet himself, whom earlier poems have suggested

[26] This assessment is perhaps encouraged by the description of *amor* as *ineptus* in this context.

is *tardus, segnis, iners,* may not be suited to following such advice. It is also possible, however, that the meaning of the words themselves changes in various contexts. Vigorous pursuit of boys in an amatory context (lack of *inertia*) might be seen as *inertia* in broader social terms.

Just as the examples following the repeated *longa dies* compare significantly with those following *hic ... hic,* so too the couplet 29–30 beginning each line with *quam cito* compares with the couplet containing the repeated *annus ... annus* (19–20). Again there are differences in each case. Although time matures the vines and turns the seasons, time also causes the colours and beauty of nature to decay quickly: *quam cito purpureos deperdit terra colores! | quam cito formosas populus alta comas!* Time, age and decay are forces against which the lover, and mortal creation in general, are powerless. The example of the horse (lines 31–2) explicitly describes the power of age, of decay (*infirmae fata senectae*), to overcome the power of mortal creatures (line 32). *Fata* recalls the inexorable power of approaching age and death at 1.1.69ff.

Vidi (line 33) implies that Priapus' advice here is based on what he has perceived for himself, rather than on report (compare the poet's appeal to his own experience at 1.2.91). The power of time (*aetas*), now directly applied to humans, is oppressive: *premeret cum serior aetas.* The only resort left to the powerless ex-*iuuenis* is lamentation: *maerentem stultos praeteriisse dies.* The past of the ageing man is defined as *stultus* relative to *amor.* The stupidity of the man's past resides in its neglect of *amor.* What is stupid and what is not are determined and defined by Priapus in terms of *amor.* Beauty, and the associated possibilities of pleasure which inspire *amor,* are destroyed by time. Priapus blames his fellow gods, suggesting they are in control of *fata: crudeles diui.*[27] *Fata* are again the power responsible for the passing of beauty (line 36), while the ugliness of the *serpens* (35) is allowed to renew itself. But *fata* themselves seem capable of being completely

[27] Again this may seem comic, since Priapus is supposedly a god himself, and was thanking the chief of gods only a few lines before.

manipulated by the gods, of whom Bacchus and Phoebus alone have the power of eternal youth (lines 37–8).[28]

The process

Tu puero quodcumque tuo temptare libebit
cedas: obsequio plurima uincet amor.
neu comes ire neges quamuis uia longa paretur
et Canis arenti torreat arua siti,
quamuis praetexens picta ferrugine caelum
uenturam †amiciat† imbrifer arcus aquam.
uel si caeruleas puppi uolet ire per undas,
ipse leuem remo per freta pelle ratem.
nec te paeniteat duros subisse labores
aut opera insuetas atteruisse manus.
nec, uelit insidiis altas si claudere ualles,
dum placeas, umeri retia ferre negent.
si uolet arma, leui temptabis ludere dextra;
saepe dabis nudum, uincat ut ille, latus.
tunc tibi mitis erit, rapias tum cara licebit
oscula: pugnabit sed tibi rapta dabit.
rapta dabit primo, post afferet ipse roganti,
post etiam collo se implicuisse uelit.   (39–56)

Tu puero quodcumque tuo temptare libebit | cedas (39–40)
instructs the poet to allow the beloved boy to control him.
The total subservience to the boy which Priapus advises here
is somewhat inconsistent with the suggestion at 21ff. that the
poet should be manipulative enough to make promises to the
boy he does not intend to keep. Although there are no absolute contradictions here, there is a tension between this fifth
component of Priapus' advice (39ff.) and the third (21ff.), just
as there was between the second (the need to take time) and
the fourth (the need for swift action), and just as there is tension and inconsistency between all this and the very first piece
of advice: don't do it! (*o fuge* ...). Priapus here, by uniting

---

[28] The *intonsus crinis* of Bacchus and Apollo here (line 38) is another instance in the
elegies where hair reflects the role or nature of the figure(s) possessing it.

apparent opposites, is presenting a comprehensive rhetorical structure which covers all options. But while heightening the humour of Priapus' advice this also undercuts his role as a decisive adviser and casts doubt upon the efficacy of the knowledge he offers.

Obsequio plurima uincet amor (line 40): once more the reader is presented with a process. In return for compliance and obedience, for abdicating control to another for an unspecified period, the lover will himself eventually gain power over the beloved (*uincet*). Or more precisely the passion, the *amor* which drives him, will gain that power. The first example of the advised abdication of power (*neu ... neges*), following the beloved on the *uia longa*, ironically recalls the poet's determination for the sake of heterosexual *amor* not to go on the *longa uia* in the opening poem. Here, for the sake of pederastic *amor*, he *would* go, exposing himself to all the dangers that implies. He would endure discomfort from heat (line 42) and rain (lines 43–4),[29] just as did the soldiers on *militia* at 1.1.1–4. As has been seen in earlier elegies, such military service involves a 'process' similar to the one which Priapus is advocating here for the sake of *amor*. But, ironically, *militia* is an option which the poet rejected for *amor* in poem one. In the end, it seems, the 'pain for gain' process cannot be escaped. Exposure to danger for *amor*'s sake is again suggested by the *leuis ratis* which the poet is advised to row *per undas, per freta*. This, like the recollection of the *longa uia* and military service generally, recalls the poet/lover's ill-fated venture in following Messalla (1.3.56), underlining the parallel between *militia* and *amor*. The poet/lover would exert power (*pelle remo*), like a galley slave, for the boy whose will, according to Priapus' advice, should control the poet (*si ... uolet* 45; *uelit ... si* 49; *si uolet* 51). It is slave-like subservience which is suggested: *duros subiisse labores | aut opera insuetas atteruisse manus* (47–8);

---

[29] The problems with the manuscript readings at this point (lines 43–4) and the various solutions proposed (most conveniently collected and discussed by Murgatroyd (1980) 308–9) do not affect the basic meaning of these lines: the would-be lover must also endure rain. This recalls Priapus' endurance of *Canis* and his exposure, *nudus*, to the cold at lines 5–6.

umeri retia ferre (50). For the poet, such activity would be unusual (*insuetas manus*). The boy on the other hand is the active partner in the relationship, as is reflected in his occupations and pastimes: the *longa uia*, the sea voyage, and at 49–50 hunting, which in itself involves control and power over the natural world (*claudere altas ualles insidiis*). The words *nec te paeniteat* (47) and *dum placeas* (50) emphasise, however, that such subservience and lack of control is part of a stratagem (a trade-off) for the compliance of the boy. The armed struggle of 51–2 parallels the power struggle between lover and non-compliant beloved of which it is part. *Ludere* recalls the 'play' of such love struggles earlier in the collection (e.g. 1.3.63–4). The consequence of *amor* upon the lover is encapsulated in the abdication of control and voluntary powerlessness which Priapus advocates, all in the hope of thus gaining the desired power over the beloved: *uincat ut ille*.[30]

Tunc (line 53) introduces the projected result of the process. The final subservience of the boy is presented as if it were the placation of a god:[31] *tibi mitis erit*. *Rapias* (re-echoed in *rapta ... rapta* 54–5) suggests a violent love-struggle of the type embodied by the inhabitants of the poet's 'lovers' Hell' in the third poem (Ixion, Tityos, and perhaps Tantalus). The suggestion of violence is reinforced by the continuance from 51–2 of the image of physical struggle in the word *pugnabit*. But it is still clearly within the power of the boy to grant or withhold the desired pleasure (*cara oscula*): *licebit ... rapta dabit. | rapta dabit.* It is the will of the boy which is being won over. There may even be a suggestion in *afferet ipse roganti* that the poet must appeal to the boy's power as he has in past elegies to the power of the gods. Priapus' assertion is that, in return for the abdication of the lover's will to the beloved, the will of

[30] Like their common exposure to weather, the exposure of the *nudum latus* is another link between the obsequious lover and the description of Priapus at lines 1–6. This may give a clue to the reason Priapus is like this: his appearance may be part of the *sollertia* rather than something which might handicap his ability to capture boys, as the poet seems to suggest in the opening of the poem. If this is so, it cheats the poet's, and possibly the reader's, first assumptions.

[31] In fact the religious process in general, as it is seen in earlier elegies, is akin to the process of wooing the boy which Priapus has just described.

the beloved himself will finally submit to the older lover (*collo se implicuisse uelit*) in gradual sequence (*primo, post ... post enim*).[32] The subjunctive, however, adds an element of un-certainty[33] and the description of the boy entangling himself about the poet's neck may recall the yoke of 16, but now on the poet's neck, and thus suggest that the poet would still in some way be controlled by the boy or by his own passion for him.

Poetry and money

Heu male nunc artes miseras haec saecula tractant!
    iam tener assueuit munera uelle puer.
at tu qui Venerem docuisti uendere primus,
    quisquis es, infelix urgeat ossa lapis.
Pieridas, pueri, doctos et amate poetas,
    aurea nec superent munera Pieridas.
carmine purpurea est Nisi coma; carmina ni sint,
    ex umero Pelopis non nituisset ebur.
quem referent Musae uiuet dum robora tellus,
    dum caelum stellas, dum uehet amnis aquas.
at qui non audit Musas, qui uendit amorem,
    Idaeae currus ille sequatur Opis
et ter centenas erroribus expleat urbes
    et secet ad Phrygios uilia membra modos.
blanditiis uult esse locum Venus: illa querelis
    supplicibus, miseris fletibus illa fauet.'   (57–72)

Priapus has supplied several suggestions for the apparently successful capture and control of the object of pederastic love. But just as the very first element of his advice suggested it was better to avoid boy-love altogether, now he undercuts the efficacy of any such *sollertia* or *artes* in the present world: *heu male nunc artes miseras haec saecula tractant* (57). The present reality of the situation (*nunc ... haec ... iam*) disempowers the

---

[32] The gradual nature of this process links it with Priapus' earlier advice at 16ff.
[33] See Murgatroyd (1980) 149.

artes which Priapus possesses,[34] and by implication the efficacy of the advice he has just given. The terms of the process by which the boy's compliance is gained are not as Priapus first represented them. This pleasure (again suggested by the adjective *tener*) is gained from the *puer* in exchange for material wealth: *iam tener assueuit munera uelle puer* (58). Commercialism of this sort is seen as the usual behaviour of such boys (*assueuit*).[35] The direct address to the man who first taught humans this particular commercial transaction describes him in terms of one who tried to gain power over love, or even the goddess, through wealth: *qui Venerem docuisti uendere*. The verb *docere* again highlights the didactic power of knowledge, at least in the case of *that* man, while Priapus himself does not even have the knowledge of who this *primus* was (*quisquis es*). All that Priapus can do is curse: *infelix urgeat ossa lapis* (60).[36]

Priapus at lines 61–2 voices his desire for poetry[37] (*Pieridas ... Pieridas*), and thus poets themselves (*doctos poetas*), to have a power which is superior to wealth in its ability to gain the sexual compliance of boys: *aurea nec superent munera*. This desire seems determined by the fact that Priapus is a poet,[38] just as the one who asked him the original question is a poet. But, as has often been seen of the poet-protagonist in earlier elegies, Priapus here can only appeal to those with the real power: *amate, pueri* (61). The unleashing of a carefully structured couplet, starting and finishing with *Pierides*, to appeal to boys to invest poetry with persuasive power, suggests

---

[34] See Stroh (1971) 113–14.

[35] It is perhaps just an extension of the usual Roman commercial ethos. See Veyne (1985) 84. Compare also Love's Weber-inspired definition of capitalism as it applied to Roman society: 'The systematic pursuit of profits through the deliberate outlay of funds upon which anticipated yields are estimated in monetary terms – i.e. capitalistically', Love (1991) 38. Substitute *in erotic terms* for the phrase *in monetary terms* and the definition re-applies itself well to an 'elegiac' capitalism.

[36] The curse itself might be considered a cliché and thus lame.

[37] This might restrict the meaning of *artes* in this context to 'arts of poetry', from the point of view of Priapus as poet at any rate.

[38] This is apparent not only from the fact that Priapus speaks in elegiac couplets, a medium forced upon him by the genre in which he appears, but by the elaborate 'poetic' language and technique of his speech; on which see Murgatroyd (1980) 131–2.

that Priapus himself is exerting all his poetic learning and power here to persuade the *pueri* of this.[39] *Doctos* recalls the didactic purpose of Priapus' words, and the general question of the reliability and power of learning and knowledge in this and earlier poems, and especially the power struggle between it and *amor*. Priapus asserts the power of poetry/song to create:

> carmine purpurea est Nisi coma; carmina ni sint
> ex umero Pelopis non nituisset ebur.   (63–4).

This suggests that poetry can notionally create wealth (*ebur*). *Purpurea coma* may also recall the *purpurei colores* and *formosae comae* of lines 29–30, setting the power of poetry to preserve things against the power of time to destroy them.[40] Continuing the reference of one couplet to another earlier one (lines 17–18 to 11–12 and 29–30 to 19–20), lines 65–6 with trees (*robora*) and water (*aqua*) recall lines 29–31 (*populus*) and line 19 (*aqua*). The reference to *stella* also perhaps recalls the *lucida signa* of line 20. This not only serves to link the different sections of Priapus' speech through shared imagery, but again, by comparison, proposes poetry as a god-supported (or at least Muse-supported) power superior to time, and the decay and final impotence of death: *quem referent Musae uiuet* (65).

Priapus again can only curse those who prefer money to poetry as the commodity by which their compliance is purchased. It is those who use, and thus control, *amor* for personal gain (*qui uendit amorem*) whom he curses. They are defined in opposition to those who are inspired by poetry (*qui audit Musas*) and thus effectively controlled by the *doctus poeta*. The terms of the curse imply a reversal of the mercenary boy's powerful position to a state of alienation and oddity (following the oriental rites *Idaeae Opis*)[41] like a slave,

---

[39] Lee (1990) ix (and note) draws attention to a similar technique in Callimachus *Epigram* 22.
[40] While these myths might exemplify the overwhelming and destructive power of *amor*, the references to Nisus, whose daughter was driven by the power of *amor* to betray him, and Pelops, who, also inspired by *amor*, resorted to treachery to win his bride, do not bode well for the poet/lover.
[41] Murgatroyd (1980) 153–4.

uncertain and unsettled (*erroribus*, line 69). The fulfilment of the curse sees the boy's self-mutilation, as he brings upon himself the sexual uncertainty[42] and powerlessness of a eunuch: *secet ad Phrygios uilia membra modos*. This state is a reflection of the state in which the boy's actions leave the poet/lover, but Priapus can only wish it upon the boy (note the subjunctives). The *artes* of the god lack effectiveness and he seems powerless to affect things as they are (*nunc . . . iam*). Instead he claims, as the poet has done in past elegies, the support of Venus' power for his appeals (*blanditiis . . . querelis supplicibus . . . miseris fletibus*). The terms of that support, however, are vague. Venus wishes them a place for *blanditiae* (*uult esse locum Venus*) and favours their existence (*illa fauet*), but does not necessarily ensure their success. What's more, these lines recall a similar claim of Venus' support by the poet at 1.2.16ff. which also used the words *illa fauet* and which, by the end of that poem, was comprehensively undercut (1.2.81–100). The power of Priapus as the poet introduced it (line 3) seemed to stem from his knowledge. His final words at lines 71–2, however, suggest that for these *sollertiae* to have any effectiveness they must first be empowered by the goddess, whose support remains doubtful.

Shifting ground

> Haec mihi quae canerem Titio deus edidit ore,
>> sed Titium coniunx haec meminisse uetat.
> pareat ille suae: uos me celebrate magistrum
>> quos male habet multa callidus arte puer.
> gloria cuique sua est: me qui spernentur amantes
>> consultent; cunctis ianua nostra patet.
> tempus erit cum me Veneris praecepta ferentem
>> deducat iuuenum sedula turba senem.
> eheu, quam Marathus lento me torquet amore!
>> deficiunt artes deficiuntque doli.

---

[42] Compare Attis' confusion of gender in Catullus 63.

> parce, puer, quaeso – ne turpis fabula fiam
> cum mea ridebunt uana magisteria.   (73–84)

The direct words of the poet which follow (lines 73ff.) force the reader to revise any assumptions made about his motives in questioning Priapus. His words now seem to imply that the advice was sought not for himself, but for one Titius: *Haec mihi quae canerem Titio deus edidit ore.*[43] The identity of this Titius is another question which is left open.[44] Again the reader's control over the poem's meaning is left incomplete. The focus of line 73 is still on the efficacy of poetry (*quae canerem*), this time specifically the song which the poet presents to Titius. This supposedly includes everything in poem four before line 73. The perspective of the reader has been shifted to a poem outside a poem. Here poetry again falls powerless. The knowledge which the poet's song gives to Titius cannot be acted upon because of the intervention of another, stronger power: *sed Titium coniunx haec meminisse uetat* (74). The power of the female figure[45] is not only strong enough to prevent Titius acting upon the advice, but can actually prevent his recollection of it. It is represented as controlling even his thoughts. The poet concedes her power: *pareat ille suae.*[46]

The poet now turns to his own position and the power and use of knowledge. He pictures himself as the teacher, celebrated like a victor: *uos me celebrate magistrum* (75). He implies that through the knowledge he has gained he can impart *practical* advice to spurned lovers, even though his failure with

---

[43] Thus the poet was not necessarily acting 'unfaithfully' towards Delia, as was at first a possibility, but acting for another.

[44] A fictitious character, a friend of the poet, a 'John Doe'-style title, the poet mentioned by Horace at *Epist.* 1.3.9ff., and even the poet, Tibullus, himself are the leading alternatives which have been suggested; on these alternatives see Murgatroyd (1980) 156; and Bréguet (1980) 66 and 69–70.

[45] The wife also represents the power of conventional, socially assimilated sexual relationships, as opposed to that of the unconventional elegiac, pederastic, *amor*-relationship.

[46] This suggests that subservience in the poet's eyes (as in his experience) is the correct behaviour towards such controlling female figures. This concession also associates the poet with the comic position of the powerless husband, a role which bears some similarity to his position in earlier poems, subservient to a dominant female.

Titius might suggest that success is less than certain. Those whom such knowledge will aid are described as *quos male habet multa callidus arte puer* (76). They are controlled, to their cost (*male habet*), by the *ars* of a boy (*multa callidus arte*). Thus there is a conflict, a power struggle, set up between the *ars* of the boy and the knowledge of the poet/*magister*, with the implication that the poet will prove more powerful.[47] The poet will himself gain in power and prestige as a result, at least among the society of lovers: *gloria cuique sua est*. The difference in the style of the fourth elegy is thus matched by a projected difference in role for the poet/lover. Didactic poetry finds its match in the figure of *praeceptor amoris*. Line 77 might seem inconsistent with the poet's earlier claim not to want praise (1.1.57). Yet here glory is redefined in terms of the society of *amantes* and the field of *amor*, rather than the military/political. Those who would consult him are reminiscent of the poet himself in earlier elegies (*me qui spernentur amantes | consultent* 77–8). There is perhaps an ironic recollection of his lack of success in love in the statement *cunctis ianua nostra patet* which is in direct contrast to the state of Delia's door at 1.2.6ff. It may be that now, newly armed with knowledge, the poet can reverse his past powerlessness. Alternatively, the recollection of that powerlessness may undermine his present claims to power. The poet's projected future role (*tempus erit*) not only sees him empowered by knowledge in the sphere of *amor*, a knowledge sanctioned by Venus herself (*me Veneris praecepta ferentem*), but also sees him triumphant over time. He will retain his power into old age (*senem*) in contrast to the powerlessness occasioned by passing time which was described earlier in the poem. He will be in a position of power, as teacher, over the *sedula turba iuuenum*, a phrase which perhaps recalls and contradicts Priapus' warning about the *turba tenera puerorum*. The fact, however, that the crowd is leading the poet (*deducat*) might imply that he would still essentially be in the control of others.

---

[47] The poet's conscious assumption of the role earlier filled by Priapus might lead the reader to expect that the poet will be as ultimately unsuccessful as the god.

Eheu, like Priapus' exclamation *heu* (at line 57) which introduces information undermining confidence in the power of his advice and his *artes* in general, adds emotional emphasis to the revelation that, just as his (and Priapus', and Venus') *praecepta* were powerless in the case of Titius, so they are in the poet's own case. Again the reader is forced to re-evaluate what the poet has said or implied before. It now appears that *quae canerem Titio* meant that, while this particular song may have been aimed at Titius, the poet's initial question to Priapus and the consequent advice may well have been for his own use. He *has* in fact been 'unfaithful' to Delia, as was the initial suggestion. The actual name of another beloved, Marathus, is now given. As at the beginning of the elegy, questions are again raised. Is the poet entirely free from control by *amor* for Delia, or has his *amor* for Marathus existed concurrently with his *amor* for Delia? Is the nature of each *amor* the same? Certainly (or as certain as is possible in the shifting world of the elegies) the poet is controlled by Marathus just as he was/is by Delia, and this results in his suffering:[48] *Eheu, quam Marathus lento*[49] *me torquet amore* (81). Didacticism and the knowledge it professes to distribute are powerless: *deficiunt artes, deficiuntque doli.* Once more, all he can do is appeal to the power of the beloved: *parce, puer, quaeso* (83). His reputation, and the social position and power which he had earlier claimed he would gain through his knowledge, are dependent upon another, Marathus (lines 83–4). The power of *amor*, and of Marathus as object of that *amor*, render the poet and his apparent 'knowledge' impotent: *mea uana magisteria.*[50]

---

[48] His function as a cause of suffering (through love in particular, with its associations of 'wasting away' and 'burning up') is inscribed in the boy's very identity through the probable derivation of the name Marathus from the Greek verb μαραίνεσθαι: see Murgatroyd (1977) 112 n.26.

[49] *Lento* suggests the lingering duration of the poet's suffering and may refer again to the disempowering force of time.

[50] Murgatroyd (1977) notes the ironic contrasts here: 'Thus in 1.4 there are two sets of contrasts, the second mirroring the first: Priapus appears initially as the usual undignified figure, but then adopts a serious and learned pose; so Tibullus appears next in the same dignified role, but finally reduced to a laughing-stock' Murgatroyd (1977) 114.

Conclusion

The repeated shifts which occur within the elegy undermine the didactic stance of the speakers and reveal the ultimate failure of didacticism in the face of *amor*. This is highlighted by the comic presentation of Priapus, Titius, and the affectation of the poet himself, as well as by the general humorous tone of the elegy, which, as in the final line (*cum mea ridebunt uana magisteria*), directly draws attention to the powerlessness of knowledge (*artes, sollertia, magisteria*) in the *amor*-struggle. The new role which the poet/lover attempts to take on, the new subject of pederastic *amor*, and the new form which the poem takes are collapsed into familiar relationships and processes. If these relationships and processes are assumed to be characteristic of the elegiac genre, their resurgence here could be seen as the overwhelming of the poem's difference by the force of elegiac convention. This would suggest again, as in the opening poem, a parallel between the power of *amor* and that of the elegiac genre, or even that the two are to be identified with one another. In each case the poet is controlled; by the power of *amor* on the one hand, and by the power of the elegiac genre to determine the content and course of his poetry on the other.[51] The structure of *amor* as power-struggle is explicitly linked in elegy four to other areas which involve control and the process of exchange, elements which are central both to Priapus' advice and to the operation of *amor* in earlier elegies. This linkage between supposedly different areas parallels the interplay of similarity and difference between the fourth elegy and the earlier poems. Just as the reading of each elegy becomes involved in the reading and re-reading of every other, so too in the fourth poem traditional areas of control (hunting, fighting, campaigning, mastering nature in various forms) merge into the power dynamics of *amor*, becoming part of the proposed exchange for the beloved's compliance. The power of *amor* subverts the separateness or difference of all other areas, erasing discrete categories, forcing them into

[51] For a fuller discussion of this in relation to poem one, see above 51–2, and 58–61.

the general operational area of power and control represented by *amor*-relationships.

The uncertain relationship between the poet/lover's passion for Marathus and his passion for Delia is reflected by the variety of critical responses to the question of their inter-relation.[52] This is part of the further destabilisation of the reader's control over meaning. This didactic poem fails to bestow secure knowledge upon the reader, just as the teachings of Priapus fail to bestow secure and powerful knowledge upon Titius or the poet himself. The instability of the reading process is highlighted by the rapidity of the 'surprises' which conclude the elegy.[53] The reader must re-evaluate the shifting possibilities which the text creates and attempt to reconstruct meaning from the unreliable[54] and often inconsistent words with which she/he is presented. Through undercutting and rearranging the reader's assumptions in this way, the fourth elegy emphasises the fragility of those assumptions and leaves several questions unresolved. This is all the more striking in a poem which, at the outset, promises secure knowledge. In this way the fourth poem demonstrates its similarity with, as well as its difference from, the earlier poems as it presents in exaggerated form a reading process common to the collection.

---

[52] These are well summarised by Leonotti (1980) 260–2 n.5. The leading suggestions are that the Marathus poems should be placed within a break (*discidium*) during the Delia relationship (Alfonsi (1946) 34); that they belong to a period before (see Wimmel (1968) especially 234–5) or after (see Riposati (1967) 39–40); or that both Marathus and Delia are fictional characters (see Della Corte (1964) 501; and Ponchont (1967) 30). No proposed solution to this debate, of course, explains the interweaving of the Delia and Marathus poems within the structure of the collection or, more particularly, the interrelation and similarity of the two relationships and the poet/lover's position within each. For a fuller discussion of these questions see below 287–8.

[53] On which see Cairns (1979) 173–5; and Bréguet (1980) 68–9.

[54] In terms of the 'reality' being created by the author. See Kennedy (1993) 15.

POEM FIVE

Real and unreal

For Cairns, the fifth elegy evokes 'a series of emotional responses in the reader, first doubt and self-congratulation, then pity, then moralising, then shock, then sympathy, then disapproval, then hatred, then pathos, and finally hope'.[1] This reading presupposes a response common to all readers which can, thus, be organised and charted, allowing final control over meaning. The elegy itself, however, encourages a reading which foregrounds the destabilisation of such attempts by both reader and poet/lover to delineate and control. Cairns' interpretation of poem five is particularly concerned with 'order' and charting sequence both 'real'. ('"historical"') and apparent ('order of presentation'),[2] but it is just such clear construction and separation of the real and the apparent which can be undercut through a reading of the fifth elegy. This reading highlights the complex involvement of the reader in the struggle for control of meaning, and the nexus of the relationships which form and reform between the reader and the poet-persona, author and text in the course of that struggle.

> Asper eram et bene discidium me ferre loquebar,
> at mihi nunc longe gloria fortis abest;   (1–2)

The poem begins with a statement which could be set in opposition to the generic characterisation of the poet/lover as *mollis*:[3] *asper eram*. This is coupled with the poet's claims

---

[1] Cairns (1979) 181.
[2] Cairns (1979) 176–7.
[3] See Cairns (1979) 178 for this observation; and Kennedy (1993) 31ff. for *mollis* as a defining term of elegy and the elegiac poet/lover.

about his own feelings and situation: *et bene discidium me ferre loquebar*. But now (*at ... nunc*), in turn, he claims that his past attitude and claims are finished: *at mihi nunc longe gloria fortis abest*. As at 1.4.77, the poet's *gloria* is empty and ineffectual. *Fortis abest* suggests that he is now weak. The contrast is again between past (*eram*) and present (*nunc*), implying that the outward appearance of the poet has changed. Now, he claims, he does not even have the ability to maintain appearances. But the text is not simply working within the opposition of past and present. The poet's slip from the generic role of the poet/lover and back again is figured in the contrast of power (*fortis*) and its absence. This, in turn, is constructed as the opposition between appearances (or words: *loquebar*; *gloria*), corresponding to his behaviour in the past, and reality, corresponding to his present lack of *fortis gloria*. The generic role of the weak and passive poet/lover is thus affirmed by, and itself helps to affirm, the elegiac rhetoric of reality.[4] But the affirmation of this 'reality' is destabilised by the unreliability of the poet's words as a guide to his 'true' feelings and situation in the past. The poet's lack of pretence in the present is defined against this false appearance in the past. But the association of the poet/lover with a false appearance cannot be so easily erased. Like the person who claims 'I used to be untrustworthy, but now I tell the truth', the admission of past unreliability casts doubt upon the poet's present profession of veracity. The instability of the 'reality' presented in earlier poems further undermines the reliability of the present. The text, by continually undercutting and modifying itself, operates within an interplay of appearance and reality. This interplay might often obscure, but can also draw attention to, its own position as a representation, as itself an appearance constructed by a poet who stands outside the text, whom for convenience I shall call 'the author'.[5] The

---

[4] On 'reality' being textually (and generically) constructed, rather than being unproblematically equated with a reality outside the text, see Wyke (1989b): '... realism itself is a quality of the text, not a direct manifestation of a "real" world', 27; and Kennedy (1993) ch.1.

[5] See Kennedy (1993) ch.1 for a more wide-ranging discussion of the question of 'reality' in elegiac texts.

emphasis in lines 1–2 on the poet's earlier pretence, his 'performance' of *gloria fortis*, points in this way to the construction of reality and its opposite by the author and the various generic forces at work in the text. In these opening lines, elegiac reality destabilises itself in the process of its own affirmation.

Discidium seems to imply that the poet and the figure from whom he is now separated *were* at some time 'together' in a harmonious, established relationship. This suggestion is not supported by the earlier poems, except poem three. There, as has been seen, the poem both of itself and in reference to earlier poems suggested that such a secure and harmonious relationship is largely an unfounded ideal of the poet. More obviously, the emphasis in poem three was on 'separation' in a very physical sense, and, the poet's fantasies notwithstanding, did not necessarily imply that any securely established relationship had been broken. The previous relationship implied by *discidium* finds no secure support in the earlier elegies. Its suggestion here, then, may raise some doubts about the reality of the situation, or at least occasion some surprise. From the outset of poem five, the unreliability and ambiguity of the poet's words, and the interplay of representations of appearance and reality within the elegiac text, are foregrounded not only through the poem's own rhetoric, but also in relation to earlier poems.

Toy-boy

> namque agor, ut per plana citus sola uerbere turben
>   quem celer assueta uersat ab arte puer.
> ure ferum et torque, libeat ne dicere quicquam
>   magnificum posthac: horrida uerba doma.
> parce tamen, per te furtiui foedera lecti,
>   per Venerem quaeso compositumque caput.   (3–8)

The metaphor of the top (*namque agor*) suggests the poet's lack of control. Transformed by *amor*, he is like a toy or a slave (he is whipped, *uerbere*). It is art or skill (*assueta arte*) which is the force behind the poet's torment and, as the image suggests, his confusion. This recalls the poet's failed *artes* in 1.4.82. Now, in contrast, *ars* empowered by *amor* is successful and painful in its effects upon its victim. The agency of the *puer* in this image may also suggest that, following on from poem four, the beloved from whom the poet is separated is a boy.[6] Whatever readers' assumptions may be at this point, *amor* seems to strip away the poet's pretence and imprint its image upon his behaviour and words, as upon his emotional state. The poet appears to concede this and suggests that, from now on, the appearance he projects will reflect the reality imposed upon him by *amor*.

The poet/lover appears to give in completely to the violent punishment (*ure ferum et torque*) exacted by *amor*.[7] The poet has resisted *amor*'s power, at least in outward appearance. The expression of this resistance is described as *magnificum*.[8] Like a wayward slave, the poet needs correction. His subservience here is all the more marked, since he calls punishment down upon himself. He gives up control of his speech and attitude: *libeat ne dicere quicquam | magnificum posthac.* His freedom of speech is curtailed by *amor*, or possibly[9] the beloved empowered by *amor*'s effect on the poet: *horrida*[10] *uerba doma*. Again, this verbal powerlessness occludes the role of the poet/author outside the text who is himself constructing this powerlessness. In contrast to his presentation within the text, the poet/author could be thought of as having power over the text. This potential contrast continues the complex

---

[6] Another possibility, that the *puer* is Cupid (*Amor* himself), would make the emphasis on love's power and control over the lover even more explicit here.

[7] The instrument of this punishment is possibly the person of the beloved to whom the poet's words may now be addressed. But the identity of the addressee of these lines, if there is a specific addressee, remains unclear. In any case, the idea of *amor* as a vengeful force is familiar from the picture of Venus in poem two, and of the *deus* at 1.3.22.

[8] This *magnificum* could be taken to refer to the boasts and ideals which the poet has expressed in earlier poems.

[9] Again this largely depends on the identity of the addressee here.

[10] *Horridum* in the poet's mind seems, like many other words in the elegies which imply an emotional response or moral judgement, to be defined in terms of *amor*: i.e. what disagrees with/is not accommodated by the effects of *amor*'s power is labelled *horridum*.

interplay among the levels of representation and reality which began in the first couplet. Yet, as lines 7–8 reveal, this surrender of verbal independence is part of a familiar process. The poet/lover, in return for this subservience to *amor* and the beloved, appeals (*parce tamen ... quaeso*)[11] for ultimate success in love. The impression of a deal being struck is enhanced by the language: *per te furtiui foedera lecti ... compositumque caput.* The poet seems to be calling in old debts.[12] But, although *compositumque caput* seems to imply an established bond, the reader might doubt how strong the bonds of dishonesty (*furtiui foedera lecti*) really are. Similarly, the appeal *per Venerem* might cast doubt on the likelihood of such an appeal/deal's success, given the picture of a Venus hostile (or at least unhelpful) to the poet in previous poems.

Doing deals

Ille ego, cum tristi morbo defessa iaceres,
  te dicor uotis eripuisse meis.
ipseque te circum lustraui sulpure puro,
  carmine cum magico praecinuisset anus.
ipse procuraui ne possent saeua nocere
  somnia ter sancta deueneranda mola.
ipse ego, uelatus filo tunicisque solutis,
  uota nouem Triuiae nocte silente dedi.
omnia persolui: fruitur nunc alter amore,
  et precibus felix utitur ille meis.   (9–18)

It is now made clear that, contrary to earlier suggestions, the beloved with whom the poet is concerned in this poem is female (*defessa*).[13] Such contradiction of earlier assumptions underlines again their unreliability. At the same time, the dependence of the text's meaning on a reader's assumptions comes to the fore here as the revelation that the beloved is

[11] This recalls 1.4.83, and many similar occasions throughout the poems.
[12] The fact that he must beg (*parce*) for the transaction to be upheld may, however, suggest that the deal is less than secure.
[13] This may already have been suggested by *furtiui foedera lecti*. Compare also 1.2.36.

female raises the same questions as poem four about the consistency of the two relationships (homosexual and heterosexual). The answers to these questions depend largely upon the reader's expectations of the elegiac genre and the consistency of an elegiac collection. Are both relationships simultaneous, or was the *amor* of poem four a brief episode? What does this suggest about the poet's claimed 'faithfulness', especially if, as the reader might expect, the woman in question is Delia? In other words, how strong are the *foedera* in terms of the poet's side of the deal?

The first words of the four couplets from line 9 to 16 (*ille ego ...ipse ... ipse ... ipse ego*) concentrate on the poet as subject. Here he asserts his claim to have been the power behind the woman's recovery from sickness. In contrast to his own position in poem three, the woman is in a position of powerlessness and vulnerability brought on by sickness (*cum tristi morbo defessa iaceres*), and it is *he* who by prayers and vows seems to have the power to revive her (*uotis meis*). The poet asserts the power of his appeal in terms which would seem to give him some control over the woman (*te eripuisse*). This contrasts strikingly with similar appeals in previous poems which have seemed ineffectual or at least unlikely to succeed. The reversal of the situation in poem three raises a further question. Assuming that the woman is Delia, did she or (if the elegies are not, as a reader might first assume, in chronological order) *would* she do the same for him? Although past behaviour, as far as the reader might determine it from previous elegies, suggests that she would not, any reading remains dependent upon assumption and is always open to ultimate uncertainty.

Dicor again recalls the report of *Delia*'s apparent concern for the *poet's* welfare at 1.3.10 and undercuts the reliability of the poet's assertion that his appeals had power. This assertion is based on unspecified report, and, as the reader has seen in the course of the collection, words are unreliable and open to misinterpretation. Although the situation effectively reverses the past condition of the poet, the means of attempting to gain power and to control a future outcome are familiar. It is a mixture of religion (*lustraui*[14] recalling the purification of the flock and shepherd in 1.1.35) and magic (the *anus* with her *carmen magicum* recalling the witch of poem two). *Carmine cum magico praecinuisset* also reasserts the power of song after its apparent failure to have any effect upon the beloved in poem four. In this case, however, it is a different kind of song, a specifically magic one. The poet's unproblematic mixture of these elements (*ter*[15] *sancta deueneranda mola*) points to their common objective: to gain power of some sort. The poet here takes a more active role than previously, sharing the ritual with the *anus*. Despite this shared role in the purification ceremony, however, he claims again that it was specifically *his* actions which actually realised such power: *ipse procuraui ne possent saeua nocere | somnia. His* power brings security from harm[16] and the comfort[17] of sleep. The poet takes the role of priest (*uelatus filo tunicisque solutis*) as in poem one. This resembles his picture of Delia at 1.3.29ff., who *resoluta comas* would give and fulfil vows for the *poet's* safety. The familiar principle underlying the use of religion and magic here[18] as means of gaining some kind of power is made explicit in these lines (15–18): the contractual process. The poet offers vows[19] in return for the goddess' power being exerted for the revival of his beloved: *uota nouem Triuiae nocte silente dedi.* He claims that his side of the bargain was fulfilled (*omnia persolui*) and, for once, it seems that the other side was kept too, that the woman survived.

The connection with lines 7–8 here, however, reveals that the poet's supposed transaction was more complex. It was in fact a two-way deal, not only between Trivia and the poet, but

---

[14] The fact that this word has been used both of religious ritual, in poem one, and of arcane ritual, in 1.2.63, further strengthens the link between the magic and religion here.

[15] *Ter* recalls as much the magic ritual of 1.2.56 as it does the *sancta* rituals of 1.3.11 and here.

[16] He renders the nightmares powerless: *ne possent ...*

[17] Sleep has been a recurrent sign of comfort and security in previous poems (see 1.1.48; 1.2.2; and 1.3.88).

[18] Both magic and religion are linked in the figure of Trivia.

[19] It is significant that he offers nine vows, since nine, as a multiple of three and hence a number of power, is also associated with both magic and more respectable religion.

between the poet and the woman.[20] He expected something
from *her* in return for fulfilling these vows and thus procuring
the power of the goddess to revive her.[21] The poet believes
that, in return for this service to the woman, he should gain
her love, and thus her submission to his desires. But, as is
implied in earlier poems, when applied to the sphere of *amor*
and the relationships determined by it, such processes break
down. If the poet's prayers did have power, it was not ultimately for his benefit, he could not control the outcome:
fruitur[22] *nunc alter amore | et precibus felix utitur ille meis.*
The poet may successfully gain the power he wanted from the
first deal (with Trivia),[23] but has absolutely no control over
the second part of the process, the deal concerning *amor* (see
lines 7–8) and control over the actions of his beloved.

Shattered dreams

At mihi felicem uitam, si salua fuisses,
 fingebam demens, sed renuente deo:
'rura colam, frugumque aderit mea Delia custos,
 area dum messes sole calente teret;
aut mihi seruabit plenis in lintribus uuas
 pressaque ueloci candida musta pede.
consuescet numerare pecus; consuescet amantis
 garrulus in dominae ludere uerna sinu.
illa deo sciet agricolae pro uitibus uuam,
 pro segete spicas, pro grege ferre dapem.
illa regat cunctos, illi sint omnia curae,
 at iuuet in tota me nihil esse domo.
huc ueniet Messalla meus, cui dulcia poma
 Delia selectis detrahat arboribus,

---

[20] See Yardley on this passage, and sick visiting in elegy generally. By displaying the
obsequium of the poet, the visit to the sick beloved recalls the transaction of the
traditional *amicitia* relationship: Yardley (1973) 283–8.

[21] It remains uncertain, however, whether or not the woman agreed to *this* deal.

[22] The pleasure which was his aim actually goes to another.

[23] Trivia, while being yet another female power figure, is significantly not a goddess
normally associated with love and might therefore be expected to take no part in
the poet's notional second deal.

et tantum uenerata uirum, hunc sedula curet,
  huic paret atque epulas ipsa ministra gerat.'
haec mihi fingebam, quae nunc Eurusque Notusque
  iactat odoratos uota per Armenios.
saepe ego temptaui curas depellere uino:
  at dolor in lacrimas uerterat omne merum.   (19–38)

The poet's ideal of happiness, of his desired state (*felicem uitam*) defined in terms of love and his beloved, forms a contrast with the true outcome of his ministrations for the woman's recovery. This contrast between ideal and fact mirrors the contrast between appearance and reality with which the poem began. His own happiness, he imagined, would be the outcome of her recovery through his agency (*si salua fuisses*). The poet now appears to recognise that such expectations were deluded (*fingebam demens*). This breakdown of the poet's expectations echoes the mis-assumptions involved in the process of reading the elegies themselves. The poet has misread the situation. This further distances the powerless poet/lover from the poet/author outside the text. On the one hand the poet/lover's imaginative re-construction of his relationship with the woman cannot impose itself upon the 'reality' which the text asserts, while on the other it is the poet/ author's authority which is determining that text's course. At the same time, equating the deluded poet/lover and the mistaken (or misled) reader may cause the superior position of the reader relative to the poet/lover to be eroded. The delusion of the poet/lover has been demonstrated to the reader over the course of the collection so far, placing the reader in a position of knowledge which has seemed to contrast with that delusion. But the similarities which become especially apparent in poem five between the poet/lover's confusion of reality and delusion and the reader's own difficulties in securely determining the parameters of 'reality' in the collection may undermine the reader's elevated position. From this perspective, the relative positions of reader and poet/lover have more in common than the reader might like to think. Just as the reader's expectations may be destabilised by the elegiac text, the expectations of the poet/lover are up against a force more powerful than his own attempts to construct and enforce meaning, the *deus, Amor : sed renuente deo.*

The categorisation of the fifth elegy as a paraclausithyron, which forms the focus of studies such as Copley's,[24] can be seen in this context to be a reading strategy which seeks to impose certainty and an understandable, and therefore controllable, shape upon the elegy by appeal to generic convention. In this goal it resembles Cairns' ordering, re-ordering and strict sequence of emotional response, or the ordered structural analysis of critics such as Lieberg.[25] But by destabilising the reader's construction of meaning, and even equating it with the delusion of the poet, the text disrupts such attempts to impose structure upon it. In doing so, the poem highlights the involvement of the reader's assumptions and expectations in the unstable process of delineating elegiac reality. The imposition of a conventional generic frame, the paraclausithyron, represents a particularly intense manifestation of such assumptions and expectations.

The details of the poet's ideal (*rura colam ... plenis in lintribus uuas ... musta*) directly recall his desired lifestyle in poem one. The delay in conclusively identifying the beloved, who is now revealed as Delia, also recalls that earlier elegy.[26] The undermining of the poet's ideal within elegy one is thus reinforced by the explicit and conscious dismissal here of such an ideal as fantasy. Paradoxically and just as in poem one, the ideal, which is determined by *amor*, is made unrealisable by that same force. The imagined picture of *Delia custos frugum* recalls Priapus' role in the first elegy, and may suggest that

---

[24] Copley (1956) 107–12. Although Copley admits that the paraclausithyron forms only a loose frame to the poem, the question of what does or does not fit the 'norm' of the genre still provides the terms of his analysis: '[Tibullus] use[s] the paraclausithyron as occasion for a poem actually dealing with other, broader erotic subjects', 111; see also Musurillo (1970) 392; and Murgatroyd (1980) 160–1.

[25] Lieberg (1986) 315–30.

[26] That an element of uncertainty concerning the identity of the beloved may have been present in the reader's mind up to this point is largely due to the immediately previous poem's reference to a beloved other than Delia. This undermines the reader's confidence that the poet would be referring to the same person (even when it was certain that person was a woman) as in the first three poems.

such a role for Delia is ridiculous and inappropriate. Delia would undergo some discomfort (*sole*).[27] She would be working for the poet (*aut mihi seruabit ... uuas*). The power relationship between the two which was seen earlier seems at first to be reversed, at least to some extent. It is indicative of *amor*'s inversion of established social norms that readers are led to see a form of male-female power-relationship which might otherwise be considered socially typical (the female subservient to and contained by the male) as an unusual reversal of the expected state of affairs. At lines 25-6 Delia is contained within a rural and domestic context: *consuescet* at 25 is significant in this regard. The poet gets her where he wants her, but in turn[28] he concedes to her the control of the farm.[29] She would oversee the stock and look after the accounts (*consuescet numerare pecus*). Thus she is *domina* at 26.

The picture of the *garrulus uerna* at play (*ludere*) in Delia's lap recalls the love struggles described as 'play' earlier in the collection (compare especially 1.3.64). Here the poet seems to be attempting to transform this into a picture of harmless affection: Delia is *amans* in return. But the use of *ludere* and *in sinu* may perhaps be suggestive of sexual play[30] and imply (whether consciously or not) the reality of Delia's 'unfaithfulness' in the poet's mind.[31] Or it may be that the poet is suggesting himself as the *uerna*,[32] underlining his slave-like subservience to Delia. But such an identification is tenuous.

---

[27] This recalls the discomfort occasioned by exposure to the sun in earlier poems: 1.1.27; 1.4.2.

[28] The idea of a transaction may again be present here.

[29] *Mihi* in line 23 may also even have the sense of 'taking my place'.

[30] For sexual connotations of *sinus* see Adams (1982) 90-1; for *ludere* see Adams (1982) 162-3. A similar play on the potentially sexualised meaning of both *ludere* and *sinus* may also be present in the second line of Catullus poem two, which describes the position of the beloved's pet sparrow (a position the poet/lover would probably like to be in himself).

[31] Objectively, there is of course no definite indication of any established relationship/pact between the poet and Delia that she is being 'unfaithful' to. The poet's claims of *foedera* are subjective and of dubious validity.

[32] He has certainly been *garrulus* ('talkative, chattering') over the course of the five elegies so far.

The couplet 25–6 also provides a small-scale syntactical example of the text's undermining of the reader's assumptions. That the subject of the first *consuescet* is Delia leads the reader to expect that she will also be the subject of the second,[33] an expectation which is cheated by the first word of the pentameter (*garrulus*).

In the poet's ideal, the religious process (*pro* ...), and the power of knowledge to exploit it (*sciet*), are strongly affirmed:

> Illa deo sciet agricolae pro uitibus uuam
> pro segete spicas, pro grege ferre dapem.   (27–8)

The terms of these processes are clear, one specific thing in return for another. Similarly, the positions of the poet and Delia within the household would be equally certain.[34] In return for taking care of the practical concerns (the work) of the farm, as shown in the previous lines, she would have absolute control over everything (including the poet): *illa regat cunctos, illi sint omnia curae.* The poet is happy to take his subservient, slave-like place, in return for life with Delia: *at iuuet in tota me nihil esse domo.* He would give up control in all other areas for power in love, to achieve his desires in *that* regard alone. The broader social relationships in which the poet and Delia would be involved would be similarly well defined and contained, as the imagined visit of Messalla makes clear. Delia would show subservience and respect to the socially superior figure of Messalla:[35]

> cui dulcia poma
> Delia selectis detrahat arboribus,
> et tantum uenerata uirum, hunc sedula[36] curet,
> huic paret atque epulas ipsa ministra gerat.   (31–4)

---

[33] For example, the subjects of the repeated verbs *flebis* (at 1.1.61/63) and *uolet* (at 1.4.45/51) remain the same.

[34] This recalls another similar domestic ideal at 1.3.83ff.

[35] Messalla is possibly also representative of superior political forces, which may imply that the political sphere functions in a similar way to the poet's ideal. This opens the way to a comparison of the absolute power of Delia in administering the mini-state of the farm (and of the poet, her subject) with that of pre-eminent political figures, such as Messalla and even Augustus.

[36] This again recalls the imagined domestic scene of poem three, and the sedulousness of Delia's old woman *custos* (1.3.83–4).

Thus, Delia is assimilated into the established social hierarchy. It is only the relationship between her and the poet which transforms and re-determines the accepted norm of the man in control (of the work especially) and the woman subservient (*in tota nihil esse domo*). Even here, in the poet's ideal, the power-relationship between him and his beloved is arranged according to the conventions of elegiac *amor* rather than those of society in general.

Again, at line 35, the poet explicitly recognises his delusion: *haec mihi fingebam.* He seems to have gained this much knowledge, this much control over his love-deluded mind, at least. But it seems of no use to him. It is not within his power to control the outcome and bring his dreams to fruition. Instead, as the image at lines 35–6 suggests, they are under the control of other violent forces: *quae nunc Eurusque Notusque | iactat odoratos uota per Armenios.*[37] Unlike the earlier *uota* (10), these ones, which try to affect *amor* and the object of that passion, are useless. The poet is unable to determine his own reality. Even the poetic reality he attempted to create in previous poems is labelled futile. Lines 37–8 directly recall the opening attempt of poem two to suppress his *amor*-induced grief with wine: *saepe ego temptaui curas depellere uino.* In this struggle it is the *dolor amoris* which overcomes the wine: *at dolor in lacrimas uerterat omne merum.*

Poet and reader

The various levels of appearance and reality become entangled here once more. The poetic representation of the poet/lover's ideal, which is asserted as unreal, can be compared to what is asserted as real, which is equally a poetic representation. This highlights the problem of privileging one poetic utterance as the 'real story' while the 'unrealised ideal' which

---

[37] *Odoratos Armenios* may recall the *Assyrii odores* of 1.3.7, linking the poet's failed hopes here with his equally unrealisable dream in poem three that funeral rites might be administered by his *mater*, *soror*, and Delia.

is opposed to it is equally a construction of the poet. This continues the paradoxical interplay of appearance and reality which was introduced in the opening lines of the poem. But the elision of the distinction between real and unreal cannot be entirely suppressed by the separation of the poet in the text, presenting one deluded representation of reality, and the author outside it, controlling the final course of the text. The interweaving of the delusions of the poet/lover with the mis-assumptions or uncertainties of the reader, and the ambiguity of the relationship between the poet-persona and the author of the collection are part of the process of reading the elegies, part of the elegiac game and humour. It is through the negotiation of these distinctions and their instability that the process of reading constructs meaning. This ongoing negotiation can itself be constructed as a power struggle. The position of the reader in this struggle mirrors the relationship of the poet-persona to the elusive reality of the poetic fiction which he inhabits. Each of these struggles is involved in the other. The reader must thread her/his way through the poet-persona's own negotiation of the real and unreal in order to establish what is fact and what is fiction in the poet-persona's world. But, in turn, the 'reality' which the reader constructs from this process itself determines how the poet-persona's relationship to fact and fiction within the text is understood. At the same time, the often ambiguous and unstable nature of the poet's statements draws attention to this process by rendering it precarious. This hermeneutic spiral and its often disorienting effects upon the reader are part of both the joy and the danger of the elegiac game. Within this spiral the positions of poet and reader come to reflect each other. The poet's attempts to distinguish between the real and the unreal shadow the reader's similar attempts. Just as the position of the reader can be compared to that of the poet, so too the poet/lover can be figured as himself a 'reader', interpreting and re-assembling his own reality. In both cases complex and unstable attempts to control meaning are at work.

Saepe aliam tenui: sed iam cum gaudia adirem
admonuit dominae deseruitque Venus.
tunc me, discedens, deuotum femina dixit –
a pudet! – et narrat scire nefanda meam.
non facit hoc uerbis; facie tenerisque lacertis
deuouet et flauis nostra puella comis.
talis ad Haemonium Nereis Pelea quondam
uecta est frenato caerula pisce Thetis.   (39–46)

The revelation at 39ff. (*saepe aliam tenui*)[38] that the poet
has betrayed his own claims of faithfulness (*foedera*) is presented, like his attempts to suppress *amor* by means of wine,
in terms of a struggle to overcome his love and gain some
power, at least in a sexual sense (*tenui*). But Venus is in full
control and through her the power of Delia (*dominae*), even in
her absence, is employed like an avenging force. The poet's
impotence can thus be taken as a symbol for, and manifestation of, the outcome of his struggle to overcome his love:
dolor, the lack of *gaudia*. The poet is unable to transform his
own state by these means, just as, according to the opening
lines, he is unable to maintain even the pretence of control.
These lines (39–40) open the possibility that Marathus is also
one of the attempted distractions from Delia. This possibility
injects a new element into the reader's response to the questions raised earlier. It would break down the strict separation
of the relationships within the collection, suggesting that the
whole is an interconnected narrative and privileging the Delia
relationship as *the* central focus of the book. It also would
further underline the powerlessness of the poet, who was just
as much under the control of the supposed 'distraction' as he
is under the control of Delia herself.

The *femina* attributes[39] the poet's powerlessness, and

[38] This 'unfaithfulness' with another woman is apparently not the torment of *amor*
which he had/has for Delia or Marathus, for in those cases the poet seems
unsuccessful in his attempts to 'hold' or in any way gain the compliance of his
beloveds. This revelation of unfaithfulness also brings into question once again
how well the poet's supposed '*foedera*' were honoured on *his* side.

[39] She also reports this to others (*dixit ... narrat*), wrongly as it turns out. This reflects badly on the reliability of report, which has already been undermined at
several points in the collection: see above, 108, 111, 157 and 161.

THE CURSE

Delia's power, to more obvious forces, such as witchcraft (*deuotum ... et narrat scire*[40] *nefanda meam*). Magical power of this sort is considered morally wrong (*nefanda*) by the *femina*.[41] The poet, however, claims that Delia's power base does not lie in words (*non facit hoc uerbis*), but in physical attraction and the perhaps somewhat mysterious force connected with it.[42] The adjective *tener* comes up again in this connection (*tenerisque lacertis*), suggesting the possibility of pleasure. The power of physical attraction is the source of her control over the poet, and it is more effective than the power of magic with which it is compared: *deuouet*. The comparison to Peleus and Thetis at this point is striking because of the rarity of mythological exempla so far in the collection. At first its significance may appear obscure. Why Thetis in particular? It is possible that the position of Peleus, whom the gods chose as the husband of Thetis, may reflect that of the poet, who seems to have no choice or control in his passion for Delia. The power of the goddess Thetis, reflected in Thetis' control of an animal not normally tamed (*uecta est frenato pisce*), may also imply the god-like power of Delia over the poet. As the variety of possible significances suggests, this rare mythological exemplum provides an especially clear point in the reader's struggle to locate meaning. The now familiar element of uncertainty allows assumptions and expectations to act upon the text, fixing meaning one way or another, but always running the danger of re-interpretation or final aporia.

The curse

Haec nocuere mihi; quod adest huic diues amator,
uenit in exitium callida lena meum.

[40] Knowledge (in this case arcane knowledge) is again thought of as a source of power.
[41] As he did at the close of poem four, the poet fears here what others think of him (*a pudet!*). Now, as he is apparently freed from delusion, his powerlessness has become a source of shame to him.
[42] This force may be connected with the power of Venus (mentioned at line 40) or *Amor*. Thus the possibility of *gaudia* with the *femina* is overcome by the greater power invested in Delia, or at least her memory, by Venus' actions: *admonuit ... deseruitque Venus* 39-40.

sanguineas edat illa dapes atque ore cruento
　tristia cum multo pocula felle bibat.
hanc uolitent animae circum sua fata querentes
　semper et e tectis strix uiolenta canat.
ipsa fame stimulante furens herbasque sepulcris
　quaerat et a saeuis ossa relicta lupis;
currat et inguinibus nudis ululetque per urbem,
　post agat e triuiis aspera turba canum.
eueniet: dat signat deus. sunt numina amanti,
　saeuit et iniusta lege relicta Venus.　　　(47–58)

The power exerted against the poet/lover has caused damage: *haec nocuere mihi.* Other powerful elements that have
contributed to his situation are now introduced. A rival lover
is supreme: a *diues amator.* Wealth provides power in love, or
at least as far as the sexual transaction is concerned. Paradoxically, the very poverty which in the first poem seemed to
be imposed upon the poet by the effects of *amor* has now disempowered him in the amatory sphere. In this respect, the
heterosexual relationship here and the homosexual relationship of poem four are the same. In both cases the lack of
money results in the poet's powerlessness to achieve his desires. The *diues amator* is able to exploit the power which his
wealth provides because of another powerful female figure,
the *lena.* It is her knowledge which has channelled the wealth
into the fulfilment of the *diues amator*'s desires, and supposedly lined her own pockets in the process (she is *callida,*
like the *puer* at 1.4.76). Again the poet sees himself as the
passive victim (*in exitium meum*), and all he can do is curse.
The terms of the curse reflect the poet's view of the effects
which the *lena*'s actions have had upon him. Just as the *dolor*
of his impotence in love has turned to tears the wine with
which he would suppress it (37–8), so he wishes the food and
drink of the *lena,* whom he seems largely to blame for his
suffering, defiled and bitter (49–50).[43] He wishes her haunted

---

[43] The *sanguineae dapes* also reflect the vicious effect the *lena*'s 'craft' has had on the
poet. It may also be an inverted reflection of the 'ideal' meal prepared for Messalla
at 31ff. Indeed, the poet's past hopes expressed at 19-34 (the affirming of domestic

by souls *sua fata querentes | semper*, just as he himself is forced
to lament his fate because of her actions or advice. It is also
possible that *strix violenta canat* suggests the agency of song,
which has so far been ineffective in love when up against such
power as the *lena*'s. In the terms of the curse such song is
re-empowered and affects the *lena* with violence (*uiolenta*) just
as the poet sees her acting upon him (*in exitium meum*).
Throughout his curse, the poet threatens the *lena* with powerlessness and vulnerability: she would be *furens* as the poet was
demens at line 19. She would be controlled by appetite (*fame
stimulante*, and also 49–50) as the poet is controlled by *amor*.
The savagery which the poet sees in the effect of her actions
upon him is reflected in the state he wishes upon her: *herbas-
que sepulcris | quaerat et a saeuis ossa relicta lupis*. Lacking in
control, both physical (*currat et inguinibus nudis . . . per urbem*)
and emotional (*ululetque*), she would be driven by savage
forces (*post agat e triuiis aspera turba canum*), just as the poet
is driven by his passion (*namque agor*, line 3). In the poet's
curse, then, the *lena*'s fate would reflect both his view of the
savage nature of her actions and the poet's own state, which
he is here largely blaming on her.[44]

The poet is confident that his curse will be fulfilled (*eueniet*).
For its fulfilment, as with other things many times before, he
must rely upon divine support, which he claims he has already
been guaranteed: *dat signa deus*. The poet's apparent willingness to lie about signs at 1.3.17ff may undermine this claim.
Similarly, the claim *sunt numina amanti* recalls similar claims
in poem two which were comprehensively undercut. The
statement *saeuit Venus* may also be based on the poet's previous experience, as suggested especially in poem two (and

and traditional religious bonds, the comfortable, fruitful picture of the farm and
Delia and the poet's containment within that secure environment) are in many
ways a reverse image of his hopes for the future fate of the *lena*, whom he considers largely responsible for the failure of those past hopes.

[44] See also Oppenheim (1908) 146ff., who argues that the *lena* is a witch and that the
curse thus envisages precisely those elements and creatures that a witch would
normally control finally turning against her. For the voice of scepticism, however,
see Musurillo, who believes 'the meaning of [this *deuotio*] ... remains obscure':
Musurillo (1970) 392.

also in poem three). But this reminiscence might equally suggest that the goddess is unlikely to support the poet here, or even to maintain the process of 'law' as he suggests (lines 57–8). Her power (as at 1.2.81ff.) has not previously appeared to be exercised along rational lines. *Iniusta lege* defines such law subjectively. It is unjust because it harms the poet. He implies that the *foedera* which line 7 claimed had been established between himself and Delia have been unjustly broken. But, even if this is so,[45] such transactions have been fragile in previous elegies unless they involved some more powerful means, such as wealth. Previously in this poem, the poet has claimed that he is undeluded, but his apparent confidence in divine support here may challenge this. Again, there is the possibility that the poet himself does not believe he has the power to realise the curse, through the god's support or otherwise, but that he is only claiming this to give his curse greater authority and scare the *lena* away. However, the lack of any obvious sign that the *lena* is being addressed, either directly or indirectly, argues against this interpretation.

The poor poet

> At tu quam primum sagae praecepta rapacis
>   desere. num donis uincitur omnis amor?
> pauper erit praesto semper tibi, pauper adibit
>   primus et in tenero fixus erit latere.
> pauper in angusto fidus comes agmine turbae
>   subicietque manus efficietque uiam.
> pauper ad occultos furtim deducet amicos
>   uinclaque de niueo detrahet ipse pede.
> heu, canimus frustra, nec uerbis uicta patescit
>   ianua, sed plena est percutienda manu.
> at tu, qui potior nunc es, mea fata timeto:
>   uersatur celeri fors leuis orbe rotae.
> non frustra quidam iam nunc in limine perstat
>   sedulus, ac crebro prospicit, ac refugit,

---

[45] As has been seen, the appeal to established *foedera* which have supposedly been infringed rests on dubious foundation: see above 160.

et simulat transire domum, mox deinde recurrit
  solus, et ante ipsas exscreat usque fores.
nescioquid furtiuus Amor parat. utere, quaeso,
  dum licet: in liquida nat tibi linter aqua.   (59–76)

So far the poet has emphasised that it is the *lena*'s fault that
he has been unsuccessful, while the *diues amator* has met with
success. This may betray a deluded, love-determined idealisa-
tion of his beloved. But with the change of addressee to Delia
herself (*at tu*, line 59), the reader is reminded that it is with her
that the ultimate power lies. The poet must, and, bereft of any
other means, can only, appeal to that power: *sagae praecepta
rapacis | desere*. The knowledge (*praecepta*) of the *lena*, unlike
the poet's own (and Priapus') at 1.4.79, has power and is followed.[46] Wealth has power over *amor*, while for the poet it
remains an unconquerable force. He himself can only lament
the fact powerlessly: *num donis uincitur omnis amor?*

The repetition *pauper ... pauper ... pauper ... pauper* (61–
5), like the previous *ipseque ... ipse ... ipse* (11–15), attempts
to assert the power which the poet (the *pauper* in question)
claims he *does* have. But, at the same time, this further underlines the contrast between the poet and the more powerful
and successful figure of the *diues amator*. The *pauper* would be
constantly present to do service, like a slave (*praesto semper*).
In tenero fixus erit latere, possibly suggesting an embrace, may
indicate the state of pleasure which the poet desires, as well as
the lover's obsession with the object of his love.[47] The poet
claims that the *pauper* is a *fidus comes*, but, as has been seen,
the extent to which the poet is *fidus* has been brought into
question. The *pauper* displays some strength (*subicietque
manus efficietque uiam*) but it is subservient to the beloved,
just as was the strength of the obsequious lover in poem four.

---

[46] It is ironic that, whereas the poet himself uselessly sought the power of a *saga* in
poem two and advised Delia to trust her, he should here suffer from the effective
power of a '*saga*' whom Delia does listen to, and whom he advises her to abandon.

[47] The statement *pauper adibit | primus* might seem ironic, since it is not the *pauper/*
poet but the *diues amator* who currently comes first. This address to Delia is not
necessarily intended as a statement of fact, however, but as a desperate attempt to
persuade her to comply with the 'poor' poet's wishes.

The picture of the *pauper* making a way for Delia through the crowd might suggest his desire to keep her from others. However, lines 65–6, with the emphasis on secrecy (*ad occultos furtim deducet amicos*), imply that the *pauper* will actually facilitate Delia's sexual adventures with others.[48] Absolutely subservient to her desires, claiming and offering his power to keep the knowledge of such meetings with *occultos amicos* hidden, the poet would remain slave-like (*uinclaque de niueo detrahet ipse pede*), while Delia would be released to engage in such sexual adventures when and where she wished. She has freedom, while he has none.

Just as, in the first half of the poem, he had claimed to be no longer deluded about his relationship with Delia and the ideals which he had previously held, so too at line 67 the poet declares that the hopes he expressed in the later stage of the poem are similarly deluded.[49] This suggests that his initial undelusion was at best incomplete, and thus casts doubt on its completeness this time. The delineation of reality and unreality within the elegy is further highlighted and complicated. The hopes and ideals which love creates conflict with the reality it seems also to determine. The poet's resistance to that reality still seems futile. Poetry/persuasion has no power: *canimus frustra*.[50] Words, as at 42, achieve nothing in the face of solid reality: *nec uerbis uicta patescit | ianua*.[51] True power rests with wealth: *sed plena est percutienda manu*.

Addressing the *diues amator* directly at line 69, the poet once more seems to have only the power to threaten (*timeto*). But his predictions here are based upon personal experience (*mea fata*). The assertion of similarity between the situations of the two lovers is open to disruption by the re-assertion of their differences: one is powerless, the other apparently

---

[48] An interpretation followed by Murgatroyd (1980) 182. But see Musurillo (1970) 393–4 n.14 for the controversy over the reading of this line.

[49] The poet thus seems to undergo a double disillusionment in the course of the poem.

[50] This recalls Priapus' claim in poem four (also introduced by *heu...*) that poetry had been stripped of its power by contemporary attitudes and the superior power of money.

[51] Compare the imperviousness of Delia's door to the poet's words at 1.2.9ff.

powerful. Perhaps aware of the inequality of their positions, the poet counters with a warning of the powerlessness-to-come of the *diues amator*. At first this is described in very general terms: *uersatur celeri fors leuis orbe rotae*. Humans are rendered ultimately powerless by *fors*, which, like *fata* and *Mors* in poems one and three, seems to have final control. A more powerful (*non frustra*) lover is imminent, the poet suggests. Lines 71–4 highlight the furtiveness (*ac crebro prospicit*), uneasiness and uncertainty (*ac refugit*) surrounding *amor*, the obsessiveness of the lover (*sedulus*) and the unreliability of appearances: *simulat transire domum*. The actions of the *sedulus* lover, in his reconnaissance, his retreat and advance, suggest that *amor* is not unlike the uncertain and dangerous *militia* referred to at the very opening of the collection.[52] The possibility that the *sedulus* lover is the poet himself having another try[53] would only weaken the threat's likelihood of fulfilment, given the poet's own failure *ante fores*, and is probably discounted by the admission of his failure at 67–8. It allows, however, the possibility that this is another case of the poet's continued delusion despite claims to the contrary. Knowledge about what will occur in the sphere of love seems (at best) difficult to achieve: *nescioquid furtiuus Amor parat*. This may undercut the poet's own claims here to be foretelling the future. But, in any case, *amor* remains in full control. Its power withholds and controls knowledge (*furtiuus*) and thus the reactions of the human protagonists.

In the final lines, the poet attempts to put himself in a superior position to his otherwise powerful rival by offering advice (*utere quaeso | dum licet*),[54] ending with a *sententia*: *in liquida nat tibi linter aqua*. As in his own experience, the poet suggests that the rival has little control over the course of events (*dum licet*), that the affairs of *amor* are uncertain and uncontrollable (*in liquida aqua*). But the poet's own past per-

[52] In this respect this passage also recalls the opening of poem two.
[53] See Putnam (1973) 107: 'perhaps even ... Tibullus' attempts to steal her back'. *Sedulus*, meaning 'painstaking' or even 'persevering', might well be applicable to the poet/lover in such a situation.
[54] Once more, this is advice tinged with an element of threat.

formance, especially as compared to the rival he is trying
to advise, and his failure as an advisor in poem four, might
undermine the reliability of his predictions here.

Conclusion

The poet cannot maintain the separation of reality and unreality which he asserts in the opening lines of poem five.
Reality and unreality, delusion and truth are confused in the
course of the text. The poet is unable to define, enforce and
control the distinction. The position of the poet/lover might
seem ironic in relation to the author outside the text, who
could, as Lieberg has shown,[55] be viewed as a controlling
figure. Such an interpretation highlights the detachment of
author from poet-persona. But, as I have tried to show, the
reader is implicated in the construction of the elegiac 'reality'
and of his/her consequent position in relation to the poet/
lover, to the author and to the text. The fifth elegy foregrounds the role of the reader's active assumptions and
expectations in determining the reading which defines these
positions. The reader's struggle for control here can be
equated with the poet's power struggles in the text, and like
the poet's struggles any reading is open to being undercut and
destabilised. This allows further similarities to be drawn between the reader's position and the poet/lover's attempts to
control the definition of reality and delusion.

The poet, at the beginning of the poem and again at the
end, asserts the complementary oppositions of past/present
and delusion/knowledge. He might appear by this to have
achieved some conclusive knowledge (and possibly self-
knowledge), but he cannot control the terms of these oppositions. In the word-world of elegy appearance (or words) and
reality remain unreconciled. The familiar mechanisms fail to
control the course of his relationship: transaction and agreement with Delia and the gods; magic and religion; and finally
words, poetry and persuasion. This emphasises, and appa-

---

[55] Lieberg (1982); see also Lieberg (1986) 24 and 27.

rently convinces the poet himself, that the translation of his desires and ideals into reality is impossible. Themselves determined by *amor*, these desires and ideals are frustrated by the very nature of *amor* of this sort. The poet is left cursing, threatening and attempting to persuade with equally doubtful likelihood of bringing those aspirations and predictions to fulfilment. At the same time, not only is the construction of any ultimate meaning from the words of the poet or the projection of any outcome within the reality of the poems destabilised, but the question of how the nature of that reality can be defined, of how it can be determined and controlled, is seen to be interwoven within the nexus of power relations formed by poet-persona, reader, author and text.

POEM SIX

Positions

Semper, ut inducar, blandos offers mihi uultus,
   post tamen es misero tristis et asper, Amor.
quid tibi saeuitiae mecum est! An gloria magna est
   insidias homini composuisse deum?
nam mihi tenduntur casses. Iam Delia furtim
   nescioquem tacita callida nocte fouet.
illa quidem tam multa negat, sed credere durum est;
   sic etiam de me pernegat usque uiro.   (1–8)

The opening of poem six proposes a general rule (*semper*) concerning *Amor*'s[1] treatment of the poet/lover. By generalising in this way, the poet seems to speak with the knowledge of an experienced victim. *Amor* is seen as an actively hostile, manipulative force (*ut inducar*). Its power to cause the poet pain (*mihi . . . es misero tristis et asper*) stems from deception. The promise of the *blandi uultus* is not fulfilled. Again it seems that love creates instability and unreliability. Appearance is deceiving. This recalls the opening of the previous poem with some irony.[2] There the poet attempted to maintain an appearance (1.5.1–2), but, because of the power of his passion, was unable to do so. In the opening lines of poem six, the elegiac 'reality' is again defined through its difference from appearance. The poet tries to take the initiative, but *Amor* is too deceptive and too strong. In poem five the poet tried to be *asper* (1.5.1), but here *Amor* is the only one who is truly *asper* (1.6.2). Although the poet's sarcastic question suggests it is

---

[1] *Amor* is here personified by the poet's direct address to it (or to *him*, if he is identified with the boy-god Cupid/Eros). Hence the capital 'A'.

[2] On the echoes of the opening of poem five in the opening of poem six see Gaisser (1971a) 204 n.7.

petty (1.6.3-4), the *gloria magna* of *Amor* is at least justified by the god's power. In contrast, the *gloria* of the poet at 1.5.2 was an empty boast. Comparison of the opening lines of the two poems suggests that the manipulation of the gap between appearance and reality is an effective weapon in the power struggle between *Amor* and the poet. The relative position of the two combatants in this power-struggle can be judged by their respective abilities to maintain a false appearance, to deceive.

The relative positions in this struggle are also delineated by the hunting motif of lines 3-6. The initiative is again taken away from the poet. In earlier poems such as one and four, it is the lover who aspires to or is advised to take the active role.[3] Here, however, *Amor* itself is shown to be the active, predatory party, hunting the poet down: *an gloria magna est | insidias homini composuisse deum? | nam mihi tenduntur casses.* Whereas the poet has aspired in previous poems to capture Delia's love without success,[4] *Amor* here *successfully* hunts the poet, entrapping and controlling him.

The method of control used by *Amor* is the elegiac woman, Delia (*iam Delia* ...).[5] She too employs secrecy and active deception (*furtim*; *nescioquid tacita ... nocte*). She is *callida*, the same term which in the fourth elegy (1.4.76) described the *puer* who has his lover at his mercy. The poet suggests that Delia is deceitful in her words as well as actions (*illa quidem tam multa negat*). But, as earlier poems have suggested (notably poems two, four and five),[6] the reliability of report is broken down under the sway of *Amor* (*sed credere durum est*). This parallels the difficulties involved in reading the distinctions between reality and unreality which the text estab-

---

[3] In poem four, for example, the lover was encouraged literally to hunt with the beloved in an effort to win the beloved's consent.

[4] See the discussion of the opening of poem two above 74ff.

[5] The instrumental role of the elegiac woman here recalls Wyke's comment that 'the elegiac texts take little interest in elaborating their metaphors in terms of female power but explore, rather, the concept of male dependency' (1989b) 42. My reading of the collection, however, attempts to show that the power-relationships and struggles at work in the text are more complex than this statement would suggest.

[6] See above, 108, 111, 157, 161 and 170 n.39.

lishes, and allows further similarities to be drawn between the positions of poet/lover and reader. Many precedents for this unreliability could be recalled; but the irony of the poet's position is underlined by the very precedent that he regards as the greatest barrier in the way of belief: *sic etiam de me pernegat usque uiro.* This may come as a surprise after the situation in other poems (especially two and five). This apparent discrepancy might undermine the reliability of *this* claim, too. The poet claims that Delia actively deceived her *uir*[7] in his favour: can the reader trust this claim any more than the poet can trust Delia's denials? But the irony of the poet's own apparent contribution to the breakdown of trust, the suggestion that he has brought his present powerlessness on himself, allows the reader to assume a superior position to the poet/ lover by regarding him as an object of ridicule.[8] In this regard it resembles much of the humour of Tibullan elegy.[9] There remains, however, an unstable tension between this assumption of an asymmetrical relationship and the similarity between the positions of poet/lover and reader which is suggested by their shared difficulties in establishing reliable meaning.

Deceptions

> Ipse miser docui quo posset ludere pacto
> custodes: eheu, nunc premor arte mea.
> fingere tunc didicit causas ut sola cubaret,
> cardine tunc tacito uertere posse fores.
> tunc sucos herbasque dedi quis liuor abiret
> quem facit impresso mutua dente Venus.
> at tu, fallacis coniunx incaute puellae,
> me quoque seruato peccet ut illa nihil.

---

[7] The *uir* here may recall the dominant figure of the *diues amator* in poem five, or the *coniunx* in poem two.

[8] On the 'measure of self-deprecatory irony' inherent in the elegist's role see Littlewood (1983) 2135.

[9] See above, 78–9 and 169.

> neu iuuenes celebret multo sermone caueto,
> neue cubet laxo pectus aperta sinu,
> neu te decipiat nutu, digitoque liquorem
> ne trahat et mensae ducat in orbe notas.
> exibit quam saepe, time, seu uisere dicet
> sacra Bonae maribus non adeunda Deae.
> at mihi si credas, illam sequar unus ad aras;
> tunc mihi non oculis sit timuisse meis. (9–24)

The potential of knowledge to empower is clear in the lines which follow. The humour of the situation stems from the poet's loss of control over the translation of knowledge into practical results. The poet has given Delia the knowledge of how to deceive those guarding her, but Delia, who is clearly in a superior position, cannot be trusted to use this knowledge for the poet's benefit:

> ipse miser docui quo posset ludere pacto
> custodes: eheu, nunc premor arte mea. (9–10)

As lines 5–6 have emphasised, Delia already has the ability to choose or discard lovers; the tricks which the poet has taught her serve only to enhance her power. Her seeming detachment gives her this power: unlike the poet, she does not appear to be bound and controlled by *Amor*. Again, the passivity and foolishness of the poet are underlined as he is unable to determine the results of his own 'art' (*premor arte mea*). This clearly recalls the impotence of *ars* in poem four.[10] The inability of the poet/lover to control the course of events which he initiates points once more to a contrast between the positions of the poet-persona and the author of the collection who is in control of each poem's course.[11] At the same time, such a self-portrayal might further encourage the reader to feel secure in his/her superior position over the poet as he is presented in the text.

---

[10] Compare the poet's efforts to ensure Delia's revival from sickness at 1.5.9ff., where the fruits of those efforts are also enjoyed by others.

[11] For earlier discussion of the interplay of these two positions see my reading of poem five above, 168–9 and 178–9.

The remaining details of the tricks taught to Delia (lines 11–14) continue to emphasise the potential of knowledge to empower (*quo posset ... ut ... posse*). Here, specifically, it is taught or learnt knowledge which is in question (*docui ... didicit*). *Fingere causas* may recall the pretence of omens as reasons not to leave on *militia* in poem three (*sum causatus* 1.3.17). Both these sets of false excuses suggest the unreliability of the claims of people as a guide to truth. This unreliability is due primarily to the personal desires of the individuals making the claims. It is those desires and not any external, objective 'reality' which determine the content of those claims. The power of deception continues to be strongly emphasised in lines 12–14. Here deception comes into its own as a powerful instrument in a situation where behaviour would otherwise be detected and restrained. Delia learns to open doors silently (*cardine tunc tacito*) and to hide the marks left by lovebites (*quem facit impresso mutua dente Venus*). In the second case, the means used to hide the marks recall the ingredients used by the witch of poem two in another display of secret knowledge and power which was ultimately of no use to the poet: *sucos herbasque*.

The change of addressee after line 14, however, demands a re-evaluation of the poet's position. At first, the poet's description of the *coniunx* (*fallacis coniunx incaute puellae*) suggests that they are both in similar positions, deceived and manipulated by Delia. The title of *coniunx*, however, might lead the reader to expect a figure with rather more control over Delia than he in fact seems to possess. The position of the *coniunx* may, thus, appear even worse, and even more ridiculous, than that of the poet.[12] The generic opposition of poet/lover to the more powerful *coniunx* or *uir* of the beloved, of the sort which is seen in poem two, is startlingly disrupted by the advice the poet then goes on to give. This is true whether the words *me quoque seruato* are understood as 'keep

---

[12] Roman men who could not control their wives were often considered objects of ridicule. See Edwards (1993) 53–4. On the expectation that husbands should control their wives see Treggiari (1991) 209–10.

watch on both of us'[13] (i.e. Delia and the poet), or 'guard against/watch out for me as well as the others [i.e. rivals]', or (in a comical piece of male-bonding against the common female enemy) 'preserve me as well as yourself'.[14] Whatever the interpretation, it is clear that the poet is actually trying to enlist the power of the *coniunx* to prevent Delia from consorting with the rivals already mentioned (*peccet ut illa nihil*). The repetition *neu ... neue ... neu ... ne* (17–20) introduces the secret communication techniques, the signs and messages which, so the poet claims, allow Delia to maintain control over the situation. Again the operative element is deceit: *decipiat*.

Delia's claim that she visits the rites of the Bona Dea highlights again the unreliability of words (*dicet*). It is appropriate, as well as convenient for her own purposes, that she involves the rites of the Bona Dea in the deceit, a sphere in which, as in elegy itself, women are dominant (*maribus non adeunda*). The poet's advice to the *coniunx* to take care (*caueto ... time*) suggests that up until now the *coniunx* was unaware of these secret signs and deceptions. He lacked the knowledge which might have allowed him to control the situation, and as a result he seems foolish. But the poet's knowledge of these secret signals and stratagems may also suggest that they were among those techniques which he himself taught to Delia. If this interpretation is followed, the poet's confession of his own role in the deception of the *coniunx* (at line 8), and the use against them both of the knowledge he has given to Delia, are converted from signs of weakness to being part of a bid for a more powerful position. The poet uses the knowledge he has of Delia's deceit to empower the *coniunx*, notionally at least. The irony of this strategy, and possibly further evidence of the poet/lover's self-delusion, is the hope that the *coniunx* will now be able to protect not only *his* interests, but those of the poet. Thus, according to this reading, the poet attempts to play on the *coniunx*'s position in order to improve his own.

Lines 23–4 bring the reader to the culmination of the poet's

---

[13] Lee (1990) 27.
[14] For a discussion of the problem see Murgatroyd (1980) 190–1.

POEM SIX

newly constructed position, the punchline made possible by
the poet's assumed role as advisor: *at mihi si credas*... The
possibility emerges that the poet's confessional stance was
designed to convince the *coniunx* that the poet is *now* being
entirely truthful, and thus to encourage the trust he now re-
quests. But, at the same time, the unreliability of trust and
belief which has saturated this and earlier poems might undermine this plea. These ambiguities are increased in the
words which follow: *illam sequar unus ad aras;* | *tunc mihi non
oculis sit timuisse meis*. The image of the poet passively following Delia like a slave (*illam sequar*) is familiar from poem
five (lines 61ff.), where the ulterior amatory purpose was clear:
the familiar trade-off of service for Delia's consent (*seruitium
amoris*). It is possible that the altars referred to in line 23 were
not inside the temple, and this is the reason why the poet
would have no need to fear divine retribution in the form of
blindness[15] for infringing a non-male ceremony. The reader
might assume that this is the impression the poet expects the
coniunx to have, and it is one possible reading of the lines.[16]
But the possibility is clearly open that, just as Delia's original
claims that she was worshipping the Bona Dea were false
(lines 21–2), so too the poet and Delia would not really be
going to the rites at all. Thus he would have no fear for his
eyes.[17]

This second reading re-positions the reader within the network of power relationships, giving him/her a superior position in relation to the *coniunx* rather than the poet. It is the
coniunx who now becomes the manipulated party, as the poet
attempts to gain some power over him, and thus some power
over Delia (as her *custos*). This re-positioning of the reader is
of course intimately connected to the re-positioning of the
poet/lover, who is now seen as the manipulator, attempting,
at least, to gain some power to achieve his desires by duping

[15] On blindness as a punishment for violating the rites of the Bona Dea see Brouwer
(1989) 261; and Smith (1913) 312. For the cult of the Bona Dea generally see
Brouwer (1989), *passim*.
[16] As Putnam (1973) 111.
[17] Putnam (1973) 111; André (1965) 68; and Murgatroyd (1980) 193.

186

the *coniunx*. The poet/lover's rejuvenated position in the power dynamic could be seen as an inversion of the situation of the opening couplet: now *the poet* is using deceit, *blandos uultus ut inducat.*

> Saepe, uelut gemmas eius signumque probarem,
> per causam memini me tetigisse manum.
> saepe mero somnum peperi tibi, at ipse bibebam
> sobria supposita pocula uictor aqua.
> non ego te laesi prudens, ignosce fatenti.
> iussit Amor; contra quis ferat arma deos?
> ille ego sum (nec me iam dicere uera pudebit)
> instabat tota cui tua nocte canis.   (25–32)

The poet follows with further examples of the tricks used to deceive the *coniunx* in the past (lines 25ff.). Such a situation of connivance between Delia and the poet is unfamiliar to the reader of the previous poems, and *memini* opens the poet's claims to the same problematic unreliability attached elsewhere in the collection to reported information, and to words more generally. The deceit is again the foremost element in the stratagems described in these lines. *Per causam* directly recalls similar excuses (*causae*) at line 11. The apparent foolishness of the *coniunx* is underlined. At lines 31–2 he is more easily deceived than his dog. Humour thus reinforces the position of the poet/lover at the expense of the *coniunx*.[18] The poet sees himself in retrospect now as the *uictor*, the successful soldier in the *militia amoris*. This suggests a similarity between the *Amor*-poet power relation and that of the poet and the *coniunx*. Both are a war-like struggle in which one party overpowers the other. The comparison is reinforced by the poet's excuse (at line 30) for his past deceptions of the *coniunx*. He was compelled by the power of *Amor*, a power spoken of in military terms which recall the opening lines (3–4): *iussit Amor; contra quis ferat arma deos?*

The poet's explicit confessional stance (*nec me iam dicere*

---

[18] Even his triumphant drinking of 'sober cups' reverses the powerless position of the inebriated poet at the opening of poem two or at 1.5.37–8.

uera pudebit) could, again, be seen as an attempt to convince the *coniunx* that he is telling the truth and should thus be trusted with Delia. The confession of past deceptions would therefore be part of a further, greater deception. The poet hopes that this confession will bring him forgiveness from the *coniunx*: *ignosce fatenti.* He claims that it was his own lack of knowledge, and his lack of control over his own actions, which harmed the *coniunx*'s interests: *non ego te laesi prudens.*

The text opens up a chain of possibilities which threaten to invade and destabilise any reading. The possibility that the poet is attempting to manipulate the *coniunx* may now combine with any doubt which the suggestions of previous elegies might cast upon the poet's claims of past success with Delia at lines 25–8. It might now seem that those claims were fabricated simply to enhance the confessional appearance of the poet's words. These claims would thus form part of an overall strategy to encourage the *coniunx* to accept the poet/lover's pose as a now truthful, trustworthy and knowledgeable advisor. The irony earlier in the poem was entirely at the expense of the poet. But now the reader, manipulated by the poet's rejuvenation of his position, may see the *coniunx* as the object of humour. Alternatively, the poet's strategy here could be seen as a desperate and possibly impractical[19] attempt to preserve his own interests through the intervention of the *coniunx*. The poet's unrealistic hopes of gaining access to Delia and the power to keep her away from rivals would thus reflect his characteristic self-delusion. The attempted manipulation of the *coniunx* would appear to be one last desperate, and perhaps somewhat pathetic, powerplay. The reader, taking a superior position in relation to both, might laugh at the poet's manipulation of the *coniunx, and* at the poet's hopes that these manipulations will be successful.

The exact positioning of the poet/lover in the power relationships formed by the sixth elegy is an implicit concern of critical readings of the poem. Wimmel's reading, for example,

---

[19] Given the poet's usual unreliability, the reader may not be convinced that the *coniunx* is as gullible as the poet paints him.

maintains the reader's superior position over a deluded, powerless poet whose suggestion of a 'bargain' with the *coniunx* is only a case of wishful thinking.[20] In contrast to this approach, Gaisser's reading of conscious irony throughout the elegy places the poet in a position of control which is clear from the language of her analysis: for example, 'The double meaning in these lines is *used* for ironic effect'[21] (my italics). In this interpretation, as with Wimmel's, it is clear that the reader's position in the power dynamic of reading depends upon the poet/lover's position in the power dynamics within the text. The reader, in 'sharing' the irony of the poet, gains a mastery over the meaning of the poem which produces a single, consistent reading: 'Thus the poem is unified in tone and presents a consistent picture of Tibullus' attitude towards his situation.'[22] The fixing of the poet/lover's position enables the reader to gain control over the meaning of the elegy. But Gaisser's reading elides the distinction between the poet-persona and the author, 'Tibullus', stabilising the poet's position by equating it with what is assumed to be the controlling role of the author.[23]

But the relation of the author to the position of the poet/lover in the elegy complicates rather than secures any attempt to construct a stable reading. The various possibilities which the text can maintain, the ambiguities of the poet/lover's position, mean that any final reading is dependent upon the reader's assumptions and is always open to uncertainty. The 'controlling' author could thus be thought of as manipulating the uncertainty of both the poet/lover's position and the

---

[20] 'Er würde dieses Amt trefflich ausfüllen und die Nachteile – er müßte als Sklave fungieren – gern in Kauf nehmen. Diese Überlegungen nehmen nach Tibulls Weise mehr und mehr den Charakter der Wunschimagination.' Wimmel (1971) 156.

[21] Gaisser (1971a) 207.

[22] Gaisser (1971a) 216.

[23] Williams, similarly, shows an ambiguity in the use of the name 'Tibullus' and the location of irony in the poem: 'In i.6 Tibullus addresses Delia's coniunx and asks to be allowed, since she has another lover, to guard her himself – a neat and amusing reversal of the usual situation', Williams (1968) 535–6; 'The poetry of Tibullus is pervaded by a gentle irony that delights in contrasts and slightly unexpected turns of phrase, and there is an Ovidian touch in i.6.15ff. where he suggests himself as a suitable guardian for her', Williams (1968) 561.

reader's position in relation to the poet. Approached from this angle, the power dynamic of reading, the relationship between reader and text, is an operation of the reader's less than secure interrelation with both the poet/lover and the author.

Authority

> Quid tenera tibi coniuge opus, tua si bona nescis
>   seruare? frustra clauis inest foribus.
> te tenet, absentes alios suspirat amores
>   et simulat subito condoluisse caput.
> at mihi seruandam credas: non saeua recuso
>   uerbera, detrecto non ego uincla pedum.
> tunc procul absitis, quisquis colit arte capillos,
>   et fluit effuso cui toga laxa sinu;
> quisquis et occurret, ne possit crimen habere
>   stet procul aut alia transeat ille uia.   (33–42)

The poet claims at lines 33–4 that the *coniunx* lacks the knowledge, and thus the power, to safeguard his *bona*. These include, primarily, his *puella*: *quid tenera tibi coniuge opus, tua si bona nescis | seruare?* His lack of knowledge presumably consists of an inability to detect such deceptions as the poet has already mentioned. This ignorance robs potency from the apparatus of restraint and control: *frustra clauis inest foribus.* Ironically, this recalls the potency of locked doors in the poet's case (for example, in poem one and poem two). If the *coniunx* is to be identified with the *uir* in poem two, this may suggest that he is not as inept as the poet claims. His doors have at least been able to keep the poet himself at bay. Similarly, Delia's power over the *uir* is emphasised. *Te tenet*, for example, implies a degree of non-physical control. Her power over him stems from deception (*simulat*) and, as with *Amor* in the first lines, false or ambiguous appearances or emotions (*absentes alios suspirat amores*). But this power is also open to undermining by the contrary suggestions of earlier poems, especially poem two, in which the *uir* seemed to have full control over Delia. This may imply that the poet is himself employing deception and false appearances, or is at least manipulating the truth, to scare the *coniunx* and convince him that he is dependent on the poet's own superior knowledge of the situation. This deception would thus form part of the poet's overall strategy to persuade the *coniunx* to put him into a better position, closer to Delia.

This possibility might be strengthened by the reprise of the 'punchline' at 37: *At mihi seruandam credas.* But now it is framed in the more familiar terms of a trade-off: *non saeua recuso | uerbera, detrecto non ego uincla pedum.* The poet offers the *uir* power over him in exchange for being entrusted with Delia. The power offered the *coniunx* is of the type normally exerted over the poet by Delia herself. It might now seem an extreme measure for the poet to submit not simply to the power of his mistress, but to her *uir/coniunx*,[24] and this, in turn, might prompt a re-evaluation of the power relation of the poet and the *uir*. At the same time, however, it is open to doubt whether the poet can be trusted to keep the terms of that deal, as I have already suggested.[25] Indeed, in the sphere of *Amor*, such processes have been seen to be fragile and often unworkable. The poet's dominance by the *coniunx* would see a reversal of their past power relation, or, rather, of the version of it which the poet has presented at lines 25–8. In return for this, the power relation between the poet and his other rivals would be similarly reversed. He would dismiss these rivals like a triumphant *uictor: tunc procul absitis.*[26] For a change it would be their *ars* (*arte*, line 39), and not the poet's, which would fall impotent.[27] The poet, lines 41–2 claim, would disempower such rivals (*ne possit crimen habere*). In a continuation of sense from *tunc procul absitis*, the poet would

---

[24] See, for example, Wimmel (1971) 156 quoted above n. 20.
[25] See my discussion of lines 23–4, above 185–7.
[26] This act of dismissal is, of course, all very theoretical and subjunctive.
[27] The rivals' art is used in relation to hair styling and dress, which are again pointers to character. The laxness of dress (*fluit effuso cui toga laxa sinu*) and elaborateness of hair style suggest (as 18) a moral laxness and calculated sexual aggressiveness.

even determine a potential rival's physical position: *stet procul aut alia transeat ille uia.*[28] But, as in lines 23–4, there is ambiguity and irony here which casts doubt upon the poet's trustworthiness. While the would-be rival's distance from Delia would prevent that rival from being accused of sexual misconduct, sole access to her would, in contrast, clearly leave the poet himself exposed to just such a charge. This is particularly true in the context of the past behaviour and desires which the poet has admitted to the *coniunx* in this very elegy. The confessional technique of the poet, for the reader as well as the *uir*, leaves itself open to contrary interpretations. On the one hand it encourages trust now that the poet is apparently telling truth even where it might damage his cause, while on the other it fosters distrust, since the poet's past deceptions create a precedent for the future.[29] Indeed, his present offer of knowledge and practical help, of a trade-off to defeat his rivals, might be just such a manipulation, a deception.

> Sic fieri iubet deus, sic magna sacerdos
>   est mihi diuino uaticinata sono.
> haec, ubi Bellonae motu est agitata, nec acrem
>   flammam, non amens uerbera torta timet.
> ipsa bipenne suos caedit uiolenta lacertos
>   sanguineque effuso spargit inulta deam,
> statque latus praefixa ueru, stat saucia pectus,
>   et canit euentus quos dea magna monet:
> 'parcite quam custodit Amor uiolare puellam,
>   ne pigeat magno post didicisse malo.
> attigerit, labentur opes, ut uulnere nostro
>   sanguis, ut hic uentis diripiturque cinis.'   (43–54)

---

[28] Most manuscripts at this point (line 42) read *stet procul aut alia stet procul ante uia*, which makes no obvious sense and seems clearly corrupt (see Murgatroyd (1980) 314–15). I have borrowed this reading of the line from Lee's 'makeshift' emendation (1990) 28, 131. The line remains problematic, but *stet procul*, which by itself suggests the poet's desire to establish physical distance between himself and his rivals, seems secure and is included by almost all editors. For a discussion of the problems of this line see Murgatroyd (1980) 314–15; and Wimmel (1971) 156–7.

[29] Gaisser (1971a) 206.

Lines 43ff. possibly suggest the poet's awareness of the ironies and weaknesses of his case, and the need to back it up with stronger measures. For the poet now claims divine sanction: *sic fieri iubet ipse deus*. The poet himself is ultimately controlled by another force, *Amor*, as in the opening lines. The god is not named here, however, and the fact that it is the priestess of Bellona (*magna sacerdos*) who gives the warning, overtly inspired by Bellona herself (*quos dea magna monet*), serves to obscure the *deus'* identity. This could be seen as a deliberate strategy on the poet's part. If he explicitly confessed that, just as in the past, it is *Amor* who still determines his actions (line 30), this might suggest that his actions now will be the same as they were then. *Est mihi diuino uaticinata sono* adds weight to the poet's appeals to the *uir*. If true, it also suggests that through the power of prophecy (the power of knowledge) the poet has some security. Knowing the future (*euentus*, line 50) gives him a stronger basis from which to act, as well as the personal authority which such knowledge brings. The choice of the priestess of the war-goddess Bellona (line 45) to deliver the determinations of the love-god *Amor* (line 51) suggests the similarities between the power-struggles involved in both spheres.[30] Similarly, the extreme self-mutilation and violent agitation of the priestess under the influence of the goddess is reminiscent of the punishments the poet is willing to undergo for *his* passion[31]

> haec, ubi Bellonae motu est agitata, nec acrem
> flammam, non amens uerbera torta timet.
> ipsa bipenne suos caedit uiolenta lacertos
> sanguineque effuso spargit inulta deam,
> statque latus praefixa ueru, stat saucia pectus ... (45–9)

It seems that it was usual for such rites as described here, and probably those of Bellona in particular, to culminate in

---

[30] It suggests *militia amoris*, or the images of violence, of predator and victim, in the hunting motif of lines 3–6.

[31] See lines 3 and 37–8; and also 1.1.55–6; 1.1.57ff.; 1.2.12; 1.2.41–2; 1.2.85–8; 1.4.81; and 1.5.3–6. More specifically, *uerbera* at line 46 recalls *uerbera* a few lines earlier at 38; and the priestess's lack of fear (*non ... timet* 46) recalls the lover's supposed lack of fear at 1.2.29ff.

prophecy. This is suggested, for example, by Seneca's attack on those who give credence to such pronouncements: *cum sistrum aliquis concutiens ex imperio mentitur, cum aliquis secandi lacertos suos artifex bracchia atque umeros suspensa manu cruentat* (*De Vita Beata*, 26,8). Bellona's authority to pronounce on erotic themes may stem from the presence in some of her temples of sacred prostitutes.[32] The poet's attribution of these words to Bellona, or rather her priestess, could thus be seen as an attempt to give religious and cultural authority to the pronouncement and to himself, who is 'faithfully' reporting it. But, as Seneca's attack suggests, the authority of Bellona's priestess is equally open to being discredited in the context of traditional Roman morality. Not only are the priestess and the rites she takes part in frenzied, but, through the association of Bellona with Ma and other eastern goddesses,[33] they are non-Roman and thus not to be trusted.[34] The very nature of the figure of Ma-Bellona, both newly imported eastern cult and ancient Roman goddess of war, suggests this ambivalence. Like the uncertainty of authority in the elegy (and the collection) more generally, authority in this passage is open to both reinforcement and undermining by the intervention of Bellona and the description of her priestess.

The mental distortion which possession by Bellona produces in the priestess (*amens*) recalls the effects of control by *Amor* as surely as does the deity's demand for blood (*sanguine ... spargit ... deam*). Unlike the poet in the past, however, the priestess remains *inulta*, protected by the goddess' power.[35] Such extreme behaviour in connection with the warning about *Amor*'s power might reinforce the suggestion that the poet is attempting to scare the *uir* into compliance.[36] But the words

[32] See Strabo's description of the Cappadocian goddess Ma, with whom Bellona was identified, 12.2.3 and 12.3.36.

[33] See Murgatroyd (1980) 198.

[34] For the rites of Ma-Bellona, and that form of religious ecstasy generally, and attacks upon them as un-Roman and immoral, see Gordon, (1990) 246–8.

[35] The passive nature of the priestess, who is controlled by the active force of Bellona, also reflects the relationship between *Amor* and the poet, particularly as it is described in the opening lines of poem six.

[36] The fierce power of the prophet incidentally reasserts the power of song (*canit*) and the *uates*, perhaps an attempt by the poet to reflect on his own position.

of the priestess appeal directly to the rival suitors and possibly, depending on the perspective(s) the reader decides to take, the poet himself. From the poet's point of view, the *quisquis* of lines 39 and 41 might be the one most likely *uiolare puellam*. From the perspective of the *coniunx*, however, the poet might be the most likely candidate. *Didicisse*[37] might recall the empowering qualities of knowledge (see lines 10ff.) and the disempowering effects of ignorance, and *attigerit* at line 53 may even recall the poet's past tricks in order to touch Delia (*tetigisse*) at line 26. The positions of the poet/lover and *coniunx* are again determined by, and in turn help to determine, the interpretation the reader takes.

The power of *Amor* is made explicit (*quam custodit Amor*). The curse of lines 53–4, which directly recalls the self-mutilation of the priestess, is intended by the poet to frighten off rivals. But, like his earlier attempt to warn rivals away (lines 41–2), the terms of the curse are equally applicable to the poet himself. In fact, recollection of the first elegy might suggest that *lapsus opum* has already happened to the poet. This might raise and in turn reinforce the possibility of a connection between the poet's loss of wealth and his control by *Amor*. In any case, the effects of *Amor* here are familiar to the poet: pain and sterility (*uulnere... sanguis... cinis*). Again the ironies of the poem affect the reader's position in relation to the poet, whether she/he reads it as conscious irony (as Gaisser does) and shares a position of control over the text with a 'knowing' poet, or sees the meaning of his verses as out of the poet/lover's control, placing the 'knowing' reader in a position superior to that of the deluded poet.

Mother love

Et tibi nescioquas dixit, mea Delia, poenas;
si tamen admittas, sit precor illa leuis.

---

[37] *Didicisse* is the reading of the manuscripts, which I follow here in contrast to Lee's text which follows Achilles Statius' emendation *tetigisse*. If correct, *tetigisse* would emphasise the connection with line 26 (and both occurrences of *tetigisse* would be the second last words in their respective lines).

non ego te propter parco tibi, sed tua mater
me mouet atque iras aurea uincit anus.
haec mihi te adducit tenebris multoque timore
coniungit nostras clam taciturna manus.
haec foribusque manet noctu me affixa proculque
cognoscit strepitus me ueniente pedum.
uiue diu mihi, dulcis anus: proprios ego tecum,
sit modo fas, annos contribuisse uelim.
te semper natamque tuam te propter amabo:
quicquid agit, sanguis est tamen illa tuus.
sit modo casta doce, quamuis non uitta ligatos
impediat crines nec stola longa pedes.   (55–68)

The poet now turns to Delia (line 55), using the threat of
divine punishment to coerce *her* into compliance (*et tibi nescioquas dixit, mea Delia, poenas*). This recalls the picture of
the poet's position which earlier elegies have encouraged the
reader to construct and expect. The sentiment of line 56 (*si
tamen admittas, sit precor illa leuis*) could also be used to reinforce a familiar role for the poet/lover. This is a character so
dominated by Delia that he is unable to curse her even with
the punishments *he* believes she does or might deserve, a
character who must resort to appeals (*precor*, line 56) in the
hope of achieving his desires. But even a reading which seeks
to assimilate the presentation of the poet/lover here with his
previous position threatens to fragment against the equally
familiar possibility that the poet's subservience to Delia is
actually a *controlled* strategy of the poet's employed in the
hope of persuading her to comply with his desires. In such a
reading the competing roles of the powerless poet and of the
poet who is both in control of his words, and attempting to
gain power through them, continue to co-exist.

Lines 57–8, however, immediately undercut any of these
assumptions:

> non ego te propter parco tibi, sed tua mater
> me mouet atque iras aurea uincit anus.   (57–8)

It is not Delia but her *mother* who has such power over the
poet (*mouet ... uincit*). The poet, continuing to re-position

himself in the power dynamic, now sees himself having the
power to pardon (*parco*), like an angry but merciful god.
Delia prompts his rage (*iras*), presumably by her behaviour
with rivals. It is her mother who controls and nullifies his
reaction. In contrast to the immediately preceding lines, this
disclosure resists assimilation by the reader. But the 'explanation' which immediately follows allows this revelation to be
fitted into a familiar structure, although unexpected in its
content. In effect, the poet's concessions to the mother are
part of a trade-off process. The mother has brought Delia to
him in the past, and the present tense of *adducit ... coniungit
... manet* might imply the possibility or hope that she still
does. In return for the mother's service the poet mollifies
his anger towards her daughter. Deception, secrecy, silence
(*tenebris ... clam taciturna ... noctu*), and knowledge (*cognoscit strepitus me ueniente pedum*)[38] combine to give her the
power to bring about the poet's desires (*coniungit ...*). By
acting virtually as his servant (61–2) she empowers him. The
reader's expectations may be further destabilised or entirely
undercut here. Not only is it contrary to the expected role of
the mother actively to arrange and effect an obviously illicit
sexual rendezvous for a man with her own daughter, but the
mother in this case seems more favourable to the affair than
the mistress, who was herself unwilling to comply with the
poet's wishes.[39] In return, the poet wishes her long life (*uiue
diu mihi*), but characteristically qualifies this by admitting his
powerlessness actually to do anything about ensuring this, to
overcome the realities of life and ageing: *proprios ego tecum |
sit modo fas, annos contribuisse uelim* (63–4).

The collapse of past expectation continues in the next line.
The poet's passion for Delia, which has dominated the poem,
is due at all times and forever (*semper*) to his affection for the
mother: *te semper natamque tuam te propter amabo.* Is the

[38] The mother's recognition of the sound also shows that she has done this many
times; Murgatroyd (1980) 202.
[39] Delia's reluctance accords well, of course, with her attitude in earlier elegies. As
Murgatroyd (1980) notes (201), these apparent revelations may also prompt the
reader to reconsider the identity of the *anus* at 1.3.83ff.

poet's continued love for Delia, despite her apparent rejection
of him, simply part of his gratitude to the mother, his side
of the trade-off for her past help (*quicquid agit, sanguis est tamen illa tuus*)? Or, as line 66 suggests, does the common blood
of mother and daughter give him hope that Delia will eventually comply, just as her mother has? Or, does the poet have
other motives behind his attitude towards the mother? This
last possibility is more easily reconciled with earlier suggestions of the poet's attempts to manipulate his direct and in-
direct addressees. In fact, as lines 67ff. suggest, he hopes for
something similar to what he desired from the *coniunx*: *sit
modo casta doce*. *Casta* is defined from the *amor*-determined
perspective of the poet. Delia's chastity in this case would presumably not exclude an adulterous affair with the poet himself.
The possibility thus emerges that the poet's claims of thanks to
the mother[40] were only (or at least largely) intended to butter
her up for the following appeal for her continued assistance.

Another strategy for assimilating the new information given
here to the situation of earlier elegies is to associate the
mother's role here with that of the *lena*.[41] This reading would
maintain Delia's resistance. The poet's promotion of the
mother's role would be explained by her ability to intercede
with Delia through the brokering of the commercial transaction which has been seen in earlier elegies (and not least in
the immediately previous one) to be the only secure means of
achieving a beloved's compliance. On the one hand, this can
be used to support the reading of conscious irony on the
poet's part, bringing out, for example, a possible double
meaning of *aurea* (i.e. 'expensive').[42] But even the reading
of irony here starts to fragment into various uncertain possibilities, as Murgatroyd suggests: 'This interpretation [i.e.
Gaisser's] is possible, but it is hard to prove (esp. in view of
63f.). If there is irony here, most probably it lies in the very

---

[40] The *mater*, like the priestess and Bellona herself, continues the line of powerful
female figures, who significantly outnumber the male figures capable of appreci-
ably affecting things.

[41] For this possibility see André (1965) 71; and Gaisser (1971a) 209–10.

[42] Gaisser (1971a) 210–11.

pretence that Delia's mother is responsible for T.'s mercy and love.'[43] On the other hand, as already observed, the association of *mater* and *lena* can be used to reconcile her role in this elegy with the situation of previous poems. This, of course, like my own reading, is based on the assumption that the reading of each poem is affected by how other poems in the collection are read. But the association of the two roles does not unproblematically resolve the tensions with earlier poems. The presentation of the poet's relationship to the *mater* here is actually in conflict with his relationship with the *lena* in poem five and with his exclusion, more generally, from participation in the monetary transactions which operate in the sphere of *amor*.[44] Despite these reading strategies, the difficulties of securely determining the position of the poet/lover in relation to the *mater* remain.

Fidelity

Et mihi sint durae leges, laudare nec ullam
    possim ego quin oculos appetat illa meos;
et, siquid peccasse putet, ducarque capillis
    immerito pronas proripiarque uias.
non ego te pulsare uelim, sed uenerit iste
    si furor, optarim non habuisse manus.
nec saeuo sis casta metu sed mente fideli;
    mutuus absenti te mihi seruet amor.
at quae fida fuit nulli, post uicta senecta
    ducit inops tremula stamina torta manu,
firmaque conductis adnectit licia telis,
    tractaque de niueo uellere ducta putat.
hanc animo gaudente uident iuuenumque cateruae
    commemorant merito tot mala ferre senem.
hanc Venus ex alto flentem sublimis Olympo
    spectat et infidis quam sit acerba monet.   (69–84)

[43] Murgatroyd (1980) 201.
[44] See Murgatroyd (1980) 201: 'in view of 65f. and the characteristic attitude of the *lena* to T.'s poverty in 1.5, it seems probable that the ref. here is to Delia's mother, who did not act in the capacity of the *lena*.'

Doce, in line 68, raises the possibility of taught knowledge or behaviour being used to restrain, as well as empower. *Quamuis non uitta ligatos | impediat crines nec stola longa pedes* illustrates her lack of restraint in the now familiar terms of hair style and dress. These lines may imply that she is not of the social or legal position to wear such dress, as some critics have suggested.[45] Alternatively, it may simply suggest that she does not submit to the expected social restraints, an interpretation which would perhaps be more suggestive of the disruptive power of the elegiac beloved. The poet desires such restraint to be exerted over Delia, if not over her appearance certainly over her behaviour. In return for this, as a trade-off, the poet gladly submits to similar restraints. In his case these restraints are spoken of in socio-legal terms: *et mihi sint leges, laudare nec ullam | possim ego quin oculos appetat illa meos.* Thus, again, the reader is presented with the familiar trade-off process.[46] Delia is offered power over the poet in return for her submitting to him and no others (as implied by *casta*). Here the power which she is offered is not only violent and physical, but it is also reminiscent of a goddess's[47] power to attack the eyesight of offending mortals in revenge (a threat referred to already in line 24).[48] The poet's passivity and submission to Delia is emphasised in lines 71–2 (*ducar ... pronas proripiarque uias*), even more so because the punishment would be undeserved (*immerito*).

The poet abdicates any power to treat Delia in a similar way. The contract of the relationship is framed in terms which recall the position of the poet/lover as it appeared in earlier elegies. The poet would not have equal rights: *non ego te pulsare uelim.* But he acknowledges the possibility of a force beyond his control which might somehow compel him to dis-

[45] For a discussion of this see Murgatroyd (1980) 203 and 7–8 ; and Williams (1968) 536.

[46] For *lex* used of a contract see *TLL* VII.1242.75ff. and the references given by Murgatroyd (1980) 203.

[47] *Siquid peccasse putet* again represents Delia's power as godlike, not only to be sinned against, but also to avenge even where she only *thinks* she has been sinned against.

[48] It also recalls Bellona's power over her self-mutilating priestess.

regard these terms and attack Delia, another power which (like *Amor*) would place the poet in a powerless and vulnerable position: *sed uenerit iste | si furor*. The punishment which the poet wishes upon himself in such a case recalls the self-mutilation of the Bellona priestess (*optarim non habuisse manus*). This further emphasises the similarities between domination by *Amor* and possession by the goddess of war.

Again, the lines which follow suggest the poet is making such concessions to encourage Delia to comply with his appeals: *nec saeuo sis casta metu sed mente fideli* (75). The importance of unenforced fidelity to the poet could be contrasted with the deception and false appearances which have been a means to power for those employing them throughout the poem. Set against this, hope for Delia's uncoerced faithfulness might be considered a flimsy and comic alternative. In the same way that the ideal which ended the third elegy was destabilised, the prominence of deception and the relationship of Delia to the poet in past elegies cast doubt upon the likelihood of fidelity, let alone its chances of enduring. This reading turns the irony back onto the poet, allowing the reader to reinforce or re-establish his/her position over the deluded poet whose desires depend upon this dubious unenforced chastity. The elegiac text destabilises itself. It encourages a reality to be constructed from it which is then used as the criterion by which that text can be challenged and undermined.[49] The *mutuus amor* which the poet hopes will ensure Delia's fidelity (*seruet*) recalls his wishes for the same in poem two (1.2.65ff.), which in that case seemed ultimately useless. Primarily, the picture of Delia which can be constructed from the poet's own words in this and earlier poems would seem to argue against the possibility of her self-imposed fidelity.

The poet uses another recurrent strategy, a threat,[50] to strengthen his appeal for *fides*. Now he himself takes on the role of prophet. Coming after his desire that Delia's love pre-

[49] Compare again Kennedy (1993) 15ff.
[50] He does this despite his claims that he does not want to force her into fidelity through fear (line 75).

serve her fidelity while he is absent (*absenti*), this recalls the situation in poem three. Lines 77–84 present an inversion of the picture of fidelity painted in a similar position (lines 83ff.) in that earlier poem. Here, too, the description centres on the loom, but the unfaithful woman is now old and powerless. Her age and poverty are emphasised (*post uicta senecta | ... inops*). She is wretched (*flentem*, line 83) and able to exert control only over the loom (lines 79–80). This reflects the powerless position in which Delia's infidelity places the poet, in the same way that the terms of the curse directed at the *lena* in poem five reflected the powerlessness her actions brought upon the poet/lover and inverted her present power. Mocked by young men[51] who may, like the poet himself, have a vested interest in enforcing fidelity through such social restraints as ridiculing the deviant, the once unfaithful old woman is said *merito*[52] *tot mala ferre*. The reason for the punishment here allows room for further irony at the poet's expense, since the threat that the unfaithful will be punished might be thought to discourage precisely that which the poet/lover is trying to encourage: Delia's unfaithfulness to her *coniunx*. Furthermore, the picture of Venus as a vigilant witness (*ex alto ... sublimis Olympo | spectat*), who avenges infidelity on behalf of men such as the poet (*infidis quam sit acerba monet*), recalls the poet's previous misjudgements of her. In poem two he also claimed that she was on his side, whereas later in the same poem she was revealed to be irrational and hostile to him.

Conclusion: exemplum

Haec aliis maledicta cadant. nos, Delia, amoris
exemplum cana simus uterque coma.   (85–6)

While the likelihood of Venus exacting such punishment may be undercut, the final couplet of poem six continues to

---

[51] This recalls the mocking of the poet in poem four with some irony. One day, the poet claims, it will be the powerful beloved who is the one laughed at.
[52] The woman's unfaithfulness contrasts with the behaviour of the poet himself in line 72 who, it is implied, will stay faithful (although 1.5.39ff. might raise some doubt of this).

assert the threat. The poet appeals to Delia not to act in a manner which would call down such a curse upon herself: *haec aliis maledicta cadant*. This final appeal to the beloved might suggest that ultimately, whether the poet's machinations and attempts through his poetry to manipulate or persuade are read as real or ironic, the power to grant or deny his wishes lies with other parties. Centrally this power lies with Delia: *nos, Delia, amoris | exemplum cana simus uterque coma.*[53] This appeal might seem somewhat pathetic, or even ridiculous, given the poet's own opinion of grey-haired love at 1.1.71–2.[54] At any rate, it seems clear that final power rests with Delia. Although he may cajole and threaten, it is to Delia that the poet/lover must finally appeal. The word *exemplum* may also draw attention to the literary nature of this entire elegiac relationship. It might suggest that the purpose of that relationship is to exemplify for readers the forces, situations and processes which it represents. This, in turn, might draw attention to the controlling figure of the author behind this literary construction. The poet/author could be thought of as the force which determines the constitution of the literary work, the 'authority' which orchestrates the reader's struggle to establish meaning from the text. According to this view, the poet/author manipulates the responses of the reader to the literary creation, and in particular the *exemplum* of the central *amor*-relationship itself, just as the poet/lover attempts to manipulate the responses of his addressees throughout the poem. While in the second case the reader is in a knowing position, aware of the poet's stratagems and their ironies, in

---

[53] This may contain a gentle hint that Delia should be more like her mother (i.e. compliant to the poet's wishes), which may in turn prompt the reader to a reassessment of the purpose of the poet's eulogising of the *mater* at 57ff.

[54] Gaisser's reading of *conscious* irony on the part of the poet, however, is not as self-evident as she suggests ('it is clear that Tibullus does not imagine that he and Delia will provide an *exemplum amoris* in their old age' (1971a) 214), and is in no way the only possible reading of these lines. Stroh, at the other extreme, does not see these lines as open to being undercut, despite acknowledging that they are an exception to the depiction of old-age love elsewhere in the collection: 'Nec Tibullus semper contemnit amorem senilem, nam in fine eius elegiae, quae ultima ad Deliam scripta est, haec leguntur (Tib.1, 6, 85sq.)' Stroh (1991) 269. Compare Stroh's discussion of aged love, described elsewhere in the Tibullan collection as foul and ridiculous, (1991) 267–9.

the first the reader her/himself appears as the manipulated and unknowing party. The last couplet may thus add one final twist to the location of authority in the elegy and to the vicissitudes of the reader's position within the power struggles set up by the elegiac text.

The continuous fluctuation of the various power relations in which the poet/lover takes part (poet-*Amor* / poet-*coniunx* / poet-*mater* / and finally poet-Delia) involves the reader in a constant process of re-evaluation; not only re-evaluation of the nature of those relationships, but also of the reader's own position in relation to the poet. Various possibilities oscillate within the text, possibilities from which any reading must actively choose. The negotiation of these possibilities makes any reading vulnerable to being undermined by other or later elements in the text which might promote alternative possibilities or modify the readings taken. The problem of the reader and the text is analogous to the problem of fidelity in the world of elegiac *amor*, seemingly impossible while simultaneously most desired. The reader must question not only the shifting words of the poet, but also the assumptions which the text has encouraged. The reality of the elegiac world is constructed from a text which over its course undermines or fragments that reality. The complications to the reader's control over meaning are further multiplied as the uncertainties surrounding the poet-persona's attempted manipulations of other characters in the text and of his position in relation to them hint at the potential manipulation of the reader by the poet/author. The final couplet brings this last possibility to the surface most clearly. The representation of the elegiac *amor*-relationship as an *exemplum* points to the poetic performance of a controlling poet/author.

POEM SEVEN

Messalla

Critical approaches to the seventh elegy, which at first appears emphatically different from the other elegies in the collection, have concentrated largely on three areas. The first concerns the political views being, or not being, expressed by the elegy, an issue which I will deal with in the conclusion to my study of the collection.[1] The second is concerned with unifying the variety of generic forms[2] and subjects[3] which appear in the poem. This approach often concentrates on relating the Osiris section to the rest of the poem.[4] The uniting of varying elements comes to be seen as a central feature of the elegy and can be related to the third major concern of recent critical approaches, the power of Messalla. The associations of that power and how it is constructed in the poem have been extensively examined,[5] and my reading here draws on these studies in turn. But the exact relation of power as it is constructed in the seventh elegy to the power relations – and the position of the poet – which can be read elsewhere in the collection is largely ignored by earlier critics of the poem.[6] The embedding of this elegy to Messalla within the collection raises questions about the similarities and differences between power as it operates in traditional Roman culture on the one hand, and the networks of power relations formed by the

---

[1] See below, 299ff.
[2] See Luck (1969) 85–6; Bright (1975) 39–45; and Cairns (1979) 171–2.
[3] See Bright (1975) 46; and Leach (1980a) 90.
[4] See, for example, Schuster (1930) 17–25; Klingner (1955) 117–36; Della Corte (1966) 329–37; Alfonsi (1968) 475–6; Gaisser (1971b) 221–9; and Bright (1975) 37–9.
[5] See especially Gaisser (1971b); Bright (1975); Konstan (1978) 173–85; Johnson (1990) 95–113; and Van Nortwick (1990) 115–23.
[6] Although see Leach (1980a) 90–1; and Van Nortwick (1990).

operation of *amor* on the other. It also raises questions about
the relationship of Messalla himself to the construction of
power more generally in the collection, and about the relationship of the poet to his patron.

> Hunc cecinere diem Parcae, fatalia nentes
> stamina non ulli dissoluenda deo:
> hunc fore Aquitanas posset qui fundere gentes,
> quem tremeret forti milite uictus Atur.
> euenere: nouos pubes Romana triumphos
> uidit et euinctos bracchia capta duces;
> at te uictrices lauros, Messalla, gerentem
> portabat nitidis currus eburnus equis.   (1–8)

The seventh elegy begins with the power of the *Parcae*. This
power secures the future – which has now become the present
(*hunc diem*) – with unassailable control: *fatalia nentes | stam-
ina non ulli dissoluenda deo*. Broad questions of power are
immediately raised. There is an echo here of the Parcae's song
in Catullus 64[7] which takes as its subject the ultimate exponent of power in war, Achilles. This may imply that the object
of *this* song possesses power similar to that of Achilles. The
expression of the Parcae's binding power through song
(*cecinere*) raises again the question of poetry/song's ability to
achieve anything effectively. The power of the Parcae's song
contrasts with the efficacy of the poet's song, which has
seemed negligible in previous poems. The ultimate power of
the spinners here also contrasts with the old powerless weaver
of the final lines of the previous poem (*tremula stamina torta
manu*). The continuance of this spinning motif might suggest
a link with the earlier poem. The *ullus deus* may even suggest
the most common *deus* of the collection so far: *Amor*. Given
these associations, then, the opening lines of poem seven
might at first seem to imply an amatory context: that now
(*hunc diem*) the poet/lover is claiming to have succeeded

[7] On the echoes of Catullus 64 here see Elder (1965) 104; and Gaisser (1971b), 223,
who observes a series of allusions which associate Messalla with powerful figures
from myth, history and literature: 'He is an Achilles, a Regillus, a Sosibius, a
Callimachus', Gaisser (1971b) 228.

despite *Amor's* hostility and in contrast to the suggestions of earlier poems.

The lines which follow, however, reveal that power here is being exercised in a military sphere.[8] This might seem to conflict with the poet's repeated rejection of warfare for love. But the mention of *Aquitanae gentes* would probably suggest to the reader that Messalla is the subject here. The military context recalls the reference to Messalla's victories in war at 1.1.53–4, or his departure, probably on campaign, referred to in the opening of poem three. The military power of Messalla is stressed: power over the enemies of Rome (*hunc fore Aquitanas posset qui fundere gentes*). It is a violent power (*forti milite*) which produces fear (*tremeret*), a symptom of powerlessness familiar from the very first elegy.[9] This power is expressed even in terms of control over the geographical features of the conquered area (*uictus Atur*).[10]

Messalla's power has the certainty of fate (*euenere*). It enhances and reflects the political power of the Roman people: *nouos pubes*[11] *Romana triumphos | uidit.* The visual (*uidit*) and physical manifestation of that power over other nations is the triumph: *euinctos bracchia capta duces.* But while these lines refer to a specific military context, they are equally applicable to an amatory one. The state of the captured leaders (line 6) directly recalls the powerless and enchained poet at 1.1.55–6, significantly like the spoils outside Messalla's house (1.1.53–4). This re-emphasises the similarities between the power of *Amor* and that of Messalla, as well as between the situation of the conquered in war, and that of the poet. Power can be seen to work on the same principles in the sphere of *Amor* as in the military/political sphere,[12] where power-relations are just as

---

[8] The Parcae empower the *day*, which is described as effectively exerting the power: *hunc cecinere diem ... hunc fore Aquitanas posset qui fundere gentes ...*

[9] See 1.1.3–4, and above, 29.

[10] This idea is reinforced in the Roman triumphal procession, where representations of rivers from the conquered region would be carried alongside slaves and other booty, as in the triumph of Germanicus over the various German tribes described at Tacitus *Annals* 2.41; see Murgatroyd (1980) 214.

[11] *Pubes*, the technical term for the male population eligible for military service, suggests the military basis of that power.

[12] This raises the possibility that one could be a metaphor of the other.

clearly marked. Messalla, now named, wears the symbols of power (*uictrices lauros*). The chariot which carries him (*portabat nitidis currus eburnus equis*) combines elements of wealth (ivory) and brightness (shining horses and possibly again ivory), which are here associated with the *triumphator*'s power. Messalla's chariot also recalls the chariot of Aurora (at 1.3.93–4). The poet hoped that Aurora's chariot would empower him by bringing the day when he will return to Delia like the god-supported hero which Messalla here seems to exemplify (*Aurora nitentem | Luciferum roseis candida portet equis* 1.3.93–4). This underlines the similarity of the mechanics of power in both situations, while at the same time emphasising the differences between the positions of the central players in each case. A third party, the *Parcae*, seems to empower Messalla (or specifically the *dies*) in a way which the poet, who repeatedly appeals fruitlessly to divine and other power figures for support, also desires in his own situation. The contrast can be drawn between the poet, who is unable to secure the power he desires, and Messalla, who is presented as embodying power. This contrast is reinforced by the involvement of the poet in the unorthodox sphere of *amor*, where traditional roles are inverted, while Messalla functions within the traditional bounds of Roman culture and values.

The previous appearances of Messalla in the collection (in the odd-numbered elegies) have been brief and have set him in contrast both to the poet and to *Amor*. In the first elegy, while Messalla is powerful in his own sphere of warfare, the poet, constrained by *Amor*, operates under a different set of demands (moral and social) which effectively lead him to claim independence from Messalla's power. The rules by which Messalla operates do not apply in the poet's situation: *te bellare decet ... Messalla* (1.1.53). In the third poem the power conflict which is implicit in the first is developed explicitly. Messalla, it is revealed, has had the power to force the poet to comply and to perform *militia*. But it is *Amor* which is finally victorious as the poet is forced by an illness strongly suggested to have been engineered by *Amor* (1.3.21–2) to abandon the expedition. Even without attributing this illness directly to the god, the counter-pull of *amor* is seen in the poet's reluctance to go, and his thoughts only of returning to Delia, not of following Messalla. Finally, all Messalla can do is sail on, powerless to take the poet from *amor's* control: *ibitis . . . sine me, Messalla*. In the fifth poem Messalla appears in the poet's unrealised desires for his life with Delia. Here he is again a powerful figure, to be served by Delia, demonstrating her assimilation into the social milieu within the established set of power relations which Messalla represents. In all three of Messalla's previous 'appearances', the relationship between poet and patron has been determined by *amor's* control over the poet. Here, in the seventh elegy, Messalla is seen as a power figure, ironically, in the same mould as *Amor*. But at the same time he operates in a context – military, social, political – opposed (as in the third poem) to that of *Amor*.

Taking part

Non sine me est tibi partus honos: Tarbella Pyrene
    testis et Oceani litora Santonici,
testis Arar Rhodanusque celer magnusque Garunna,
    Carnutis et flaui caerula lympha Liger.   (9–12)

Against the background of the earlier elegies, the poet's claim at line 9, *non sine me est tibi partus honos*, might come as a surprise, conflicting with the reader's expectations. The poet's avowed preference for the *militia amoris* over the more conventional *militia* might undermine the poet's claim. The unreliability of the poet's words and the fragility of belief in general as it has been shown in the collection so far provide the reader with plenty of scope for mistrust. Furthermore, the conflict between the poet's claim and the situation in previous elegies is emphasised by the specific verbal parallel with the opening of poem three, where Messalla's expedition *was* explicitly *sine me*. If the uncertainties of this statement are suppressed and it is taken as an accurate reflection of the poet/lover's 'reality', it undercuts the definition of his role as lover in opposition to soldier in poems one and three, and re-asserts the greater power of the demands of *militia*, which had up to now remained suppressed by *amor*'s power over the poet.

The problem of reconciling this unexpected and exceptional poem with the other poems in the collection is highlighted by this line, the possibilities it allows, and the various critical strategies employed to explain it. An implicit separation, in the work of critics such as Klingner, Gaisser, Bright, Ball, Konstan, and more recently Johnson,[13] of the 'historical' Tibullus, who is taken to be the direct speaker of poem seven, from the poet-persona of earlier elegies, allows any need to reconcile the tensions between poem seven and the rest of the collection to be dispensed with or ignored. In one respect, the distinction which this approach draws between 'public' poetry in elegy seven and the poetic world of earlier in the collection forms the basis of the contrasts between the power and spheres of operation of the poet/lover and Messalla mentioned above. But it does not prevent interrelation between the poems or render their relationship unproblematic. The emphatic contrast between the poet/lover and Messalla itself draws attention to this interrelation, and the presence of Messalla and the forces he represents in earlier poems explicitly places the patron in the world of the poet/lover (and vice versa). This does not allow the poet of poem seven to be so unproblematically divorced from the poet/lover of earlier poems. Sullivan sees the relationship between the poet's claims here and those elsewhere in the collection as simply demonstrating 'the inconsistency of Tibullus' attitude to war'.[14] Alternatively, the western campaign (referred to in lines 9–12) can be separated from the eastern campaign referred to in poem three. Line 9 of poem seven, therefore, may refer to an earlier experience of *militia* before the poet came under the influence of *amor*'s power.[15] A further possibility

[13] Klingner (1955); Gaisser (1971b); Bright (1975); Ball (1975) 729–44, and (1981) 135–42; Konstan (1978); and Johnson (1990).
[14] Sullivan (1972) 32; see also Little (1982) 311 n.203; and Levin (1982) 497.
[15] The existing *Vita*, which claims Tibullus did take part in a western campaign, is of course much later and cannot be trusted on this point since the biographer's – or his source's – information may in fact be gleaned from the poem itself; and, in any

which could be used to reconcile the 'inconsistency' here was first raised by Jacob Hammer, and has been assimilated into a reading of the collection as a whole by Leach. This is the possibility that it is the poet's poetry which, at least in part, constitutes his share in his patron's *honos*.[16] *Canam* at line 13, for example, might be taken to suggest the power of song[17] to contribute to such *honos* by celebrating the patron's victories. The explicit statement at line 9 that the poet has shared in Messalla's honours in the *past* might, however, suggest that the *present* celebration of Messalla's achievements in poem seven is not part of that share. Likewise, the reasonably brief references to Messalla in poems one and three hardly seem to constitute a poetic celebration which qualifies as a share in his *honos*, and there seems no evidence or even suggestion within this or the earlier poems that some earlier celebratory piece by the poet exists. The various possibilities opened by this line and the poem as a whole add further uncertainty to the poet's position, and destabilise the reader's control over the role by which the elegiac poet is to be defined.

Regardless of these difficulties of interpretation, the poet's statement at line 9 is most obviously an attempt to attach himself to the power figure Messalla.[18] In the process the poet claims for himself some of the power connected, especially in this poem, with his patron's victories. Such a claim, if

case, the reality or otherwise of the historical Tibullus' participation in the campaign is irrelevant to the poet's treatment of those 'facts' in the context of the collection.

[16] For this possibility see Hammer (1925) 70ff.; also Hammer (1926/27) 128. Konstan proposes that the line refers to the poet's participation in the patron's triumph (Konstan (1978) 174), although this pre-supposes the poet's participation in the campaign. Leach sees this poem's place in the collection as 'moving [the] book in the direction of reality', and believes that while the poem 'join[s] together ... many opposites' and 'subtly impos[es] its own ideal order upon reality', by the end of the poem 'the fictional world dissolves wholly into the real', Leach (1980a) 90–1. While differing from my study in her approaches to the collection as an *ars poetica*, Leach does view the issue of control as central and believes that poem seven is part of the movement by which the poet's 'control over his fate ... is at last brought into accord with reality', 93.

[17] This follows the reintroduction of the power of song in potent form in the very first line of the poem.

[18] '[The poet] proceeds to associate himself clearly with Messalla's achievement and public recognition', Galinsky (1969) 77.

accepted, would improve the poet's own position. It would greatly enhance his previously powerless appearance. Thus the poet/lover, unable to possess any power within the amatory sphere, must reach outside that sphere and associate himself with the military, political, social authority and power of Messalla in order to improve his own position. This not uncommon aspect of the patronage relationship (enhancing the position of the client by association with the powerful patron) is thus re-contextualised within the world of the elegiac lover. The tension between this and the poet's earlier claims, and the problem of relating the seventh poem to poems earlier in the collection, could thus be viewed as part of the negotiation of the power dynamic between the poet and the patron, and of the relation of the public sphere in which Messalla operates to the elegiac 'reality' in which the poet/ lover's role is developed.

In support of his claims, the poet calls the regions of Messalla's victories to witness (*testis ... testis*).[19] The geographical allusions (lines 9ff.) also demonstrate the extent of the victories and, on the analogy of *uictus Atur*, suggest that the land, like the people, has been conquered. The power of *Rhodanusque celer magnusque Garunna* enhances the power of those who now have unrivalled dominion over them.[20] Line 13 seems to extend the poet's claim to share in Messalla's *honos. An te, Cydne, canam* suggests an alternative to, or a continuation of, the listing of geographical features at 9–12 which the poet claimed as *testis* of his contribution to Messalla's honour. Later, the poet refers explicitly to the process of authorial choice: *quid referam ...* (17). This might suggest a double power dynamic at work in the poem, between both poet and patron, and poet and reader. The irony

---

[19] Ironically, of course, geographical features cannot talk. Here, however, the poet by using this motif may be attaching his work to a tradition of works celebrating the deeds of great men; see Cicero, *De Or.* 3.167, where a fragment is quoted, probably from Ennius' *Scipio*: *Testes sunt Campi Magni*; and see also Catullus 64.357.

[20] The description of the *Liger* (the modern Loire) as *Carnutis et flaui caerula lympha* may also set up a contrast between the colour (blond and blue) of the conquered and the white brilliance (line 8) of the *uictor*.

that in explicitly asking whether he should tell of the various
details the poet does, of course, tell of them further underlines
the poet's control over the reader, to whom he reveals only
what he chooses.[21] The question *quid referam* may also imply
that these details are already known. But the poet remains in
control over their presentation. He chooses which to emphasise and which not to emphasise (*quid referam*). This gives him
at least some degree of control over the image of Messalla
which the reader receives, and thus over Messalla's reputation. The suggestion that the poet, who is seen to be powerless
in the face of *Amor*, Marathus and Delia,[22] has some even
minor control over the politically, socially and militarily[23]
powerful figure of Messalla would be an unexpected and radi-
cal modification of the poet's power as it was seen in earlier
poems. This might open the further possibility that the claim
of line 9, and its apparent incongruities with the poet's earlier
boasts,[24] be read as humorous. It may be simply another
indication of the poet's ridiculous attempts to associate himself with power, similar to his claims to be supported by
Venus in the second elegy or his enlistment of the authority of
Bellona and her priestess in poem five. Alternatively, the picture of an author in control of the poetic presentation of his
subject suggested by the poet's Pindaric stance here might
validate Leach's judgement that in the seventh poem 'the elegist drops his mask a bit'.[25] This would make suddenly explicit the power dynamic between author and reader which
I have discussed in my readings of earlier poems.[26] Such a
direct intimation of authorial control would destabilise the
reader's superior position over the powerless poet by suggesting that the reader too is being manipulated. It thus points to

[21] The revelation only now of the poet's part in Messalla's western campaign, and
despite the statement of his preference for a life controlled by *amor* rather than one
of *militia* in earlier poems, might illustrate this power of selectivity.
[22] And his poetry was similarly powerless in these cases; see above 151, 176 and 178.
[23] It is military power, of course, which forms the basis of his power in other areas.
[24] See especially *non ego laudari curo* at 1.1.57.
[25] Leach (1980) 90.
[26] See, for example, my reading of the fifth elegy above, especially 156–8, 168–9 and
178–9.

another level of the involvement of this 'public' poem in the construction and operation of power in the collection.

The Nile

> An te, Cydne, canam, tacitis qui leniter undis
> caeruleus placidis per uada serpis aquis?
> quantus et aetherio contingens uertice nubes
> frigidus intonsos Taurus alat Cilicas?
> quid referam ut uolitet crebras intacta per urbes
> alba Palaestino sancta columba Syro?
> utque maris uastum prospectet turribus aequor
> prima ratem uentis credere docta Tyros?
> qualis et, arentes cum findit Sirius agros,
> fertilis aestiua Nilus abundet aqua?
> Nile pater, quanam possim te dicere causa
> aut quibus in terris occuluisse caput?
> te propter nullos tellus tua postulat imbres,
> arida nec pluuio supplicat herba Ioui.   (13–26)

Again the description of the geographical and, now, man-made features in lines 13–22 gives the impression that dominion has been gained not only over these rivers and mountains (*Cydne ... Taurus ... Nilus*) and towns (*crebras urbes ... turribus ... Tyros*), but over the elements which cluster around these in great variety: calm water (*tacitis undis ... placidis aquis*), cold air (*aetherio ... frigidus*), vast ocean (*maris uastum ... aequor*), heat (*arentes ... agros*), and fertility (*fertilis Nilus*). The power of the elements figured in the description enhances the power of those who have dominion over them: i.e. Rome and its representative, Messalla.[27] Taurus is a source of sustenance to the Cilicians (*intonsos Taurus alat Cilicas*);[28] the doves of Syria gain security through the divine power[29] which makes them sacred (*intacta ... sancta co-*

---

[27] And also, perhaps, the author who assimilates them into his poetry.
[28] Again here people are characterised by their hair style (as were the Carnutes at line 12).
[29] The identification of Astarte with Venus may also suggest that the power of love has been brought under this dominion; see Putnam (1973) 121.

lumba); the power of knowledge is imparted by the Tyrians not only through watching the sea (*prospectet*), but by teaching trust[30] in ships (*prima ratem uentis credere docta*); and the Nile demonstrates its power to overcome the violent power of Sirius (*findit agros*).

The description of the Nile at lines 21–2 recalls the poet's desire to avoid the heat of Sirius at 1.1.27–8. It is the god-like power of the Nile which is emphasised in the lines which follow.[31] The poet lacks the knowledge to explain the source of the Nile's power:

> Nile pater, quanam possim te dicere causa
> aut quibus in terris occuluisse caput?   (23–4)

This power (emanating from the *caput*) is maintained through secrecy (*occuluisse*). The flooding of the Nile takes the role of the sort of divine aid which the poet has appealed to in past poems, especially in poem one where those appeals were also set in an agricultural context:

> te propter nullos tellus tua postulat imbres,
> arida nec pluuio supplicat herba Ioui.   (25–6)

The recollection of the forms of power which the poet has desired in previous poems not only emphasises the power of the Nile but contrasts it with the powerlessness of the poet. As the power of the Fates supports Messalla, and Messalla's power supports the *pubes Romana*, so the Nile's power in an agricultural sphere supports the Egyptian people, who are also referred to as *pubes* at line 27, significantly underlining the similarity.

Osiris

> Te canit atque suum pubes miratur Osirim
> barbara, Memphitem plangere docta bouem.

---

[30] The fragility of trust, matched here with the unreliability of seafaring, is a theme familiar from earlier elegies: see above on trust/belief, 86–8, 90–1, 100, 137, 182; and on seafaring above, 115.

[31] This may also reflect the crucial position of Egypt in the Roman Empire.

primus aratra manu sollerti fecit Osiris
et teneram ferro sollicitauit humum.
primus inexpertae commisit semina terrae
pomaque non notis legit ab arboribus.
hic docuit teneram palis adiungere uitem,
hic uiridem dura caedere falce comam.
illi iucundos primum matura sapores
expressa incultis uua dedit pedibus.
ille liquor docuit uoces inflectere cantu,
mouit et ad certos nescia membra modos.
Bacchus et agricolae magno confecta labore
pectora laetitiae dissoluenda dedit.
Bacchus et afflictis requiem mortalibus affert,
crura licet dura compede pulsa sonent.
non tibi sunt tristes curae nec luctus, Osiri,
sed chorus et cantus et leuis aptus amor,
sed uarii flores et frons redimita corymbis,
fusa sed ad teneros lutea palla pedes,
et Tyriae uestes et dulcis tibia cantu
et leuis occultis conscia cista sacris.   (27–48)

Lines 27–8 suggest an exchange (a trade-off) of worship for
the benefits supplied by the Nile's power. Once more it is song
(*te canit*) which is the instrument that releases this power. It is
not necessary to read *suum . . . Osirim* as implying that the
Egyptians worship the Nile as a manifestation of Osiris[32] in
order to see the similarities between the exchange processes in
the cases of the god and the river. The knowledge of the exotic
form of Osiris-worship through the Memphis bull (*Mem-
phitem plangere docta bouem*) enables the Egyptians to exchange this worship for the power Osiris has bestowed upon
humans through a series of innovations (lines 29ff.). The primacy of Osiris in these areas (*primus . . . primus . . . primum*)
emphasises that this knowledge was unavailable before him.
Through his knowledge and skill (*manu sollerti*) he creates
instruments of power over the land (*aratra*). The exertion of

---

[32] For this reading see Murgatroyd (1980) 220–1.

this power is violent, attacking (*ferro*) the defenceless (*teneram*) earth in a line reminiscent of similar attacks on the earth in the *Georgics*,[33] and slaughtering leaves with agricultural weaponry: *uiridem dura caedere falce comam*. The vines are joined to poles, *teneram palis adiungere uitem*, and the grapes are *expressa*. The power of knowledge is continually stressed as Osiris both teaches humans ways of exploiting and controlling nature (*pomaque non notis legit ab arboribus.* | *hic docuit . . .*), and teaches the earth itself to be controlled. Osiris' gift of wine in turn empowers people. The power of *liquor*, described at line 39 and again at 41 by the metonymic name of the god Bacchus,[34] is described as the source of song (*ille liquor docuit uoces inflectere cantu*). The chain of power and the process of empowering developed here, and given emphatic primacy (*primus . . . primus . . . primum*), could be seen as paradigmatic. It recalls the force of Messalla and his deeds, empowered by the *Parcae* which opened the poem, and represents an ideal which the poet himself has hoped to achieve.

Ironically, the wine also controls the partaker (*mouit*). This control, however, brings joy and even an element of certainty as the drinker dances *ad certos modos*. The power of wine as described in lines 39–42 is beneficial to the partaker, overcoming exhaustion, just as the power of the Nile overcomes Sirius' ravaging effects or Messalla overcomes the enemies of Rome:

> Bacchus et agricolae magno confecta labore
> pectora laetitiae dissoluenda dedit.   (39–40)

The power of wine releases the farmers (*dissoluenda*) from the impotence of exhaustion. The appearance of *agricolae* recalls poem one and the poet's desire for a rural life in poem five. Similarly, the power of wine to overcome human affliction at lines 39–40 and at 41 (*Bacchus et afflictis requiem mortalibus affert*) recalls, and seems to be contradicted by, the poet's own failed attempts to be consoled by wine in poems two and five.

---

[33] For example, *Georgics* Bk. 2.22–5 and 367–70.
[34] The description of wine by the conventional name of Bacchus is particularly appropriate given the god-like power of *liquor* in this passage.

That mortals so aided in lines 41-2 are in chains (*crura licet dura compede pulsa sonent*) also recalls the poet's situation, enchained by love, at 1.1.55-6, and that this power of wine has not been available to the poet because of the superior power of *amor* (see especially 1.5.37-8).

This recollection of the poet/lover's position draws attention to the contrast between it and the description of Osiris which follows at lines 43-8. Osiris appears as a lover himself, and although it is *leuis amor*, perhaps implying its fickleness,[35] that love is painless and, unlike the poet's, apparently successful: *non tibi sunt tristes curae nec luctus*. The picture of the ideally in-control lover is enhanced by echoes of the lovers' Elysium pictured by the poet in 1.3.59-66: the *chorus et cantus*, and the *uarii flores*. As in the lovers' Elysium, song is prevalent: *dulcis tibia cantu*. The adornment of Osiris at lines 45-7 as a Dionysian god[36] highlights the combination of powerful agricultural benefactor and powerful lover in the one divine figure.[37] The poet, too, has been seen both as would-be farmer (in poems one and five) and as lover.[38] His failure in both cases (because of the greater power of *amor* and thus of his beloveds) contrasts with Osiris, just as the poet's powerlessness in general contrasts with Messalla's power. This suggests that, in both the agricultural and amatory aspects of Osiris, the poet may be constructing ideals according to his own aspirations, and that, like his agricultural pretensions in the first elegy and the fifth, these aspirations are essentially determined by *amor*. Like the powerful Nile, the source of Osiris' power is protected by secrecy (*et leuis occultis conscia*

---

[35] The fickleness might, in fact, be on Osiris' part. *Leuis amor* would thus suggest a lack of obsessive enslavement to *amor* which may be the key to Osiris' success.

[36] Osiris has already been identified with Bacchus through the invention of wine at lines 35ff.

[37] Osiris is also a male power figure in contrast to his sister Isis, whose female power is referred to in poem three.

[38] The similarities are perhaps not surprising to the reader, since there has already been an attempt at a link between the poet (or at least his aspirations) and Osiris in poem three with the presentation of Delia's appeal to Isis. There the separation of the two divine lovers echoed the separation of the poet and Delia and reflected the poet's hope that, like Osiris and Isis, he and Delia would be reunited through her faithfulness. In that case too there appeared to be a gulf between the aspiration and reality.

cista sacris), which is also a source of power in love, as has been clearly seen in the previous poem and earlier elegies in the collection.

Not only is the power of Osiris comparable to Messalla's, but it is set in the context of Messalla's dominion over Osiris' homeland (as its inclusion within the sequence of conquered lands from line 9 onwards suggests). Messalla has dominion over the barbarians (*barbara*, line 28) of Egypt. But ironically, through the poet's choice and manipulation of motifs and subject matter, Messalla's power is seen in relation to a foreign god's power. What's more, the importance of *amor* (along with an overtly agricultural, non-military context) is returned to the foreground despite the apparent conflict between the political/social sphere of Messalla and *amor*'s sphere of control. In contrast to the poet/lover in previous elegies, however, Osiris is in control over *amor* rather than controlled by it, complementing the ideal military and political superiority of Messalla with a detached superiority in love.

Celebration

Huc ades et Genium ludis Geniumque choreis
    concelebra et multo tempora funde mero.
illius et nitido stillent unguenta capillo,
    et capite et collo mollia serta gerat.
sic uenias, hodierne: tibi dem turis honores,
    liba et Mopsopio dulcia melle feram.
at tibi succrescat proles quae facta parentis
    augeat et circa stet ueneranda senem.
nec taceat monumenta uiae quem Tuscula tellus
    candidaque antiquo detinet Alba Lare.
namque opibus congesta tuis, hic glarea dura
    sternitur, hic apta iungitur arte silex.
te canat agricola a magna cum uenerit Vrbe
    serus inoffensum rettuleritque pedem.
at tu, Natalis, multos celebrande per annos,
    candidior semper candidiorque ueni.   (49–64)

The poet explicitly brings Osiris and Messalla (or, in particular, Messalla's Genius) together at what the reader now clearly sees is a birthday celebration:[39] *huc ades et Genium ludis Geniumque choreis | concelebra.* The echoes of the lovers' Elysium here underline the fact that *ludi* and *choreae* are as appropriate to the ideal situation for the lover as they are for the manifestation of military power in the triumph.[40] Similarly the shining hair (*nitido capillo*), which recalls the brightness of the *uictor* at line 8, is appropriate to the Dionysian-Osirian lover (*nitido stillent unguenta capillo*); and the *mollia serta* could as easily be the garlands in Venus' temple or on Delia's door as those around the neck of the *uictor*'s Genius. The description of the birthday celebration brings all these aspects together. The world of *amor* and the world of the Roman public celebration are merged, just as Osiris (the foreign lover/god) is called upon to join with the Genius of the great and powerful Roman general in celebration at lines 49ff. This fusion is reflected in the uncertainty concerning which god is being addressed in these lines. The addressee at line 49 seems most likely to be Osiris, following on from the immediately previous lines, but the identity of the deity addressed at line 53 is more doubtful.[41] The non-specific nature of the address allows it to be applied to Osiris, the Genius or Natalis, and serves to blur their identities and functions together. The poet's appeal for the presence and power of this unspecified deity at line 53 (*sic uenias hodierne*) is set in the terms of the usual process. It directly recalls the kinds of offerings made by the poet in poem one in the hope that divine power would

---

[39] On the delayed revelation of the poem's function as a birthday celebration see Bright (1975) 32.

[40] There is, however, a contradiction, or at least a tension, between the cultural and military power of Osiris and Messalla, and the pre-technological, pre-power-struggle world of the Golden Age as presented in poem three (or even the poet's ideal rural life with Delia in poem five). This may raise the question of how well these figures fit into the poet's ideals as previously expressed. Of course the ideal results of the poet's aspirations to the sort of power embodied by Osiris or Messalla, or to a Golden Age world, would mean essentially the same thing: a removal of his powerlessness, either through a growth in power or an end to the necessity for power struggle altogether.

[41] On the difficulties of establishing the identity of the addressees here see Murgatroyd (1980) 226–9.

be granted for his benefit: *tibi dem turis honores,* | *liba et Mopsopio dulcia melle feram.* These *honores,* given by the poet for the sake of Messalla, are the divine equivalent of Messalla's *honos* which the poet claims he contributes to at lines 9ff. The public equivalent of this is the triumph, the Roman people's trade-off to Messalla for the exertion of his power on their behalf.

Such power relations and exchanges exist also within the family (lines 55–6). The children growing in their own power, as the poet wishes of Messalla's children (*tibi succrescat proles*), in turn increase the father's power through reputation (*facta parentis* | *augeat*),[42] and themselves honour him in old age (*circa stet ueneranda senem*). The *facta* or *monumenta* (as at lines 57ff.) which empower or benefit others in the social sphere also enhance the benefactor's honour and reflect on his power: *nec taceat monumenta uiae* ... Appropriately, one of the points along the road which Messalla repairs (*candida* ... *Alba*) recalls the brightness associated with the *uictor* earlier in the poem. In the reconstruction of the road Messalla appears, like Osiris, to contribute his power/wealth (*opibus* ... *tuis*) and skill (*arte*) for the security of others (the safety of the farmer at lines 61–2 whose *pes* will be *inoffensus*). Again an *agricola* is the beneficiary of Messalla's gift here, as was the case with Osiris' gift of wine at line 37. The presence of the farmer in the context of Tusculum may seem contrived, since the area was primarily known for its rich villas where wealthier Romans might retreat *a magna urbe* rather than for its peasant farmers. This might open up tensions in the assimilation of various potentially conflicting elements which critics have observed in the poem.[43] The presence of a farmer in a suburban setting may point to the artificiality of Messalla's link with Osiris and the rural world, or of the poet's aspirations to include Messalla and his world in a stable rural milieu relatively free of discordant power struggle and in line with the poet's own rural ideals. These tensions have been highlighted in relation

---

[42] This interpretation of the phrase *facta parentis augeat* follows Postgate (1922) 97.
[43] See Leach (1980a) 90; and Bright (1975) 46.

to both the fifth poem and the seventh by Van Nortwick. He argues that these tensions are inherent in Messalla's 'presence in the pastoral world[, a presence which] is always potentially destructive', and concludes that 'Tibullus was keenly aware of the fragility of his dream, and of the paradoxes that lay at the center of that dream.'[44] In the case of the road, the exertion of this power is again described in harsh, even violent, terms (*congesta ... hic glarea dura | sternitur, hic ... iungitur ... silex*). Most strikingly, the *uia* has been described throughout the collection as an instrument for the aggressive acquisition of power. It has always appeared as a channel for military and commercial ventures, directly opposed to the rural world (compare especially 1.1.25ff.).

The association of Osiris and Messalla continues at line 61 as *te canat* recalls line 27, linking the praising of Osiris and the praising of Messalla. This highlights once more the process of exchange, which is similar in each case. Power is exerted in return for honours/praise/veneration. This includes the honour and praise available from poetry which, in turn, has the power to enhance the reputation and thus social standing or power of the individual. The elegy ends with an example of such poetic veneration (lines 63–4). The poet desires that the brightness associated in this poem with victory and power, and here attributed to Messalla's *Natalis*, increase with the years (*candidior candidiorque*).

Conclusion

The seventh elegy brings into direct and explicit contact the broader networks of power relations and exchanges in the military, political, social and agricultural/geographical spheres, and draws attention especially to the specific power relation of the poet and Messalla. Goldhill in his study of fame in archaic Greek lyric, focusing on Ibycus fr.263 (Page), writes: '"To what degree is the *kleos* of the subject of the poem subject to the *kleos* of the poet/poem?" is a question raised by the final

[44] Nortwick (1990) 123.

lines of Ibycus' poem and replayed again and again in the encomiastic literature of Greece and Rome.'[45] The poet of Tibullus 1.7, by suggesting the place of praise and similar *honos* in the power exchange between client and patron (or beneficiary and benefactor), claims some power for himself and his poetry. In the process he more closely defines the relationship of poet and patron as a reciprocal power-exchange. This also draws out the role of the poet/author as the constructor of praise, and of the text more generally; it suggests more explicitly than in previous elegies the dependence of the *reader* on the poet's words for the construction of meaning, just as the patron might depend, at least partly, on the poet's words for the construction and dissemination of his fame. The power of the poet/author here is thus asserted on several interrelated levels.

But the focus of the poem is the power of Messalla, as Johnson has observed: 'Power in the service of the *res publica*'.[46] Messalla himself is represented as an ideal power figure in military, political and social terms, even assimilating (although not without tension and contradiction) the power of the ideal divine farmer/lover through his association with Osiris. Osiris, with whom Messalla is linked,[47] provides an ideal representation of the power, security and pleasure in love (in a rural context) which the poet/lover has been seen to desire without success. It is an ideal constructed by the poet, which conforms well with the desires and preoccupations of the poet/lover in earlier poems.[48] The power of Messalla is echoed in the powers of the Fates, the Nile, Osiris, and wine, which chart chains of power gained by one figure from another back to the apparently arbitrary and unassailable will of the *Parcae*, or the mysterious source of the Nile. Messalla emerges as a power figure in complete contrast to the appa-

---

[45] Goldhill (1991) 119.

[46] Johnson (1990) 105.

[47] For more on the association of Osiris and Messalla see Gaisser (1971b) 221ff.; and Bright (1975) 46.

[48] Compare the conclusion of Leach: 'These alliances and assimilations exist only within the fictional world of the poem which has thus subtly imposed its own ideal order upon reality', Leach (1980a) 91.

rently powerless figure of the poet seen in earlier poems. Given Messalla's association with the poet's picture of the lovers' Elysium in poem three and his dream of a rural life with Delia in poem five, the power of the patron here may represent an ideal which the poet, in some ways, aspires to.

The poem's blending of Roman public and military affairs, the rural world (and the physical world in general), and the sphere of love suggests similarities in the operation of power in all of these areas. The poem's collapsing of distinctions between these spheres has drawn the attention of several critics. Konstan points to 'Man's violence against innocent nature'[49] which is inherent to Osiris' rural power, just as violence is the basis of Messalla's military power. Gaisser, similarly, points out that the peaceful achievements in the poem depend on power achieved through violence: 'the road-building itself, however emblematic of peace, cannot be completely dissociated from war, for it was paid for out of Messalla's booty (*opibus congesta suis* 59)'.[50] The pervading language of power and control, which I have attempted to highlight in my reading of the poem, suggests that the operation of power cuts through such distinctions as war and peace. A common dynamic of power unites all these otherwise distinct categories. This adds significance to the critical assertion that the poem involves 'the joining together of many opposites'.[51] The bringing together of these various elements within the dominion of Rome and under the auspices of the unifying figure of Messalla 'who brings order out of parts'[52] sets up the Roman state as the ultimate exponent of this culture of power struggle.

But while, on the one hand, Roman power and Messalla, '*Romanitas* incarnate',[53] could be thought of as absorbing all else within the realities of power which they are seen to represent and exploit, on the other Messalla himself can be assimilated into the world of elegiac *amor*. As Van Nortwick has observed of Messalla's appearance both in poem five and

---

[49] Konstan (1978) 183.   [50] Gaisser (1971b) 228.   [51] Leach (1980a) 90.
[52] Bright (1975) 46.   [53] Johnson (1990) 95.

in the seventh elegy, the patron is associated with the role of the lover through the sexual symbolism of Delia's attitude towards the patron in the poet's ideal of poem five,[54] and the sexual connotations of the portrait of Osiris,[55] who is linked with Messalla in the seventh elegy: 'Both here and in poem 1.5, the poet brings Messalla into the tender world of love elegy.'[56] This view sees Messalla as a lover, albeit an ideally powerful one (more like the *diues amator* than the powerless and passive poet). But it is also possible to view the patron in the role of the beloved. This similarity, which has already been suggested by 1.1.53–6 and the similar demands made of the poet by both patron and beloved in poem three, is evident in the almost identical terms in which the power of patron and beloved are constructed. The association of Messalla with the power of a god, not only through links with Osiris, but through the association of the *triumphator* with Jupiter,[57] parallels the links of the beloved with divine power. Other related verbal parallels, such as the garlands of Messalla's Genius recalling the garlands of Delia's door, reinforce this link.

But the positions of the patron and the beloved are linked more conclusively through the relation of the poet to them. The construction of the relationship in terms of an exchange is common to both. As the poet offers his service and submission to the beloveds in the hope of receiving their compliance in return, so in poem seven he offers the celebration of Messalla's power and, in exchange, associates himself with that power and the construction of the patron's fame. This accords well with the similarity of the power relationships between poet and beloved and between poet and patron suggested by previous elegies.[58] In this context, the poem celebrating the patron would fit easily with the other elegies as

---

[54] Van Nortwick (1990) 116–17.

[55] Ibid. 118.

[56] Ibid. 119, although his conclusion on why the poet does this ('in an attempt to draw creative, fertile energy from the great world of Roman manhood') is vague and unconvincing.

[57] See Versnel (1970) 56–93.

[58] See above 48, 109 and 130.

another poem directed at another 'beloved'. While the similarities in the construction and operation of power link the seventh elegy with earlier elegies, and the world of Roman power with that of elegiac *amor*, the question of which of these is to be privileged as the principal sphere of that power is left open. Is Messalla to be absorbed into the paradigm of power represented by the elegiac beloved, or is the power of *amor* to be seen as just part of the culture of power struggle dominated by, or even identified with, the *Romanitas* which the patron represents? The negotiation of this issue one way or another reveals, in turn, the reader's own involvement in the construction of power in the collection. This suggests another level of the elegiac contest (beloved of critics) between the traditional demands of Roman society and the imperatives of elegiac *amor*.[59]

[59] For a representative critical view of this contest see Lyne (1980) 68ff.

POEM EIGHT

Knowledge

Wimmel, in his reading of the eighth poem, has traced the way that the text demands continual re-evaluation as new information realigns the reader's understanding of the poet's words.[1] Cairns similarly focuses on the 'technique of delayed information'[2] and the reader's struggle with it in the effort to establish final meaning. But both ultimately reach a point in their readings where an overview or reconstruction of the poem can be established.[3] The elegy, however, destabilises even this sort of attempt to gain final control over the meaning of the text. In examining this process of destabilisation, a parallel can be established with another focus of critical attention in the poem, the poet's assumed role of *magister* (or *praeceptor*) *amoris*.[4] The parallel between these two central areas of concern for critics of the poem emphasises the interrelation of knowledge and power, both in the position which the poet attempts to establish for himself and in the reader's relationship to the text.

> Non ego celari possum quid nutus amantis
>   quidue ferant miti lenia uerba sono,
> nec mihi sunt sortes nec conscia fibra deorum,
>   praecinit euentus nec mihi cantus auis:
> ipsa Venus magico religatum bracchia nodo
>   perdocuit, multis non sine uerberibus.

---

[1] Wimmel (1968) 49–80. He calls this process '[die] schrittweis[e] Exposition des Gedichts'.

[2] Cairns (1979) 147.

[3] See Wimmel (1968) 76–80; Cairns (1979) 150–1.

[4] See Cairns (1979) 138 and 147ff.; Murgatroyd (1977) 114–15; also Wheeler (1910) and (1911).

desine dissimulare: deus crudelius urit
quos uidet inuitos succubuisse sibi.
quid tibi nunc molles prodest coluisse capillos
saepeque mutatas disposuisse comas?
quid fuco splendente genas ornare? quid ungues
artificis docta subsecuisse manu?
frustra iam uestes, frustra mutantur amictus
ansaque compressos colligat arta pedes.
illa placet, quamuis inculto uenerit ore
nec nitidum tarda compserit arte caput.   (1-16)

In the opening lines the poet claims for himself knowledge
in the sphere of love. Ironically, this is described in terms of
powerlessness (*non ... possum*), which perhaps suggests that
the poet had no control over his acquisition of that knowledge; he has it whether he likes it or not. The recollection in
this opening of the secret signs between lovers which the poet
has already claimed to be master of in the sixth poem (1.6.19–
20; compare also 1.2.21–2) might suggest that this poem, too,
is concerned directly with the poet's own amatory affairs,
possibly, as in poems six and two, involving Delia. In these
opening lines of poem eight, the poet again sets up the conflict
between knowledge and deception which has already been
drawn in the context of *furtiuus amor* in previous poems of the
collection. He claims a power to understand secret communi-
cations. This power, in lines 3–4, is compared to the conventional divine/magical[5] power of prophecy (*sortes ... fibra ...
cantus auis*). The poet's knowledge, however, is gained from a
different, unconventional source. This source is Venus' power
over the poet: *ipsa Venus magico[6] religatum bracchia nodo |
perdocuit*. His arms (*bracchia*) are bound, like a military captive (compare 1.7.6), but his sufferings (*multis non sine uer-
beribus*), which recall the slave-like position he has been
placed in by love's power at 1.1.55–6 and elsewhere, have
brought him knowledge.

[5] This recalls the priestess of Bellona's prophecy of *euentus* concerning *Amor* (compare 1.8.4 and 1.6.50).
[6] The reference to magic here recalls the power of the *saga* in poem two.

This is the now familiar trade-off, a process delineated in the very first lines of the collection and repeatedly after that. Some measure of power is gained in return for suffering and lack of control. The knowledge he has obtained seems to place the poet in a superior position to the person he now addresses: *desine dissimulare* (7). For once, it seems, the exchange has been completed and the poet has achieved some power from it. With the command, *desine dissimulare*, the poet asserts his power to see through any dissimulation. Again, the recollection of the deceits and infidelity of Delia in previous poems may suggest that she is the addressee here. In the erotic context the picture of a malicious, avenging god (a *deus* who *crudelius urit*) suggests *Amor*. This is a god who, like the poet, sees through pretence (*uidet*) and punishes (*urit*) those who do not willingly submit to his power (*inuitos succubuisse*). As with similar threats in earlier poems, this could suggest a warning to the uncompliant mistress to succumb willingly[7] or face punishment from the vengeful god.[8] Any attempt by the beloved to stand up to the power of the god would see *Amor* finally triumphant, like a master torturing a disobedient slave (compare *urit* to *ure* at 1.5.5). The superior position which the poet's claim of hard-won knowledge gives him adds authority to this statement. Comparison with similar tactics in earlier elegies, both the claims of knowledge in poem six and the use of threats throughout the previous poems, might suggest that this claim of authority is part of the poet's overall strategy to gain the compliance of the addressee. As such, it is open to being undermined by the apparent failure of such strategies in past elegies or to being itself refigured as a deception. As in the opening lines of the fifth elegy, the opposition set up at the outset of poem eight between deception and truth is open to being broken down.

Just as dissimulation is useless to the addressee, so too is the attempt to create a false, more attractive (and thus more

---

[7] Thus *Amor*'s power would be employed for the poet's benefit.

[8] *Crudelius* also suggests that, while the unwilling will be worse treated, even those who come under love's sway willingly are treated badly.

powerful) physical appearance (lines 9–14). *Quid ... prodest*
recalls the supposed uselessness of wealth without love at
1.2.78 (*quid ... prodest*), and the attempt to control personal
appearance (*coluisse*; *disposuisse*) results in the same powerlessness (note the emphatic repetition of *frustra ... frustra*). It
only results in inconstancy (*saepeque mutatas ... mutantur*),
suggesting uncertainty and insecurity, as well as fickleness. It
is seen as a kind of deception (*artificis* 12). Ironically perhaps,
given the poet's own claims, knowledge (*docta ... manu*) is
also finally useless. The attempted manipulation of personal
appearance is portrayed as a struggle, in language equally
descriptive of armies, battle (*disposuisse ... colligat*) and violent force (*compressos*). There may also be a suggestion of the
force used by the farmer to control the land:[9] *docta subsecuisse manu* (compare *facili ... manu* 1.1.8).

The close reminiscence of Propertius 1.2.1–8 may lead any
reader familiar with that poem to suspect that the addressee
here is likewise the poet's mistress adorning herself for the
sake of rivals. Following this reading, *illa placet* may point to
another woman whose contrasting behaviour is meant by the
poet as an example to the addressee. Such a woman is a
powerful attracting force, offering the possibility of pleasure
(*placet*), without the extra and useless power of art (*inculto ...
ore* line 15; *arte* line 16),[10] and without the false splendour
(*nitidum caput*; like *fuco splendente* at 11) which contrasts with
the true brightness surrounding figures of power in the immediately previous poem. The similarities shared with the Propertian passage might suggest that the addressee is adorning
herself to attract rivals for the sake of gain (see *uendere* at
Prop.1.2.4), as might the past behaviour of Delia. But the
suggestion of Tib.1.8.7–8 also encourages the possibility that
the addressee is now in love and is adorning herself to attract
her own beloved. The ability of the poet to see through dissimulation, to spot these adornments and trace their cause, is
of course a practical example of the knowledge gained from

---

[9] Compare the first elegy and the echoes of the *Georgics* there; see above, 32–3.
[10] Compare Propertius 1.2.8ff.

experience claimed at lines 1–6. The powerlessness of the addressee (*frustra*) ironically recalls the 'advisor's' own (*frustra*) at 1.5.67. More than simply 'delaying information',[11] the text seems to suggest several distinct possibilities to the reader.

Identities

Num te carminibus, num te pallentibus herbis
    deuouit tacito tempore noctis anus?
cantus uicinis fruges traducit ab agris,
    cantus et iratae detinet anguis iter,
cantus et e curru Lunam deducere temptat,
    et faceret si non aera repulsa sonent.
quid queror, heu, misero carmen nocuisse? quid herbas?
    forma nihil magicis utitur auxiliis,
sed corpus tetigisse nocet, sed longa dedisse
    oscula, sed femori conseruisse femur.   (17–26)

At lines 17ff. the poet considers whether the addressee is controlled by an *anus* (18), a *saga*, but it is still unclear what that control consists of. The instruments of supposed control are familiar from the picture of the *saga* in poem two (*carminibus ... herbis ... deuouit*). Again the emphasis is on the power of song (*cantus ... cantus ... cantus*), recalling the poet's own contrasting failure to achieve anything through song (compare in particular *canimus frustra* 1.5.67). Again this power works through secrecy and obscurity (*tacito tempore noctis*). It is described in terms of power over natural forces, again with strong suggestions of deceit and theft (*uicinis fruges traducit ab agris*). It is also described in terms of control over passions (*iratae detinet anguis iter*), and in its power over the moon (*e curru Lunam deducere temptat*)[12] it is seen as taking part in a power struggle with the potentially more powerful *aera repulsa*.[13] The poet's raising of the initial question (*num*

---

[11] See Cairns (1979) 147ff.

[12] This may suggest power over chastity (a distinguishing quality of Diana/Luna) as well as a power which rivals that of a god, Luna.

[13] The opposition of noise (*sonent*) to secrecy and silence also suggests the conflict of deceit and knowledge.

... *num* 17–18) and the picture of the power of magic which
follows suggest that he is searching for the source of power
which has caused the addressee's behaviour (*te ... te*). But
what are the ultimate aims of that behaviour? Its direct manifestations (lines 9–16) could as easily be aimed at the poet's
rivals (to attract paying customers) as at one particular beloved. Similarly, the poet's statement at lines 7–8, by analogy
with his practice in past poems, might as easily be a knowing
threat as a knowing statement of what has already occurred.
The opening lines (1–2) might suggest the former, that the
poet has detected something, but this could still be understood
as a general statement of the poet's expertise in love. Read in
the light of the picture of Delia at 1.6.17ff., the poet's statement at 1.8.1–2 might not necessarily imply a single *loved* one,
but possibly one or several suitors for whom the addressee
feels less than the all-controlling obsessive love which the
comparison with bewitchment suggests. The poet has claimed
the power of magic to bring such a love (*mutuus amor*) at
1.2.65, although there it seemed finally powerless to do so in
Delia's case. This recollection might suggest that the poet is
deluded here as well.

But the lines which resolve some of these ambiguities also
create others, and, casually, state something for which the
reader has not been prepared. While confirming that *carmina*
and *herbae* are not, in the poet's opinion, the powers responsible for the damage (*nocuisse*), *misero* reorganises the reader's
understanding of the preceding lines as completely as the now
apparently male addressee changes his hairstyle and cloak at
lines 10 and 13. It now seems that the poet is speaking purely
as an advisor. He has taken up the role of *magister amoris*
which he tried to adopt, and failed to maintain, at the end of
poem four (a link which might undermine his claims in *this*
poem). In this case, however, the poet claims that his knowledge comes not from a set of *praecepta* given to him, but from
his own experience. The naming of Venus as the source in
both cases, however, might collapse this distinction, and suggest that the two sets of knowledge are synonymous. More
significantly, it now appears that the addressee's position is

similar to the poet's own in previous poems. This lends greater specificity to the poet's claim at lines 5–6. The poet has already learned from experience what the addressee is going through now. Furthermore, the suggestion that the addressee has been dissimulating (*desine dissimulare*) can now be related more securely to the poet's opening claims: the addressee has attempted to hide the fact that she or he is in love, but the poet's own hard-won powers of discernment have overcome the pretence. Lines 7–8 can now be re-read as a knowing summary of what the addressee has already undergone (or, rather, is already undergoing) apparently unwillingly. The possibility is now raised that *illa* at line 15 refers to the addressee's beloved, whose own behaviour contrasts with the addressee's elaborate attempts to gain her favour by adorning himself. The power struggle which this re-reading suggests, between the addressee and his beloved, is similar to that of the poet and his beloved, even if the methods may not be. In this power struggle the *puella*'s power, which the poet asserts is stronger than magic (*nihil magicis utitur auxiliis*), stems from the possibility of sexual pleasure she represents:

> Forma nihil magicis utitur auxiliis,
> sed corpus tetigisse nocet,[14] sed longa dedisse
> oscula, sed femori conseruisse femur.   (24–6)

This complicated realignment of the reader's understanding of the dramatic situation of the poem and the roles being fulfilled by the poet, the addressee and the mysterious *illa* of line 15 may contribute, and has been taken by critics such as Cairns[15] to contribute, to a more secure control over the meaning of the poem. But that realignment, by undercutting the assumptions which the text has up until now encouraged, might rather emphasise the reader's lack of control over the meaning of the text. This might leave the reader uncertain of any reading taken from the text, in that it is liable to be

---

[14] Again *amor* is described as a harmful force, recalling the poet's own sufferings.
[15] 'Only at lines 23ff. does it become clear that the addressee is a former beloved boy who is in love with *illa* and whose cosmetics, once useful in attracting male lovers, do not impress the girl whom he now loves.' Cairns (1979) 139.

destabilised at any point. The potential for uncertainty is heightened by the further ambiguities which these lines create. A question may be raised, for instance, as to whether all the preceding lines were addressed to the same figure. If not, who is the other addressee – the male figure's beloved? And where does the address to one stop and the address to the other begin – line 9? line 7? The reader's control over this text still remains particularly tenuous.

Indeed, just as the dramatic situation of the poet and addressee has apparently been resolved, the addressee changes (at line 27) to the figure in whose power the original addressee now is (*nec tu difficilis puero tamen esse memento*). But, again casually, the word *puero* further re-aligns the reader's understanding, this time by opening rather than closing possibilities. The effeminate[16] nature of the addressee's behaviour at lines 9ff. might have suggested a *puer* of the type in poem four, a view which might be strengthened by the poem's other reminiscences of the fourth elegy, especially the poet's role as *magister amoris*. But a concern for hair, clothes, footwear and appearance were also marks of all of the poet's rivals competing to win Delia at 1.6.39–40. Now that a *puer* is specified, however, the reader may remember the poet's position in poem four, and question the exact relationship of poet and *puer* here. Whether or not it is assumed at this stage that the *puer* is Marathus himself,[17] the boy is now ironically in the same position with the *puella* as the poet was with a boy in the fourth elegy.

Déjà vu

Nec tu difficilis puero tamen esse memento;
    persequitur poenis tristia facta Venus.
munera nec poscas; det munera canus amator
    ut foueat molli frigida membra sinu.

---

[16] On the effeminate characteristics of the addressee here see Murgatroyd (1980) 239.
[17] However, the fact that the poet (at the end of poem four) showed no signs of escaping Marathus' power might easily suggest this.

carior est auro iuuenis cui leuia fulgent
    ora nec amplexus aspera barba terit.
huic tu candentes umero suppone lacertos
    et regum magnae despiciantur opes.   (27–34)

The similarity of the *puer*'s position and the poet's relationship with Delia is further underlined. The poet's appeal to
the *puella* not to be *difficilis* recalls his experience with the
difficilis ianua at 1.2.7. So too, the threat of Venus' punishment is a technique he has also used (with a significant lack of
success) against Delia and those who keep her from him (see
1.5.56–7). Line 28 suggests a legalistic trade-off: no *tristia
facta* brings no *poena*.[18] But the failure of Venus' power to
support the poet when he has claimed her as an authority in
the past (see 1.2.81ff.),[19] and her apparent disregard for such
rational processes[20] as this (see 1.2.99–100),[21] might undercut
the claim that *persequitur poenis tristia facta Venus*. It is precisely in the sphere of Venus' power that such processes have
been seen to collapse.

Lines 29ff. recall the poet's own position in poems two and
five, where Delia favours a *diues amator*, and the expressions
of Priapus in the fourth elegy. The poet appeals against the
use of a financial transaction as the trade-off for the *puella*'s
compliance: *munera nec poscas*. Such a trade-off is more appropriate to the *canus amator* (29–30) who has nothing else to
offer (only *frigida membra*). In such a case only the old man
would gain a benefit (*ut foueat*) from the sexual exchange, and
thus must use money as his side of the trade-off. The *puer*,
however, has a better (*carior*) currency to exchange in his
beauty.[22] Both money and beauty fulfil the same role in the
trade-off. It is significant that, like gold, the boy's beauty is

---

[18] Punishment can thus be seen as the other side of the familiar reward-for-service
    process.
[19] See above, 96.
[20] This is suggested by her apparently unmerited 'punishment' of the poet in the
    second poem.
[21] See above, 98–9.
[22] The poet is practical and does not expect the *puer* to have no rivals, perhaps
    because he is not directly involved himself and can be more cold and pragmatic.
    He himself, of course, wanted exclusive rights to Delia (poems two and five).

described as shining (*fulgent*), just as the *puella* has *candentes lacerti* at line 33. But in the case of the *iuuenis* pleasure would be exchanged for pleasure. It is emphasised that with the *puer* there would be no discomfort (*nec amplexus aspera barba terit*). This is a superior exchange to one involving wealth, or so the poet, who has himself suffered from the preference for wealthy lovers, asserts to the *puella*:

> huic tu candentes umero suppone lacertos
> et regum magnae despiciantur opes.   (33–4)

There is a direct parallel between line 34 here and the final line of the first elegy (*dites despiciam*). But whereas in the first elegy the poet's desire to discard wealth in favour of rural *paupertas* was revealed to be effectively engineered by *amor*'s influence over him, here a clear choice is set up between sexual pleasures, which the poet considers superior, and wealth. This proverbial,[23] moral language (*regum magnae despiciantur opes*) ironically asserts (as in poem one) an *amor*-determined moral code. It is not because of any intrinsic moral worthlessness of wealth that the poet asserts this position, but because sexual pleasure is viewed as *relatively* superior. The preference of *puellae* for wealth in earlier poems, however, might undermine his hopes in this apparently similar case.

> At Venus inuenit puero concumbere furtim,
>   dum timet et teneros conserit usque sinus,
> et dare anhelanti pugnantibus umida linguis
>   oscula et in collo figere dente notas.
> non lapis hanc gemmaeque iuuant quae frigore sola
>   dormiat et nulli sit cupienda uiro.
> heu sero reuocatur amor seroque iuuentas
>   cum uetus infecit cana senecta caput.
> tum studium formae est; coma tum mutatur ut annos
>   dissimulet uiridi cortice tincta nucis;
> tollere tum cura est albos a stirpe capillos
>   et faciem dempta pelle referre nouam.

---

[23] On the proverbial nature of this sentiment see Smith (1913) 350.

at tu, dum primi floret tibi temporis aetas,
utere: non tardo labitur illa pede.   (35–48)

The poet again claims the authority of Venus at line 35, this time as an *exemplum*, a role model for the *puella*. Venus' power over the boy in this *exemplum* is clear. As such amatory power often does, it involves secrecy and deceit: *at Venus inuenit puero concumbere furtim.* It is a conflict between Venus and the *puer*. He is afraid (*dum timet*) like a soldier (compare 1.1.3), and the language of lines 36–8 recalls the language of battle (*conserit ... pugnantibus linguis*) and violence (*figere*).[24] He is her hunted prey whom she finally 'devours': *in collo figere dente notas.* By describing love for a boy as a position of power taken by no less a power figure than Venus herself, the poet suggests that the *puella* would be able to maintain her power over the *puer* even by giving in to his desires. The depiction of Venus here can thus be seen as part of the poet's attempt to manipulate the *puella* into compliance.

Another part of that strategy, familiar from earlier passages such as 1.6.77ff., follows: the threat of future suffering if the beloved does not comply with the lover's desires. Again wealth (*lapis ... gemmaeque*) is ultimately powerless. It lacks the pleasure which submission to male desire (the demand of their *amor*) supposedly offers. The alternative to this submission, the poet argues, is ultimate discomfort and solitude: *quae frigore sola | dormiat et nulli sit cupienda uiro.* Thus the poet makes the *puella*'s pleasure seem dependent on male desire instead of vice versa. This is contrary to the power relationship seen in earlier elegies, where male desire places the man in the power of the beloved. The poet adds another factor to the threat, the power of passing time (*sero ... sero*), which comes like a disease and cannot be overcome (*uetus infecit cana senecta caput*). This encourages the *puella* to take the 'opportunity' of complying now. In age *amor* exerts its power (*reuocatur amor*), but it is too late (*sero ... sero*), the *puella*'s

---

[24] The fact that the *puer* has *teneri sinus*, while again suggesting the pleasure to be gained from him, also makes Venus' violence, against a *tener* opponent, seem all the fiercer.

power to attract has gone (as line 40 states). Instead, knowledge and deception alone must be used (*tum studium formae est ... dissimulet*). The result is ridiculous[25] and leads, as at 9ff., to inconstancy and insecurity (*mutatur*). In the pursuit of this attractive (and thus powerful) appearance the old woman acts with violence to herself in a bizarre, unnatural way:

> tollere tum cura est albos a stirpe capillos
> et faciem dempta pelle referre nouam.   (45–6)

She thus suffers punishment for the suffering she has inflicted on her lover by not complying. In this, and in the picture of the old woman as a whole, the poet recalls his previous predictions, especially 1.6.77ff. This suggests not only that the position of the *puer* is the same as the poet's was in that earlier poem, but that the poet's techniques of persuasion have not changed. The apparent lack of success associated with these techniques in the past (*canimus frustra*) might weaken the poet's claim to have learnt from his past experiences. Lines 47–8 sum up the direction of his argument, enlisting the power of time (*non tardo labitur illa pede*) to gain the *puella*'s compliance.

The 'advice' offered in lines 41–6 further complicates the question of who is addressed at what point. *Tum* may draw the reader's attention to the contrast not only between present youthful beauty and future aged ugliness, but between necessary adornment in the future (*tum*) and the present unnecessary adornment of the addressee at lines 9ff. But uncertainty remains about whether the poet is conscious of this contrast and the addressee (the *puella*) is the same in each case.

Turning the tables

> Neu Marathum torque. puero quae gloria uicto est?
>   in ueteres esto dura, puella, senes.
> parce, precor, tenero. non illi sontica causa est,
>   sed nimius luto corpora tingit amor.

---

[25] This recalls the poet's picture of the universally ridiculed old lover at 1.2.91ff.

uel miser absenti maestas quam saepe querelas
  conicit, et lacrimis omnia plena madent.
'quid me spernis?' ait, 'poterat custodia uinci;
  ipse dedit cupidis fallere posse deus.
nota Venus furtiua mihi est – ut lenis agatur
  spiritus, ut nec dent oscula rapta sonum.
et possum media quauis obrepere nocte
  et strepitu nullo clam reserare fores.
quid prosunt artes, miserum si spernit amantem
  et fugit ex ipso saeua puella toro?
uel cum promittit subito sed perfida fallit
  et mihi nox multis est uigilanda malis?
dum mihi uenturam fingo, quodcumque mouetur
  illius credo tunc sonuisse pedes.'   (49–66)

Neu Marathum torque provides, or at least confirms, information which rearranges again the reader's understanding of
the poem and the poet's position.[26] The *puer* is now explicitly
revealed as Marathus, and the direct reminiscence of 1.4.81
(*quam Marathus lento me torquet amore*) underlines the irony
of his position, which is similar to that in which he placed the
poet. But the poet's position could be viewed as equally ironic.
He is helping the very person who put him in such a painful
position and withheld the compliance he now seeks from the
puella for Marathus. An alternative interpretation of the
entire elegy is now possible: that the poem itself, the poet's
advice to and help for Marathus, may be part of a trade-off in
return for Marathus' compliance with the poet's desires. In
any case, as in the sixth elegy, the role of advisor and the
power to give aid would seem to enhance the position of the
poet, who has previously been powerless and himself forced to
appeal to others for help.

Like the power of the poet's beloveds, the girl's power over
Marathus resembles that of a master over a slave (*torque*) or a
conquering general over a captive (*puero quae gloria uicto*

---

[26] See Wimmel (1968) 67: 'der nebenbei gefallene Name Marathus rückt doch alles in
neues Licht.'

est?).[27] The power of a conquering general is further suggested by the poet's request at lines 50–1: *in ueteres esto dura, puella, senes. | parce, precor, tenero.* This suggests a trade-off[28] of a sort. The *puella* may be harsh to the older lovers who (as has been suggested at lines 29ff.) can themselves offer only money, not pleasure, and in return she should spare the younger man who does offer pleasure (note *tener* again). But, as in previous poems, the poet can finally only appeal to the power of the *puella* to accept these terms (*parce*). In the end it is the *puella* who has the power, just as *amor* has control over Marathus' body and manifests itself there: *nimius luto corpora tingit amor.*

The picture of Marathus which the poet gives at lines 53–66 emphasises again not only the powerlessness of the boy, but also his similarity to the poet in previous poems. The suffering and wretchedness of his position (*miser absenti maestas quam saepe querelas | conicit*) is expressed, like the poet's at 1.5.38, in tears. The poet presents Marathus' direct speech, supposedly in order to excite the *puella*'s pity (compare line 51). But the words of 'Marathus' recall those of the poet himself. The god-granted power to deceive is available to overcome any obstacle: *poterat custodia uinci; | ipse dedit cupidis fallere posse deus* (55–6). The speaker has the knowledge to control the situation: *nota Venus furtiua mihi est* (57). This recalls the aid and knowledge supposedly given by Venus at 1.2.15ff. But, as in that poem, the lover is helpless before the final obstacle, the non-compliance of the girl herself: *quid ... spernis?* (55). The *rapta oscula* at line 58 suggest again the violent struggle of love. But while Marathus, like the poet, might have the knowledge and skill (of deception and secrecy) to achieve these things (*possum media quauis obrepere nocte*[29] *| et strepitu nullo clam reserare fores*), lines 61–2 demonstrate the central controlling power which renders these *artes*[30]

---

[27] This recalls the power of *Amor* over the poet at 1.6.3–4.
[28] The sense of a contract being made is enhanced by the use of the legalistic *esto*.
[29] This recalls the poet's claim at 1.2.29–30.
[30] This carries on the theme of the impotence of art, recalling most specifically 1.4.57 and 82.

impotent: the *puella*, who in this case is hostile (*saeua*) to the lover:

> quid prosunt artes, miserum si spernit amantem
> et fugit ex ipso saeua puella toro?   (61–2)

Marathus' repeated questions (*quid ... quid*) seem a mark of his confusion and impotence in this situation, suggesting a lack of knowledge on his part, in contrast to the stance of the poet/advisor. But, ironically, the failure of Marathus' *artes* here (line 61) directly recalls the failure of the poet's *artes* to affect Marathus himself (*deficiunt artes* 1.4.82). The deception which is a source of power in the amatory sphere is used against the boy. Deals break down: *cum promittit subito sed perfida fallit* (64). The result for Marathus is suffering, manifested (as in poems one and two) in sleep-deprivation: *mihi nox multis est uigilanda malis?*[31] Like the poet (*fingebam ... fingebam* 1.5.20–35) *amor*'s effect on him causes Marathus to imagine what he is powerless to bring about (*uenturam fingo*). This renders his interpretation of events, that which he believes to be the case, unreliable: *quodcumque mouetur | illius credo tunc sonuisse pedes* (65–6). He is powerless to do anything *but* imagine – imagine, complain and appeal – like the poet before him. The insistent similarities between the poet's past (and possibly present) situation and the present situation of Marathus, the similarities between the poet's approach to persuading the *puella* here and in the past, might suggest that here also the poet's appeals will be powerless, that his claimed knowledge (lines 1–2) will effectively achieve nothing.

> Desistas lacrimare, puer. non frangitur illa,
>   et tua iam fletu lumina fessa tument.
> oderunt, Pholoe, moneo, fastidia diui,
>   nec prodest sanctis tura dedisse focis.
> hic Marathus quondam miseros ludebat amantes,
>   nescius ultorem post caput esse deum.

---

[31] Whereas at 1.2.78 the vigil (*nox uigilanda*) illustrates the powerlessness of wealth without love, here Marathus' beauty and the poet's knowledge and persuasive technique seem equally useless. The power rests ultimately with the beloved.

saepe etiam lacrimas fertur risisse dolentis
et cupidum ficta detinuisse mora.
nunc omnes odit fastus, nunc displicet illi
quaecumque opposita est ianua dura sera.
et te poena manet, ni desinis esse superba.
quam cupies uotis hunc reuocare diem! (67–78)

The failure of his appeal to the *puella* is acknowledged
at line 67 as the poet, turning back to the *puer*, calls an end
to the attempt to gain her pity: *desistas lacrimare*. This may
imply that the tears were part, perhaps a contrived part, of the
strategy to gain the girl's compliance.[32] The assault upon her,
of which the poem itself has been the instrument, has failed
(*non frangitur illa*). The poet, consistent with the possibility
that he is still concerned with Marathus' beauty himself, advises him to save his eyes (line 68). At line 69 the poet returns
to the *puella*, who is now named as Pholoe.[33] As in many
of the preceding poems, the poet can only end with a threat,
for the realisation of which he must rely on other powers:
oderunt, Pholoe, moneo, fastidia diui. Such a divine moral
code, which would finally justify the positions of Marathus
and the poet, would render Pholoe's appeals for the gods'
power as futile as the poet's and Marathus' appeals to *her*
power have been: *nec prodest sanctis tura dedisse focis.* The
poet's threat, like the knowledge he claimed in the opening
lines, is supported by past experience. He now explicitly
makes the comparison which the reader has almost certainly
already made: *hic Marathus quondam* ... Marathus was also
once in a position of power which enabled him to ridicule his
lovers (*ludebat amantes* ... *lacrimas fertur risisse dolentis*) and
use deception to manipulate them (*cupidum ficta detinuisse
mora*).

The word *fertur* (line 73), and the supposed reliance on report for the information of these lines, might also highlight
the fact that the reader is depending on the words of a poet
who has been shown to be unreliable and may have ulterior

---

[32] As suggested by Murgatroyd (1980) 252.
[33] This recalls the delayed revelation of Delia's name in the first elegy; see above 49.

motives for the impression he gives or the details he chooses to tell. A certain selectivity could be seen to operate in these lines themselves. The question might be raised, for example, as to why the poet mentions *amantes* without admitting he was one.[34] This might suggest the poet is ashamed, or that admitting this would weaken the superior position he is struggling to establish as a knowledgeable and detached advisor.

The poet describes in moral terms the fate of Marathus, who lacked the knowledge (*nescius*) to amend his actions (he is being punished by an *ultor deus*). The underlying argument of these lines is that Pholoe, to whom the poet has just given the necessary knowledge to escape such a fate, should not follow Marathus' example. For once it seems that the power of *amor* is working on the poet's side, to avenge Marathus' treatment of him. *Amor* now determines Marathus' attitude and behaviour:

> nunc omnes odit fastus, nunc displicet illi
> quaecumque opposita est ianua dura sera.[35]   (75–6)

The irony that Marathus, once the cause of such emotions and behaviour, is now repeating the history of the poet/lover might suggest that the poet is gloating here. But the fact that he has here attempted to aid Marathus, while appearing to be no more successful than he did in his own case, tempers this. The poet's new role may seem just as ironic. The past experience of Marathus, however, gives the poet's parting warning of punishment (*et te poena manet*) more weight than usual. It is emphasised that the *puella* can escape this fate in return for her compliance with Marathus' wishes (*ni desinis*[36] *esse superba*), yet another trade-off of sorts. As in the case of Marathus, the poet suggests, *amor* will ultimately change the

---

[34] This piece of information might, for instance, have further backed up the poet's claims to know from experience and add strength to the threat.

[35] There may be a suggestion here that Marathus' attitude towards the poet has also changed, in the poet's favour, but the exact nature of their relationship at this point in the collection remains uncertain.

[36] It is significant that many of the poet's instructions to his addressees involve stopping (*desine; desistas; desinis*). This suggests that his desire to modify their behaviour stems partly from his own desire to control, to restrain, and thus to gain some power for himself (as their advisor) in so doing.

desires of Pholoe (*cupies*) and *she* will be the one appealing for divine aid (*uotis*): *quam cupies uotis hunc revocare diem. Hunc diem,* the day she could have acted to prevent the punishment, contrasts with another high profile *dies* in the opening lines of the previous poem. The *dies* in poem seven saw the realisation and expression of Messalla's power. But that contrasts sharply with the powerlessness of Pholoe which, according to the poet here in poem eight, will be caused by her actions on *hic dies.*

This warning to Pholoe recalls the poet's statement at lines 7–8: *deus crudelius urit | quos uidet inuitos succubuisse sibi.*[37] This may further complicate the reader's impression of who is being addressed, and where. It might suggest that it was Pholoe who was being warned in these earlier lines. There is, however, no stronger evidence that she was the addressee of these lines, and, if she was, it is uncertain when the address turned to Marathus. This only succeeds in creating more uncertainty, opening further equally indefinite possibilities for the reader, whose preference for one version over the next is dependent on the assumptions and expectations brought to and taken from the text.

Conclusion

The interrelation of knowledge and power in the elegy can be traced both in the self-positioning of the poet-persona and in the relationship of the reader to the text. However unsuccessfully he may fulfil it, in poem eight the poet takes upon himself the role of *magister amoris*. The superior position this might have seemed to give him in relation to the addressees is undercut, however, by the apparent failure of the knowledge he claims for himself to achieve his aim of persuading Pholoe to comply. As in previous poems, knowledge is seen to have no practical power in the sphere of *amor*. Similarly, the irony which emerges from the transformation of Marathus into a lover in the mould of the poet himself is prevented from

---

[37] In this case too the threat involves the desire that the addressee's current behaviour should cease: compare *desine* (line 7) and *desinis* (line 77).

reflecting entirely favourably on the poet's position since he is here serving the interests of Marathus. This suggests that, despite his stance, the poet/lover is still, in some way, in the boy's power.

The reader, similarly, finds a problematic relationship between knowledge and control of the text. The gradual revelation of information which Wimmel and Cairns have observed gives the reader no secure understanding of the text's meaning. New ambiguities or competing possibilities are raised just as others are apparently resolved. The reader's 'knowledge' is shown to be dependent on assumptions which are liable to be undercut at later points in reading, even when they seemed to be strongly encouraged by the text or by the reader's own knowledge of previous Tibullan poems, elegiac conventions in general or other factors. The resultant realignment, or re-reading, which this process necessitates provides no more secure a control over meaning than previously. A similar process of reading can be seen in the earlier elegies,[38] but in the eighth poem it seems especially prominent and is paralleled by the position of the poet-persona, who sets up, through his assumed role of *magister amoris*, a relation of knowledge to power which is not upheld in the course of the poem. In the same way, the reader is unable to translate securely the 'knowledge' provided by the words of the poet into control over the meaning of the text.

---

[38] Compare especially the reading of poem five above, and in particular 156–8, 168–9 and 178–9.

POEM NINE

Wealth and *foedera*

The prominence of wealth as a force in *amor*-relationships has received detailed attention in the studies of the ninth poem by critics such as Leonotti[1] and Wimmel.[2] As in previous poems, wealth is not only a powerful element in the exchange for the sexual compliance of the beloved, but overcomes and takes the place of non-monetary exchanges. Lyne[3] and, in more detail, de Verger[4] have focused upon this conflict in their examination of the *foedus* between poet and beloved and its failure in this poem. But the comparison of these two structures (the *foedus* and the exchange of wealth) can be extended. Both of these processes employ a similar structure in an attempt to achieve the stabilisation and control of the *amor*-relationship. This structure, and the success of wealth in this regard, draw parallels with processes in other, non-erotic spheres. Both the *foedus* and the role of wealth can thus be fitted within the power structures which have been seen at work in *amor*-relationships in previous elegies. The similarities which they highlight between the operation of *amor*-relationships and other areas suggests a general and pervasive paradigm for the construction of power.

> Quid mihi, si fueras miseros laesurus amores,
>   foedera per diuos clam uiolanda dabas?
> a miser, etsi quis primo periuria celat,
>   sera tamen tacitis Poena uenit pedibus. (1–4)

---

[1] Leonotti (1980) 259–70, who views this theme as 'il pericolo dei doni', 269.
[2] See especially Wimmel (1968) 89–90.
[3] Lyne (1980) 170–1.
[4] de Verger (1987) 335–46.

As in earlier elegies, it is not at first clear who the addressee of the opening couplet of poem nine is. The poet implies that a pact has been broken (*foedera uiolanda*). In the sphere of love (*miseros amores*) the security promised by such pacts breaks down. *Laesurus* makes it clear that the beloved is male and, after poem eight, the reader is naturally encouraged to assume that Marathus is again the beloved in question.[5] The beloved is in control, even at the time the pact was made: *si fueras miseros laesurus amores*. Secrecy is the instrument of the beloved's control (*clam*). Although the poet now seems to see through the pretence, he is still the victim (*miseros laesurus amores*) and is left questioning, seemingly confused and powerless: *quid mihi* . . .

A miser might, at first, seem to refer to the poet himself, but the context of lines 3–4 suppresses this assumption. The *miser* appears to be the unfaithful male lover. Lines 3–4 form a direct contrast with the concluding lines of the last poem. While poem eight concluded with the poet threatening Pholoe with punishment on Marathus' behalf (*poena* 1.8.77), here he is threatening Marathus with a similar punishment (*poena* 1.9.4). It is even more ironic that in poem eight the poet had used Marathus as an *exemplum* of someone who had *already* suffered such a punishment (1.8.71ff.). That such punishment *had* actually occurred was a foundation stone of the poet's authority in that poem. Now it appears that such 'punishment' has done nothing to modify Marathus' behaviour, as the poet claimed in poem eight. This not only suggests that the *poena* with which the poet now threatens the beloved will be equally powerless to change the situation (assuming it does in fact occur), but it also undermines the poet's authority in the previous poem in retrospect.

Far from the knowledgeable *magister amoris*, whose experience had allowed him to observe the patterns and processes involved in the sphere of love, the poet now seems to have gained or learnt nothing. The processes he described now

---

[5] For the assumption that the beloved in this case is Marathus see McGann (1983) 1991; and Murgatroyd (1977) 111.

appear to collapse or fail to produce the expected effect. Just as the reader's assumptions and expectations have been cheated or modified in past poems, now the poet himself does not get what he seemed confidently to expect. The pact between the poet and the beloved has broken down because of deceit (*quis primo periuria celat*). Deceit has been continually associated with *amor* throughout the collection. The poet's suggestion that punishment will eventually follow offence (*sera tamen tacitis Poena uenit pedibus*) now lacks authority and might seem unlikely.

This complex interaction between poems eight and nine[6] emphasises the process which takes place not only between each poem in the collection, but within individual poems themselves. This is the process of re-evaluation which destabilises any reading of the collection as the suggestions of previous poems or lines are undercut or modified. The obvious resonances between the two adjacent poems emphasise in immediate form the possibilities for interconnection and interaction between all the poems of the collection and the consequences of this for the reading process.

Profit and punishment

Parcite, caelestes: aequum est impune licere
    numina formosis laedere uestra semel.
lucra petens habili tauros adiungit aratro
    et durum terrae rusticus urget opus.
lucra petituras freta per parentia uentis
    ducunt instabiles sidera certa rates.
muneribus meus est captus puer: at deus illa
    in cinerem et liquidas munera uertat aquas.
iam mihi persoluet poenas, puluisque decorem
    detrahet et uentis horrida facta coma.

---

[6] For another perspective on this interaction see Murgatroyd, who sums it up as the 'contrast between the detached "praeceptor" in 1.8 and the naïve and involved lover in 1.9 ... the amusing contrast between uninvolved precepts and the reality of personal involvement', Murgatroyd (1977) 118.

uretur facies, urentur sole capilli,
  deteret inualidos et uia longa pedes.
admonui quotiens 'auro ne pollue formam:
  saepe solent auro multa subesse mala.
diuitiis captus si quis uiolauit amorem,
  asperaque est illi difficilisque Venus.
ure meum potius flamma caput et pete ferro
  corpus et intorto uerbere terga seca.   (5–22)

At line 5 the poet again appears to be an apologist for
Marathus. He appeals to divine power with the familiar word,
parcite, on the boy's behalf. Significantly, the excuse he gives
(*aequum est impune licere | numina formosis laedere uestra
semel*) seems an attempt to equate harm to himself (*miseros
laesurus amores*) with damage to divine authority (*numina ...
laedere uestra*). The appeal to the gods also perhaps suggests
that the boy's punishment or pardon is within the poet's re-
quest. The association of the poet with such a source of power
might now seem ironic and ridiculous following the undermining of his authority which the situation delineated in the
opening lines produced. Such irony might in turn suggest a
further reading of lines 5–6. This qualification may be a cover,
an excuse in case the punishment promised at line 4 does not
eventuate (or has no effect). Punishment will only be avoided
this time, the poet warns (*semel*, being saved for the final,
emphatic word in the couplet). But the poet's authority has
been damaged, and his lack of power over the boy lies at the
source of these lines.

As if trying to fit the boy's behaviour into an established
pattern or process, the poet now gives a series of *exempla*
which reveal what he considers to be the reason for the boy's
infidelity: *lucra*. Indeed, the parallels which the poet gives all
involve the process familiar from the first lines of poem one:
hardship, hard work or vulnerability exchanged for wealth,
for power. The *rusticus* exerts force (*urget*) and control (*habili
tauros adiungit aratro*) in hard work (*durum terrae ... opus*),
enduring this discomfort in a trade-off for *lucra*. In exchange
for *lucra*, ships undergo vulnerability (*instabiles ... rates*)

whilst under the control of other forces (*ducunt ... sidera certa*).[7] The poet assumes that the *puer*, following the conventional, expected processes, has experienced a similar lack of control for the sake of money: *muneribus meus est captus puer*. The poet, once again, can only appeal for divine intervention to counteract the power of wealth: *at deus illa | in cinerem et liquidas munera uertat aquas.*[8] The power of wealth is common to all the areas described in lines 7–10. The similarities of the processes involved in achieving the aim of profit (what McGann calls 'the universality of the pursuit of profit')[9] link these areas to the sphere of *amor* through emphasis of the common structures by which power is defined and achieved in each case. The construction and operation of power thus transcends, once more, the differences between supposedly separate spheres of activity.

The poet still hopes that such processes (like offence/ punishment or service/reward) will remain stable: *iam mihi persoluet poenas. Persoluet* suggests a debt-process, the boy's 'payment' consisting of a destruction (pay-back) of those assets which he had exchanged for *lucra* (*coma; decus*). Accordingly, the wind and dust of lines 13–14 fulfil, in a way, the ash and water prayer of lines 11–12. The boy will suffer slave-like punishment (*uretur facies, urentur sole capilli*), a reversal of the current power-relation between him and the poet. The poet asserts that the search for gain which the *puer* has apparently followed, and which is exemplified in line 16 and elsewhere in the collection by the *longa uia*, will demand the exchange of hardships: *deteret inualidos et uia longa pedes.* The analogy of the search for profit in other areas is applied to the case of the *puer*, allowing the poet to threaten him with the inevitable payment of hardship which such profit usually demands. The poet thus attempts to affirm the conventional process (as exemplified in lines 7ff.) as an instrument to sup-

---

[7] Even the waters are subject to a chain of command: *freta per parentia uentis.*

[8] This recalls the prophecy concerning *Amor*'s power given by the priestess of Bellona at 1.6.53–4. Again here the poet seems to rely on the power of *Amor* (the *deus*), who now appears not to have come to his aid in the past.

[9] McGann (1983) 1992.

port his own authority, to prop up his own power, which has seemed to be failing under the power and control exerted by the *puer* and, more generally, *amor*.

With the words *admonui quotiens* the poet again tries to adopt a more powerful, knowing, prophetic position. He uses predominantly moral language in his warning. He speaks of pollution (*auro ne pollue formam*), suggesting that the boy's beauty is a sacred object. Again the exchange of hardships for gold is asserted and placed in opposition to *amor* (*saepe solent auro multa subesse mala*). The poet suggests a power-struggle between wealth and *amor*, in which the control of *Amor/ Venus* over the individual is finally more powerful: *diuitiis captus si quis uiolauit amorem*[10] *| asperaque est illi difficilisque Venus* (19–20). The poet's *amor*-determined morality and his final reliance on Venus' power are again highlighted. But it seems that the boy, unlike the poet in poem one, has chosen the trade-off for gain (wealth and power) rather than submission to *amor*, defining and exploiting his position as the object of love (the beloved) rather than taking the position of lover. The enlistment of Venus' authority against the boy's choice is put under strain by the picture of Venus elsewhere in the collection and her apparent lack of aid when the poet has appealed for it in the past. It is clear that the boy himself was not put off by such appeals to Venus, since these lines (from 17) report the poet's words in the past and the warning was useless.

The 'punishment' or revenge which the poet hopes for involves a loss of power on the part of the boy worse than the punishments described in lines 21–2, which are of a type usually meted out to slaves:

> ure meum potius flamma caput et pete ferro
> corpus et intorto uerbere terga seca.[11] (21–2)

---

[10] Again the power of *Amor* is underlined by reminiscence of the priestess of Bellona's prophecy in 1.6.

[11] This may again suggest a *foedus* of a sort on the poet's part, if Ramírez de Verger's perception of an echo of the gladiatorial *auctoramentum* oath in these lines is correct: de Verger (1986) 109–10.

According to the poet, the boy by choosing the exchange of his beauty for wealth will in fact be involved in another process. The boy will also, ultimately, pay for that wealth with the *mala* of submission to *Amor*/Venus. It is significant that the poet thinks of the punishment from his own point of view (*meum* 21). He has already felt control by Venus in such terms (see burning, 1.2.100; torture, 1.4.81; and both together, 1.5.5). He has also desired such a slave-like position in exchange for being near his beloved (see 1.6.37–8). It had seemed that Marathus was in such an *amor*-controlled position as regards Pholoe in poem eight, but this now appears to have had no effect on the power-relationship between himself and the poet, despite what the poet seemed to claim at 1.8.71–6. Venus' power was no aid to the poet in the past and, while that power seems real, the poet has no control over how it might be exerted. As in poem two, the normal, supposedly typical and stable patterns, such as offence/punishment, seem not to apply.

Past deceptions

Nec tibi celandi spes sit peccare paranti:
  scit deus occultos qui uetat esse dolos.
ipse deus tacito permisit saepe ministro
  ederet ut multo libera uerba mero.
ipse deus somno domitos emittere uocem
  iussit et inuitos facta tegenda loqui.'
haec ego dicebam: nunc me fleuisse loquentem,
  nunc pudet ad teneros procubuisse pedes.
tunc mihi iurabas nullo te diuitis auri
  pondere, non gemmis uendere uelle fidem,
non tibi si pretium Campania terra daretur,
  non tibi si Bacchi cura Falernus ager.
illis eriperes uerbis mihi sidera caeli
  lucere et pronas fluminis esse uias.
quin etiam flebas, at non ego fallere doctus
  tergebam umentes credulus usque genas.   (23–38)

PAST DECEPTIONS

The poet now focuses on the power of deceit, again posing the power of the *deus* against it at lines 23–8 (*deus ... ipse deus ... ipse deus*). The deceiver gains power, or hopes to gain power, through secrecy (*nec tibi celandi spes sit peccare paranti*). But the poet claims that the power of the god, his knowledge (*scit*), is stronger (*scit deus occultos qui uetat esse dolos*). The god's power (*permisit ... iussit*) through the instrument of wine (*mero*) or sleep (*somno*), overcomes and controls those who would otherwise be silent (*tacito ... ministro*). Those who would employ deceit are disempowered (*domitos ... inuitos*) in the familiar power-struggle between knowledge and secrecy. As has been seen, however, the poet's authority has been undermined and this brings into doubt his assurance that the god's power *will* be contributed to tip the balance of the power-struggle. It seems that Marathus himself was not convinced.

Now the poet is ashamed of his past words and behaviour. His words were powerless (*haec ego dicebam* 29). His attempts to manipulate the boy emotionally (*me fleuisse*[12] *loquentem | nunc pudet ad teneros procubuisse pedes* 29–30) now seem futile. The contrast between *nunc ... nunc* and *tunc* (29–31) emphasises that, despite the poet's claim to knowledge in the previous poem, he lacked foresight. He trusts in the pact which the boy made with him (*tunc mihi iurabas*) agreeing not to engage in the commercial exchange (*uendere uelle fidem*). The boy swears not to betray his *fides* to the poet in exchange for gems, gold and land (lines 31–4). The last two items recall the opening lines of the collection, where gold and lands together constituted wealth and power. The measure of gold (*auri ... pondere*) and *pretium* of land emphasise the commercial nature of the deal which the boy forswears. But the poet is entirely manipulated by the *puer*. His belief is controlled:

> Illis eriperes uerbis mihi sidera caeli
> lucere et pronas fluminis esse uias.   (35–6)

---

[12] This recalls Marathus' own use of tears in an attempt to persuade Pholoe at 1.8.67.

253

This suggests the fragility of belief under the influence of emotional and other mental factors. The motifs of stars and rivers, as well as the violence of the language (*eriperes*), also strongly recall the power of witches, which, in the second poem, included power over belief. The poet claims that the *puer* has similar power. Ironically, the boy's attempt to manipulate the poet emotionally through tears (*quin etiam flebas*) is successful in contrast to the poet's own futile tears at line 29. The poet now admits his *lack* of knowledge regarding the deceptions of love, in direct contrast to his claims in poems eight and six: *at non ego fallere doctus*. He sees himself as *credulus*, characteristically trusting in the conventional pacts and processes which have so often failed in the sphere of *amor*. The poet's own use of deception in past poems may raise the possibility that the poet is trying here to project an image of himself (to emphasise the pathos of his situation) for a purpose: to manipulate the boy emotionally. But his past failures in this respect only point further to his powerlessness.

> Quid faciam, nisi et ipse fores in amore puellae?
>   sic precor, exemplo sit leuis illa tuo.
> o quotiens, uerbis ne quisquam conscius esset
>   ipse comes multa lumina nocte tuli!
> saepe insperanti uenit tibi munere nostro
>   et latuit clausas post adoperta fores.
> tum miser interii, stulte confisus amari;
>   nam poteram ad laqueos cautior esse tuos.
> quin etiam attonita laudes tibi mente canebam,
>   et me nunc nostri Pieridumque pudet.
> illa uelim rapida Vulcanus carmina flamma
>   torreat et liquida deleat amnis aqua.
> tu procul hinc absis, cui formam uendere cura est
>   et pretium plena grande referre manu.   (39–52)

At line 39, the poet states that, as in poem eight, the boy is in love with a girl. This further strengthens the assumption that the *puer* here *is* Marathus. The poet sees this relationship as an opportunity for revenge, for the affirmation of the offence/punishment process which he has been hoping for from the early lines of the elegy: *quid faciam, nisi et ipse fores in amore puellae?*[13] The poet appeals (*sic precor*) for the pattern to be repeated and the process of punishment in return for transgression, of revenge from his point of view, to recur: *exemplo sit leuis illa tuo.* The continued appeal to *exempla* of different types in this poem suggests the poet's desire for stable and understandable[14] patterns of behaviour.

But lines 41ff. undercut the poet's hopes. It is revealed that through the poet's own agency the compliance of the boy's beloved has been attained on a regular basis (*O quotiens . . .*). This clearly recalls poem eight, where similar attempts on the poet's part had seemed unsuccessful. It now appears that this impression may have been incorrect. Ironically, while acting on the boy's behalf the poet has himself employed deceit and secrecy (*uerbis ne quisquam conscius esset . . . nocte . . . latuit clausas post adoperta fores*).[15] While powerless to help himself, he exerts these efforts for another, like a slave. He is in this other's control. The situation here recalls what was (or would have been) the situation with Delia and *her* lovers at 1.5.65–6. These reminiscences further emphasise the similarities between the power-structures of the two relationships (poet with Delia and poet with Marathus). Here the poet offers these services as an exchange (*munere* at line 43 recalls *muneribus* at line 11). Again lack of knowledge leads to the poet's downfall: *tum miser interii, stulte confisus amari.* The process which the poet had expected (*munera* for *amor*) breaks down as the boy prefers a different form of *munera*. The poet's lack of foresight is all the more striking given Priapus' direct

---

[13] This recalls Pholoe's infidelity at 1.8.63.

[14] The use of set patterns of behaviour, such as are described by *exempla*, as a means of explaining and understanding actions and events is important to the success of the poet/lover's strategies for gaining the beloved's compliance, since, if behavioural patterns in the sphere of *amor* were rendered comprehensible and predictable, a more stable base for knowledge and thus action would be provided.

[15] Equally ironically, this is the only time when closed doors are a sign of the poet's power and control of the situation rather than the opposite.

POEM NINE

warning to the poet at 1.4.57ff. concerning boys' preference
for cash. As a result the poet is powerless and in the boy's
control: *ad laqueos*[16] ... *tuos.*

The recollection of Priapus' warning in the fourth elegy is
underlined at 47ff. by the failure of poetry to achieve anything
in the sphere of love.[17] The content of the poet's poetry, like
the words the reader is now reading, was determined by his
amor towards Marathus. The poet/lover is mentally controlled
by that *amor* (*attonita* ... *mente*). His shame (*pudet* 48 as at
line 30) underlines the powerlessness which converts his own
past deeds into his present distress (*nunc*). As at lines 11–12,
he wishes for the power of elemental forces (*flamma*; *aqua*) to
intervene and destroy his shame. It may be significant that
here he appeals not to the power of Venus or *Amor*, but to
that of Vulcanus, who was himself both the dupe and then the
avenger of unfaithful, deceitful love between Venus and Mars.
As well as suggesting a parallel between Vulcanus and the
poet himself any perceived allusion to the story of the god's
revenge upon the adulterous couple may have another more
ironic implication. It may suggest to the reader that, contrary
to what the poet suggests in earlier lines, Venus herself, as an
adulteress, might be thought to support rather than punish
infidelity.[18] The poet desires freedom from control and humiliation by the boy (*tu procul hinc absis*).[19] But it seems that
only money and commercial transactions (*uendere* ... *et pretium* ... *referre* at lines 51–2, recalling lines 31–2) ensure
stability in love. The poet tries to rely upon other *munera*,
such as service, *carmina* and the profession of his own *amor*,
but he is powerless to achieve the boy's compliance: *cui
formam uendere cura est* | *et pretium plena grande referre manu*
(51–2).

[16] The poet/lover here is depicted as the hunted victim.
[17] *Pieridumque* (line 48) directly recalls 1.4.61–2.
[18] Venus might also be thought to support *furtiuus amor* in general, as at 1.2.36, and
thus to stand in direct contradiction to the sentiment of 1.9.23–8.
[19] It might be significant that it is not the poet who makes the move, but the boy who
is expected to go while the poet remains still and passive.

Husband, wife and sister

At te, qui puerum donis corrumpere es ausus,
    rideat assiduis uxor inulta dolis,
et cum furtiuo iuuenem lassauerit usu,
    tecum interposita languida ueste cubet.
semper sint externa tuo uestigia lecto
    et pateat cupidis semper aperta domus.
nec lasciua soror dicatur plura bibisse
    pocula uel plures emeruisse uiros.
illam saepe ferunt conuiuia ducere baccho
    dum rota Luciferi prouocet orta diem.
illa nulla queat melius consumere noctem
    aut operum uarias disposuisse uices.
at tua perdidicit, nec tu, stultissime, sentis
    cum tibi non solita corpus ab arte mouet.
tune putas illam pro te disponere crines
    aut tenues denso pectere dente comas?
istane persuadet facies auroque lacertos
    uinciat et Tyrio prodeat apta sinu?
non tibi sed iuueni cuidam uult bella uideri,
    deuoueat pro quo remque domumque tuam.
nec facit hoc uitio, sed corpora foeda podagra
    et senis amplexus culta puella fugit.   (53–74)

At line 53 the poet turns to the more powerful male lover, and again speaks of his beloved in terms of moral indignation (*corrumpere es ausus*). The reader at this point, if his/her assumptions are based upon the pattern of the poet's responses to similar 'situations' in previous poems, might expect a series of largely impotent curses. The curses which do in fact follow take advantage of male anxiety, threatening the same humiliation (*rideat*) which the other man has forced the poet to undergo because of loss of power over the beloved. In the case of the poet's rival it is loss of power over his *uxor* that the curse threatens. Deceit would be used against this man, as it was against the poet (*assiduis ... dolis ... furtiuo ... usu*). The woman would take the initiative, as she tires out her young man: *iuuenem lassauerit.* She would have the power, just as the poet's beloveds have, to cause the man great distress. The poet's rival would be deprived of the pleasure expected from the conventional power-relation of *uir* and *uxor: tecum interposita languida ueste cubet.* This would lead to vulnerability, insecurity and powerlessness in his own house and his own bed:

> semper sint externa tuo uestigia lecto
> et pateat cupidis semper aperta domus.[20]   (57–8)

The poet then turns to another female connected with the man, his sister.[21] The poet's choice for the focus of his attack exploits the fact that, in a public context, the women of his family are an object of anxiety for the male. The potential humiliation which public opinion can bring (*dicatur* 59; and *ferunt* 61) makes the man publicly vulnerable through the females associated with his household. Over these women, so the poet suggests, he has no power; even less over his wife, whom he might be expected to have under his control more than his sister:[22]

> Nec lasciua soror dicatur plura bibisse
> pocula uel plures emeruisse[23] uiros.   (59–60)

Dicatur and *ferunt* also suggest the husband's lack of knowledge. It seems that only *he* is deceived, just as at lines 54–5. The woman in lines 61–2[24] has control (*ducere*) in a setting where it is unconventional for a woman, especially a married

---

[20] The husband would thus lose the power-struggle against the lovers who are waiting, like the poet in earlier poems, *ante fores.*

[21] The *soror* may also possibly be his wife's sister, his sister-in-law; it is ambiguous.

[22] On the expectation that Roman husbands would control their wives see Edwards (1993) 53–8.

[23] *Emeruisse* again suggests some form of transaction. Compare an interesting parallel usage, in connection with prostitution, in Plautus *Bacchides,* 42–3: *Bacchis 1: haec* [the other Bacchis] *ita me orat sibi qui caueat aliquem ut hominem reperiam, | ut istunc militem – ut, ubi emeritum sibi sit, se reuehat domum.*

[24] There is also some ambiguity as to whether the sister or wife is meant by *illam,* again forcing the reader to rely on his/her own assumptions one way or another until *at tua* at line 65.

one, to have control: *illam saepe ferunt conuiuia ducere Baccho*. The juxtaposition of this with Lucifer's bringing of the dawn suggests that hers is a similar power; she leads on the *conuiuia* (*ducere*), while Lucifer brings on the day: *rota Luciferi prouocet orta diem*. Her power is seen as threatening and devouring: *illa nulla queat melius consumere noctem*. She is an unstable, uncertain, changing force (*operum uarias disposuisse uices*). In this respect she presents a contrast to the stable, controlled, and restrained position of women and objects of love in general which is apparently looked upon as ideal by the poet. The suggestion that the rival is (or should be) publicly humiliated by the unrestrained behaviour of his wife and sister also implies that all conventional male society desires and expects the position of women to be one of stability and restraint, under male control. At the same time, however, these lines also demonstrate that male desire, like that of the sister's and wife's lovers or the poet's own desire for his beloveds, is often directed towards just such an unstable, uncertain and uncontrollable figure. Control over the beloved is the male ideal, but at the same time it is the uncontrollable which attracts male desire. These lines thus exploit the two sides of male desire which have formed the central contradiction of the poet/lover's position and rendered him powerless in both the central *amor*-relationships of the collection.

As the poet describes it at lines 65–6, the wife has the knowledge (*at tua perdidicit ... ab arte*), while the husband is cast as ignorant and unsuspecting (*nec tu, stultissime, sentis | cum tibi non solita corpus ab arte mouet*).[25] This recalls the poet's relationship with Marathus, *stultissime* directly echoing description of the poet as *stulte* at line 45. (In the rival's case, however, the superlative suggests that the situation is even worse.) The poet's sarcastic questions at lines 67–70 seem to place the poet in a superior position and underline the husband's lack of knowledge and thus power to act (*tune putas*

---

[25] Compare the superior position which the poet attempted to take in advising the *coniunx* in poem six.

POEM NINE

...). These questions also suggest that the wife's efforts are not exerted for her husband's sake, that *his* is not the power concerned: *tune putas illam pro te disponere crines? ... istane persuadet facies ...?* Again hair and dress are a key to behaviour and character. The wife's efforts are being exerted (*disponere*; *pectere*) for another, but the husband, so the poet claims, is unable to see it. The woman's power is exerted for another, who apparently controls her behaviour: *non tibi sed iuueni cuidam uult bella uideri.* This also suggests the poet's superior knowledge over the man whose household is at the mercy of the wife (line 72). The poet knows what is going on, while the husband himself does not. From this superior position the poet threatens that the woman's power might be exerted on behalf of her lover like a destructive force, a sacrifice (*deuoueat*) to him (*pro quo*): *deuoueat pro quo remque domumque tuam.* The husband's own powerbase, his wealth and household (*remque domumque*), is unconventionally and humiliatingly in the power of his wife, whose behaviour in turn seems to be determined by *amor*.

The cause and blame for the wife's behaviour are transferred by the poet to the husband (*nec facit hoc uitio*). The suggestion is that her behaviour is a form of punishment in two senses: indirect punishment for the rival's supposed 'corruption' of Marathus, and direct punishment for his own physical repulsiveness and powerlessness, which the poet emphasises: *sed corpora foeda podagra | et senis amplexus culta puella fugit.* The conversion of the adulterous *uxor* into a *culta puella* (or, as the poet now suggests, vice versa) adds humorous emphasis to the extent of the husband's supposed foulness which prompts such faithlessness from his wife. Moreover, the poet's suggestion that the man is somehow responsible for his wife's own corruption, whether half serious or not, points to the poet's manipulation of the picture of the man and his household to discredit his rival, who would otherwise appear more powerful and thus more successful than the poet. The rival's corruption of his wife also parallels his corruption of Marathus. Everyone the foul rival touches, the poet suggests, becomes unfaithful.

Vindication

Huic tamen accubuit noster puer! hunc ego credam
  cum trucibus Venerem iungere posse feris.
blanditiasne meas aliis tu uendere es ausus?
  tune aliis, demens, oscula ferre mea?
tunc flebis cum me uinctum puer alter habebit
  et geret in regno regna superba tuo.
at tua tum me poena iuuet, Venerique merenti
  fixa notet casus aurea palma meos:
HANC TIBI FALLACI RESOLVTVS AMORE TIBVLLVS
DEDICAT ET GRATA SIS DEA MENTE ROGAT.

(75–84)

The poet's ulterior motive, and the past unreliability of his
words and supposed superior knowledge, might suggest that
the poet's threat and sarcastic warning is an elaborate fabri-
cation, another ultimately useless, perhaps even pathetic, attempt to affirm the offence/punishment process. But the central irony of the poet's image of 'the other man' is made
explicit at line 75: *huic tamen accubuit noster puer*. The poet
has lost the power struggle for the *puer* to this man. The worse
he describes that man, the worse it reflects on himself and his
own failure. The boy has not followed the pattern suggested
by the *culta puella*. He has not fled from the rival's foulness.
This prompts the poet to believe, at least rhetorically, that
other such 'natural' patterns, even the stable boundaries of
species, might be broken down: *hunc ego credam | cum truci-
bus Venerem iungere posse feris*. The poet can only question
indignantly and powerlessly (*uendere es ausus?*). The things
which he claimed for himself (*blanditias meas ... oscula mea*)
have been taken from him. This is emphasised by the repetition *aliis ... aliis*. The power belongs to others. The *puer* does
not follow the expected pattern. At least the *puer* does not
follow the pattern expected by the poet, according to *his* picture of the other man, and *his amor*-determined outlook, which
vehemently opposes the commercial transaction which the boy
has chosen. Thus the boy is branded *demens* by the poet.
    The poet asserts that he will eventually have some emo-

tional power over Marathus (*tunc flebis*), but the cost of that power is submission to another: *cum me uinctum puer alter habebit*.[26] The *alter* will take over the original *puer*'s power, apparently winning a power struggle with him where the poet himself could not: *geret in regno regna superba tuo*. But the poet is still controlled as he was even in poem one (*me uinctum*). He does not seem to have developed or gained any knowledge from his experiences: despite the claims of poem eight, his actions are still determined by *amor*. The poet himself concentrates on the view that this is a punishment for Marathus' behaviour (*poena* 81), a re-affirmation of established processes: the familiar offence/punishment process with which the poem began. This prospect gives the poet pleasure: *at tua tum me poena iuuet*.

Despite the doubts surrounding Venus' support in the past, the poet claims that it will be Venus' authority which brings this punishment (*Venerique merenti*). Accordingly, the poet promises the fulfilment of one final pact or process: in return for her power being granted to bring about such *poena*, the poet will dedicate an *aurea*[27] *palma* to the goddess. This recalls similar exchanges underlying the religious process in the first poem. In the promised inscription the poet sees himself freed from control exerted by *amor* (*fallaci resolutus amore*), although this might appear to be contradicted by the very terms of that release: *me uinctum puer alter habebit*. Again this suggests the poet's lack of understanding, which seems set once more to render him powerless. Apparently unaware of this contradiction, the poet concludes with the hope that his offering will fulfil his side of the transaction: *grata sis dea mente rogat* (84).

Conclusion

By the end of poem nine the poet/lover's claims (made in poem eight) to have gained knowledge, and thus power to act, from his experiences are comprehensively undercut, since he

---

[26] Compare Virgil, *Eclogues* 2.73, where Corydon pledges to make a similar move from passion for one boy to an identical passion for another.

[27] This gold recalls the gold used as currency in other exchanges in the poem.

seems prepared to repeat behaviour which has left him powerless and under the control of other forces in the past. The interaction of the two poems which Murgatroyd[28] draws attention to and which prompts Cairns to link them together ('they are contiguous poems sharing themes and situation')[29] encourages a reading of the collection which assumes and observes the interconnection of poems and the complicated effects of this on the construction of meaning from the texts. The patterns of the poet's behaviour and relationship with the beloved remain the same as in previous poems. The similarity of his subservient and deluded position in both the pederastic and the heterosexual poems is underlined by parallels such as between 1.9.41–4 and 1.5.65–6. Lyne argues that the poet/lover's subservience is even more emphatic in the case of the boy than in the case of Delia,[30] but the grounds of the similarity between the poet/lover's position in each lie in the assumed similarity in Roman culture between the power relationships involved in love of a boy and love of a woman.[31] In the Tibullan poet/lover's case both relationships represent an inversion of the conventional positions of the two participants in this power structure.

Similarly, the processes, pacts and exchanges (the *foedera*) which function in other spheres of society, which bring stability and which the poet seems to desire, are seen in this poem to break down entirely.[32] They are not valid in the sphere of love. But, at the same time, it is precisely the dominant process operating in other areas of activity which is validated by its reproduction in the sphere of *amor*: it is only the pursuit of wealth, *lucra*, which seems to operate in the expected manner, and it is only the possession and exchange of such wealth which brings any stability to the position of the lover. Despite direct experience of this, the poet continues to appeal to non-

---

[28] Murgatroyd (1977) 118.
[29] Cairns (1979) 209.
[30] Lyne (1980) 174–5.
[31] On which see Veyne (1985) 26, 29–30; these similarities are discussed in more detail in the Conclusion below, 287–8.
[32] As Ramírez de Verger has demonstrated: see de Verger (1987), especially 337–9 and 343–6.

monetary versions of the exchange process to the end of the poem. The reader, who has, supposedly, gained some knowledge of how (elegiac) *amor*-relationships operate from the elegies themselves, might assume from this 'knowledge' a superior position in relation to the poet/lover as he seems to continue in his delusion. This superior position is directly connected to the humour of the piece, as it is to that of other elegies, as it enables the reader to laugh at the poet's character and situation. But even this superior position might be rendered insecure in the light of the failure of knowledge in the last two elegies and the general instability throughout the collection so far of any position the reader might construct from the text.

POEM TEN

Peace, love and understanding

The prominence of *pax* in the final elegy has immediate consequences for a reading of power struggle in the collection. Solmsen and Pillinger have emphasised the centrality of *pax* to the poem and its opposition to the culture of power struggle.[1] Pillinger reinforces this opposition through linking the appearance of *Pax* in this elegy with the proem of Lucretius' *De Rerum Natura*:

[T]he Epicurean impulse to quietism and pacifism, the pursuit of *ignobile otium*, of inner peace and detachment from worldly designs and ambitions – these are qualities that have more than a distant affinity with attitudes expressed in the poetry of Tibullus.[2]

Similarly, the reminiscences of Virgil's *Eclogues* and *Georgics* which Wimmel[3] and others have observed in detail underline a contrast which is shared, in various forms, by all these texts. That is the contrast between the world of Roman power on the one hand and on the other freedom from the power structures and struggles inherent in that world. In poem ten *pax* is associated with the poet/lover's rural ideal. As Boyd puts it, it is 'a peace which guarantees that Tibullus' rural landscape will thrive'.[4] For Leach, this 'become[s] the basis for a stable philosophy that gives a coloring of permanence of life'.[5] *Pax* suggests the suppression of power struggle. This, and the replacement of the uncertainty and powerlessness of

---

[1] Solmsen (1962): 'Now *pax* or *Pax* as we find her celebrated in Tibullus I,10 has no relation to imperial policies and none either to the equivocal slogans or formulas used to justify Rome's rule over other nations', 298; see also Pillinger (1971) especially 205-7.
[2] Pillinger (1971) 207.
[3] Wimmel (1968) 171-4; and also Leach (1978) 98; and Cartault (1909) 117-23.
[4] Boyd (1984) 279.
[5] Leach (1980a) 92.

the poet-persona with assertions of stability and permanence, encourages a re-assessment of the structures and relationships of power which are presented in the collection.

Gaisser and Solmsen[6] have also pointed to the 'sub-ordination' of *amor* in the poem: 'In 1.10 and 1.1 *amor* is by no means represented as the poet's principal theme.'[7] As in the seventh elegy, this subordination allows other areas, in this case particularly *rura*, to be foregrounded and inter-connections between the various themes to be created. The power structures and the processes which operate within these areas provide the common ground on which such inter-connections (similarities and differences) are formed. These interconnections and the prominence of themes and spheres other than *amor* throughout the elegies suggest that a focus of the collection may lie in the operation of these power struc-tures and processes generally rather than simply in *amor*, *rura*, or any other single sphere or theme.

The misuse of power

Quis fuit horrendos primus qui protulit enses?
　quam ferus, et uere ferreus, ille fuit!
tum caedes hominum generi, tum proelia nata;
　tum breuior dirae mortis aperta uia est.
an nihil ille miser meruit, nos ad mala nostra
　uertimus in saeuas quod dedit ille feras?
diuitis hoc uitium est auri, nec bella fuerunt
　faginus astabat cum scyphus ante dapes.
non acres, non uallus erat, somnumque petebat
　securus uarias dux gregis inter oues.
tunc mihi uita foret, ⟨Valgi⟩ nec tristia possem
　arma, nec audissem corde micante tubam.　(1–12)

As many critics have remarked,[8] the first lines of poem ten recall the rejection of *militia* which opens the first poem. In

---

[6] Solmsen (1962) 306–7; and Gaisser (1983) 72.
[7] Gaisser (1983) 72.
[8] For the links between the first and tenth poems see especially Boyd (1984) and Gaisser (1983).

the opening lines of the first elegy the poet made a relative choice between *militia* and an apparently simple rural lifestyle. Later in the poem this 'choice' was revealed to be a rejection of the conventional Roman career structure, described as the exchange of discomfort and vulnerability for wealth and power, in favour of domination by *amor*. The *militia* process was not criticised or dismissed as wrong in itself. The first lines of poem ten, however, suggest an examination and rejection of the nature of war in itself, apparently independent of any relative lifestyle choice. The *enses* of the opening line are *horrendi*. The creative power of the inventor[9] (*primus qui protulit*) has produced only fear, discomfort and uncertainty. The description of that inventor as *ferus* at line 2 emphasises this impression of an uncontrolled power for destruction. The reader might assume, on the evidence of the first poem, that it will eventually be revealed that these words, too, are determined by *amor*'s overwhelming influence over the poet. The pun *ferus et ferreus* might even suggest that this, as many other passages in the elegies, is a rhetorical construction aiming to impress and persuade the addressee. The uncertainty of who the addressee is (is it one of the poet's beloveds?) further encourages such an assumption.

The creation of the sword and war itself is blamed, in a succession of clauses following *tum* at lines 3–4, for destruction (*caedes*; *proelia*), discomfort and insecurity (*breuior dirae mortis aperta uia est*). Once more, the mention of *uia* and its associations in earlier poems might suggest that, just as in the past, the poet is now only resentful of war because it is the cause of separation from his beloved (compare poems one and three). But the difference in the poet's approach here is underlined by the following line: *at nihil ille miser meruit*. He views the unleashing of such apparently uncontrolled power as a fault to be apportioned, rather than simply an option to be rejected in favour of another. He is characteristically concerned to assert the exchange of offence/punishment, or in this

---

[9] Compare the power of creators elsewhere in the collection, such as Osiris in poem seven, and the treatment of earlier times in general (for example 1.1.39ff.).

case offence/blame, to be sure people get what they deserve (*meruit*).[10]

The poet suggests at lines 5–6 that a power struggle which should be between humankind and nature, in particular between humankind and wild beasts, has been distorted into the struggle of human against human.[11] This type of struggle, in more or less violent forms, has underpinned and dominated the entire collection to date: *nos ad mala nostra | uertimus in saeuas quod dedit ille feras?* The word *feras*, recalling *ferus* at line 2, underlines this point. The victims and power-wielders, by becoming the same (both are now of the *hominum genus*, line 3), have effectively made themselves *ferae*. This wild, bestial nature is a mark of the uncontrolled misuse of the power of the *ensis* and violence in general. These lines may also suggest that power struggle in general grows out of the desire for protection (as from wild beasts) and certainty which, in an uncertain and insecure world, can only come from a position of greater power. This also implies that power struggle itself, through its creation of insecurity and uncertainty in the world, generates more power struggle, presenting a picture of society as an ever expanding organism of conflict and power relations.

The poet's diagnosis of the cause of this misuse of power (*diuitis . . . auri*) directly recalls poem one (*diuitias* 1.1.1)[12] and the process described there: *militia* begun and endured in return for wealth and the power it brings. Here, however, the pursuit of wealth is not simply an unwanted option left to an *alius*, but is condemned as a *uitium* (the meaning is underlined by the play on the words *diuitis* and *uitium*). The language is thus more moralistic than in poem one. The alternative to the

---

[10] This suggests a debt or legal guilt.

[11] This recalls the Golden Age described in poem three and its contrast to a contemporary age of power-struggle and destruction: *nec ensem | immiti saeuus duxerat arte faber* (1.3.47–8). There is also a close similarity between the description of the *saeuus faber* in poem three and the opening line of poem ten, although the poet does not seek to apportion blame in the third elegy or to examine in such detail the source of conflict.

[12] This also directly recalls *diuitis auri* at 1.9.31, where the wealth is the result of the *puer*'s compliance with the wealthy lover.

power struggle for wealth is again provided by a rural world, although here it is entirely a world of the past. *Nec bella fuerunt ... non arces, non uallus erat* recalls once more the Golden Age described in poem three (1.3.47). At such a time there was no power struggle between humans. There was no exchange of discomfort and vulnerability for wealth and power, since there was no wealth.[13] It was a time of comfort. This is suggested, as in previous poems, including the opening elegy (compare 1.1.4), by the availability of sleep (*somnum-que*). It was also a time of security and freedom from anxiety (*securus*) in a rural setting which is rural only because it pre-dates the urban world and the wars and violent power strug-gles which accompany the wealth necessary for such an urban, commercial world. This rural setting recalls the poet's wishes in poem one, but here it is explicit that such freedom from the struggle for power and wealth cannot be achieved in the present but belongs to the past (*tunc mihi uita foret*). Only in the past would the poet escape the power struggles which contemporary society forces him to take part in: *nec tristia nossem | arma*. Only then could he have escaped the fear, dis-comfort and insecurity (*corde micante*) which these struggles bring. This suggests again that contemporary society involves and is based upon power struggles and wealth/power-gaining processes, the most violent example of which is war.

It is highly uncertain whether Heyne's emendation *Valgi* at line 11 is correct.[14] But if it is, it eliminates the possibility that the poet is trying to persuade a beloved. Instead it suggests that the poet is addressing a friend, like Propertius in poems one, four, five and others of his first book (addressed to Tullus, Bassus, Gallus etc.). This might encourage the reader to see the poem as an example of the poet's personal beliefs being confided to a 'neutral' figure possibly similar to himself.

---

[13] This implies that humans will naturally struggle for wealth and power if it is available, since only its unavailability will prevent their struggles.

[14] See Murgatroyd (1980) 324, who supports the reading *uulgi*, transmitted by the oldest complete manuscript of the poems, the Ambrosianus. The meaning of this line would thus be: 'Had I been alive then, I would not have known the harsh arms of the multitude (i.e. the warfare which the multitude favours).'

These words may thus be an index to the poet's own central attitudes and thought, although the undermining of belief in the poet's words throughout the collection to this point might destabilise this assumption. At any rate, an address to a 'Valgius' at this point remains in doubt.

Then and now

> Nunc ad bella trahor, et iam quis forsitan hostis
>   haesura in nostro tela gerit latere.
> sed patrii seruate Lares: aluistis et idem
>   cursarem uestros cum tener ante pedes.
> neu pudeat prisco uos esse e stipite factos:
>   sic ueteris sedes incoluistis aui.
> tunc melius tenuere fidem, cum paupere cultu
>   stabat in exigua ligneus aede deus.
> hic placatus erat, seu quis libauerat uuam
>   seu dederat sanctae spicea serta comae;
> atque aliquis uoti compos liba ipse ferebat
>   postque comes purum filia parua fauum.
> at nobis aerata, Lares, depellite tela
>   . . . .
>   . . . .
> hostiaque e plena rustica porcus hara.
> hanc pura cum ueste sequar, myrtoque canistra
>   uincta geram, myrto uinctus et ipse caput.   (13–28)

Lines 13–14 balance the immediately preceding couplet's description of the contemporary dangers and discomforts which life in the past would avoid (*tunc*) with a description of what the poet faces in the present (*nunc*). The poet is passive and sees himself as treated violently (*trahor*). He is being forced into *militia: nunc ad bella trahor*. It now appears that the poet is personally and immediately affected by the forces he has described in the previous lines, that his attack on war reflects his own position, facing uncertainty, and vulnerability: *quis forsitan hostis | haesura in nostro tela*[15] *gerit latere*. This

---

[15] *Tela* recalls the condemnation of the invention of the *ensis* in the opening lines.

may further encourage the assumption that the poet is rejecting war because, as in the first poem, his own *militia* threatens
separation from his beloved. So, it might seem, his attitude is
once again determined by *amor*. The emphasis here, however,
is on the danger and uncertainty he must endure (lines 13–14).
The *Lares* (the safe, secure, domestic gods of poem one) are
appealed to for protection: *sed patrii seruate Lares*. *Patrii*
emphasises the link between household gods and an earlier era
of the type envisaged by the poet at lines 7ff. This is echoed
by an earlier phase of the poet's life, his vulnerable childhood
(*tener*), when the power of the *Lares* protected and nourished
him: *aluistis et idem | cursarem uestros cum tener ante pedes*.
Then, as in the pre-war, pre-urban world, there was security
and certainty.[16] The protecting power of the *Lares* makes
human power struggle unnecessary,[17] just as the absence of
wealth (and thus of the motive for warfare) negated the
human power struggle in the earlier 'golden' age. The infancy
of the poet thus parallels the infancy of humankind.

Again, the power of the gods is gained through a process of
exchange. In this case a simple form of worship is offered,
easily available and requiring no struggle to provide it (*prisco
... esse e stipite factos*). The poet hopes that this exchange will
be valid (*neu pudeat*). This suggest a fear that the terms of the
process may have changed since the earlier age, in alignment
with the change in the importance to humankind of wealth:
sic ueteris sedes incoluistis aui. The possible mutability of the
terms of such vital processes is in itself an indication of the
uncertainty inherent in contemporary life. Lines 19ff. further
expand upon the breakdown of these once stable processes. In
the past stability secured trust (*tunc melius tenuere fidem*). In
previous, more stable times wealth and the power associated
with it were absent (*cum paupere cultu*) and the terms of
the exchange between humans and the gods were fixed and
simple: *stabat in exigua ligneus aede deus*. This depiction of

---

[16] 'Past and present come together in this image with its implications of continuity
and stability', Leach (1980a) 92.
[17] In the poet's vulnerable childhood state any participation in such struggle or
response to threat would have been impossible.

paupertas and the apparently secure religious processes of the past recalls the poet's wishes in the first elegy. Doubts raised in that poem about the sincerity or restraint of the poet's *paupertas*, and about the true reliability of the exchange between the poet and the gods, already pointed to the un-achievability and ineffectiveness of these factors in contemporary life. Poem ten makes this explicit. The reader may expect that the power of *amor*, which was finally seen to motivate the poet's desires in poem one, is again the force which prompts him to long for these things (line 11). A revelation of the poet's position such as at lines 51ff. of poem one might be expected.

The stability, availability and consequent ease of the terms of religious exchange are emphasised: *hic placatus erat seu quis libauerat uuam | seu dederat sanctae spicea serta comae.* The power of the gods is exerted on behalf of the offerant (*uoti compos*) and the offering itself is depicted in the secure context of a family ritual: *postque comes... filia parua.* Yet, as the poet has emphasised, this state lies in the past. Doubts are raised, therefore, about the likelihood *in the present* of the *Lares* answering his appeal for protection (line 15) which is now re-iterated: *at nobis aerata, Lares, depellite tela* (25). The change in the terms of the appeal itself reflects the shift from the sta-bility of a pre-power-struggle world: *depellite tela.* Although the extent of the lacuna after line 25 is unknown, lines 26ff. seem to be a description of the offering (*hostiaque*) to be ex-changed in return for the *Lares'* intervention. There may, thus, be no great gap in sense between lines 25 and 26 as they now stand. If this assumption is true, it may be surprising that, as at lines 17–18, the poet relies on the same form of offerings[18] as in the (now apparently out-dated) past: *hostia-que e plena*[19] *rustica porcus hara.* This is particularly true fol-lowing the emphasis placed by the poet on the shift which has occurred in the context and terms of such an exchange. The

---

[18] The offering in this case is, however, perhaps a little more elaborate.
[19] This might seem unlikely given the poet's claims in the first elegy that he *lacked* such plenty, that such plenty was itself a thing of the past.

poet presents the *Lares* with a rural offering (*rustica*), and he himself takes part in the ritual (*sequar*).[20] The ritual itself, with its purity of clothing (*pura ueste*) and the repeated motif of binding (*myrtoque canistra | uincta geram, myrto uinctus et ipse caput*), reflects the poet's desire and expectation of a certain and secure process of interchange between man and gods. The insistence on binding (*uincta*; *uinctus*), in fact, recalls the poet's earlier restriction by the bonds of *amor*'s power (compare 1.1.55). This points to the similarities of the power relations defined by the poet's submission to worship of the gods in the hope of gaining their favour and thus their help, and by the poet's enchainment before his mistress' house in the hope of gaining her compliance.[21] The breakdown of such processes in the sphere of *amor* has been marked in earlier poems. The suggestion of the poet in the first elegy, and especially his explicit remarks in this poem, seem to make it clear that the stability of such processes is a thing of the (now almost mythical) past. The poet can only plead that such an exchange may be valid: *sic placeam uobis*.

Another *alius*

Sic placeam uobis. alius sit fortis in armis,
    sternat et aduersos Marte fauente duces,
ut mihi potanti possit sua dicere facta
    miles et in mensa pingere castra mero.
quis furor est atram bellis arcessere Mortem!
    imminet et tacito clam uenit illa pede.
non seges est infra, non uinea culta, sed audax
    Cerberus et Stygiae nauita turpis aquae.
illic percussisque genis ustoque capillo
    errat ad obscuros pallida turba lacus.

[20] Whom is the poet physically following? Is it just the *hostia*? Or is it the swineherd, or, on the analogy of 1.5.27–8, is it even possibly *Delia*? This information, which might have considerably re-arranged our understanding of this elegy, is, however, lost in the lacuna between lines 25 and 26.

[21] The similarity of the poet's relationship with *Amor*/Venus and the *Lares* is also suggested by the repeated use of myrtle, sacred to Venus. But here myrtle is being offered not to Venus but, presumably, to the *Lares*, perhaps suggesting a change of primary allegiance on the poet's part.

quis potius laudandus hic est quem prole parata
occupat in parua pigra senecta casa? (29–40)

The recollection of the opening lines of the first elegy in
alius sit of line 29 recalls the new central determinant of a
more violent, commercial process which underlies the actions
of the *alius fortis in armis* at 1.10.29. This is the pursuit of
wealth: the *diuitias fuluo auro* and *iugera multa* of 1.1.1–2
which form the power base in post-Golden-Age society. The
picture of the *alius* at lines 29–30 of poem ten, moreover,
strongly recalls the picture of Messalla at 1.1.53–4 and especially in the seventh poem. He is a figure of power (*fortis*), a
soldier overpowering enemy leaders: *sternat et aduersos Marte
fauente duces* (compare 1.1.53–4 and 1.7.6). Yet, whereas such
behaviour was depicted as perfectly valid in itself in poem one
(*te bellare decet* lines 53–4), and as the exertion of great power
on behalf of the Roman people in poem seven, here not only
are warfare, its motives and consequences condemned in far
less qualified terms (lines 1–7), but the actual description of
the successful veteran soldier belittles the ultimate achieve-
ment of his power: *ut mihi potanti*[22] *possit sua dicere facta |
miles et in mensa pingere castra mero.* This also links the
soldier with the lover, who, the poet has previously claimed,
similarly uses marks on the table to communicate secretly
with his/her beloved (1.6.19–20). This may suggest that war is
an ultimate, violent realization of the type of power struggles
mapped out in the sphere of *amor.* But while in the case of
lovers this communication gave them the power of secrecy, in
the case of the conventionally more powerful soldier it suggests the ultimate futility of his occupation.

The lines which follow underline this futility of the martial
power struggle. The poet sees this struggle, paradoxically, as a
form of lack of control (*quis furor*). This reference to power
used in an uncontrolled and inappropriate way picks up the
themes of the opening lines of the poem (lines 1–6). Now the
poet portrays violent struggle for power and wealth as, in fact,

---

[22] The poet himself is seen enjoying the pleasure of the wine.

power exerted on behalf of another force, *Mors* : *quis furor est atram bellis arcessere Mortem!* The pursuers of a war are pictured as lacking control and as being instead controlled by a passion for *Mors* in a similar manner to the lover's domination by *Amor*. *Mors* is also seen here as an unstoppable force employing the same tactics of secrecy as the lover earlier in the collection (*tacito clam ... pede*), but with apparently far greater success: *imminet et tacito clam uenit illa pede*. The comfort and security associated with rural life are negated by death's power: *non seges est infra, non uinea culta*.[23] The afterlife is associated with further violence (*audax | Cerberus; percussisque*[24] *genis*), discomfort (*Stygiae nauita*[25] *turpis aquae*) and uncertainty (*errat ad obscuros ... lacus*). *Mors* appears as a power which cannot be opposed and needs no support. In the face of this power opposed to humankind, the soldier's alliance with death is depicted as a power misused, like the *ensis* itself in lines 5–6. In contrast, the power best used (*potius laudandus*) is that which most successfully resists death (*pigra senecta*), at least for a while. By re-allocating praise, which in the past has been associated with power and particularly military success,[26] the poet effectively depicts the quiet, rural life as the more powerful position.

The *laudandus*

Ipse suas sectatur oues, at filius agnos;
   et calidam fesso comparat uxor aquam.
sic ego sim, liceatque caput candescere canis,
   temporis et prisci facta referre senem.   (41–4)

---

[23] On this line's suggestion of the vulnerability of the poet's rural ideal see Boyd (1984) 278.

[24] The conjectured *pertusisque*, which may well be correct (see Murgatroyd (1980) 324–5), would also suggest the violence associated with death and the afterlife, referring to cheeks 'perforated' or 'bored through' either by the effects of a funeral pyre (as Murgatroyd suggests) or the natural decay which follows death.

[25] Navigation and the sea are associated with vulnerability and discomfort in previous poems (compare especially 1.3.37ff.).

[26] As it was, for example, in the poet's rejection of the military life at 1.1.57: *non ego laudari curo*.

The *laudandus* is securely placed in a family context (*prole parata ... filius ... uxor*).[27] His resources are small but they are within his, or his family's, control (*ipse suas sectatur oues, at filius*[28] *agros*). Comfort, too, is available to him in exchange for his work (*et calidam fesso comparat uxor aquam*). The depiction of the *laudandus* as a powerful figure is enhanced by the recollection here of Messalla surrounded by his children in old age at 1.7.55–6. The presence of the *uxor* and the secure role and position of each member in the family unit excludes the insecurity and lack of control which has characterised the poet/lover under the influence of *amor* in earlier elegies. The *laudandus* and his *uxor* present a conventional male/female social relationship and thus, because of the very nature of that conventional social bond, a male-biased power relationship. This is also suggested by the portrayal of the *uxor* 'serving' the man at line 42, a detail which recalls the assimilation of Delia into more conventional social relationships through her serving of Messalla as part of the poet's ideal at 1.5.31–4.

The poet himself hopes for such a life: *sic ego sim*. It is the opposite of the insecure, powerless lifestyle of the *amor*-controlled poet seen in previous poems. The growing brightness of the man's hair (*caput ... candescere canis*) again recalls the poet's depiction of the *uictor* in poem seven and his hopes for Messalla at 1.7.64. This further associates the *laudandus* with Messalla and points to the power held by such a figure, a power which is here re-set in a rural, peaceful context.[29] Unlike poem one, the demands of *amor* have not yet been shown to underlie and effectively prevent the poet's desires from being fulfilled. But, also unlike the first poem, it has been emphasised already in poem ten that the security which the poet now hopes for belongs to a past world. The chances of re-establishing that security seem slim in a present where, as all

---

[27] On the meaning of *prole parata* as 'with his children at hand' see Race (1981) 146–7.

[28] This also suggests the security of the line of descent.

[29] This perhaps recalls the poet's attempt to set Messalla in a rural context through association with Osiris.

ten poems have demonstrated, the sort of processes around which the poet would structure his ideal lifestyle have become unstable. The place of such processes seems to have been taken by violent, disruptive and, more importantly, commercial exchanges and power struggles. The contrast between the two worlds is further emphasised by the picture of the old man recounting *facta* (*temporis et prisci facta referre senem*) just as the *miles* had boasted of *facta* in a mock-heroic way at lines 31–2. But the fact that they are *temporis prisci facta* may further suggest that such an ideal lifestyle could itself only be realised in a past age.

Pax

> Interea Pax arua colat. Pax candida primum
> duxit araturos sub iuga curua boues.
> Pax aluit uites et sucos condidit uuae,
> funderet ut nato testa paterna merum.
> Pace bidens uomerque nitent, at tristia duri
> militis in tenebris occupat arma situs.
> rusticus e lucoque uehit, male sobrius ipse,
> uxorem plaustro progeniemque domum.   (45–52)

This ideal lifestyle, without the violent power struggles embodied by war, is summed up in the poet's wish not simply for his own protection from war, but for general peace: *interea Pax arua colat*. That *Pax* appears in a rural setting, and in fact as a rural god (*arua colat ... primum*[30] | *duxit araturos sub iuga curua boues*), suggests again that the poet's motive for desiring a rural life in this case is a wish to be free of power struggles beyond his control. Such struggles are typified by war and, by contrast with rural *Pax*, associated with an urban, post-Golden-Age society. This also draws attention to the contradictions between the rural world of *Pax* here and the rural world in which the warrior Messalla is set in the

---

[30] Presenting a more appropriately used power of the creator, opposed to the destructive power of the sword's inventor in the opening lines.

POEM TEN

closing lines of poem seven and by his association with the
farmer-god Osiris earlier in the same poem.[31]

The absence of the need to struggle for power, especially
with fellow humans, is the element emphasised in the description of the intervention of *Pax* in human affairs from line 45.
Pax's manipulation of the oxen, a skill which she is the first to
develop (supposedly for the use of humans), is described in
terms of domination and control: *duxit araturos sub iuga
curua boues*. (Like the self-possessed old man of the previous
lines or the powerful victor of poem seven, *Pax* is *candida*.)
She takes control of the cultivation and thus the support and
nourishment of rural folk: *Pax aluit uites et sucos condidit
uuae*. The power struggle here is against nature, but *Pax*
ensures the ease and success of human efforts. This brings
security, exemplified by the stable continuation of the family
line (*funderet ut nato testa paterna merum*) which was significantly broken, for whatever reason,[32] in poem one. The concern for the correct use of human power, which first appeared
in the poet's attitude towards the *ensis* at lines 5–6, is now
developed into broader expression at lines 49–50: *Pace bidens
uomerque nitent, at tristia duri | militis in tenebris occupat arma
situs*. At lines 45–8, *Pax* has been seen to ensure the effectiveness of the instruments through which humans exert
power over nature. Those instruments express their power
through the familiar motif of brightness (*nitent*), while in
contrast the instruments of commercial power struggle between humans are themselves overpowered and restrained: *in
tenebris occupat arma situs*. However, the poet's insistent de-

---

[31] Compare the contrast, suggested by Solmsen (1962) 298 (quoted above, note 1),
between the world of contemporary Roman power embodied in Augustan *Pax*
and the picture of *pax* in this poem. In contrast see Leach (1978): 'reconciling
imagination and reality, [the poet] brings his book to its resolution in an image of
Roman harmony with Augustan Pax spreading her influence over the countryside,' 97–8. See also Cairns (1979): 'his praise of peace could be read as praise of
what Augustus had achieved for Italy, despite the wars still going on abroad,' 104.
See below, 282–5, for a fuller discussion of the contrast between the ideal and
reality.

[32] This may be due to the poet's neglect of his estate because of his domination by
amor, or to land-confiscations of some sort (see above, 37 and 40). Both possibilities could be looked upon as varieties of the power struggle which are seen here in
poem ten and in earlier poems to be characteristic of the contemporary world.

278

sire for peace (*Pax ... Pax ... Pax ... Pace*), along with his description of his own impending *militia*[33] at line 13, points to the fact that peace has *not* yet been achieved and does *not* now appear imminent. The *rusticus* of lines 51ff. is pictured returning from a conventional religious setting (*e lucoque*) which recalls the poet's desire for a stable relationship between gods and mortals. The *rusticus* enjoys the pleasure of wine (*male sobrius ipse*) probably at a festival.[34] But the secure, domestic family context of this *rusticus* (*uehit ... | uxorem plaustro progeniemque domum*)[35] seems fragile; a possibly unachievable ideal in the contemporary world.[36]

An end to struggle?

Sed Veneris tunc bella calent, scissosque capillos
    femina perfractas conqueriturque fores.
flet teneras subtusa genas, sed uictor et ipse
    flet sibi dementes tam ualuisse manus.
at lasciuus Amor rixae mala uerba ministrat,
    inter et iratum lentus utrumque sedet.
a lapis est ferrumque, suam quicumque puellam
    uerberat: e caelo deripit ille deos.
sit satis e membris tenuem rescindere uestem,
    sit satis ornatus dissoluisse comae,
sit lacrimas mouisse satis. quater ille beatus
    quo tenera irato flere puella potest.
sed manibus qui saeuus erit, scutumque sudemque
    is gerat et miti sit procul a Venere.
at nobis, Pax alma, ueni spicamque teneto,
    profluat et pomis candidus ante sinus.   (53–68)

---

[33] This is an unexpected development after the apparent abortive end to the poet's military career in poem three, and suggests the persistent and irresistible demands of the contemporary world and the processes which dominate it.

[34] Hence *e lucoque*; the festival being an affirmation of community as well as religious certainties and securities.

[35] The textual integrity of this passage is, however, disputed. See Courtney (1987) 29–30, who argues for the deletion of lines 51–2.

[36] On the unachievability of the ideal see Boyd (1984) 278, and Lyne (1980) 153–4.

At line 53 another familiar force erupts into the ideal: *sed Veneris tunc bella calent*. This might raise the expectation that, as in poem one, *amor*'s effective determination of the poet's attitudes and aspirations will now be revealed. But the description of the sphere of love as *Veneris bella* associates it with the power struggles of war and the contemporary age already rejected by the poet. Its sudden appearance (*sed ... tunc*) seems disruptive and opposed to the ideal rather than determining it as in the first poem.[37] In the opposition of past versus present, *Pax* vs *bella*, absence of power struggles among humans versus the commercially and power motivated struggles of contemporary society, *amor* is firmly placed on the side of *bella* and violent struggle. This violence is clear in lines 53–4: *scissosque capillos | femina perfractas conqueriturque fores*. This recalls love-as-war seen at the end of the first elegy (1.1.73ff.). But this is no longer seen as something which is both similar in nature and set in opposition to *militia*. Rather, in the context not only of poem ten but of the power struggles of the collection as it has developed, this violent conflict within the *amor*-relationship is seen as entirely the same as *bella*. It is a disruptive struggle for power. Although here it is specifically physical violence in love, this might now seem only an ultimate expression of the conflict and struggle which has surrounded *amor* throughout the ten poems. While the male has the physical power, the female clearly has the emotional control, and the outburst of physical violence is effectively turned against him. *Dementes manus* suggests a lack of control under the influence of *amor*, which has been characteristic of the poet himself, although not in his case expressed in physical violence: *sed uictor et ipse | flet sibi dementes tam ualuisse manus*. *Amor* is a creator of struggle and violent division, and *Amor*, like *Mors*, appears unstoppable and entirely in control: *at lasciuus Amor rixae mala uerba ministrat*. Alongside and akin to the conflict between *Pax* and

---

[37] In the opening elegy the force of *amor* did effectively make the poet's desires unrealisable, and it was also clear that it was his domination by that passion which largely motivated those desires (see above, 50ff.).

Martis bella there is now seen the struggle for domination between *Pax* and *Amor* (*Veneris bella*), and *Amor* like war seems the more powerful opponent: *inter et iratum lentus utrumque sedet.*

The link between *amor* and war is further emphasised at line 59: *a lapis est ferrumque.* The man's attempt to control his beloved through physical power is described in the same terms as the poet has previously described a master's treatment of a slave, illustrating the power relation: *suam quicumque puellam | uerberat.* The man himself is described in the same terms as the creator of the sword (*ferreus* at line 2, *ferrumque* at line 59). Like the invention of the sword at lines 5–6, excessive violence is seen as a misuse of power, and it is described as disrupting the secure religious structure which the poet has expressed as part of the peaceful rural lifestyle he desires: *e caelo deripit ille deos.*[38]

The poet does not entirely reject the use of physical force within the *amor*-relationship, but is concerned with the limits of such power (*sit satis ... sit satis ... sit ... satis*). Now violent destruction, though not levelled directly against humans (*e membris tenuem rescindere uestem ... ornatus dissoluisse comae ... lacrimas mouisse*), becomes an expression of the male's power over the female, an assertion of a more or less conventional male-biased power relationship. This is suggested in the male's mock-heroic power over the woman's emotions: *quater ille beatus | quo tenera irato flere puella potest.*[39] The mock-heroic tone of these lines might suggest that the poet is in fact ridiculing such a power relationship, although its nature seems similar to the conventional male-dominated relationship of man and *uxor* desired by the poet at 1.10.42, a relationship of the type which the poet himself has been unable to achieve throughout the elegies.[40] However

---

[38] This is also expressed in terms which recall the power of a witch and her struggles with nature and divine power, which have also been seen in the context of *amor*-relationships in previous poems (see 1.2.43ff., and 1.8.17ff.).

[39] Compare the poet's aspirations to make Delia cry at 1.1.61ff.

[40] The joke may thus be on the poet for expressing in such elevated, longing terms a position of power over the beloved which he has been conspicuously unable to achieve throughout the collection.

this point is interpreted, it seems clear that the poet rejects excessive power and its misuse as disruptive in the same sense that the power struggle of war is disruptive (*scutumque sudemque*): *sed manibus qui saeuus erit, scutumque sudemque | is gerat et miti sit procul a Venere.*[41] It is significant that the male's lack of control, which was an element of excessive power at lines 53–8 (particularly line 56), is eliminated in the restrained use of male power at lines 61–4, as is the woman's consequent emotional power over the man. Effectively, then, there would be no power struggle, and certainly no one-sided control of the male by *amor* such as the poet has experienced. Instead the male would hold a dominant position in the relationship, expressed by his controlled use of physical force.

In the final lines of the poem the poet asserts again what in particular he desires: *at nobis, Pax alma, ueni. Pax* embodies and brings about the rural security and certainty which the poet desires. (Again brightness is a feature of this: *candidus sinus*.) Part of such security is the ease with which rural produce is distributed: *profluat et pomis candidus ante sinus.* This is a world where power struggles of the type which the poet has seemed unsuited for and unsuccessful at are absent. *Pax candida* replaces the brightness of military victors and brings security by exerting her power as a provider, as well as protector, on behalf of rural folk. But, as the poem itself has emphasised, *Pax*'s sphere of influence belongs to the past. Finally the poet, himself being powerlessly dragged off to war, can only appeal for an end to power struggles, both of war and *amor*. In both such struggles he has conspicuously failed, a failure charted through the collection and brought to the final powerless desire to escape expressed in poem ten.

Conclusion: ramifications

The contrast between the ideal of peace and the reality of *nunc ad bella trahor*, between the desire for freedom from power

---

[41] It is ironic, of course, that despite his wishes here, the poet himself has found Venus far less than *mitis*.

struggle and the operation of a culture based upon it, is emphasised by the pastoral motifs observed in the poem by some critics.[42] Elder and Lawall[43] have noted the essential conflict in Tibullan pastoral between ideal and reality: 'a confrontation between a misty dream world and the actual world of Rome'.[44] Although the ideal in poem ten is rather more specific than the 'misty dream world' which Lawall suggests, its unrealisability is emphasised, reflecting the essential contrasts upon which the pastoral genre is founded. Halperin has described this as 'the most traditional contrast ... between the little world of natural simplicity and the great world of civilization, power, statecraft, ordered society, established codes of behaviour, and artifice in general'.[45] Citing Halperin's view and applying it to Tibullus, Van Nortwick concludes: 'This is the contrast that Tibullus exploits relentlessly in his elegies, and here is where we must look for the link between pastoral and love elegy.'[46] Like the pastoral world of Virgil's *Eclogues*, the structures and demands of Roman power (of the power with which Rome has become equated) overwhelm the poet's ideal in Tibullus 1.10, as the reality of *nunc ad bella trahor* occasions, and hangs over, the prayer for peace which ends the collection.

The final poem of the collection forces the reader to question and re-evaluate the whole in a number of ways. The 'Delia' sequence of poems is now seen to be completed at poem six and can now be considered in its entirety and compared with the other central amorous theme, the 'Marathus' sequence which ended in poem nine.[47] With the final poem, the culture of power struggle and aggressive commercial exchange, equated with a contemporary 'iron' age, is rejected

---

[42] For example, Pillinger's characterisation of the poet's ideal here as one of 'bucolic ease', Pillinger (1971) 204; or the reminiscences of the *Eclogues* referred to above, 265. One dissenting voice is that of Solmsen, who denies the presence of pastoral elements in Tibullan poetry, Solmsen (1962) 302-4.
[43] Elder (1962) 79ff.; and Lawall (1975) 87-100.
[44] Lawall (1975) 94.
[45] Halperin (1983) 64-5.
[46] Van Nortwick (1990) 121.
[47] For a more detailed examination of the implications of this, see below, 287-8.

entirely by the poet, who has failed to master the processes and demands of such a world. Unlike the first elegy, where the poet's desire for a rural life was finally revealed to be determined by *amor*'s control over him, in poem ten the power struggles of *amor* are ranked with the power struggles of war, and the poet desires a more restrained *amor*-relationship of a type he was unable to achieve in earlier poems. The depiction of struggle throughout the collection has led to the poet's rejection of struggle, wealth and power in general. The nature of his desire seems determined by his own failures rather than by control exerted over him by *amor*, which is itself seen as a force for conflict.[48]

Military power is rejected, not in relation to *amor*, but in itself, as a disruptive, destructive contemporary force. This inevitably reflects on the figure of Messalla. Messalla, like Delia and Marathus, is absent from the poem. But imagery within the poem, as well as the theme of martial struggle and the poet's impending *militia*, recalls the depiction of Messalla in earlier elegies. Poem ten encourages a re-evaluation of the poet's relationship with his patron. By rejecting not only warfare but the whole culture of power-acquisition, the poet, effectively if not consciously, undercuts Messalla himself, whose own power has been seen in poems one, three and seven to be based upon military prowess. Not only this, but the poet's desire for a world free of human power struggle and differentiation also seems to deny the implicit power relationship of poet and patron, such as exists between himself and Messalla. Although the poet's hopes appear unlikely to be realised, the reader is led to question the poet's attitude to Messalla himself along with the world of contemporary military/political power which he inhabits.

Related to this are the implications which the poet's final emphasis on war and his desire for peace have for the reader's understanding of the entire collection's context and meaning. The eruption of war after the apparent universal triumph of

---

[48] Ironically, however, it might be said that *amor* in its very nature in fact *caused* his failures, and thus his final attitude.

Messalla in the seventh elegy suggests the disruption of the contemporary political world and its failure[49] to control the power struggles inherent in its nature. The poet's insistent desire for peace, and his indication of the equivalence of warfare and the struggles of *amor* not only in the tenth elegy but throughout the collection, suggest that the poet's experiences with *amor* might reflect by analogy on the nature of the broader socio-political world and its workings.[50] Poem ten suggests that the importance of power, the instability of conventional processes, and the importance of commercial exchange are characteristic of both worlds. The concerns of the collection encompass both of these worlds, which, it seems to suggest, are in many essential ways the same. This is the force behind much of the irony and humour of the collection: that something like elegiac *amor* which inverts conventional relationships and might be thought of as peripheral to traditional Roman elite culture is not only placed centre-stage but is equated with the central structures and processes by which that culture operates. This has already been suggested by similarities between the amorous sphere and the military/ political sphere as seen in poem seven and elsewhere. But it is in poem ten that this equivalence finds strongest expression, encouraging the reader to draw conclusions in retrospect about the workings and implications of the broader social, military and political situation from the elegies just read.

---

[49] Even if the elegies are not considered as a chronological sequence, the recurrence of the motif of war suggests its repeated, if not continual, eruption.

[50] For a more detailed discussion of these questions, see below, 300ff.

CONCLUSION

Powerplay

From the top to the bottom – from the world of the most powerful senator to that of the humblest slave – Roman society was sharply stratified. Divisions of status underlay all social and political life.[1]

The very notion that a patronal benefit requires a client response in the short-term implies an inherently self-regulating process in which the principle of reciprocal exchange maintains not only a given structure of power but – because it is personalised – particular groups or persons as the powerful.[2]

In Rome, as in other societies, religious institutions and practices reflected the power relations within the community and provided justification for the existing order.[3]

Sexual relationships were constructed as relationships of domination and subordination, of superiority and inferiority, in Roman moral and social discourse.[4]

The construction of relationships in terms of power, which these statements suggest is an inherent aspect of Roman culture in general, can easily be accommodated to a reading of Roman elegy. The *amor*-relationship, the element of elegiac discourse most commonly focused upon by critics, can be rendered as a relationship of domination and subordination. The beloved is dominant, in control of the poet/lover. This, it has been observed, produces an inversion of the dynamic of gender relations normally constructed in Roman discourse. Edwards, in the context of Roman moral discourse generally, sums this up: 'The usual elegiac scenario presents the man (conventionally the dominant partner) as slave to the woman

---

[1] Beard & Crawford (1985) 40. [2] Johnson & Dandeker (1989) 227.
[3] Garnsey & Saller (1987) 163. [4] Edwards (1993) 70.

– a piquant inversion of relations of domination as traditionally conceived, which also serves to problematize the relationship between power and sexual desire.'[5] This, by its very
abnormality, might tend to throw the structure and operation
of the norm into greater relief. The differences between these
relationships lend fresh emphasis to the similarities.

The *amor*-relationships in Tibullus' first book of elegies can
easily be read in these terms, and an approach to the text in
this way suggests a complex and wide-ranging skein of power
relations and their effects. The poet's domination by Delia
extends not only to his sexual desires, but to his social and
moral choices. The first elegy gradually collapses the assertion
of autonomous ethical choice made in the opening lines: the
poet's rejection of *militia* in favour of rural life. The determinant is not ethical choice, but *amor*. The power of Delia,
figured as physically restraining the poet at lines 55–6, is revealed to be the cause of the poet's 'rejection' of *militia* (lines
53–6) and his 'choice' of lifestyle. The dynamic which operates in the first elegy is not driven by ethics, it is driven by
power. The poet is passive, captured, bound and held by the
power of *amor*, and thus by *amor*'s instrument, the beloved.
It is this power, and the poet's position within the power-
relationship, which determines his choices, location, feelings
and responses.

The similarities between the relationship with Marathus
and that with Delia can also be read as indicative of parallel
power dynamics. The position of the poet at the end of poem
four (lines 81–4) and in the ninth poem mirrors the powerlessness of his relationship with Delia. Veyne, in his examination of homosexuality in Roman society, emphasises the
similar terms in which love of boys and love of women were
understood: 'the one was the same as the other, and what one
thought of one went for the other as well.'[6] The terms are
those of power-relations, of active and passive, of domination
or subordination: 'To be active was to be male, whatever the

[5] Edwards (1993) 65 n.4.   [6] Veyne (1985) 26.

sex of the compliant partner. To take one's pleasure was virile, to accept it servile – that was the whole story.'[7] This framework of sexual relationships maps easily onto the *amor*-relationships of Tibullan elegy. Both in the relationship with Delia and that with Marathus, *amor* leaves the poet/lover in the position of the passive, servile partner, in contrast to the norm.[8] This difference from the norm, and the similarity in this respect between the presentation of the heterosexual and pederastic relationships, can be located in their operation as power-relationships.[9]

The reading of the *amor*-relationships I have been suggesting creates resonances with other relationships in the elegies, which particular uses of language such as the *seruitium amoris* or *militia amoris* motifs highlight. For example, the motif of *seruitium amoris*, the interchangeability of the terms of slavery and those of *amor*, does not only underline the powerlessness of the poet/lover in both the Delia and the Marathus relationships (compare, for example, 5.61–6 and 9.41–4). It does not only reinforce the reading of *amor*-relationships as power-relationships. It also signals a parallel between the operation of *amor* and of other common social relationships.

Read in terms of a power dynamic, the relation of poet to patron is perhaps the most obvious parallel with the operation of the *amor*-relationship. The seventh elegy suggests similarities to the poet/lover's relationships with his beloveds not simply in the asserted power of Messalla, but in the language used to describe the patron's power. In some cases this extends to direct echoes of the beloved's power: the chains of 7.6 compare to those of 1.55–6, where the poet was also explicitly

---

[7] Veyne (1985) 29–30; also Edwards (1993) 70–3.

[8] 'Woman was passive by definition' Veyne (1982) 29–30.

[9] The powerful figures of Delia and Marathus, empowered by the poet's *amor* for them, correspond to the divine power figures, Venus and Cupid, who embody *amor*'s power. The correspondence is underlined by the similarity of the poet's appeals to both sets of forces as well as by the religious offerings and service which he bestows upon his human beloveds: compare especially the garlands which he hangs upon the doors both of Ceres (1.15–16) and Delia (2.14) with the garlands which are hung in the temple of Venus (2.83–4). Also, Cupid or Amor is often described in literature as a *puer*, and is referred to as *puer* at 5.4, just as Marathus is often referred to as *puer* in the collection.

comparing himself, as the spoils of Delia, to the spoils of war amassed by Messalla (1.54). The prominence of the 'Osiris hymn', and the links made there to the amorous sphere (see, for example, 7.43), suggest a parallel between that sphere and the one in which Messalla operates. The relationship of social domination and subordination between patron and poet itself reflects the power dynamic of the *amor*-relationships. Part of the poet's ideal in the fifth elegy (lines 31–4) involves Delia's serving of Messalla, significantly reversing the dominance of the beloved in the *amor*-relationship by submerging it in the dominance/subordination dynamic of the more conventional social relationship of patron and client. The immediate differences between the beloveds and Messalla add force to the similarities, and the similarities lie in the parallel positions of Messalla and the beloveds in their respective power-relationships. The appearance of a poem apparently in praise of a socially, politically, militarily powerful figure such as Messalla in the midst of a book of love poems may come as an initial surprise to the reader. But such surprise, if it occurs, only adds force to what, in another respect, is the appropriateness of a poem to such a figure of power alongside other poems concerned with similar figures of power. In turn, the placement of such figures 'side by side' in the elegiac collection, and sometimes in the same poem, draws out such similarities, encouraging the reader to compare and to observe connections. These connections, of course, raise questions concerning the text's involvement in the affirmation or subversion of this power structure in relation to Roman politics and society more generally, questions to which I will return later.

The similarities which can be seen here are placed within a broader network of parallel relationships and processes. The collection does not begin directly with *amor*, but with the opposition of *militia* to a pious, rural lifestyle. Both of these lifestyles can, in turn, be seen as separate and even radically different from the sphere of *amor*. In the ethical implications of *militia* and a rustic life, however, and in the operation of *militia*, *rus*, and *amor* as seen in the first elegy, this separation and asserted difference can be elided. Not only are the roles of the *miles* and the *rusticus* closely identified in Roman ethical discourse, but the relationship of the soldier to military service, or to his general,[10] and of the farmer to the gods of the countryside parallel the relationships between the poet/lover and the beloveds. The powerlessness and vulnerability of the soldier during military service are emphasised in the opening lines, as they are in the third and tenth poems (compare especially 3.49–50; 10.11–14). Similarly, the farmer whom the poet seeks to identify himself with is largely dependent on the intervention of the gods to ensure the success of his ideal (compare specially 1.24; 1.33–6),[11] and the fate of the poet's estate in the past might put this intervention in doubt.

Religion as it appears more generally in the collection can be seen to operate within a power structure similar in shape to the *amor*-relationship and explicitly recalled by it in the language used to define the position of the beloved in relation to the poet/lover. The poet assumes or, more often, appeals to the power of various deities at many points throughout the ten poems. The gods are expected or entreated to aid the poet, or the beloved on the poet's behalf, by bestowing their power through knowledge, protection, or other forms of intervention. Venus' supposed protection of and bestowal of useful knowledge upon lovers (2.15–24 and 35–42), and the invocation of the authority of the goddess Bellona's priestess to warn away potential rivals (6.43–56), are two more developed examples of this, but there are also many briefer appeals (often linked through use of the recurrent verb *parco*)[12] which suggest the poet's dependence on divine power. In return for this divine aid the poet gives religious service: offerings, prayers, rituals. In other words, piety. A parallel can be constructed

---

[10] The relationship between *miles* and general becomes more obvious in poem three.

[11] See also the quasi-divine role of *Spes* at 1.9–10. It is the poet's expectation of divine support granted in return for prayer and offering that, in his mind, justifies this hope (1.11–14).

[12] The imperative forms *parce* and *parcite* occur eleven times in Tibullus Book One alone, compared to only five occurrences in all the works of Propertius combined.

here with the relationship of subordination and dominance between poet/lover and beloveds. This parallel is reinforced by the common motifs of offering and service given or pledged by the poet/lover. One particular example of this is the hanging of similar[13] garlands both on the doors of Delia (2.14) and at temples or shrines (1.12). The similarities of the language used in both cases (of the religious and of the erotic) reflect the parallel power structures of the two supposedly separate spheres.

In other areas, too, the language of *amor*, and thus the power relationships constructed and set in operation by that language, are paralleled in the language of what are otherwise represented as separate and distinct spheres. As referred to above, the motifs of *seruitium amoris* and *militia amoris* are the most obvious and extensive forms of linguistic linkage. As a result their role in elegy more generally has been extensively explored by critics.[14] While the observation that similar language is being used of different spheres of action or experience affirms in one respect the separateness of those spheres, it simultaneously draws attention to the similarities. This, of course, raises the question of which sphere is to be privileged over the other: is the structure of slavery, for example, a paradigm for the *amor*-relationship, or vice versa? It is one thing to read the various social relationships and spheres which parallel *amor* as suggesting something about the nature of the elegiac, erotic relationship, and another to read *amor*, as it is constructed in the elegiac text, as having implications for those other spheres. While it is tempting to read *amor* in Tibullus' first book as paradigmatic,[15] the similarities of these various relationships and spheres point rather to a common construction of power, a common framework by which power can be understood and thus presented.

[13] These garlands may even be identical, as is suggested by the charge that the poet/lover may have been stealing garlands from Venus' temple to hang on Delia's door (2.83–4).

[14] See for example Lyne (1980) 71–81, and (1979); Murgatroyd (1975), and (1981); Copley (1947); Veyne (1988) 132–50.

[15] For this suggestion, see above 66.

CONCLUSION

The exception and the rule

This framework delineates not only the relationship of domination and subordination present in the power dynamic, but the process by which power is gained, maintained and exercised. This process can be read in the description of *militia* in the opening six lines of the collection. The exchange of military service, involving hardship and danger in a trade-off for wealth, is set up as an opposite to the ideal rural life of the poet. But this assertion of difference can be collapsed by emphasis on the structure of this exchange, or trade-off. The relationship between the projected poet/farmer and the gods can also be viewed in just such terms. As observed above, the poet suggests that in return for prosperity he venerates, or will venerate, the gods by offering them votive gifts and first fruits (1.9–16; 1.19–24; 1.35–8). Just as the two lifestyles are linked in Roman moral discourse, religious service and military service can be seen to operate in similar ways, despite the assertion of opposition which opens the collection.[16] In the tenth elegy, the rural offerings are made in return for protection from the dangers of war, further collapsing the assertion of difference between farmer and soldier. In each case, starting from a position of powerlessness, service is offered to gain the desired outcome. The power represented by wealth, prosperity and security can only be achieved through this exchange. It presents a structure for achieving and defining power, whether of the successful, wealthy soldier, or of the prosperous and secure farmer.

This structure can easily be applied to the *amor*-relationship. The abasement or vulnerability (the powerlessness) of the poet/lover[17] offered in return for the power of achieving his desires and bringing security to the relationship with the beloved is a common idea in erotic poetry and, in particular,

---

[16] See above, 27–34, for this assertion of opposition in the opening lines of the first elegy.
[17] Here the motifs of *seruitium amoris* and *militia amoris* can also be collapsed into one another, as can the lifestyles of the farmer and soldier in the first and final elegies.

292

the first Tibullan collection. Service is offered in return for the desired compliance of the beloved: powerlessness is exchanged for power (compare 1.55–6; 1.73–6; 2.73–6; 4.39–56; 5.9–16; 5.61–6; 9.41–4). This is the assumed, or at least hoped-for, process set up by the poet/lover.

Its recurrence in various spheres might be seen as an affirmation of this process as a pervasive structure for the achievement, operation and, thus, conceptualisation of power in Roman society. This recurrence might seem to present the 'service' and the resultant subservience of the individual, which are necessary in various fields for the successful operation of Roman social structures, as the price to be paid for eventual success and, thus, power. But the application of this process to elegiac *amor* places it under pressure. As the poet presents it, the process operates securely in the realm of *militia*, as is suggested not only by the assertion of the opening lines of the collection, but also by the position of the powerful, successful *ferreus* in poem two (2.67–72), and even the position of Messalla himself. It is also asserted in relation to the farmer, for whom it includes the hardship involved in working the land, a form of toil which is directly equated with the hardship undergone in hope of the beloved's compliance at 2.73–6. This comparison further elides the differences between the two spheres. This process also operates in the sphere of trade. The processes involved in both the case of the farmer and that of the trader are, in fact, directly identified with one another at 9.7–10, the aim being again wealth (*lucra*). But, when applied to the erotic sphere, this process of service and vulnerability exchanged for profit appears to break down. It fails to bring the result which is expected: the compliance of the beloved. It does not win the poet/lover any control over the *amor*-relationship. This is explicit in both the heterosexual (5.59–68) and the pederastic (9.41–51) relationships.

The exchange process in the fields of *militia* and agriculture can, of course, be put under similar stress. Military service can end in death, and the rural gods can fail to deliver a good harvest. Indeed, a comparison between the breakdown of this process in the sphere of *amor* and its potential failure in these other areas is suggested through the figure of the poet/lover himself. The poet/lover's involvement with military service and farming both draw attention to the potential breakdown of the exchange. In the opening poem, the decline of the poet's rural estate is explicitly referred to at 1.19–20 and this casts doubt upon the likelihood that the gods' power will be directed for the prosperity of that estate in the future, as the poet seems to expect it will. In the same way, the poet/lover's experience of *militia* as it is reflected in the third poem ends in sickness and the immediate prospect of death, and when he is forced to go on military service in the tenth poem, the poet himself draws attention to the threat of death (10.13–14). The poet/lover assumes in his description of the rural world that the exchange process will be complete. He also presents other figures involved in the *militia* process (the *alius* of poem one, the *ferreus* of poem two, and Messalla) as having successfully exploited the trade-off. But in the poet/lover's case the breakdown of this process in the fields of *militia* and rural life is emphasised, as it is in the sphere of *amor*. Through the figure of the poet/lover the similarity between the stress put on this process by *amor* and its operation in other areas is suggested. This allows an analogy to be made, in contrast to the poet's assumptions and his presentation of the process' successful function in other spheres as something different from its breakdown when applied to the domain of *amor*. The text allows *amor* to be seen as both/either analogous and/or anomalous to those other areas.

Other sources of power to which the poet/lover turns, both within and outside the conventional process, similarly fail before *amor*'s complete control. This failure can be seen not only in the poet's attempt to assert ethical autonomy in the first poem, but also in his claims to power throughout the collection. His claims to be supported by Venus' power in the second elegy are undercut (compare especially 2.35–42 and 2.81–2, 2.99–100), and the elegy as a whole involves the undercutting of the poet's implications that Delia, empowered simply by the knowledge which Venus provides (2.15–24), will be willing to comply with his desires. This destabilises similar claims of the poet's later in the collection, as in the sixth poem where he claims authority for his words from the high-priestess of Bellona (6.43–56) and suggests that he and Delia will be an *exemplum* of *amor* into their old age (6.85–6). The language of this final claim links it with other attempts to imaginatively reconstruct and control the power dynamic of the relationship: the dream of homecoming which concludes the third elegy (3.89–94), and the ideal expressed in poem five (5.19–34). The failure of desire and imagination to control the relationship is explicitly stated in this last example (5.35–6) and is reflected in the literary failure of the poet/lover in the struggle with *amor*. *Canimus frustra* (5.67) underlines the powerlessness of poetry as a persuasive force,[18] as do the complaints of Priapus in the pederastic context (4.57ff.). The poet's claims to knowledge in the erotic sphere, primarily of the techniques of *furtiuus amor*, are similarly ineffectual, giving him no control over his situation either with Delia[19] or Marathus.[20] More peripheral means to power are equally overpowered by *amor*: the poet's desire for Delia prevents him from employing magic to free himself from *amor*'s power (2.65–6), and his claims to have magical assistance (2.43–64)[21] are useless without Delia's compliance. The poet is represented as entirely powerless, a position within the relationship equated with great suffering (see, for example, 2.81ff., 4.81–4, 5.3–6, 6.1–4). Both less orthodox means, such as magic, and more conventional sources of power, like the gods, persuasion, and even the poet's ability, as he presents it, to imaginatively control his literary world and the direction of the text, break down when applied to the *amor*-relationship.

---

[18] As observed by Stroh (1971) 112ff.

[19] See, for example, poem six, lines 9–22, where the lessons the poet teaches Delia actually worsen his position, and the 'superior' knowledge displayed in his address to the *coniunx* has been and remains unable to improve his powerless situation.

[20] Compare the claims to knowledge at 8.5–6 ánd the continued powerlessness of the poet in poem nine.

[21] This powerlessness, despite the poet's various claims to power, often culminates in his appeal either for power to be exercised on his behalf or for power detrimental to his interests *not* to be exerted. Such appeals recur throughout the collection: in particular, *parce/parcite*, addressed variously to gods, humans and animals, recurs like a familiar refrain eleven times in the ten poems.

As has been remarked above, this breakdown can be read most clearly in terms of the service or exchange process, a structure for social relationships that was pervasive in Roman culture. The implications of this breakdown can be read, for example, in the passage previously cited as an example of the *seruitium amoris* trade-off: 5.61–6. The service offered here by the *pauper* closely resembles that of the poorest rank of *cliens*, the *adsectatores*, 'whose devotion or obligation is to one patron only and who therefore stay at his side all day, clearing the way for him and making themselves useful however they can.'[22] This passage thus invokes the fundamental social power-relationship of client-patron, together with the related relationship of *amicitia*,[23] to which the *amor*-relationship, at least as it is idealised by the poet/lover, has often been compared.[24] But this relationship breaks down: the beloved does not fulfil her part of the exchange (5.67–8). Beyond the suffering of powerlessness which is a feature of depictions of the elegiac poet/lover more generally, and beyond the inversion of conventional gender relations involved in this, the irrational, anomalous nature of the *amor*-relationship is asserted through its failure to conform to, or be affected by, the structure which is at the same time affirmed as the conventional process by which power is distributed and understood.

But, at the same time as the elegiac *amor*-relationship can be read as anomalous in this respect and its operation viewed as irrational, there is common ground between the presentation of the breakdown of this conventional process in the erotic sphere and the central means by which this process in its various forms was defined and conducted in Roman culture. In both cases the interrelation of wealth and power is instrumental. Money is asserted as the means to control in the *amor*-relationship in both the Delia and the Marathus poems.

---

[22] Wiseman (1982) 29.
[23] See Saller (1989), 49–62, for the similarities between patronage and *amicitia*. For a more recent, and different, view of *amicitia*, however, see Konstan (1997) 122–48.
[24] See Lyne (1980) 24–41; Copley (1972) 78–96; and Alfonsi (1945) 372–8; compare also the *'foedus'* of *amor*: Reitzenstein (1975) on Catullus; and Freyburger (1980), 105–16 on elegy.

Money gains the compliance of the beloved (4.58–60; 5.47ff.; 9.11ff.). In one respect, this could be seen as maintaining the dominant position of the beloved in the *amor*-relationship, demanding and receiving the gifts for his/her compliance. But it can also be read as a realignment in terms of the conventional power relationship. The beloved, now like the client, provides the service, while the rich lover, taking the position of the socially dominant patron, provides *munera*.

There is a correspondence between this view of the *amor*-relationship as a commercial exchange and Roman economic activities more generally. Paul Veyne, describing the elegiac mistress's demands for gifts, draws attention to this correspondence:

> ... these women were not venal (*vénales*), although they were mercenary (*intéressées*), because they were Roman women and Roman society was so mercenary, anti-Semites could have taken Rome rather than the Jews for their obsession. Which means simply that economic activities were not the specialization of a few professionals, nor were they characteristic of one particular social class. In Rome, rich people all did business wherever they could, senators all lent money at usurious rates, and making deals among the nobles was even more widespread than at the end of our own ancient régime, except that it was not hidden. This multiformed omnipresence of seeking gain took the place of the absent bourgeois class.[25]

In poem nine, the exchange of erotic service for money is explicitly grouped with other examples of the same process (farming and trade), reinforcing its correspondence with Roman social norms (9.5–11). Wealth was a defining force in Roman conceptualisations of power, determining the social stratification which delineated not only who was eligible to hold public office, but also the power dynamic between social classes and between individuals.[26] Through the identification

---

[25] Veyne (1988) 84; Love (1991); for the commercial activities of the senatorial class see D'Arms (1981) 48–71, and Finley (1985) 53–7.

[26] As in relationships such as *clientela* and/or *amicitia*. For an overview of wealth as a determinant of eligibility for office-holding and class status see Beard & Crawford (1985) 43–7; on inequality of status as a determinant of the positions within the relationships of *clientela* and *amicitia* see the third point of Saller's definition of patronage, 'it must be asymmetrical, in the sense that the two parties are of unequal status and offer different kinds of goods and services in the exchange' (Saller (1982) 1), and the similarities in this respect of *amicitia*, '*amici* were subdivided

of wealth with power in the erotic sphere, the power structure of the *amor*-relationship can be re-assimilated into the power structures and processes of Roman society. It can be seen as an assertion of the conventional relationship of exchange, of service for money or similar *beneficia*, which, in its more formalised manifestations, such as the client-patron relationship, provided the terms in which power was understood and negotiated.[27]

I stated earlier that it was tempting to view *amor* as paradigmatic, representing in an inverted and exaggerated form the power structures which can also be seen at work within other spheres of Roman society. I suggested this possibility in my reading of the opening poem. But, viewed from the perspective of the whole collection, it can be seen instead that it is through its operation as both representative *and* anomalous that the *amor*-relationship asserts these structures and processes. By conforming to *and* disrupting them, by the interplay of similarity and difference, it delineates the way they define, support and channel power. Similarly, the poet/lover of the collection is located both within and outside these structures and processes. This is the irony of his position. While *amor* prevents him from pursuing the normal processes by which power (wealth) might be amassed, this also leaves him powerless to gain his desire within the *amor*-relationship itself. The conventional process for gaining power which he is able to follow (the exchange of service for gain) breaks down in the sphere of *amor*. The form of the exchange process which actually succeeds in the erotic context (the exchange of wealth) is the very one which the poet is prevented from taking part in by the control which *amor* exerts over his ethical choices. The conventional process upon which the operation of Roman society generally seems to be based (in the spheres of military service, farming, trade, religion, patronage) is disrupted. But

into categories: *superiores, pares,* and *inferiores*' (Saller (1989) 57). For a subtle examination of the use made by the Roman elegist of the 'protocols and moral code' of *amicitia*, see Gibson (1995).

[27] On the similarities between the patron-client relationship and the elegists' representations of the beloved-poet/lover relationship see Gibson (1995) 65–8.

at the same time that process is also affirmed by the simple necessity for the power that only it can bring in the form of wealth, prosperity, and security.

An end to power?

The poet/lover's failed struggle for power within the *amor*-relationship is mirrored in the final elegy, as it is in the third, by his powerlessness before the demands of *militia* (see especially 10.13). It is in this context that he hopes finally for an end to the struggle for power; in other words, an end to the processes (such as *militia* or the farmer's struggles with the land) by which power is achieved. Thus, he hopes, the intermediate hardship, powerlessness and insecurity which these processes involve will cease. This end to power struggle is represented by the figure of *Pax*, who embodies not simply an end to *militia* but an easy rural prosperity (10.45–50, 10.67–8) which recalls the Golden Age, when the land gave its produce without the need for the process of struggle normally associated with the life of the farmer. The Golden Age is recalled explicitly both in poem ten (10.7–12) and in poem three (3.35–48), where the poet is similarly in a position of powerlessness occasioned by *militia*. In both cases, the Golden Age, like the land under the auspices of *Pax*, is free of power struggle and the need for the related processes by which success and wealth are gained. Not only war and the farmer's need to struggle for the control of nature and the produce of the land but also the parallel process of trade are absent from the Golden Age as presented in the third elegy. In all these respects, the ideal is explicitly contrasted to the present and the culture of power struggle by which present society operates. On one level, the poet/lover's reaction against this culture of power struggle can be understood as a reflection of his own failure in these struggles, his inability to exploit the related structures and processes, and his consequent lack of control in various respects. Yet the explicit contrast between the present culture of power struggles and the ideals of *Pax* or the Golden Age is especially prominent in the concluding elegy, making it effectively the final statement of the collection, and this contrast also raises questions. What might the operation of power in the collection imply about contemporary Roman social and political concerns and circumstances?

As I have argued, *amor* can be related to the military and political spheres through similarities in the construction and operation of power in all these areas. The implications which this presentation of *amor* might have for the construction of power in Roman culture more generally have been discussed above. In the third poem, however, the power of *amor* can be seen to come into direct conflict with the demands of the Roman state. This poem can be read as a power struggle between the demands of *amor* and those of Messalla, a conflict already suggested in the first poem (at 1.1–6 and 1.53–6), which *amor* effectively wins. Read in this way, the reassertion of the demands of *militia* in poem ten (10.13) could be taken as a final affirmation of these demands and the power structures and processes which support them. The poet's rejection of these structures and processes, while it might appear to subvert the principles which underpin the operation of contemporary political and military structures and careers, could rather be seen to underline the anomalous position of the poet. The emphasis on the poet's own powerlessness and exclusion from the normal processes affirms those structures and processes as the norm. They are the means by which a Roman citizen not wishing to exclude and disempower himself in the manner of the poet/lover must proceed. The *ferreus* of poem two, who rejects Delia in favour of a military career, presents just such a contrast to the powerless, subservient poet/lover.

But the reappearance of war in the final poem after the assertion of Roman triumph through the agency of Messalla in the seventh elegy brings into question the success and stability of that triumph. The continued necessity for war might cast doubt upon the ability of these state-sanctioned power struggles to bring lasting security. Indeed, the recurrence of *militia* in the final poem ends the collection with the threat and insecurity of war, rather than the state of power and security asserted in poem seven. This provides another parallel

between the depiction of the *amor*-relationship and the operation of the Roman state. In both cases, the processes expected
to bring power and security, whether war, or the devotion and
service of the poet/lover to his beloveds, fail. The insecurity of
war recurs, and the compliance and loyalty of the beloved are
not produced. According to *this* reading, the interpenetration
of the sphere of *amor* with that of politics would subvert
rather than affirm the conventional structures by which the
Roman state accumulates, defines and asserts power.

The powers that be

One further area remains where the operation of power in the
collection may have implications for the construction of
political power in Rome. The absence of Augustus from the
elegies of Tibullus, in contrast to those of other elegists, has
been commented upon by a number of critics. This is often
used as evidence of the poet's (or Messalla's) political lean-
ings.[28] But the intrusion of *amor* into the area of politics collapses the distinctions between them through the similarities
of the power relationships at work in both cases. This suggests
a general pattern for the operation of power which has unavoidable implications for a figure as intimately involved
in the contemporary renegotiation of power at Rome as
Octavian/Augustus. As I have already suggested, the repetition of the structure of the patron-client relationship in the
amor-relationship both destabilises the conventional structure,
suggesting the possibility of the breakdown of the exchange
relationship through its breakdown in the sphere of *amor*, and
affirms that structure as the norm and the patron-client rela-

---

[28] For example, Little (1982) 314: 'In this circle, reserve towards the new regime may
have been a fashionable sentiment'; or Cancelli (1986) 250: 'L'ostilità di Tibullo
per il nuovo regime non era sfuggita ai più attenti studiosi, solo che si tendeva a
interpretarla per lo più come effetto dell'influenza su di lui di Messalla, con l'in-
congruenza di non avere più solido argomento per definire le idee politiche di
Messalla, come non lige od ostili ad Augusto, se non il sentimento politico stesso
della poesia di Tibullo'; or Davies (1973) 35: 'Tibullus sees Messalla's achievements as glorious in themselves, not as part of the wider military programme of
Augustus.'

tionship as the legitimate form of it in contrast to the dys-
functional form it takes in the *amor*-relationship. The clearest
expression of the conventional patron-client relationship in
the collection, the relationship of the poet with Messalla,
highlights these tensions. In poem seven, the poet asserts his
contribution to Messalla's achievement, and thus his part of
the patron-client exchange (7.9). However, when in conflict
with the demands of *amor*, the poet's obligations to Messalla,
such as accompanying him on *militia*, are neglected (1.53–6)
or overcome (poem three). Again, this breakdown might
either place pressure on the conventional relationship structure, or reaffirm it, through emphasis on the anomalous position of the poet. The breakdown of the structure can draw
attention both to the fact that the structure is not working and
to the model of how it should work in *normal* circumstances.

These tensions might have implications for the position of
Augustus. Critics such as Little[29] have focused upon the
poet's choice of the personal patron, Messalla, as the representative of this conventional power relationship in the collection, perhaps in rivalry to Augustus. Similarly, the almost
universal nature of Messalla's power over West and East in
the seventh elegy, and his associations with Egypt, whose
annexation Augustus represented as one of his own greatest
achievements,[30] might also be thought to rival the claims of
Augustus. But, at a more fundamental level, the interplay of
power relationships and related processes within the collection
could be thought to reflect upon the *princeps*'s own involvement in these power structures and the reorganisation of these
around him which was taking place in contemporary Rome.
As Andrew Wallace-Hadrill has pointed out, 'Roman imperial power has at its root a transformation of the patronage
structures of republican Rome.'[31] The importance of these
power structures, and their renegotiation, to the position of

[29] Little (1982); Ball (1981) 135–42.
[30] See *Res Gestae* 27.24; and Cancelli (1986) 247–9.
[31] Wallace-Hadrill (1989b) 79.

Octavian/Augustus[32] gives significance to the tensions and contradictions in these structures caused by the interplay of *amor* and the other spheres of power in the collection. The absolute power of *amor* and the anomalous operation of conventional power structures when subjected to that power would thus have resonances with the very visible,[33] intensive and extensive contemporary realignment of power taking place at Rome: 'Thus the network of patronage realigns and all strands converge on the emperor at the centre.'[34] These resonances open up an immediate social and political significance for all the pressures and potential for breakdown which can be seen in the *amor*-relationship. As I suggested above in relation to the operation of these power structures in Roman society, this reading also allows the reaffirmation of imperial power as the norm in contrast to the abnormal power relationship delineated by elegiac *amor*.[35] But Tibullus' first collection was produced at a significant moment in the reconstruction of power at Rome, and a reading of it which focuses on these relationships and structures cannot escape comparison with contemporary Roman concerns and circumstances. To state this more generally: given its concern with unorthodox forms of power and their relation to the conventional power relationships, structures and processes of Roman society, it is perhaps not surprising that the genre of erotic elegy developed and flourished in the early years of the imperial period.

[32] The *princeps*'s name-change around the time that Tibullus' first book was published stands as a neat emblem, as well as a component part, of his realignment of these power structures.

[33] On the changing expression of power in the visual imagery of Rome at the time see Zanker (1988): 'through visual imagery a new mythology of Rome and, for the emperor, a new ritual of power were created' (4); 'The great power struggle and its consequences were everywhere evident in the city' (24–5).

[34] Wallace-Hadrill (1989b) 81.

[35] Similarly, on the one hand the assertion in the final elegy that *pax* is still a hope for the future rather than a present reality might be seen to subvert Augustus, whose propaganda relied heavily on the association of the new order with the bringing of *pax* (see Gruen (1986) 51–72). But at the same time and by the terms of the same propaganda, this could be taken as an affirmation of the need for an Augustus to constantly *re*-assert *pax*.

Reading Tibullus Book One

The reading of Elegy, and of Tibullus Book One specifically, is not only involved in the construction of these power relationships and the network of associations and implications which they open up, but is itself implicated intimately in what could be described as a 'power relationship'. This relationship can be figured as one between reader and poet, or between reader and text, and operates in the gathering or construction of meaning. The power struggles of professional critics are, of course, an exaggerated expression of this process, as various critical models vie to be privileged as *the* meaning of the text.[36] But it has been my contention that the text of Tibullus Book One is disruptive to this process.

The text does not unproblematically resolve itself into a biographical narrative, but can, rather, be viewed as a performance on the part of a poet detached from any narrative which the poems might suggest. If the 'Albius' of its first line is identified with the poet Tibullus, Horace's *Epistle* 1.4 may highlight some of the complexities of the elegiac poet's relationship to the text. Horace presents a picture of Tibullus detached not only geographically, at Pedum, but also in the nature of his pastimes, writing being grouped with philosophical musings and silent strolls in the woods:

quid nunc te dicam facere in regione Pedana?
  scribere quod Cassi Parmensis opuscula uincat,
an tacitum siluas inter reptare salubris,
  curantem quicquid dignum sapiente bonoque est?   (Horace, *Ep.*1.4.2–5)

The contrast between the poet whom Horace portrays and the poet/lover of Tibullus Book One further emphasises the distance between the author of the elegies and the persona of the poet/lover presented in those ten poems: *di tibi diuitias dederunt artemque fruendi* (*Ep.*1.4.7). If an analogy with the first elegiac book of Propertius can be made, *diuitias* may be a direct pun on the practice of referring to collections of poetry by

---

[36] 'Criticism of all kinds is subject to analysis in terms of "a will-to-power"' Martindale (1993) 39.

their first word.[37] Whether or not this is the case, the explicit possession of wealth effectively detaches the author, Tibullus, from the poet/lover, 'Tibullus', presented in the collection of elegies. The opening presentation of Albius as a *critic* of poetry (*Ep*.1.4.1) further suggests detachment from literature, rather than the direct equation of poetry with the life of the poet.

This detachment has been recognised by various critics of elegy in the last ten years who have reacted against the biographical equation of poetry and life which had previously underlain the reading strategies of the majority of scholars and, thus, determined their methods of constructing meaning from the elegiac collections. Veyne, for example, replaces the autobiographical framework for meaning with one built of generic imperatives:

What therefore was Roman erotic elegy? A fiction no less systematic than the erotic lyrics of the troubadours or Petrarchian poetry. The contingency of what might have been autobiographical events is replaced by the internal necessities of a certain form of creation.[38]

Maria Wyke has also drawn attention to the difficulties of identifying elegiac representation with contemporary reality,[39] and Duncan Kennedy, conveniently for my purposes, has highlighted precisely this problem of equating the two Tibulli in the context of his examination of the Delia poems: 'One cannot impose a closure on Tibullus 1.2 by referring to the person Tibullus, for "Tibullus" is an exploration of the roles, poetic and erotic, the elegy dramatizes.'[40]

The problems for the construction of meaning from elegiac texts suggested variously by Horace, Veyne, Wyke and Kennedy form the background to my reading of Tibullus' first book of *Elegies* and my representation of the construction of meaning from that text as a power struggle. Attempts to read

[37] For the use of *Cynthia*, the first word of Propertius Book One, as a title for that collection see Martial 14.189. On the use of opening words as titles for poems see Kenney (1970).

[38] Veyne (1985) 85.

[39] Wyke (1989).

[40] Kennedy (1993) 22; see also Kennedy (1993) ch. 5.

the poems as a narrative of either the course of the various relationships, or the position and motivation of the poet/ lover, are disrupted by the ambiguities, changing directions, and undermined expectations which any reading of the text is prey to.

Some of these elements are best seen in a first reading of the collection, and allow the reader to take control of meaning on re-reading. For example, the expectations created by the opening of the collection, that the poet has made an autonomous choice of a rural lifestyle for traditional, pious, moral reasons (undermined in the course of the poem), can be reconstructed and re-assimilated into a framework of meaning for the poem as a whole by the reader on re-reading. Similarly, smaller instances, such as the image of the *puer* in the opening lines of poem five which, coming immediately after the fourth elegy, might encourage the reader to expect a poem about pederastic *amor*, can be effaced in retrospect or on second reading. In this way, Francis Cairns reconstructs poem eight, among others, from an overview of all the 'essential information ... presented ... at various convenient points',[41] thus taking control over the meaning of the poems by hindsight of the Tibullan techniques of 'Informing'[42] and 'Deceiving'.[43] Of course, all reading involves hindsight of this sort and texts are in the process of being re-read even as they are being read. This draws attention to the role of knowledge (in this case the reader's) in the construction of meaning, and points to the parts which the different sets of knowledge and experience of each reader may play in determining their reading of the text. This can be seen in Cairns' use of his knowledge of Plato, Xenophon, Pindar, Theocritus and 'Hellenistic techniques' to reconstruct a meaning for poem eight,[44] just as it can be seen in my own use of Horace, Veyne, Wyke and

---

[41] Cairns (1979) 145. For his reconstruction of poem eight see Cairns (1979) 147–51, and for a more schematic reconstruction of one of the poems of the first book (poem five) see Cairns (1979) 176–7.
[42] Cairns (1979) ch. 6.
[43] Cairns (1979) ch. 7.
[44] Cairns (1979) 150–1.

Kennedy above, and the use of Lucretius, Cicero, Horace and Virgil in the opening of my reading of the first poem.

Other elements of ambiguity or the disruption of the process of constructing meaning are less amenable to assimilation by the reader. Indeed, even some of the points mentioned above as being open to re-assimilation into any reading can also create more unresolvable dificulties. As I attempted to suggest in my own reading of poem eight, the points of 'essential information' which are brought together by Cairns to construct a reading of the poem in hindsight are open to further destabilisation. The possibility of continued uncertainty over the addressee of various lines remains open.[45] Similarly, the relationship between the poet and the *coniunx* in poem six, and the extent of the poet's attempted manipulation of the power relationship there, also remain indefinite. Any conclusive reading is suspended, and as a result the position of the reader in this manoeuvring, the *reader's* command of the situation, is destabilised.[46] This suggests another level to the nexus of power relations in which the reader is involved.

Earlier I stated that what I have been calling the power relationship at work in the process of reading the elegies can be figured as a relationship between reader and text or between reader and poet. The second of these formulations opens further complications beyond those suggested in the critical discussion of the detachment of the poet-persona from the author of the poems which is referred to above. In one respect the reader is constantly placed in a superior, knowing position in relation to the deluded, powerless poet-persona, although at times, such as the opening of the first elegy or in poem six, the reader's control over meaning is (or is later shown to have been) insecure. At the same time, however, the undermined expectations and the shifting position of the reader within this power dynamic suggest that this position is being manoeuvred by a poet who, in contrast to the powerless persona he projects, is in control of the course of the poems. This underlines

---

[45] See my reading of poem eight above, especially 233–4, 238 and 244.
[46] See my reading of poem six above, especially 188–90 and 204.

the irony of the claims of the powerlessness of poetry made by the poet in a situation which is itself constructed by poetry and the poet (see, for example, 5.67). The reader's superior position in relation to the powerless poet-persona always operates within the power dynamic between reader and detached poet-author. Or, figured differently, this position is a product of both the reader's manipulation of, and the reader's manipulation by, the elegiac text. There are further complications to this dynamic, of course, since this poetic performance is dependent on its reception. Before this dynamic can operate, a poet needs an audience, just as he needs a patron to ensure distribution of his work.[47] In this way, the complications of the power relationship between reader and text, and reader and poet, spiral out of control, and my own attempts to construct a framework of 'power relations and processes' in which the text can be understood are equally open to being figured as part of this powerplay.

This view of both the relationships presented within the text, and the process of reading that text, as interconnected power dynamics leads naturally to the equation of *amor* with the writing of elegy itself which Ovid makes explicit in his first book of *Amores*.[48] It adds a further dimension to the connection observed by critics such as Veyne: 'To love is to be an elegiac poet ... To love is to write and to be loved, to be read.'[49] Elegy itself can be read as operating through power relations, placing the reader within this dynamic where the construction of meaning may be disrupted or deferred and his/her own position destabilised or left insecure or ambig-

---

[47] For this dependence for distribution see White (1978) 85.
[48] See especially *Amores* 1.1.25–30. On Ovid and the relation between *amor* and elegy see Kennedy (1993) 82: 'The applicability of the term *amores* both to the object of love and to the form in which that object is represented within a discourse where the domain of "love" is worldwide (cf. Ovid *Amores* 1.1.15, *an, quod ubique, tuum est?*), where everything is seen in terms of "love", renders the act of making love and the act of writing about it open to being seen as manifestations of a single sphere of activity.' See also Myerowitz on the equation of art and love in the *Ars Amatoria*: 'In Ovid's poem on love, the question becomes what is art, rather than what is love ... Seen from this point of view, the best lover would be the best artist,' Myerowitz (1985) 36.
[49] Veyne (1988) 108 and 112.

uous, just as the poet/lover, 'Tibullus', struggles to control his position in a similar dynamic. According to this model, the reading of elegy becomes not just a 'witty genre, a literary game' where the relationship between poet and reader is unproblematic and neutral, as Veyne sees it,[50] but a far more dynamic process where the reader's position is constantly being negotiated, constructed and destabilised within the power relations set up by the text. As the knowledge and assumptions of the reader act upon his/her reception of the power structures at work within the text (the construction of them as conventional or anomalistic, their implication within contemporary social or political power dynamics) the reader, too, is involved within a power struggle, a struggle which opens his/her reception of the text to disruption and destabilisation. This model presents a different Tibullus from the harmless, 'cultured', *tersus atque elegans* Tibullus of so many modern commentators.[51] Such a model for reading Tibullus' first book of *Elegies* adds new and unexpected meaning to Ovid's judgement:

> carmina quis potuit tuto legisse Tibulli?   (Ovid, *Rem. Am.* 763)

---

[50] Veyne (1988) 154; compare Kennedy's criticism of Veyne's position: 'The most obvious manifestation of this is Veyne's characterisation of elegy as a form of entertainment (and so its effects are not to be described as "real"), in particular his description of elegy as a game in which author and readers agree on the rules, and, by implication, agree on the interpretation. However, seeing elegy as a semiotic system pure and simple, as a "game", forswears any investigation of why it might have been viewed either as "entertaining" or as "shocking", why it might have "mattered". That is, it seeks to abstract elegy from the discursive situation in which it was produced and the assumptions which it exploited, the discursive situation by which it was shaped and in which it was received.' Kennedy (1993) 96.

[51] So, for example, Ball: 'Tibullus the elegist, the gentle young writer who differed considerably from his more resolute fellow Augustans' (1989) 12. On this tendency of modern Tibullan criticism, and the contribution of Quintilian's famous tag to the formation of the myth, see Elder (1962). Elder himself, however, like many critics since, cannot escape the temptation to apply the soft-focus lens to Tibullus, albeit differently tinted: 'In the final analysis, we realise that we have been listening to someone who could not "keep pace" with his companions – thank heaven for such men – and who knew this fact and felt torment therefrom. In fine, we have been listening to an Augustan who heard the distant call of Thoreau's "different drummer".' Elder (1962) 103.

BIBLIOGRAPHY

Adams, J.N. (1982) *The Latin Sexual Vocabulary*, London

Alfonsi, L. (1945) 'L'amore-amicizia negli elegiaci latini', *Aevum* 19: 372–8

(1946) *Albio Tibullo e gli autori del "Corpus Tibullianum"*, Milan

(1968) 'A proposito della digressione tibulliana su Osiride', *Aevum* 42: 475–6

André, J. (1965) *Tibulle. Elégies, Livre Premier*, Paris

Ariès, P. & Béjin, A. eds. (1985) *Western Sexuality: Practice and Precept in Past and Present Times*, translated by A. Forster, Oxford and New York

Ball, R.J. (1975) 'The Structure of Tibullus 1.7', *Latomus* 34: 729–44

(1979) 'Tibullus' Structural Strategy: the external ordering', *Prudentia* 11: 1–6

(1981) 'The Politics of Tibullus: Augustus, Messalla and Macer', *GB* 10: 135–42

(1983) *Tibullus the Elegist: A Critical Survey*, Göttingen

(1989) 'Recent Structural Studies on Tibullus', *The Augustan Age* 9: 1–15

Barthes, R. (1974) *S/Z*, translated by R. Miller, London

(1979) *A Lover's Discourse: Fragments*, translated by R. Howard, London

Beagon, M. (1992) *Roman Nature: The Thought of Pliny the Elder*, Oxford

Beard, M. & Crawford, M. (1985) *Rome in the Late Republic: Problems and Interpretations*, London

Beard, M. & North, J. eds. (1990) *Pagan Priests: Religion and Power in the Ancient World*, London

Bénéjam, M.J. (1980) 'L'Age d'Or de Tibulle' in *L'Elégie Romaine. Enracinement – Thèmes – Diffusion*, Paris, 91–103

Ben-Porat, Z. (1979) 'Method in *Mad*ness: Notes on the Structure of Parody based on MAD TV Satires', *Poetics Today* 1: 245–72

Betensky, A. (1979) 'The Farmer's Battles' in Boyle ed. (1979): 108–19

Blau, P.M. (1964) *Exchange and Power in Social Life*, New York

Boyd, B.W. (1984) '*Parva Seges Satis Est*: The Landscape of Tibullan Elegy in 1.1 and 1.10', *TAPhA* 114: 273–80

Boyle, A.J. ed. (1975a) *Ancient Pastoral: Ramus Essays on Greek and Roman Pastoral Poetry*, Berwick, Vic.

(1975b) 'A Reading of Virgil's *Eclogues*' in Boyle ed. (1975): 187–203

ed. (1979) *Virgil's Ascraean Song: Ramus Essays on the Georgics*, Berwick, Vic.

Bradley, K.R. (1994) *Slavery and Society at Rome*, Cambridge

BIBLIOGRAPHY

Bréguet, E. (1980) 'L'Elégie I, 4 de Tibulle' in *L'Elégie Romaine. Enracinement – Thèmes – Diffusion*, Paris, 65–71
Bright, D.F. (1971) 'A Tibullan Odyssey', *Arethusa* 4: 197–214
(1975) 'The Art and Structure of Tibullus 1.7', *GB* 3: 31–46
(1978) *Haec mihi fingebam: Tibullus in His World*, Leiden
Brouwer, H.H.J. (1989) *Bona Dea: the Sources and a Description of the Cult*, Leiden
Brouwers, J.H. (1978) '*Ferreus ille fuit*. Sens et structure de Tibulle 1, 2, 67–80', *Mnemosyne* 31: 389–406
Bulloch, A.W. (1973) 'Tibullus and the Alexandrians', *PCPhS* 19: 71–89
Cairns, F. (1972) *Generic Composition in Greek and Roman Poetry*, Edinburgh
(1975) 'Horace, *Epode* 2, Tibullus 1.1 and Rhetorical Praise of the Countryside', *MPhil.* 1: 79–91
(1979) *Tibullus: A Hellenistic Poet at Rome*, Cambridge
Cameron, A. ed. (1989) *History as Text*, London
Campbell, C. (1973) 'Tibullus Elegy I. 3', *YCIS* 23: 147–57
Cancelli, F. (1986) 'Spunti Ideologico-Politici in Tibullo' in *Atti del Convegno Internazionale di Studi su Albio Tibullo (Roma – Palestrina, 10–13 maggio 1984)*, Rome, 233–50
Cartault, A. (1909) *Tibulle et les auteurs du corpus Tibullianum*, Paris
Cilliers, J.F. (1974) 'The Tartarus Motif in Tibullus Elegy 1, 3', *AClass* 17: 74–9
Cloud, D. (1993) 'Roman Poetry and Anti-Militarism' in Rich & Shipley eds. (1993): 113–38
Conte, G.B. (1994a) *Latin Literature: A History*, translated by J.B. Solodow, Baltimore and London
(1994b) *Genres and Readers: Lucretius, Love Elegy, Pliny's 'Encyclopedia'*, translated by G.W. Most; Baltimore and London
Copley, F.O. (1947) '*Servitium Amoris* in the Roman Elegists', *TAPhA* 78: 285–300
(1956) *Exclusus amator: A Study in Latin Love Poetry*, Madison, Wis.
(1972) 'Emotional Conflict and its Significance in the Lesbia-Poems of Catullus' in Quinn ed. (1972b): 78–96
Courtney, E. (1987) 'Problems in Tibullus and Lygdamus', *Maia* 39: 29–32
Culler, J. (1982) *On Deconstruction: Theory and Criticism after Structuralism*, Ithaca
D'Arms, J.H. (1981) *Commerce and Social Standing in Ancient Rome*, Cambridge, Mass.
Davies, C. (1973) 'Poetry in the "Circle" of Messalla', *G&R* n.s.10: 25–35
Dawson, C.M. (1946) 'An Alexandrian Prototype of Marathus?', *AJPh* 65: 1–15
Day, A.A. (1938) *The Origins of Latin Love Elegy*, Oxford
Della Corte, F. (1964) *Tibullo*, Genoa
(1966) 'Tibullo e l'Egitto', *Maia* 18: 329–37

311

Derrida, J. (1978) *Writing and Difference*, translated by A. Bass, London
Dettmer, H. (1980) 'The Arrangement of Tibullus Bks 1 and 2', *Philologus* 124: 68–82
Dissen, L. (1835) *Tibulli carmina*, Göttingen
Doncieux, G. (1887) *De Tibulli amoribus*, dissertation, Paris
Dorey, T.A. ed. (1964) *Cicero*, London
Douglas, A.E. (1964) 'Cicero the Philosopher' in Dorey ed. (1964): 135–70
Dover, K. (1978) *Greek Homosexuality*, Cambridge, Mass.
Eagleton, T. (1983) *Literary Theory: An Introduction*, Oxford
Edwards, C. (1993) *The Politics of Immorality in Ancient Rome*, Cambridge
Eisenberger, H. (1960) 'Der innere Zusammenhang der Motive in Tibulls Gedicht 1, 3', *Hermes* 88: 188–97
Elder, J.P. (1962) 'Tibullus: *Tersus atque elegans*' in Sullivan ed. (1962): 65–105
(1965) 'Tibullus, Ennius and the Blue Loire', *TAPhA* 96: 97–105
Felman, S. (1982a) 'Turning the Screw of Interpretation' in Felman ed. (1982b): 94–207
ed. (1982b) *Literature and Psychoanalysis*, Baltimore
Finley, M.I. (1985) *The Ancient Economy*, 2nd edn., London
Fisher, J.M. (1983) 'The Life and Work of Tibullus', *ANRW* 2.30.3: 1924–61
Foucault, M. (1972) *The Archaeology of Knowledge*, translated by A.M. Sheridan Smith, London
(1976) *A History of Sexuality vol. 1: Introduction*, translated by R. Hurley, London
(1980) 'Two Lectures', in Gordon ed. (1980): 78–108
French, M. (1985) *Beyond Power: On Women, Men, and Morals*, London
Freyburger, G. (1980) 'Le *Foedus* d'amour' in *L'Elégie Romaine. Enracinement – Thèmes – Diffusion*, Paris, 105–16
Gaisser, J.H. (1971a) 'Structure and Tone in Tibullus 1,6', *AJPh* 92: 202–16
(1971b) 'Tibullus 1.7: A Tribute to Messalla', *CPh* 66.4: 221–9
(1983) '*Amor, rura* and *militia* in Three Elegies of Tibullus: 1.1, 1.5 and 1.10', *Latomus* 92: 58–72
Galinsky, K. (1969) 'The Triumph Theme in Augustan Elegy', *WS* 3: 75–107
Garnsey, P. & Saller, R. (1987) *The Roman Empire: Economy, Society and Culture*, London
Gibson, R.K. (1995) 'How to Win Girlfriends and Influence them: *amicitia* in Roman love elegy', *PCPhS* 41: 62–82
Gold, B.K. ed. (1982) *Literary and Artistic Patronage in Ancient Rome*, Austin
Goldhill, S. (1991) *The Poet's Voice: Essays on Poetics and Greek Literature*, Cambridge
Gordon, C. ed. (1980) *Power/Knowledge*, Brighton

Gordon, R. (1990) 'Religion in the Roman Empire: the civic compromise and its limits' in Beard & North eds. (1990): 246–8
Gotoff, H.C. (1974) 'Tibullus: *Nunc Levis est Tractanda Venus*', *HSPh* 78: 231–51
Grondona, M. (1975) 'L'elegia 1.10 di Tibullo nelle sue corrispondenze strutturali con 1, 1, 3 e 7', *A&R* 20: 323–62
Gruen, E.S. (1986) 'Augustus and the Ideology of War and Peace' in Winkes ed. (1986): 165–73
Hallett, J.P. (1973) 'The Role of Women in Roman Elegy: Counter-cultural Feminism', *Arethusa* 6.1: 103–24
Halperin, D. (1983) *Before Pastoral: Theocritus and the Ancient Tradition of Bucolic Poetry*, New Haven
Hammer, J. (1925) *Prolegomena to an Edition of the Panegyricus Messallae: The Military and Political Career of M. Valerius Messalla Corvinus*, New York
    (1926/7) 'Tibullus 1.7.9', *CW* 20: 128
Hanslik, R. (1970) 'Tibulls Elegie 1, 3' in Wimmel ed. (1970): 138–45
Henderson, A.A.R. (1969) 'Tibullus, Elysium and Tartarus', *Latomus* 28: 649–53
    (1987) 'Tibullus 1.2.1', *LCM* 12.2: 21
Henderson, J.G.W. (1991) 'Wrapping up the Case: Reading Ovid, *Amores* 2,7 (+8) I', *Materiali e discussioni* 27: 37–88
    (1992) 'Wrapping up the Case: Reading Ovid, *Amores* 2,7 (+8) II', *Materiali e discussioni* 28: 27–83
Hutcheon, L. (1984) *A Theory of Parody*, New York
Iser, W. (1978) *The Act of Reading: a theory of aesthetic response*, translation, London
    (1980) 'The Reading Process: A Phenomenological Approach' in Tompkins ed. (1980): 50–69
Jacoby, F. (1905) 'Zur Entstehung der römischen Elegie', *RhM* 60: 38–105
    (1910) 'Tibulls erste Elegie', *RhM* 65: 22–87
Johnson, B. (1982) 'The Frame of Reference: Poe, Lacan, Derrida' in Felman ed. (1982b): 457–505
Johnson, T. & Dandeker, C. (1989) 'Patronage: relation and system' in Wallace-Hadrill ed. (1989a): 219–45
Johnson, W.R. (1990) 'Messalla's Birthday: The Politics of Pastoral', *Arethusa* 23: 95–113
Kennedy, D.F. (1992) '"Augustan" and "Anti-Augustan": Reflections on Terms of Reference' in Powell ed. (1992): 26–58
    (1993) *The Arts of Love*, Cambridge
Kenney, E.J. (1970) 'The Incomparable Poem "ille ego"?', *CR* 20: 290
Klingner, F. (1955) 'Tibulls Geburtstagsgedicht an Messalla (1.7)', *Eranos* 49: 117–36
Koenen, L. (1976) 'Egyptian Influence in Tibullus', *ICS* 1: 127–59

313

Konstan, D. (1978) 'The Politics of Tibullus 1,7', *RSC* 26: 173–85
  (1997) *Friendship in the Classical World*, Cambridge
Lattimore, R. (1942) *Themes in Greek and Latin Epitaphs*, Urbana
Lawall, G. (1975) 'The Green Cabinet and the Pastoral Design: Theocritus, Euripides, and Tibullus', *Ramus* 4: 87–100
Leach, E.W. (1978) 'Vergil, Horace, Tibullus. Three collections of ten', *Ramus* 7: 79–105
  (1980a) 'Poetics and Poetic Design in Tibullus' First Elegiac Book', *Arethusa* 13: 79–96
  (1980b) 'Sacral-Idyllic Landscape Painting and the Poems of Tibullus' First Book', *Latomus* 39: 47–61
  (1995) Review of Conte (1994b), *CP* 90.2: 200
Lee, G. (1990) *Tibullus: Elegies*, Leeds
Leonotti, E. (1980) 'Per una interpretazione di tre elegie di Tibullo (I 4, 8, 9)', *Prometheus* 6: 259–70
Levin, D.N. (1982) 'War and Peace in Early Roman Elegy', *ANRW* 2.30.1: 418–538
Lieberg, G. (1982) *Poeta Creator*, Amsterdam
  (1985) *'Poeta creator* : some religious aspects', *Liverpool Latin Seminar* 5: 23–32
  (1986) 'Tibullo e lo strutturalismo: analisi dell'elegia 1,5' in *Atti del Convegno Internazionale di Studi su Albio Tibullo (Roma – Palestrina, 10–13 maggio 1984)*, Rome, 315–30
Lilja, S. (1965) *The Roman Elegists' Attitude to Women*, Helsinki
  (1983) *Homosexuality in Republican and Augustan Rome*, Helsinki
Little, D. (1982) 'Politics in Augustan Poetry', *ANRW* 2.30.1: 254–370
Littlewood, R.J. (1970) 'The Symbolic Structure of Tibullus Book 1', *Latomus* 29: 661–9
  (1983) 'Humour in Tibullus', *ANRW* 2.30.3: 2128–58
Love, J.R. (1991) *Antiquity and Capitalism*, London
Luck, G. (1969) *The Latin Love Elegy*, London
Lyne, R.O.A.M. (1979) *'Servitium Amoris'*, *CQ* n.s.29: 117–30
  (1980) *The Latin Love Poets: from Catullus to Horace*, Oxford
McGann, M.J. (1983) 'The Marathus Elegies of Tibullus', *ANRW* 2.30.3: 1976–99
Maltby, R. (1991) *A Lexicon of Ancient Latin Etymologies*, Leeds
Martindale, C. (1993) *Redeeming the Text*, Cambridge
Miller, P.A. (1994) *Lyric Texts and Lyric Consciousness: The Birth of a Genre from Archaic Greece to Augustan Rome*, London & New York
Mills, D.H. (1974) 'Tibullus and Phaeacia: A Re-interpretation of 1.3', *CJ* 69: 226–32
Morris, P. ed. (1986), *The Bakhtin Reader*, London
Murgatroyd, P. (1975) *'Militia Amoris* and the Roman Elegists', *Latomus* 34: 59–79

(1977) 'Tibullus and the Puer Delicatus', *AClass* 20: 105–19

(1980) *Tibullus I, a commentary*, Pietermaritzburg

(1981) '*Servitium Amoris* and the Roman Elegists', *Latomus* 40: 589–606

Musurillo, S.J. (1967) 'The theme of time as a poetic device in the elegies of Tibullus', *TAPhA* 98: 253–68

(1970) '*Furtivus Amor*: The Structure of Tibullus 1.5', *TAPhA* 101: 387–99

Mutschler, F-H. (1985) *Die poetische Kunst Tibulls*, Frankfurt

Myerowitz, M. (1985) *Ovid's Games of Love*, Detroit

Nicastri, L. (1984) *Cornelio Gallo e l'elegia ellenistico-romana*, Rome

Ogilvie, R.M. (1970) *A Commentary on Livy Books 1–5*, Oxford

Oppenheim, D.E. (1908) 'APAI (Zu Tibull 1.5)', *WS* 30: 146–64

Palmer, R.B. (1977) 'Is There a Religion of Love in Tibullus?', *CJ* 73: 1–10

Parker, W.H. (1988) *Priapea: Poems for a Phallic God*, London and Sydney

Pieri, M-P. (1986) 'Il dio Priapo in Tibullo 1,4: spunti bucolici d'un elegiaco' in *Atti del Convegno Internazionale di Studi su Albio Tibullo (Roma – Palestrina, 10–13 maggio 1984)*, Rome, 69–88

Pillinger, H.E. (1971) 'Tibullus 1.10 and Lucretius', *CJ* 66: 204–8

Ponchont, M. (1967) *Tibulle et les auteurs du Corpus Tibullianum*, Paris

Postgate, J.P. (1922) *Selections from Tibullus*, London

Powell, A. ed. (1993) *Roman Poetry and Propaganda in the Age of Augustus*, Bristol

Powell, B.B. (1974) 'The Ordering of Tibullus Book 1', *CPh* 69: 107–12

Putnam, M.C.J. (1970) *Virgil's Pastoral Art: studies in the Eclogues*, Princeton

(1973) *Tibullus, a commentary*, Norman

Quinn, K. ed. (1972a) *Approaches to Catullus*, Cambridge

(1972b) *Catullus: an Interpretation*, London

Race, W.H. (1981) '*Prole parata* at Tibullus 1.10.39', *AJPh* 102: 146–7

Reitzenstein, R. (1975) 'Das *foedus* in der römischen Erotik' in *Catull*, Darmstadt

Rich, J. & Shipley, G. eds. (1993) *War and Society in the Roman World*, London and New York

Riposati, B. (1967) *Introduzione allo studio di Tibullo*, Milan

Rose, M.A. (1993) *Parody: Ancient, Modern and Post-Modern*, Cambridge

Ross, D.O. (1975) *Backgrounds to Augustan Poetry: Gallus, Elegy and Rome*, Cambridge

Saller, R.P. (1982) *Personal Patronage under the Early Empire*, Cambridge

(1989) 'Patronage and Friendship in Early Imperial Rome: drawing the distinction' in Wallace-Hadrill ed. (1989a): 49–62

Scaliger, J.J. (1577) *Catulli, Tibulli, Propertii noua editio*, Paris

Schiebe, M.W. (1981) *Das ideale Dasein bei Tibull und die Goldzeit-Konzeption Vergils*, Uppsala and Stockholm

Schuster, M. (1930) *Tibull-Studien*, Vienna

Smith, K.F. (1913) *The Elegies of Albius Tibullus*, New York

Solmsen, F. (1962) 'Tibullus as an Augustan Poet', *Hermes* 91: 295–325
(1979) *Isis Among the Greeks and Romans*, Cambridge, Mass.

Stroh, W. (1971) *Die römische Liebeselegie als werbende Dichtung*, Amsterdam
(1991) 'De amore senili quid veteres poetae senserint', *Gymnasium* 98: 264–76

Sullivan, J.P. ed. (1962) *Critical Essays on Roman Literature: Elegy and Lyric*, London
(1972) 'The Politics of Elegy', *Arethusa* 5: 17–34
(1976) *Propertius, A Critical Introduction*, Cambridge

Todorov, T. (1990) *Genres in Discourse*, translated by C. Porter, Cambridge

Tompkins, J.P. ed. (1980) *Reader-Response Criticism: From Formalism to Post-Structuralism*, Baltimore & London

Tracy, V.A. (1976) 'The Poet-Lover in Augustan Elegy', *Latomus* 35: 575–81

Treggiari, S. (1991) *Roman Marriage: Iusti Coniuges From the Time of Cicero to the Time of Ulpian*, Oxford

Van Nortwick, T. (1990) '*Huc Veniet Messalla Meus*: Commentary on Johnson', *Arethusa* 23: 115–23

Van Sickle, J. (1980) 'The Book-Roll and Some Conventions of the Poetic Book', *Arethusa* 13.1: 5–40

Veremans, J. (1983) 'Tibull und der Isis- und Osiriskult' in *Festschrift für Robert Muth*, Innsbruck, 547–57

de Verger, A. Ramírez (1986) 'A Note on Tibullus 1.9.21–22', *AJPh* 107: 109–10
(1987) 'La elegia 1.9 de Tibullo', *Veleia* 4: 335–46

Versnel, H.S. (1970) *Triumphus: An Inquiry into the Origin, Development and Meaning of the Roman Triumph*, Leiden

Veyne, P. (1985) 'Homosexuality in Ancient Rome' in Ariès & Béjin eds. (1985): 26–35
(1988) *Roman Erotic Elegy: Love, Poetry, and the West*, translated by D. Pellauer, Chicago

Volpi, G. (1749) *Albius Tibullus, Eques Romanus*, Padua

Vretska, K. (1955) 'Tibulls Paraklausithyron', *WS* 68: 20–46

Wallace-Hadrill, A. ed. (1989a) *Patronage in Ancient Society*, London
(1989b) 'Patronage in Roman Society: from Republic to Empire' in Wallace-Hadrill ed. (1989a): 63–88

Wheeler, A.L. (1910) 'Erotic Teaching in Roman Elegy and the Greek Sources: Part 1', *CPh* 5: 440–50
(1911) 'Erotic Teaching in Roman Elegy and the Greek Sources: Part 2', *CPh* 6: 56–77

Wheelis, A. (1990) *The Path Not Taken: Reflections on Power and Fear*, New York and London

White, P. (1978) *'Amicitia* and the Profession of Poetry in Early Imperial Rome', *JRS* 68: 74–92

(1993) *Promised Verse: Poets in the Society of Augustan Rome*, Cambridge, Mass.

Wilhelm, F. (1896) 'Zu Tibull (I 4)' in *Satura Viadrina*, 48–58. Breslau

Williams, G. (1968) *Tradition and Originality in Roman Poetry*, Oxford

(1982) 'Phases in Political Patronage of Literature in Rome' in Gold ed. (1982): 3–27

Wimmel, W. (1960) *Kallimachos in Rom*, Wiesbaden

(1968) *Der frühe Tibull*, Munich

ed. (1970) *Forschungen zur römischen Literatur, Festschrift zum 60 Geburtstag von Karl Büchner*, Wiesbaden

(1971) 'Quisquis et occurret ne possit crimen habere stet procul (Zu Tibull 1, 6, 41/42)', *Hermes* 99: 156–63

(1976) *Tibull und Delia. I: Tibulls Elegie 1,1*, Wiesbaden

(1983) *Tibull und Delia. II: Tibulls Elegie 1,2*, Wiesbaden

Winkes, R. ed. (1986) *The Age of Augustus*, Louvain

Wiseman, T.P. (1982) *'Pete nobiles amicos*: Poets and Patrons in Late Republican Rome' in Gold ed. (1982): 28–49

Wood, N. (1988) *Cicero's Social and Political Thought*, Berkeley

Wyke, M. (1989a) 'In Pursuit of Love, The Poetic Self and a Process of Reading: Augustan Elegy in the 80s', *JRS* 79: 165–73

(1989b) 'Mistress and Metaphor in Augustan Elegy', *Helios* 16: 25–47

(1989c) 'Reading Female Flesh: *Amores* 3.1' in Cameron ed. (1989): 111–43

Yardley, J.C. (1973) 'Sick-Visiting in Roman Elegy', *Phoenix* 27: 283–8

(1978) 'The Elegiac Paraclausithyron', *Eranos* 76: 19–34

Zanker, P. (1988) *The Power of Images in the Age of Augustus*, translated by A. Shapiro, Ann Arbor

Zelzer, K. (1988) 'Zur Person des "Rivalen" bei Tibull 1, 2, 67 (65)f.', *WS* 101: 259–64

GENERAL INDEX

addressees 50, 198, 232, 234, 267, 269
  of uncertain identity 220, 238, 244,
  247, 307
adornment (personal) 230, 233, 238
ageing *see* old age
agriculture 44, 214, 217, 249, 282, 293,
  297–8
amicitia 163 n.20, 296, 297 n.26
Amor / amor 68, 82–3, 97, 99–100, 109,
  115, 119–20, 122–3, 141, 142 n.26,
  164–5, 168, 171 n.42, 180, 187,
  193–5, 206–10, 218–20, 224–6, 229,
  236–7, 240, 243, 250–2, 254–6, 260,
  262–3, 266–7, 271–5, 278 n.32,
  280–2, 284–5, 288–90, 293–5, 298,
  300–3, 308
  and death 87
  and *militia* 67–8
  and rural life 67–8, 137
  as generic inevitability in elegy 51
  in Propertius 51–4
  heterosexual similar to pederastic 139,
    154, 172, 255, 263, 287–8, 293
  inverts established social norms 166,
    168
  pederastic 132, 134–55, 287–8, 306
  power of 52, 54, 137, 154
  re-figuring of 'heroic' in terms of 119,
    130
amor-relationships 12, 21, 25, 98–9,
  246–7, 255, 259, 263–4, 280–1, 284,
  286–93, 295–303
anus 126–7, 162, 197 n.39, 231
appeal (entreaty) 42, 56–9, 64, 67, 77,
  79, 80, 84–5, 104, 111, 117, 125–6,
  133, 146, 148, 150, 153, 160–1, 175,
  196, 201, 203, 215, 220, 239–40,
  242, 244, 241, 249–50, 255, 264,
  272, 288 n.9, 290, 295 n.21
  see also parce / parcite
appearance 177, 230, 234, 238
  and reality 157–60, 164, 168–9, 178,
  180–1
ars / artes 116, 147–8, 150, 152–3, 158–
  9, 183, 191, 230, 240–1

assumptions *see* expectations and
  assumptions (of reader)
Augustus 167 n.35, 278 n.31, 301–3
author *see* poet/author
authority 194, 203–4, 229, 247–51, 253

Bacchus 144, 217, 218 n.36
Bakhtin, Mikhail 18
Barthes, Roland 4
beauty 235–6, 238, 242, 251–2
belief 86–8, 90–1, 96, 100, 108, 137, 182,
  186, 209, 215 n.30, 241, 253–4,
  269–70
Bellona (Ma) 193–4, 198 n.40, 200
  n.48, 213, 250 n.8, 251 n.10, 290,
  295
Blau, Peter 21–2
Bona Dea 185–6
Bradley, Keith 19–20
brightness 130, 208, 221–2, 230, 236,
  276, 278, 282

Cairns, Francis 9–12, 69, 156, 165, 227,
  233, 245, 263, 306
carmina see song
Ceres 36, 48, 79, 288 n.9
certainty 43–4, 107, 271, 273, 282
  lack of 150, 230, 267–8, 270–1, 275
children 221, 276
clothing *see* dress
comfort 65, 269, 275–6
comic tone 133, 136–7, 141, 143 n.27,
  154
commerce 249–50, 274, 277–8, 293,
  297–9
coniunx 76, 81, 85–6, 90–1, 182, 184–95,
  258–60, 295 n.19, 307
Conte, Gian Biagio 17
Cupid 159 n.6, 288 n.9 *see also Amor*
curses 76–8, 148–50, 172–4, 179, 195,
  202–3, 257

death 57–8, 104–5, 118–19, 143, 294
  see also Mors

213, 214 n.29, 220, 228, 232, 235, 237, 240, 251–2, 256, 262, 280, 282 n.41, 288, 290, 291 n.13, 294
Veyne, Paul 12–13, 287–8, 297, 305, 308
uia 117, 221, 224, 267
  longa 39–40, 42, 47, 60–1, 114, 121, 145–6, 250
violence 240, 269, 281–2
  misuse of 268, 274–5, 277, 280
uir see coniunx

war 47, 207, 209–10, 267, 269–71, 274–5, 277, 280–2, 284–5, 292, 299, 300–1
  inconsistencies in Tibullan attitude to 210–11
wealth 27–9, 93–4, 148–9, 172, 174–6, 198–9, 230, 235–7, 240, 246, 249–53, 255–6, 260, 263, 268–9, 271, 274, 284, 292–3, 296–9

vulnerability associated with 43, 47, 64–5
  see also trade-off
weeping 105, 107–9, 240, 242, 254, 281
wife *see uxor*
wine 74–5, 168, 217–18, 221, 223, 253, 274 n.22, 279
witches *see* magic
Wimmel, Walter 7, 68, 129, 188–9, 227, 245–6, 265
women 105, 185, 258–9
  as power figures 88, 198 n.40
  conventional subservience to male 53, 166, 276
  in Elegy 89–90, 181 n.5
  male fear of 60
  power over male in *amor*-relationship 54, 60, 151, 166, 168
  traditional virtues of 127–9
Wyke, Maria 13–16, 89–90, 305

INDEX OF PASSAGES DISCUSSED

Major discussions are indicated in **bold** type

For EU product safety concerns, contact us at Calle de José Abascal, 56–1°,
28003 Madrid, Spain or eugpsr@cambridge.org.

www.ingramcontent.com/pod-product-compliance
Ingram Content Group UK Ltd.
Pitfield, Milton Keynes, MK11 3LW, UK
UKHW010350140625
459647UK00010B/978